CW00687065

"For decades evangelicals have been absorbing relational theism and have assumed that it is consistent with the biblical witness. Craig Carter exposes this faulty assumption, revealing social trinitarianism's radical inconsistency with Scripture's own presentation of the triune God. Thankfully, Carter also knows the antidote and summons us back to classical Christianity. Only by taking *ressourcement* seriously and sitting with hermeneutical humility at the feet of the Great Tradition can we escape the captivity of modern manipulations of the Trinity."

—**Matthew Barrett**, Midwestern Baptist Theological Seminary; author of *Simply Trinity*

"With an insider's knowledge of modern 'relational theism,' Carter is able to bring into sharp relief the choice that the church faces in its doctrine of God, a choice as vital as the one it faced in the fourth century. Will it return to trinitarian classical theism, or will it collapse God into the world and consign itself to the degenerate oblivion faced by pagan modernity and the liberal theological project that piggybacks upon it? Carter blends exegesis with sweeping cultural analysis to provide by both instruction and example an inspiring vision of the Christian doctrine of God as it should be done."

—**Garry J. Williams**, director of the Pastors' Academy at London Seminary

"By revisiting the doctrines behind classical theism—Nicene orthodoxy—Carter takes readers on a journey to the past on a path that leads to the future. We have much to learn from the Nicene fathers: the exegesis, theology, and metaphysics that inform their doctrine of God is biblical and true. For those who love classical theism, this book serves as a welcome enchiridion; for those who are drawn to revisionary doctrines of God, this book serves as a worthy dialogue partner; and for anyone who wants to know the God of Scripture, this book is must reading."

—**J. V. Fesko**, Reformed Theological Seminary, Jackson, Mississippi

Contemplating God
with the
Great Tradition

Contemplating God

with the

Great Tradition

Recovering Trinitarian Classical Theism

Craig A. Carter

Foreword by Carl R. Trueman

B
Baker Academic
a division of Baker Publishing Group
Grand Rapids, Michigan

© 2021 by Craig A. Carter

Published by Baker Academic
a division of Baker Publishing Group
PO Box 6287, Grand Rapids, MI 49516-6287
www.bakeracademic.com

Printed in the United States of America

All rights reserved. No part of this publication may be reproduced, stored in a retrieval system, or transmitted in any form or by any means—for example, electronic, photocopy, recording—without the prior written permission of the publisher. The only exception is brief quotations in printed reviews.

Library of Congress Cataloging-in-Publication Data
Names: Carter, Craig A., 1956– author. | Trueman, Carl R., writer of foreword.
Title: Contemplating God with the great tradition : recovering trinitarian classical theism / Craig A. Carter ; foreword by Carl R. Trueman.
Description: Grand Rapids, Michigan : Baker Academic, a division of Baker Publishing Group, [2021] | Includes bibliographical references and index.
Identifiers: LCCN 2020037103 | ISBN 9781540963307 (paperback) | ISBN 9781540964410 (casebound)
Subjects: LCSH: Trinity—Biblical teaching. | Trinity—History of doctrines. | Theism.
Classification: LCC BT109 .C37 2021 | DDC 231/.044—dc23
LC record available at https://lccn.loc.gov/2020037103

Unless otherwise indicated, all Scripture quotations are from The Holy Bible, English Standard Version® (ESV®), copyright © 2001 by Crossway, a publishing ministry of Good News Publishers. Used by permission. All rights reserved. ESV Text Edition: 2016

21 22 23 24 25 26 27   7 6 5 4 3 2 1

In keeping with biblical principles of creation stewardship, Baker Publishing Group advocates the responsible use of our natural resources. As a member of the Green Press Initiative, our company uses recycled paper when possible. The text paper of this book is composed in part of post-consumer waste.

To my students at Tyndale University,

who patiently listened as I thought my way through
the ideas in this book,
and especially to those who discovered along the way
that they were classical theists

Contents

Foreword

Recent years have witnessed an unexpected but most welcome development within the ranks of conservative Protestant theology: the recovery of the classical doctrine of God as expressed in the early church creeds and the great confessions of the magisterial Reformation. For some generations, particularly evangelical Protestant theology has been dominated by biblical scholars who pursue the theological endeavor on the basis of biblical exegesis with little or no engagement with the theological tradition of the church. While this is perhaps understandable, given the Protestant commitment to "Scripture alone" as the norming norm of theology, it has also proved highly problematic in at least two ways: (1) ironically, it has served to detach evangelical Protestant thought from the orthodox Protestant tradition, and (2) it has done so because (again ironically) it has unwittingly adopted the antimetaphysical stance of the dominant Kantian trajectories of Western thought since the Enlightenment.

One example of this trend is the redemptive-historical method of interpretation that is now the default in many Reformed and evangelical circles. Building on the important truth that the Bible tells one basic soteriological story culminating in Christ, this approach has done sterling service in saving the Old Testament from both dispensationalism and a reductive moralism. But in focusing on the redemptive storyline, it has also tended to prioritize the narrative economy of God's actions over the eternal ontology of his being and has thereby collapsed the transcendent into the immanent. It is not that the redemptive-historical approach is incorrect; rather, it is that it does not say enough and tends to ignore questions of metaphysics and ontology that (ironically) the Bible's own narrative itself raises.

This lack is often reflected in the default piety that always worships God for what he has done and rarely or never worships him for who he is. Of course, the former is vital—the Psalms are replete with praise for God's acts of creation, providence, and salvation. But they also contain references to his intrinsic holiness and glory. Our piety—and therefore the theology on which our piety rests and that motivates it—must also give due weight to God's glorious, holy, praiseworthy being. It was, after all, exposure to God in his thrice holiness in the temple and not any specific act of God that drove an awestruck Isaiah to the ground in worship.

In this context, the recent renaissance of interest in the classical, creedal doctrine of God is to be welcomed. This is the teaching that has generated beautiful liturgies, fortified the church, and nurtured Christians for centuries. And yet many Christians are likely still perplexed by classical theism. They may be unfamiliar with J. P. Gabler and Adolf von Harnack, but they still share their suspicion that the abstruse and abstract language of Nicene trinitarianism and such ideas as immutability and impassibility subvert the reading of Scripture in order to buttress a doctrine of God that owes more to pagan philosophy than God's self-revelation.

In such a context, Craig Carter is doing sterling service for the church. In his earlier volume, *Interpreting Scripture with the Great Tradition*, he made a compelling case for today's church to move beyond the narrow interests of the guild of contemporary evangelical biblical scholarship and seek once again to reconnect with how the church itself has read and understood the Bible over the centuries. In the present volume, Carter builds on *Interpreting Scripture* but presses in a more theological and methodological direction, seeking to demonstrate how classical theism is both demanded by the Bible's teaching and a constitutive element in how we read the Bible.

His proposal of a first and second exegesis is persuasive: the initial findings of biblical interpretation are used to establish theological syntheses that are then fed back into a further reading of the text. It does justice both to the concern that our doctrine of God be drawn from the Bible but also to the fact that who God is in himself should then refine and enrich our understanding of what the Bible says. Paying particular attention to the Trinity and to the book of Isaiah, Craig makes a compelling case (in line with the catholic, premodern approach of the church to such matters) that this approach is consistent with the Bible and a means of confronting us with the glorious and transcendent God who, though revealed in the economy of creation and salvation, yet transcends that economy and is indeed worthy of worship for his very being. And Craig also underscores that this kind of approach is born and conducted and terminates upon adoration of and devotion to the Triune God, who needs nothing to be glorious and complete and yet has condescended to create finite creatures for joyous communion with him.

This is a book for Protestants—especially us Reformed Protestants who have perhaps placed too exclusive a focus on redemptive history—to read, ponder, and apply.

Carl R Trueman
Grove City College

Acknowledgments

As I mentioned in the dedication, I want to thank my students at Tyndale University. I have been blessed with some excellent students, who have been intellectually curious, spiritually awake, and ready to engage with deep ideas. Of course, not all students are like that, but one takes the good with the bad. When I see students go on to study for advanced degrees and know that they will far surpass me in their scholarship, I feel a sense of satisfaction in having done my job as a teacher. I find that I learn by teaching and am motivated to think more deeply about theology by the questions the students ask.

I also want to thank the administration of Tyndale for two sabbaticals, during which I was able to give sustained attention to this project. Teaching undergraduates is time-consuming, and I am grateful to have had relatively few administrative assignments over the past few years, which has helped the writing process as well.

I want to thank the people of Westney Heights Baptist Church, where I have served as Theologian in Residence since 2008. This church has been extremely supportive of my vocation as a theologian, and as I have taught its Sunday school class and adult classes in hermeneutics and Old Testament survey, its members have helped to keep me grounded and in touch with what it means to do theology in the church and for the church. In particular, the men's Bible class that meets on Thursday evenings has prayed for me and supported me in my writing over the past few years, and I owe them my gratitude.

I wish to thank David Nelson and the team at Baker Academic for taking on this project and doing such a professional and excellent job on it. My theological conversations with David have helped me in articulating what I am trying to say and in developing my ideas. It is a great pleasure to have a theologically perceptive editor.

Dale Dawson has been a wonderful conversation partner on many issues related to this book over the entire time I have been writing it. We talk theology almost nonstop for a week every November as we travel to and from the annual meeting of the Evangelical Theological Society and many times throughout the year. I am also grateful to the friends who took time to read an earlier version of the manuscript in the summer of 2019, including Grant Sutherland, Dale Dawson, Ryan Hurd, Paul Bruderer, and Steve Harris. Their feedback was very helpful. I am also grateful to Carl Trueman for providing a generous foreword.

My wife, Bonnie, has also been a wonderful source of feedback and reflective criticism. She has been very patient and supportive of my work, and for this I remain grateful and indebted. She also did the indexing for this book, for which I am grateful.

Abbreviations

General and Bibliographic

ANF	*The Ante-Nicene Fathers*. Edited by Alexander Roberts and James Donaldson. 10 vols. New York: Christian Literature, 1885–96. Repr., Peabody, MA: Hendrickson, 1999.
ad	to, toward; in Aquinas's *Summa*, it marks a reply to a numbered objection
art(s).	article(s)
ca.	*circa*, about
chap(s).	chapter(s)
esp.	especially
ESV	English Standard Version
etc.	*et cetera*, and the rest
KJV	King James Version
LEB	Lexham English Bible
NPNF¹	*A Select Library of Nicene and Post-Nicene Fathers of the Christian Church*. Edited by Philip Schaff. 1st series. 14 vols. New York: Christian Literature, 1886–90. Repr., Grand Rapids: Eerdmans, 1956.
NPNF²	*A Select Library of Nicene and Post-Nicene Fathers of the Christian Church*. Edited by Philip Schaff and Henry Wace. 2nd series. 14 vols. New York: Christian Literature, 1890–1900. Repr., Peabody, MA: Hendrickson, 1999.
p(p).	page(s)
q.	question
sec(s).	section(s)

Old Testament

Gen.	Genesis		Num.	Numbers
Exod.	Exodus		Deut.	Deuteronomy
Lev.	Leviticus		Josh.	Joshua

Judg.	Judges	Lam.	Lamentations
Ruth	Ruth	Ezek.	Ezekiel
1–2 Sam.	1–2 Samuel	Dan.	Daniel
1–2 Kings	1–2 Kings	Hosea	Hosea
1–2 Chron.	1–2 Chronicles	Joel	Joel
Ezra	Ezra	Amos	Amos
Neh.	Nehemiah	Obad.	Obadiah
Esther	Esther	Jon.	Jonah
Job	Job	Mic.	Micah
Ps(s).	Psalm(s)	Nah.	Nahum
Prov.	Proverbs	Hab.	Habakkuk
Eccles.	Ecclesiastes	Zeph.	Zephaniah
Song	Song of Songs	Hag.	Haggai
Isa.	Isaiah	Zech.	Zechariah
Jer.	Jeremiah	Mal.	Malachi

New Testament

Matt.	Matthew	1–2 Thess.	1–2 Thessalonians
Mark	Mark	1–2 Tim.	1–2 Timothy
Luke	Luke	Titus	Titus
John	John	Philem.	Philemon
Acts	Acts	Heb.	Hebrews
Rom.	Romans	James	James
1–2 Cor.	1–2 Corinthians	1–2 Pet.	1–2 Peter
Gal.	Galatians	1–3 John	1–3 John
Eph.	Ephesians	Jude	Jude
Phil.	Philippians	Rev.	Revelation
Col.	Colossians		

Prologue

How My Mind Has Changed

The story of how this book came to be written goes back to my doctoral studies under John Webster at the University of Toronto School of Theology in the early 1990s. John was still in his Barth phase at that time; he was publishing a lot on Barth and getting famous in the process. I chose to study Barth as the major theologian for my program and John Howard Yoder as my thesis topic. Yoder was a Mennonite who had studied under Barth in Basel and written a book on Barth's ethics of war. Yoder also had been an acquaintance of my favorite seminary professor, J. K. Zeman, who had attended Barth's seminar in Basel with Yoder in the late 1950s. I began to study Yoder in 1992, and by 1999 I had completed my thesis, which was then published as *The Politics of the Cross: The Theology and Ethics of John Howard Yoder*.[1] I followed it up with a book titled *Rethinking Christ and Culture: A Post-Christendom Approach*, in which I argued for a Barthian-Anabaptist approach to social ethics.[2] However, by the time that book was in print, I was experiencing doubts on multiple levels about both Barth and Yoder, doubts that only grew in seriousness as time went on.

From 1992–2004 I was heavily involved in academic administration, serving as vice president and academic dean at two small Christian universities. Finally, in 2004–5 I had a full-year sabbatical, after which I began to teach full-time. As I thought about my next writing project, I envisioned writing a book on the doctrine of God in which I would argue for a relational understanding of God as the basis for social ethics. Having obtained a contract, I went off to do research. I had been reading Colin Gunton, John Zizioulas,

1. Grand Rapids: Brazos, 2001.
2. Grand Rapids: Brazos, 2007.

Stanley Grenz, Miroslav Volf, and J. Denny Weaver, and I gradually got deeper into revisionist views of God. As time went on, however, I began to become alarmed by the things I was reading.

It gradually dawned on me that this revisionist road led logically to some form of theological liberalism. I had more or less swallowed a relational view of how God interacts with the world, which sees a two-way influence between God and the world, with both affecting each other. I had also accepted the idea that the relational understanding of God's essence was rooted in the Nicene doctrine of the Trinity as expounded by the Cappadocian fathers. The idea was that the essence of God is relationality, or love between the members of the godhead, which presupposed a concept of three persons, each with a will and each in a relationship to the other two. Thus social trinitarianism grounded relational theism. I wanted to write a book about how this understanding of God provides a basis for social ethics. For a time, it seemed to me that all this was a profound way of rooting the doctrines of the church and the kingdom of God in the very nature of God himself. But up to this point, I had never thought that doing so meant deviating from Nicene orthodoxy.

As my doubts developed, however, I began to see that for many theologians, the logic of viewing God in this way led to a denial of God's wrath and the doctrine of final judgment. That changed the whole gospel message. Are people really lost? Do they need to repent and believe in order to be saved? Is salvation a matter of heaven or hell, or is it a matter of social justice here and now? Even if you say it is both, is that really where the logic leads in the end? The love of God is viewed by many as incompatible with God's justice and wrath against sin. Of course, there are many cultural pressures calling the whole idea of original sin into question, so it is popular to say that God is love and then define love as little more than liberal tolerance. But that is the path to moralistic therapeutic Deism and the end of Christianity.[3]

The idea of pacifism was being used by some to redefine the concept of God as "the nonviolent God,"[4] and once that was accomplished, then anthropology, sin, judgment, atonement, salvation, the mission of the church, and

3. This term was coined by C. Smith and Denton in their book, *Soul Searching*. The book describes the religious beliefs of American teens based on wide-ranging and extensive research. Moralistic therapeutic Deism, the dominant belief system of today's youth, can be summarized in five points: (1) a god exists who created and ordered the world and watches over human life on earth; (2) God wants people to be good, nice, and fair to each other, as taught in the Bible and by most world religions; (3) the central goal of life is to be happy and to feel good about oneself; (4) God does not need to be particularly involved in one's life except when God is needed to resolve a problem; (5) good people go to heaven when they die.

4. J. Weaver, *Nonviolent God*.

the nature of the kingdom of God were all negatively affected.[5] One good thing to come out of all my reflections and growing doubts, however, was that I came to see how thoroughly the doctrine of God influences all other doctrines. My fascination with the Nicene doctrine of God only grew, even as my relational concept of God crumbled.

In my earlier work, I had argued that Yoder's concept of following Jesus in the way of peace was simply the ethical implication of an orthodox confession of Jesus as divine, and I had also argued that pacifism was rooted in the Nicene doctrine of God. But now I began to wonder if the revisionist view of God really was compatible with historic, Nicene orthodoxy. Obviously, I was aware of the many heretical concepts of God proliferating in liberal Protestantism today. Maybe the most radical forms of relational theism were not arbitrary deviations from orthodoxy but merely a further step down the same road I and many other evangelicals were traveling. Was not the openness of God theology a logical development of what I was reading? Was I on the way to becoming a process theologian? That seemed preposterous, yet I could not help wondering if I was just being temperamentally conservative rather than rigorously logical, and this concerned me deeply. I'm afraid I have never been enough of a postmodernist to carry logical contradictions around in my head without experiencing severe cognitive dissonance. Having been a student of Clark Pinnock in the early 1980s, I was well aware that drastic theological changes usually occur gradually in stages rather than all at once.

At this point, I began to read the fourth-century fathers for myself, which was a life-changing experience. Reading the primary sources carefully is dangerous when all you want to do is to get your book done and use the sources to justify your own preconceptions. The safest course is to refrain from reading anything written before the twentieth century. (To paraphrase C. S. Lewis, a young revisionist cannot be too careful about his reading.)

Eventually I came to the conclusion that the twentieth-century revisionist theologians who were advocating various forms of relational theism and subjecting classical theism to withering critique were themselves snared in highly questionable modernist philosophical assumptions and were in danger of losing touch with the classical orthodox tradition and the biblical roots of that tradition. This was quite ironic, since the revisionists typically used Scripture to refute and revise the tradition. But to me it began to seem as if modern hermeneutics was controlled by certain philosophical assumptions that derive from Kantian and Hegelian metaphysics.

5. For an example of the slide into liberalism and the loss of contact with true, Nicene orthodoxy, see McLaren, *New Kind of Christianity*.

Eventually I realized that *everyone* utilizes metaphysical assumptions in exegesis and that the choice is not between metaphysics or not but rather between unconsciously assumed metaphysics and critically revised metaphysics. It is, after all, highly arbitrary to assume that Hellenization is bad but Hegelianization is just fine. It began to look as if the modern revisionists were far more uncritical of the dominant metaphysical assumptions of their culture than the fathers had been of the dominant metaphysical assumptions of their culture. As I read the fathers—especially Athanasius, the Cappadocians, and Augustine—and patristic scholars such as Khaled Anatolios, Lewis Ayres, John Behr, Paul Gavrilyuk, Robert Wilken, and Frances Young, I gradually came to the conclusion that the fourth-century fathers had utilized certain metaphysical concepts in a careful and critical manner, in some cases redefining words and in other cases making precise distinctions, in order to restate the biblical message in ways that preserved the meaning of the Bible and defended that meaning against heresy. I marveled at the care they took in handling the concepts with which they dealt and at how clear their thinking was.

My world was turned upside down, but I gradually came to realize that it was now actually right side up. Many scholars have noted that the supposed corruption of early Christian theology by Greek philosophical ideas is a theory that has run its course and been found to be untenable. But I would go further and say that the nineteenth-century German liberals who invented and promoted this theory were in fact engaged in a kind of projection, insofar as they were accusing the church fathers of doing in their historical context exactly the sort of thing the modern liberal Protestants were doing in their historical context. It is actually liberal theology that has imported unrevised pagan metaphysics into theology. Modernity rejects the theological metaphysics of Nicaea and replaces these ideas with pagan metaphysical ideas that were considered and rejected by the church fathers. While Aristotle was being ushered out the front door, Epicurus and Zeno were sneaking in the back door.

What I have come to call "the liberal project" is the attempt to revise Christian doctrines one by one so as to make them fit into the metaphysics of modernity. The liberal project has two branches, each with a conservative expression and a liberal expression. One branch is the modern project of *historical criticism* stemming from Spinoza; it takes a radical form in liberal higher criticism in the Enlightenment and eventually ends up in Bultmann's program of demythologization and the Jesus Seminar. It also comes in a conservative version, in which basically conservative scholars seek to work within the constraints of historicism. The other branch of the liberal project is *revisionist theology* stemming from Schleiermacher, and it takes a radical form in process theology and Hegelian panentheism. It also comes in a conservative version in the form of what Brian Davies terms "theistic personalism"[6] and the various revisions of classical theism described by James E. Dolezal as "theistic mutualism."[7] Both Spinoza and Schleiermacher were pantheists, and the entire liberal project is oriented toward reconceiving God in a way that leaves behind genuine biblical transcendence as a figment of Greek metaphysics. The liberal project leads to a neopagan view of God and to the return of ancient mythology in place of a biblical metaphysics.

In a culture dominated by pagan metaphysics, the cosmos is all that exists. Carl Sagan enunciates the quintessentially modern confession of faith (disguised as science) at the beginning of his book when he says, "The cosmos is all there is or ever was or ever will be."[8] In such a worldview, it is possible to speak of God as identical with the whole of the cosmos, and so we find pantheism all over the world in various cultures, from India to Greece to the modern West. It is also possible to speak of God as a being within the cosmos, and the possibilities range from the extremely powerful disembodied Mind of Deism to the anthropomorphic figures of the Greco-Roman pantheon or the gods of Norse mythology. These gods can be superhumans or divinized humans, or they can be personifications of the forces of nature. In some cases, they are believed to exist literally, and in other cases they may be thought of as metaphors for natural forces.

Many pagan societies contain a majority of uneducated people who believe in literal gods and also an educated elite that takes a pantheistic view but may participate in the popular religion to avoid controversy.[9] But what we never see—not in the ancient Near Eastern context in which the Old Testament was written, not in the Greco-Roman world of the New Testament, and not in the great non-Christian cultures like China and India—is a view of God as the transcendent Creator of all things, who is in the process of guiding history to its appointed destiny in Christ. In fact, the concept of linear history *itself*

6. Theistic personalism is the view that God is a being among beings within the cosmos, a person like us only greater in magnitude, power, wisdom, etc. See Davies, *Introduction to the Philosophy of Religion*, 9–16. We will discuss this idea at length later in this book.

7. Theistic mutualism is the idea that God and the world change each other as a result of a mutual relation in which they participate. In "hard theistic mutualism," change is forced on God by the world; in "soft theistic mutualism," God sovereignly chooses to allow the world to change him in some way. In both cases, the impassibility of God is denied, and immutability is either denied or redefined in an incoherent manner. See Dolezal, *All That Is in God*, 1. Dolezal conflates theistic personalism and theistic mutualism, whereas I see them as closely related but distinguishable. We will discuss these matters thoroughly as we go along.

8. Sagan, *Cosmos*, 1.

9. That was the situation Augustine encountered with many Platonist philosophers of his day and he is highly critical of them for engaging in polytheistic worship when they clearly knew better. See Augustine, *City of God* 8.13 (I/6, 257–58).

arises only out of biblical revelation and depends for its coherence on belief in a transcendent Creator. The uniqueness of the biblical doctrine of God was becoming more and more obvious to me, as was the gap between this orthodox view of God and the relational god of contemporary revisionist theology.

Relational theisms such as process theology and panentheism represent a drift toward pantheism, and the various forms of social trinitarianism and theistic personalism represent a drift toward polytheism. The pressure on Christian theologians to move in these directions is not really coming from the Bible. It is coming from the desire to articulate a doctrine of God that makes sense to a culture in which the concept of divine transcendence has been rejected as unscientific. The choice, it seems to me, is between a Nicene doctrine of God that affirms the transcendence of God and a modern doctrine of God that leaves transcendence behind. But part of the problem we face is that, in order to affirm transcendence, one has to accept the existence of irreducible mystery in our doctrine of God, which seems hard for many modern theologians, including many evangelicals, to do.

The orthodox Nicene tradition generated a doctrine of God in which the three persons (*hypostases*) share one being (*ousia*) and constitute one God. The mystery of God means that the immanent (or eternal) Trinity is incomprehensible to human reason and that what is revealed in the economy (that is, in history) is all true so far as it goes but does not reveal all of God's eternal being. How could it? How could the finite comprehend the infinite? The distinction between the immanent and the economic Trinity is absolutely crucial if we wish to avoid idolatry. There is only one God—the holy Trinity—but our minds cannot grasp all that God is. Theology is contemplation of the Triune One who creates the cosmos, speaks and acts as the sovereign Lord of history, and who alone is to be worshiped. Contemplative theology thus leads to worship.

In the process of puzzling over how to restate the meaning of biblical texts in order to convey as clearly as possible the truth about the one whom we worship, it is necessary to engage with certain metaphysical ideas. This is especially so when we attempt to clarify how God relates to the creation. *Creatio ex nihilo* becomes a crucial doctrine with centrally important metaphysical implications for the creator-creature distinction.

The fathers saw theology as a spiritual discipline leading to sanctification, not as a game of solving puzzles or as a way of mastering knowledge of God. For them, "all truth is God's truth,"[10] so they were unafraid to engage their culture in dialogue. They engaged in dialogue with the best of Greek philosophy

10. A. Holmes, *Idea of a Christian College*, 25.

in their day and formulated a set of metaphysical doctrines that can be called Christian Platonism, which functioned as the metaphysical framework in which biblical exegesis was done. Christian Platonism is not simply a matter of redefining Christianity in terms of Neoplatonism; actually, Neoplatonism is one kind of Platonism, and Christian Platonism is a rival kind. Historically, Christian Platonism eventually superseded Neoplatonism.

Christian Platonism is a label that can be applied to the theological metaphysics that grows out of fourth-century pro-Nicene theology and becomes integral to classical Christian orthodoxy. Augustinianism is the seminal source of Christian Platonism in the West, and Thomism is one form of Augustinianism. The specific form of Christian Platonism I find most compelling is the "Reformed Thomism" exemplified by Reformed scholastics like Francis Turretin, Puritans like John Owen, and in our day the later John Webster.

Reformed Thomism is a form of Augustinian theology developed during the Protestant Reformation that views the doctrine of God outlined by Thomas Aquinas in the first forty-three questions of the *Summa Theologica* as an exemplary expression of the trinitarian classical theism at the heart of classic Nicene orthodoxy. Reformed Thomism affirms the Reformation *sola*s[11] and views them as a needed correction of medieval errors, especially in soteriology, ecclesiology, and sacramental theology. Reformed Thomism understands the *sola*s to be more firmly grounded in the Nicene doctrine of God than were the medieval deviations that the *sola*s were designed to oppose. To preserve orthodoxy, Reformed Thomism finds it necessary to grapple with certain metaphysical doctrines, such as *creatio ex nihilo*, as it contemplates the being of God and all things in relation to God. Ultimately, *creatio ex nihilo* is the foundation and source of the great gospel truth "grace alone." Reformed Thomism embraces mystery and analogical language for God and rejects rationalism and univocal language for God. Reformed Thomism distinguishes conceptually between the immanent and economic Trinity, while affirming that there is only one God in three persons both in eternity and in God's own self-revelation in history. Reformed Thomists affirm the major Reformation confessions, such as the Westminster Confession of Faith, the Heidelberg Catechism, the Canons of the Synod of Dort, and the Belgic Confession. Baptists who embrace Reformed Thomism affirm the Second London Confession of Faith of 1689.

John Webster, especially in his later writings, has been very influential in modeling how to do Reformed Thomism in the contemporary situation.[12]

---

11. *Sola gratia* (grace alone), *Sola fide* (faith alone), *Sola Christus* (Christ alone), *Sola Scriptura* (Scripture alone), *Soli Deo gloria* (glory of God alone).

12. See Scott Swain's comments about Webster: "John is the supreme contemporary exemplar of dogmatic theology in a (shall we call it?) Reformed and Thomistic key, and an encouragement

Reformed Thomism is currently enjoying something of a renaissance in writers such as Michael Allen and Scott Swain,[13] Richard Muller,[14] Carl Trueman,[15] J. V. Fesko,[16] James Dolezal,[17] Steven J. Duby,[18] and those influenced by the Alliance of Confessing Evangelicals, the Davenant Institute, the Greystone Theological Institute, the Institute of Reformed Baptist Studies, and other like-minded organizations that seem to be springing up on a regular basis these days.

Contemporary interest in Reformed Thomism is an example of *ressourcement* in an age of grave cultural decline. It is a natural response to the crisis of late modernity in which postmodern relativism has dissolved all metaphysics into the will to power. The corrosive influence of neo-Marxist and postmodern ideas have led to the collapse of natural theology and the natural moral law and now threaten the concept of natural scientific law itself. It seems to me that these developments completely discredit the modern critique of premodern classical metaphysics because modernity has utterly failed to sustain any viable alternative to classical metaphysics. Nihilism cannot support a flourishing culture.

As modernity collapses, it is critically important that we recover classical orthodoxy. However, late modern metaphysics makes impossible the kind of biblical interpretation that generates classical orthodoxy, because late-modern thought arbitrarily rejects out of hand the metaphysics of Nicaea. So the problem of modernity is actually a metaphysical crisis as well as a doctrinal and hermeneutical problem, and these three things are so intertwined that they need to be tackled together. Reformed Thomism is a logical, coherent, biblically based school of thought, which has the potential to generate the fresh and vital kind of theology that needs to be done in what we could term the post-postmodern or postcritical era now dawning.

The pro-Nicene theology of the fourth century emerged on the basis of a certain type of biblical interpretation. The modernist rejection of the metaphysical framework or "sacramental ontology"[19] in which this way of reading

---

to many of us who aspire to fulfill the theologian's vocation faithfully and intelligently" (*God of the Gospel*, 7).

13. See Allen and Swain, *Reformed Catholicity*.

14. Muller, *Post-Reformation Reformed Dogmatics*.

15. See Trueman, *Creedal Imperative*.

16. Fesko, *Reforming Apologetics*.

17. In addition to Dolezal's *All That Is in God*, mentioned above, see also his *God without Parts*.

18. Duby, *Divine Simplicity*, and his *God in Himself*.

19. This term is used by Hans Boersma in a series of important books to describe essentially the same thing that I call "Christian Platonism." See esp. Boersma, *Nouvelle Théologie*; Boersma, *Heavenly Participation*; and Boersma, *Scripture as Real Presence*.

Scripture flourished has led many modern thinkers to assume that we cannot read the Bible that way anymore. As I worked my way through these issues, I found the question of hermeneutics becoming more and more complex and also, at the same time, more and more important. I realized that it would be insufficient merely to demonstrate that modern doctrines of God—like Moltmann's dynamic panentheism, for example—were incompatible with Nicaea. This is true and easily done; one can look at Stephen Holmes's work, for example, to see things spelled out rather clearly.[20] But what is to be said in response to the claim that patristic exegesis was inferior to modern exegesis and therefore that Nicaea has to be revised according to newer, better ways of interpreting of the Bible?

The surprising answer is that modern historical criticism actually is inferior to premodern exegesis, not superior to it.[21] The church has always understood the Bible to have a spiritual sense in addition to the literal sense, which is an extension of the literal sense and not a contradiction of it. But I found myself having to go deeper into the hermeneutical question to make that case, and eventually I had to admit that I was writing two different books. So I separated out the material on hermeneutics as a separate book.[22] Having made the best argument I could for the hermeneutical approach of the Great Tradition, I have now tried to put that approach into practice in the theological interpretation of Scripture done in the present book. This book is thus based on the previous one in that it seeks to do theology in the way the previous book recommended as the classic approach to doing theology.

I am currently involved in writing a major commentary on Isaiah for the International Theological Commentary series (T&T Clark). In it I attempt to interpret this centrally important biblical book using the classical approach to biblical interpretation that has been used throughout church history by theologians in the Great Tradition. My book on hermeneutics and this one on the doctrine of God are meant to support and prepare the way for the highest form of theology, which is done in the form of commentary on Scripture. The modern separation of exegesis and hermeneutics from doctrine is a recent innovation and a serious weakness of modern theology. The way forward is to break down the hyper-specialization that weakens our attempts to hear God speaking clearly in his Word.

Lewis Ayres's *Nicaea and Its Legacy: An Approach to Fourth-Century Trinitarian Theology*[23] has been extremely important to me, and I have used

---

20. S. Holmes, *Quest for the Trinity.*
21. See the seminal article by Steinmetz, "Superiority of Pre-critical Exegesis."
22. Carter, *Interpreting Scripture with the Great Tradition.*
23. Oxford: Oxford University Press, 2004.

it several times in a seminar I offer on fourth-century theology. One reason it is so important is that Ayres sees so clearly how wide the gap is between fourth- and twentieth-century theology, and he shows convincingly how poorly modern theologians understand pro-Nicene theology. It is dangerous for Christian theologians to be orthodox in the sense of wishing to confess the trinitarian theology of Nicaea and yet be so historically illiterate and so philosophically ignorant that they do not understand why the fathers in this formative period said what they said, with whom they were debating, and what issues were at stake. Knowing only the form of the words of the creed is not exactly of no value whatsoever, but it is inadequate. In such a situation, one is at risk of not understanding when or how contemporary thought goes off the rails and leaves orthodoxy behind. This is the perilous condition of much of what remains of Christian orthodox theology today.

I admit to having been part of the problem. I am painfully aware of how little I understood the fourth-century debates over the doctrine of God until the past fifteen years. In addition to my own laziness, I also blame deficiencies in my education. The designers of my seminary curriculum obviously thought that the study of patristic theology and exegesis was totally unimportant. My doctoral program at Toronto required a course in liberation theology but none in patristic theology! That pretty much sums up in a nutshell what is wrong with the modern academy. I can only be thankful that I did get an honors BA in the history of philosophy in which we read nothing but primary sources, and this has been the most useful part of my education. But there is no future for orthodox theology unless pastors and professors make it a priority to understand the classical tradition of Nicene orthodoxy. This is part of what motivates me to write this book.

As I become increasingly aware of the distance between Nicene orthodoxy and much of contemporary evangelical theology, I realize my need for deeper roots in a living tradition. Thomas Oden argued that if members of various denominational traditions were each to burrow down to the roots of their own traditions, they would find themselves closer to one another as a result. This is because the various Christian traditions converge the further back in time we go.[24] Instead of looking for the lowest common denominator in the present, he recommends looking for the oldest and most fundamental traditions as a strategy for true ecumenism. But trying to go all the way back to the

---

24. Thomas Oden is the author of many books that have influenced me. But let me mention three: *After Modernity . . . What?*; *Requiem*; and *Rebirth of Orthodoxy*. His greatest contribution, however, was his vision for, and general editorship of, the Ancient Christian Commentary Series published by InterVarsity Press. This was a monumental accomplishment, for which he will always be remembered with gratitude.

Bible while ignoring the patristic, medieval, and Reformation periods is not effective. If we wish to be orthodox and not merely repeat ancient heresies, we need to know historical theology. I have, therefore, gone deeper into my own Baptist roots and studied the seventeenth-century Reformed Baptist tradition in England. The Second London Confession of 1689 shapes my identity as a confessional Protestant. I also am privileged to have held the office of Theologian in Residence in my local Baptist church for over a decade now, in addition to serving as professor of theology in an evangelical university. So I am accountable to a local church and not just to the academy. My theological work is not that of a freelance thinker. Instead, it is a part of a living tradition of classical orthodoxy that stretches back to the New Testament apostles, who proclaimed that Jesus Christ is the fulfillment of the Old Testament Scriptures. I have gone from wanting to revise classical orthodoxy to joyfully and wholeheartedly celebrating it; in this book I aim to defend it.

Part One

Defining Trinitarian Classical Theism

One

Classical Orthodoxy and the Rise of Relational Theism

> Because God is simple, he is absolutely and not merely contingently other than the world. . . . The otherness of God is not an instance of correlativity or complementarity. . . . Creatures are not related to God as to a thing of a different genus, but as to something outside of and prior to all genera.
>
> John Webster[1]

For the past decade, I have been contemplating the meaning of two curious facts about the history of Christian theology. The first is that prior to the Enlightenment, virtually no Christian theologian thought that there was any tension, let alone a contraction, between the immutability and impassibility of God, on the one hand, and the fact that God has acted in history to judge and save, on the other. The second is that by the late nineteenth century the problem of how to reconcile divine immutability and impassibility with what the Bible says about God's actions in history had become a pressing question, and in the twentieth century there was a virtual stampede of Christian theologians from many different traditions seeking to qualify, modify, or even deny outright the immutability and impassibility of God in the name of being "biblical." Nobody thought it was a problem until suddenly everybody

---

1. Webster, "*Non ex Aequo*," 120.

thought it was a problem. How did this change occur? Why did it occur? What does it mean for the future of orthodox Christianity?

Classical Theism versus Relational Theism

Classical theism is the historic orthodox doctrine of God, and it says that God is the simple, immutable, eternal, self-existent First Cause of the cosmos. God creates the world and acts on it, but the world cannot change God in any way. Relational theism is a term that we can apply to a number of different doctrines of God, all of which affirm that God changes the world and the world changes God. Surely it is obvious that these two conceptions of God are as different as day and night. We are talking about two different concepts of what God is.

On the one hand, there is the transcendent Creator, whose being is qualitatively different from created being and who is unknowable in his unique being except by means of his own gracious self-revelation and then only insofar as the limited capacity of the human creature allows. As John Webster says in the quotation that heads this chapter, God is not part of the world, and this means not only that God is not a being within this world but also that God does not exist *alongside* the world as the complement to the world. God and the world do not stand on some common plane that allows them to be in a relationship with each other as two creatures stand in relation to each other. God is totally other than the world in his divine being. Historic orthodoxy, including both Eastern Orthodoxy and Western Christianity in both its Roman Catholic and Protestant forms, has viewed divine simplicity as a way of stating the radical otherness of God rather than as a univocal statement about the nature of divine being. It is a signifier of mystery, not a rational definition. The famous denial of "real relations" between God and creation by Thomas Aquinas means not that God cannot act on the world but only that the world cannot act on God. God brings about change in the world, but the world does not bring about change in God. He writes, "Since therefore God is outside the whole order of creation, and all creatures are ordered to Him, and not conversely, it is manifest that creatures are really related to God Himself; whereas in God there is no real relation to creatures, but a relation only in idea, inasmuch as creatures are referred to Him."[2] This

2. Thomas Aquinas, *Summa Theologica*, I, q. 13, art. 7 (1:66). See Davies (*Thought of Thomas Aquinas*, 75–79) for a discussion of what Thomas means here. Davies shows that Thomas's point is the same as that of Webster in the above quotation: God is utterly other than the world and not in any way limited by, conditioned by, or otherwise changed or affected by the

is an affirmation that the relationship is not between two entities of similar being but between the immutable and perfect self-existent God, on the one hand, and the world of change and imperfection that is itself wholly dependent on God, on the other.

The modern era, however, has witnessed a sustained challenge to the traditional view of God as simple, immutable, impassible, and outside of time. This challenge has taken a number of different forms, some relatively radical and others relatively conservative with regard to the classical tradition. On the radical end of the spectrum we see the weak, pleading, cajoling God of process theism, who, as part of the cosmos himself (or itself?), is incapable of directing history by his power to its appointed end. This God changes along with the world and interacts with it in such a way that God changes the world and the world changes God. Process theologians think that the omnipotence of God must be denied lest God be responsible for evil. For example, Catherine Keller, speaking of what she terms "the contradiction growing in the heart of monotheism," says, "If the God of justice is to be counted all-powerful, that God must be held accountable for all injustice."[3] The God of the various forms of relational theism cannot prevent evil, but he/it can and does suffer along with the creation. In his dynamic panentheism, for example, Jürgen Moltmann views "the suffering of Christ as the suffering of the passionate God."[4] Divine love is redefined as God's voluntary suffering along with the creation. This suffering god can thus rightly be said to be, in more than one sense, pathetic.

On the (relatively) conservative end of the spectrum, we see many less-radical proposals, which nevertheless are reacting to the same basic problem of the supposed incompatibility of divine immutability with divine action in history. Brian Davies has coined the term "theistic personalism" to describe those who reject classical theism and view God as a "being among beings," that is, a person like us only greater, older, wiser, more powerful, and immortal—a sort of disembodied mind similar to Descartes's conception of himself, only greater than us by degree. Davies cites Richard Swinburne, who defines God as "a person without a body."[5] Swinburne believes that God is within time[6] and that the Trinity is a "collective" of three "individuals, whose

---

world. This is an idea that is central to Eastern and Western and Roman Catholic and Protestant theology down through the entire history of theology. If it seems unfamiliar and esoteric today, that is merely an indication of how out of touch contemporary theology is with its own roots.

3. Keller, *Face of the Deep*, 127.

4. Moltmann, *Trinity and the Kingdom*, 22.

5. Davies, *Introduction to the Philosophy of Religion*, 9ff.

6. Swinburne, *Christian God*, 131–32.

unity consists in the fact that each of them are members of a genus (kind) named 'divine.'"[7] This "social trinitarianism" was rejected by the pro-Nicene fathers of the fourth century, who were responsible for developing the Nicene doctrine of God, but it is making a big comeback today.[8] A slightly less radical proposal, but one that arises from similar concerns, is the open theism of Clark Pinnock and others. In this theology, God waits to see what creatures do and then responds because God has made "a kind of covenant of non-coercion with creatures," which means that there are "certain metaphysical constraints that God cannot avoid."[9] In open theism the limits on God's power are seen as self-imposed and voluntary on his part, which makes this view much closer to orthodoxy than process theology. Pinnock calls his view "a species of free will theism" that is in opposition to "the strong immutability central to the Thomistic model."[10] James E. Dolezal discusses a number of conservative Calvinist theologians who have moved in the direction of what he calls "theistic mutualism" in order to meet the objection that an immutable and impassible God is incapable of having a real relationship with us. As an example, he cites Bruce Ware, who Dolezal believes has conceded too much ground in responding to the open theists. Ware, Dolezal argues, concedes the main point that ontological change occurs in the being of God and wishes only to insist that the cause of this change is the sovereign will of God.[11] It seems that many conservative evangelical and Reformed theologians feel a great deal of pressure to make similar concessions to relational theism in the current climate.

Relational theism takes many forms, resulting in models of God that vary considerably from each other. But if we look closely, we can see that all of them spring from the same source—namely, the supposed contradiction between the transcendent God of classical theism and the biblical God who speaks and acts in history to judge and to save. In surveying the proposed solutions to the problem, one gets the feeling that some theologians would have difficulty refuting the devasting assessment that they have destroyed God in order to save him. By this I mean that the solution to the problem is worse than the problem itself. Weakening the radical otherness and transcendence of God in order to bring God closer to us and ensure that we have a "real" relationship with him fails in the stated goal of making possible a

---

7. Swinburne, *Christian God*, 180–81.

8. Ayres, *Nicaea and Its Legacy*. See chap. 14, which expounds Gregory of Nyssa's rejection of social trinitarianism.

9. Pinnock, *Most Moved Mover*, 137.

10. Pinnock, *Most Moved Mover*, x, xi.

11. Dolezal, *All That Is in God*, 27–28. See Ware, "Modified Calvinist Doctrine of God," 85–92.

relationship between the transcendent God and human beings precisely to the extent that, by denying God's simplicity and immutability, God becomes a being different from what he actually is. Having thus created a god in our own image capable of functioning alongside us within the cosmos, we certainly are capable of having a two-way relationship with him, but we still do not have a relationship with the one true God of the Bible and of historic Christian orthodoxy. It is not with God but with an idol that we now enjoy a relationship. Rather than coming close to the God of the Bible, we have merely become idol-worshipers.

The crucial difference between the classical doctrine of God and modern relational theism has to do with the distinction between God and the world. Both classical theism and relational theism assert that God speaks and acts in history to judge and save. Where they differ is in their respective understandings of the nature of the God who does these things. In the quotation at the head of this chapter, John Webster speaks of how God differs from the world. In classical theism there is a strong emphasis on the otherness of God; God is not seen as an extension of the world in any way, and the world is not seen as an extension of God in any way. The being of the world and the being of God are not continuous but radically different. God alone is creator of all that is not God. This contrasts with all forms of pagan religion and many types of Greek philosophy, in which the being of God and the being of the cosmos are continuous.

One crucial way of expressing this difference has been to speak of God as acting causally on the world while denying that the world acts causally on God. This is because God is creator and the world is creation. The being of the world is contingent on God in a way that the being of God is not contingent on the world. This asymmetrical relationship is crucial to the preservation of God's uniqueness. Classical theism speaks of God's aseity, which means that he is self-existent and thus dependent only on his own being. But creation is contingent on God, which means that it is totally dependent on God both for its origin and also for its continuation in existence. In modern relational theism, the simplicity and aseity of God are denied, and God is seen as existing in a relationship to creation similar to the kind of relationship one creature has with another. Quite often as well, God is understood to be in time with us and therefore participating in the ongoing change that characterizes creatures. Characteristic of all relations between creatures is the mutual influence of creatures on each other, resulting in change on both sides. But in God the relation is one way only: God causes and changes creatures, but creatures do not cause or change God. Why not? Because God's being is unique to himself and unlike our own. When relational theism affirms two-way relations of causality and change between God and creatures, it eliminates the uniqueness of God and brings him down to the level of a creature. The dispute between classical theism and relational theism is not about details or obscure points of metaphysics; at stake is nothing less than the creator-creature distinction. To get this issue wrong is to fall into idolatry.

In this book, I want to explain as simply and clearly as possible how and why this sea change in our understanding of the nature of God occurred and why relational theism is a dead end intellectually, spiritually, and culturally. I want to demonstrate the superiority of the historic, classic, orthodox, Nicene view of God as the true teaching of Holy Scripture. Those who hold to one version or another of the new relational understanding of God view themselves as "progressives" and see their views as surpassing the older understandings of God in much the same way as modern science surpasses primitive superstitions about how the world works. However, from my perspective, something like the opposite actually is true. The modern relational view of God is merely a reversion to the pagan mythology that existed in the world before Abraham; there is nothing progressive about it.

It is the divine self-revelation to Abraham, Moses, David, and the prophets culminating in the coming of Jesus Christ that constitutes the only true progress that has ever been made in the human understanding of God. On nearly every page the Old Testament testifies to how radical that revelation of God as the transcendent Creator was and how difficult it was for the children of Israel to detach themselves from the grip of pagan mythological thinking long enough for the new revelation of the transcendent Creator to establish itself and take root among them. The Christian church has also struggled mightily throughout history to absorb and preserve the astonishing revelation contained in Holy Scripture. In the fourth century, the Arian crisis led to the church nearly losing the biblical thread and reverting back to paganism, but in God's providence the church was able to hold on to the scriptural revelation of God as the transcendent Creator and articulate that understanding in the Niceno-Constantinopolitan Creed of AD 381. Today we are living through a period of struggle similar in magnitude to the one that occurred in the fourth century. The modern period has seen a major challenge to the orthodox understanding of God, one that the church currently is coping with hesitantly and clumsily.

One complicating factor today is the great apostasy within the world center of Christianity, namely Western Europe, which has occurred over the past three centuries. It may well turn out to be the case that the classically orthodox faith will not survive much longer in Europe except as the faith of a persecuted minority but will instead flourish and take root in the growing churches of the global South. Since Europe has been the place where the church has done much of its best thinking over the past millennium, this means that the global church lacks the in-depth theological resources that would be helpful in this crisis. However, the fact that the Holy Spirit moves in power in the growing churches of the global South more than makes up for the lack of great universities and well-educated theologians. Once Europe itself lacked these resources, but the work of Spirit-filled gospel preaching caused the church to reflect more deeply on its faith and resulted in the growth and flourishing of colleges, seminaries, and universities. This process is already happening in our day in the global South, and in due course the intellectual center of world Christianity will likely shift to Africa and other parts of the global South. What happened in terms of intellectual life in Europe between, say, the tenth and nineteenth centuries was not something baked into the genes of the European races; rather, it was a culture created and nourished by the gospel. Wherever the gospel goes, Christian culture grows. Race is as irrelevant as geography to this historical process. The future of Nicene orthodoxy is in Africa and Asia, not in Europe and North America (unless a massive revival breaks out in those places). Before signing up to massive revisions in doctrine, theologians facing the challenge of relational theism ought to consider the nature of our social situation and take into account the fact that we live in a culture that is systematically rejecting the gospel.

Most Western theology in the twenty-first century, apart from conservative and orthodox exceptions, has embraced various forms of relational theism. In so doing, vast swaths of the Roman church and most of the historic Protestant denominations have cut themselves off from their own confessional roots. This is the painful reality that this book seeks to lay bare. The obvious question that arises from this bleak diagnosis is what this fact means for the church, for the gospel, and for Western culture. What does it mean that most academic theology done today in Western universities and in the leading seminaries of the historic denominations is based on some sort of relational theism? To answer this question, we first need to gain greater clarity on how relational theism differs from classical orthodoxy. I believe that most people, including conservative evangelical scholars, have only a dim awareness of the seriousness of the issues involved in this historic theological shift. We need to understand what classical theism is and how it relates to biblical trinitarian theology. We also need to understand how deeply biblical the roots of classical orthodoxy really are. The main purpose of this book is to explain the true nature of our situation so that we understand what is at stake in the challenge that relational theism poses to classical theism.

Contemplating God with the Nicene Fathers

There are three problems with a lot of contemporary theology that we would do well to avoid. First, modern theology tends to discuss the doctrine of the Trinity separately from the doctrine of the attributes of God. This is a problem because the doctrine of the Trinity can float free of its moorings in the nature of God and can take on pagan, unbiblical baggage without anyone realizing it. Second, modern theology often is far too impatient with mystery and much too quick to declare a contradiction when, in fact, it is only confronting a paradox. Just because things become complex does not necessarily mean we are doing anything wrong. Third, modern theology tries to jump over the history of theology and interpret the Bible in modern terms without realizing when it is just repeating old mistakes all over again. In this book, I hope to avoid these three pitfalls by paying sustained attention to the key century from the Council of Nicaea in AD 325 to the death of Augustine in AD 430. This is the formative period when the classical Christian doctrine of God took shape and was expressed in the Niceno-Constantinopolitan Creed of AD 381, which is more popularly known as the Nicene Creed.

The best way to think of the classically orthodox definition of God is to see it as the union of classical theism and trinitarian theology. Classical theism and biblical trinitarianism came together during the fourth century in the context of the Arian debates. This period of controversy was the context for the genesis of the Nicene doctrine of God, which is the heart of classical orthodoxy as expressed in the Nicene Creed. Fourth-century pro-Nicene theology combined a commitment to divine immutability and simplicity, on the one hand, with a trinitarian account of how God operates in history, on the other. Combining these two understandings of God was an intentional strategy designed to do justice to Scripture. The Nicene fathers believed that they needed to be concerned both with what was termed "theology" and also with what was termed the "economy." So they spoke of what we would call the ontological or immanent Trinity as well as the economic Trinity. These terms refer to God in his own eternal being (the ontological Trinity) and to God in his revelatory actions in history (the economic Trinity). There is only one Triune God, but to be clear about our meaning, we speak of him in different ways.

Our most important knowledge of God comes from his self-revelation in the economy, that is, in history. God acts in history (e.g., the exodus, the resurrection of Christ), and he inspires his prophets to explain the significance of those acts (the testimony of Scripture). But fourth-century pro-Nicene theologians sought to go beyond descriptions of God's actions in history and make statements about the nature of God in himself; that is, they sought to make statements about the eternal being of God on the basis of revelation. It is not enough to speak only of God's actions in history. Why not? Because we seek absolute truth about God, not merely an account of how he has acted so far. By this I mean that theology seeks to rest our faith on the very being of God, not merely on the account of his acts. Some theologians talk as if it were more biblical to speak only of the economy, and they dismiss the hard work of relating the economy to theology as unnecessary speculation. In patristic and scholastic theology, speculative theology is a good thing, but in modern theology, the term has acquired a pejorative connotation. We need to recover the premodern sense of speculative theology and see why it is spiritually beneficial. Scripture is our model here.

Modern theologians often mistakenly think that they are imitating the Bible itself when they focus only on God's acts in history. But the Bible itself grapples with the relationship between God's self-revelation in history and God's eternal being in himself. The prophets of Israel were well aware of the natural fear we have that, given the intractable evil of the human heart, God might one day decide that enough is enough and that the messy experiment with human beings should come to an end. In other words, the confidence that God will continue to be gracious to us needs to be grounded in something more than the *will* of God; if God's promises are to be taken as absolutely certain, our confidence must be grounded in the *being* of God. Can we trust God to keep his promise to David in 2 Samuel 7 that a descendent of David will sit on the throne of David forever? This was Isaiah's problem. The problem of the book of Isaiah is encapsulated in the uniquely Isaianic phrase "the Holy One of Israel." Israel's God is holy and therefore must separate himself from all sin and punish it. Israel, however, is unholy and therefore must go into exile and suffer punishment for sin. But if exile is coming and the city of Jerusalem, the temple, and the throne of David must all fall, how can God's promise to David be kept? The extreme pressure of the problem arises from the fact that a holy God has made an unconditional promise to an unholy people. Isaiah sees that the holiness of God is a matter of the being of God, not just the will of God. Is grace also a matter of the being of God or merely a matter of God's will? All the prophets felt the burden of this problem, and their preoccupation was therefore with the nature of Israel's God, not merely with his actions up to that point in history.

This is why the book of Psalms resounds with exclamations about the very being and nature of God:

> Praise the LORD!
> Oh give thanks to the LORD, for he is good,
>   for his steadfast love endures forever! (Ps. 106:1)

"The LORD is good" (Ps. 100:5). That is the bedrock conviction on which the faith of Israel rested. In Psalm 106 the psalmist recounts the checkered history of the people of Israel, a history marred by continuous sin (v. 6), forgetfulness (vv. 7, 13), idolatry (v. 19), lack of faith (v. 24), and immorality (v. 28). More than once during this sorry history, the psalmist recalls that the LORD was tempted to destroy and abandon his people (vv. 23, 26), and the LORD's anger burned against them (vv. 29, 32). Instead of destroying the inhabitants of Canaan as they were commanded to do (v. 34), God's people mixed with the nations and learned to worship idols (vv. 35–36), even to the point of joining in with the pagans in the abominable practice of child sacrifice (vv. 37–39). The LORD's anger against his people led to their being oppressed by the nations (vv. 41–42), but the LORD always delivered them. The psalmist is sure that it was the steadfast love of the LORD, not any sort of merit on the part of Israel, that caused the LORD to act in mercy. From the perspective of the exile, the psalmist musters up the nerve to call on the LORD to "gather us from among the nations that we may give thanks to your holy name and glory in your praise" (v. 47). On what basis does the psalmist dare to ask this? Certainly not the merit of the people of Israel; rather, it is because of who God is. The psalm ends by affirming the LORD, the God of Israel, who is unchanging "from everlasting to everlasting" (v. 48). What, primarily and most importantly, is he eternally? He is good. The goodness of God is the foundation of faith.[12]

From a human point of view, it would be easy to lose heart and give in to despair in the face of Israel's continual apostasy—from the golden calf at the foot of Sinai to the worship of Assyrian gods in the Jerusalem temple under Ahaz—and it was necessary to ground hope in something other than history. Is there a basis in the nature of God for our hope of grace and redemption? The question of the nature of God was central to the faith of the Old Testament, and it remained central to New Testament theology and to the faith of the early church. It is one thing to say that God has acted mercifully in the past (in the economy); it is another to say that God is characterized by steadfast love (ḥesed) in his very being (ontology). Viewed from this perspective, the doctrine of immutability takes on a whole different complexion. What might have been perceived as a matter of abstract speculation is suddenly revealed to be a crucial matter of faith. For fourth-century pro-Nicene theologians, the debates we study today as the Arian crisis and the formation of Nicene trinitarianism were as much an issue of personal faith versus unbelief as they

12. For an edifying elaboration of the truth that the goodness of God is the preeminent claim of the Psalter about God, see C. Holmes, *Lord Is Good*.

were a complex philosophical problem. They were not merely one or the other but both at the same time.

Thus one of the main topics of contemplation for the pro-Nicene theologians of the fourth century was how the utterly simple, unchanging, eternal, perfect God could be Father, Son, and Holy Spirit. How could the Son be simple and immutable while also becoming man? The Arians gave up trying; they suggested that we view the Father as the eternal, simple, unchanging, perfect one and then see the Son and Spirit as the ones who act in history. Thus they placed the Son and Spirit outside the simplicity of God. The pro-Nicene fathers considered this to be a denial of their essential deity and therefore to be heretical and blasphemous. One of the major contributions the Cappadocian fathers made to Nicene orthodoxy was to work out an account of the Trinity in which all three persons are understood as partaking of the divine simplicity.[13] A potential conflict was introduced into the Triune God by the Arians that threatened the unity of the divine being unless some way could be found to include the three persons of the Trinity within the divine simplicity. This required sustained reflection both on what simplicity is and what it is not. The eternal being of God, which is the being of Father, Son, and Spirit, is simple.[14]

The doctrines of immutability and impassibility say that God does not change in his essence. These doctrines, however, are not stand-alone doctrines; they actually are part of an intricate web of beliefs that make up what is often called "classical theism" or "the classical doctrine of God." Classical theism refers to what can be known about God by reason working on general revelation. By philosophical reasoning about nature, we can know that God necessarily must exist as the First Cause of the universe and that God is simple, immutable, eternal, and self-existent. But we cannot know that this God has acted so as to create, judge, become incarnate, and redeem the fallen creation except by special revelation. Special revelation comes to us today in Holy Scripture. Although some attributes of God, such as immutability and eternity, can be known by natural theology, other attributes of God, such as love and mercy, can be known only by special revelation. The Nicene doctrine of the Trinity was formulated to affirm that the Triune God—Father, Son, and Holy Spirit—has the attributes of simplicity, eternity, aseity, perfection, and immutability. The fathers were convinced that Scripture teaches both of these sets of attributes—that is, both the philosophical attributes and the personal

---

13. For the best recent account of how they did this, see Radde-Gallwitz, *Transformation of Divine Simplicity*.

14. I will discuss this issue in more depth in chap. 7.

attributes. Contemplation of the Spirit-interpreted acts of God in history, as found in Scripture, led the pro-Nicene theologians of the fourth century to conclude that we can have absolutely certain, though not comprehensive, knowledge of the eternal nature of God. The economic Trinity reveals the ontological Trinity truly, though not exhaustively.

So the best way to understand the formation of the Nicene doctrine of God is to see it as bringing together what would later be called "classical theism" (derived both from general revelation and from special revelation) with trinitarian theology (known only from Holy Scripture) to allow the full meaning of the truths of general revelation to be understood more fully *in the light of* special revelation. Today the so-called god of the philosophers often is denigrated as being incompatible with the personal God of the Bible, and classical theism is considered unimportant at best and harmful to the biblical doctrine of God at worst. Theological speculation about the immanent Trinity and the being of God in itself is thought to be utterly unrelated to the Christian life and irrelevant to preaching. After all, it is said, how many sermons have you heard on the doctrine of divine simplicity? My hope is that, having read this book, you will see why the early church fathers, medieval scholastics, Protestant Reformers, and post-Reformation scholastics and Puritans thought that the issue of classical theism is vitally important to worship, spirituality, and Christian confidence in God. It is actually the basis of our hope of eternal salvation. We may not preach divine simplicity every Sunday, but divine simplicity undergirds the gospel we do preach every Sunday, and the truth of classical theism, coupled with biblical trinitarian theology, makes it possible to confess the gospel as absolutely and eternally true.

The Decline of Classical Orthodoxy in Modernity

During the seventeenth and eighteenth centuries, many of Europe's elites turned away from special revelation and from the Christian faith itself. There was a growing conviction that there is a contradiction between what reason can know about God and what is taught in the Bible about God. To put it as concisely as possible: if God is immutable, he does not act in history; on the other hand, if he acts in history, he is not immutable. So why did the church teach that God can at the same time be immutable and also act in history? Why then was this sort of contradiction, along with the rest of historic orthodoxy, so widely held for over a millennium by so many thinkers? The answer the advocates of Enlightenment came up with was that no rational person would ever have believed this kind of contradiction except for the pressure applied to philosophers and theologians by the institutional church. This is the origin of the Enlightenment drive to overturn the authority of the church in the name of reason. This crusade began to make serious inroads into Western cultural consciousness in the nineteenth century and burst into dominance in the twentieth century.

In the nineteenth century, we see the rise of the myth of the romantic hero. This is the individual who challenges the establishment, the single heroic thinker who refuses to bow to political pressure to conform but who instead rebels in the name of free thought and reason. We also see a widespread tendency—beginning in the nineteenth century and mushrooming in the twentieth century—to view the pursuit of truth as incompatible with the constraints of any sort of creed or doctrinal authority. The scientist must be an iconoclast who challenges dominant ideas in the culture. Finally, we also see the rise of the myth of warfare between science and theology, in which progress in intellectual thought is held back by the forces of reaction- ary churchmen bent on stifling challenges to established ways of thinking. Christianity was increasingly portrayed as self-contradictory, anti-reason, and politically reactionary. Human progress was said to require the triumph of reason over superstition, education over ignorance, and science over theology. Revelation came to be seen as an impediment to reason instead of being complementary to reason.

During the period of the Enlightenment, the three problems in modern theology that we noted in the previous section began to affect theology. First, the tendency to pit the God who speaks and acts in Scripture against the im- mutable and simple God of classical theism resulted in the separation of the attributes of God from the Trinity. Initially, this brought about the eclipse of the doctrine of the Trinity between the eighteenth and nineteenth centuries and the rise of Deism. Then when the doctrine of the Trinity was brought back to the forefront of theological thought in the twentieth century, it was done in a way that separated it from classical theism. As a result, the so-called twentieth-century revival of trinitarian theology was more a massive revision of the classical doctrine of God than a revival of it. We will discuss problems with the twentieth-century doctrine of God in more detail in chapter 9, but for now it is important to note that what the fourth-century fathers did by uniting the simple, immutable God with the biblical God who speaks and acts in history was ignored by twentieth-century theologians.

Twentieth-century theology, for the most part, tended to be preoccupied with the economic Trinity while ignoring the immanent Trinity. There was a desire for a doctrine of God based entirely on biblical themes, but what came to prominence was a doctrine of God that lost its grip on divine transcendence, thereby losing what is most distinctively and uniquely biblical in the process. The lesson from this is that if we want to be truly biblical, we need to pay attention to the relationship between our concept of God's self-revelation in history and God's eternal being in himself. Toward the end of the twentieth century, and in the early part of the twenty-first century, a movement led by John Webster emerged that called for theology to refocus on the being of the immanent Trinity, that is, on the attributes of the Triune God.

Second, there is a much lower tolerance for mystery and paradox in modernity than in historic orthodoxy. Here the moderns are closer in spirit to the Arians of the fourth century than to the Nicene fathers. As in the Arian controversy of the fourth century, orthodoxy is today seen as obscurantist and overly complicated, whereas the heretical alternative is seen as rational, clear, and reasonable. It needs to be pointed out, however, that the common assumption that our doctrine of God should be easily understandable is badly flawed. We can expect rational clarity if all we want is a God who is a larger version of ourselves, that is, a God who differs from creatures only by degree and not in kind. But if God is essentially different from us in kind, not just in degree, then his being necessarily must be mysterious to us and beyond the rational capacity of the creature to grasp. The great problem then becomes how even to speak about God at all. How can human language be adequate to express the mystery that is the transcendent Creator? Paradox and limits on our understanding should be expected. Worship, not rational comprehension, of God is the end of such theology. A rationally comprehensible God will inevitably turn out to be either identical with the cosmos as a whole or a being within the cosmos with us. Either way we end up worshiping the creature instead of the Creator.

Third, modern theology has lost its living connection to fourth-century Nicene theology. Lewis Ayres writes, "In many ways the argument of my last chapter is not that modern Trinitarianism has engaged with pro-Nicene theology badly, but that it has barely engaged it at all. As a result the legacy of Nicaea remains paradoxically the unnoticed ghost at the modern Trinitarian feast."[15] We can see how true this is in various ways. The study of patristics has not been regarded as essential preparation either for systematic theologians or for pastors, and this creates problems in understanding and passing on classical orthodoxy. The decline in the study of Greek philosophy by theologians also renders them unable to comprehend what the fourth-century debates were all about. But on a deeper level, the Enlightenment insistence that we not "read in" the theology of the ecumenical creeds as we exegete

---

15. Ayres, *Nicaea and Its Legacy*, 7.

Scripture has been internalized to such a degree even by confessing orthodox theologians that exegesis has been done within the framework of modern metaphysical assumptions that are very different from (and incompatible with) those with which the fourth-century fathers worked. This has led to attempts to combine trinitarian theology with various metaphysical systems that are not just different from the ones employed by pro-Nicene theology of the fourth century but are actually contradictory to the ones used in the fourth century. In some cases, twentieth-century theologians actually employ the very metaphysical doctrines that the fourth-century fathers explicitly and consciously rejected as they sought to refute Arianism.

Holding together classical theism and trinitarian theology requires tolerance for mystery and sustained attentiveness to the nuances of the philosophical and theological debates of the fourth century. Classical theism without trinitarian theology gives us the god of the philosophers, that is, the remote and impersonal god of Deism, who does not speak or act and who, crucially, cannot save us. But trinitarian theology without classical theism results in a God who is part of the cosmos with us, differing from creatures only by degree and not by nature. Such a god is no more able to save us than the Deist god. The so-called trinitarian revival of the twentieth century was not a revival of Nicene orthodoxy.[16] The reason twentieth-century theology failed to revive Nicene orthodoxy was that it was an attempt to have a Nicene doctrine of the Trinity without classical theism. Many forms of relational theism attempt to pass themselves off as biblical by affirming the doctrine of the Trinity, but they reject classical theism. The result of that experiment was an entirely new thing in the history of theology, something never seen before, namely, pagan trinitarianism.

When relational theism replaces classical theism, the result is a reversion into the pagan mythology that was in the world before God called Abraham out of Ur and began to reveal himself to him and his descendants. It is the combining of pantheism and polytheism, with the added wrinkle that the number of deities worshiped is limited to three instead of an unspecified number. Many ancient cultures have combined pantheism and polytheism in this way; one need only think of Hinduism, for example. What this means is that, strange as it may sound, modernity has more in common with the mythological worldview of the ancient Near East than it has with the God revealed in Scripture and the biblical doctrine of God enshrined in Nicene orthodoxy.

16. For a good treatment of this point, see S. Holmes, *Quest for the Trinity*. I will come back to this book and to this point in chap. 9.

This may seem like a radical thesis to the true believer in modern progressivism, but the grounds for taking modernity seriously as progress are becoming weaker with every passing year. Western culture has peaked and is in moral, religious, and even demographic decline. The astonishingly large gap between contemporary theological movements such as ecological panentheism and the Nicene orthodoxy of the past millennium and a half has to be explained somehow. Why are old ideas such as pantheism so attractive to moderns? If we have progressed so far, why does our view of God so clearly resemble primitive ancient Near Eastern concepts? For understanding the meaning of contemporary currents in the doctrine of God, nothing seems more relevant and instructive than the history of ancient Israel as depicted in the Old Testament books of the Prophets: both the Former Prophets (Joshua–Kings) and the Latter Prophets (Isaiah–Malachi) of the Hebrew Scriptures. The long war against Baal worship left the postexilic community of Israel in much the same position as the United Kingdom at the end of World War II: victorious but exhausted, impoverished, and severely diminished in strength. The church today in Western culture exhibits a worrisome degree of weakness in its tepid response to the rise of relational theism. Rather than thinking that the war against pagan doctrines of God was won long ago, we need to realize that this war will never end until the second advent of our Lord Jesus Christ.

One frequently encounters the view that modern science is providing needed resources for the development of Christian theology by helping theology come to grips with the nature of the cosmos. But I think this view is less helpful than an alternative way of looking at the situation. It seems preferable to view modern science as having developed, over the past two centuries, an interpretation of nature from within a pantheistic metaphysics. From this perspective, it appears that many of those on the cutting edge of the science-theology dialogue are attempting to revise the Christian doctrines of God and creation so as to make them fit within the pantheistic metaphysics that has replaced the theological metaphysics of Nicaea since the Enlightenment.[17] What is emerging from the contemporary science-theology dialogue is no doubt a very rationally clear and comprehensible understanding of God, but that is precisely why it should be doubted that it could ever be reconciled with historic Christian orthodoxy.

I contend that the understanding of God found in the Old Testament— the theology preached by the Hebrew prophets—is faithfully restated in a different philosophical context by the pro-Nicene theologians of the fourth century and is presupposed by the whole of confessional orthodoxy ever since.

17. For more on this, see chap. 8.

But in modernity, this understanding of God, which I refer to as trinitarian classical theism, is exerting less and less influence; in the liberal Protestant denominations, it has virtually been lost. Modern theology does not merely come to conclusions different from those of classical theology; it has an entirely different starting point and an entirely different method. It is, in short, a different religion altogether.[18] Just as Israel in Old Testament times was negatively affected by the surrounding pagan religions, so the Western church is struggling against the influence of the pagan ideas that surround us today. I will explain why this is the case and how we might think more clearly about modern theology *in order to overcome it.* The path to real future progress in theology runs through the past. How far back do we need to go? We need to go far enough back to avoid the disastrous wrong turn that mainstream Western philosophical and theological thought took in the eighteenth century. Our goal is not, of course, to dwell permanently in the past, for that is simply impossible. On the contrary, our goal is to recover valuable resources from the past that can help us grow in our understanding of the transcendent Creator in the future. This is a project of *ressourcement.*

Toward the Recovery of Classical Theological Method

Perhaps no dictum today is so widespread and so widely agreed on by the entire spectrum of biblical scholars from liberal to conservative as the one saying that we must be absolutely sure not to read our dogmas into the Bible. In the Enlightenment period, a central line of attack against traditional orthodox theology was that the church was guilty of reading the dogmas of the ecumenical creeds into the Bible. In his inaugural address at the University of Altdorf in 1787, J. P. Gabler argued for a distinction between biblical and dogmatic theology. He began his address by lamenting the "fatal discord of the various sects" and deplored what he called "the depraved custom of reading one's own opinions and judgments into the Bible."[19] He asserted that "the sacred books . . . are frequently and in many places veiled by a deep obscurity."[20] But as a typical Enlightenment figure, his proposed solution was to read the Bible as a human book written by ordinary human beings, and he expressed confidence that if we investigate the historical situation in which the books were written, we can determine what the human authors meant in the original situation.

18. This was asserted a century ago by Machen in his classic *Christianity and Liberalism.* He was prescient.

19. Sandys-Wunsch and Eldredge, "J. P. Gabler," 134.

20. Sandys-Wunsch and Eldredge, "J. P. Gabler," 135.

But he insisted that we focus on human authorial intent only: "Let us not by applying tropes forge new dogmas about which the authors themselves never thought."[21] The word "tropes" here, as Sandys-Wunsch notes, is "a technical term referring to allegorical or similar methods of extracting a 'spiritual' meaning from the text."[22] So the emphasis was to be on the Bible as a human document, and the responsibility of the interpreter was not only to under-stand it in its historical context but also to distinguish between meaning that was only for "some particular era or testament" and meaning that has to do with "the unchanging testament of Christian doctrine" because it expresses "universal ideas."[23] He claims that we must distinguish between what in the Bible is "truly divine" and what is "merely human."[24] Inspiration, he assumes without argument, is only partial:

> In this way it may finally be established whether all the opinions of the Apostles, of every type and sort altogether, are truly divine, or rather whether some of them, which have no bearing on salvation, were left to their own ingenuity. . . . Thus, as soon as all these things have been properly observed and carefully ar-ranged, at last a clear sacred Scripture will be selected with scarcely any doubtful readings, made up of passages which are appropriate to the Christian religion of all times. . . . For only from these methods can those certain and undoubted universal ideas be singled out, those ideas which alone are useful in dogmatic theology.[25]

As far as Gabler is concerned, the problem has been that dogmatic theology uses too much of the Bible in its formulations and needs to restrict itself to those biblical concepts that express what he terms "universal ideas." But in fact, the phrase "universal ideas" is just inflated Enlightenment rhetoric for the metaphysical biases of the eighteenth century. Gabler unintentionally makes this clear when he writes, "The nature of our age urgently demands that we teach accurately the harmony of divine dogmatics and the principles of human reason."[26]

Gabler's vision for biblical theology is for modern scholars to treat the Bible as a human book and bracket out divine revelation of the kind of truth the human author could never have attained in any other way but by inspira-tion. He wants to search the Scriptures for instances where the Bible agrees

21. Sandys-Wunsch and Eldredge, "J. P. Gabler," 140.
22. Sandys-Wunsch and Eldredge, "J. P. Gabler," 140n1.
23. Sandys-Wunsch and Eldredge, "J. P. Gabler," 142.
24. Sandys-Wunsch and Eldredge, "J. P. Gabler," 143.
25. Sandys-Wunsch and Eldredge, "J. P. Gabler," 143.
26. Sandys-Wunsch and Eldredge, "J. P. Gabler," 144.

with the metaphysical and ethical assumptions of his own age and extract those as the basis for dogmatic theology. In this way, Christian theology will become identical with the ideas popular in modern Europe, which are supposedly derived from pure reason alone. Needless to say, this new Christian dogmatic theology will be quite unlike the orthodox heritage enshrined in the ecumenical creeds and the Reformation confessions.

We see four key moves here. First, there is a hint that the problem of various denominations disagreeing about the right interpretation of Scripture is rooted in the nature of the Bible itself. This is implied in the statement that the Bible contains much that is obscure, and it is also implied in the account given of limited inspiration. Apparently, sometimes the inspired writers were left to their own devices in matters not essential for salvation. Second, inspiration is defined as a matter of "inspired writers" rather than as the New Testament defines it in terms of inspired texts (2 Tim. 3:16–17). Third, there is the insistence that the focus of exegesis be human authorial intent only and not divine authorial intent, despite the New Testament's clear teaching that both are present in the Scriptures of Israel (1 Pet. 1:10–12). Fourth, the "universal ideas" of the Enlightenment era replace the Bible's own metanarrative as the conceptual framework in which the Bible is to be interpreted. For Irenaeus and Athanasius, as for the apostles, the Bible is a unified book centered on Jesus Christ, and the overarching narrative—including creation, fall, redemption, and consummation—comes out of the Bible and becomes the context for sound biblical exegesis. For Gabler, this overarching narrative is replaced by Enlightenment ideas generated by universal reason.

In *Interpreting Scripture with the Great Tradition*, I argued that the Bible must be interpreted as a unified book centered on Jesus Christ and that this unity comes from divine inspiration. I further argued that reducing the meaning of the biblical text to the conscious intention of the human author in the original situation constitutes a denial of inspiration and leads to the domestication of the Bible. Only by recognizing the spiritual meaning of the text, which is an extension of the literal meaning, can we do justice to the divine authorial intention that is present in the text as a result of inspiration. The dictum that we must not read dogma into the Bible originates in an Enlightenment context in which inspiration is limited, the single-meaning theory espoused, and the unity of the Bible effectively denied. This should give us pause.

What I want to suggest in this book builds on my previous work by arguing that the dictum "We must not read dogma into the Bible" is wrong if it is taken in the way that Gabler means it. Of course, there is a relatively trivial and obvious sense in which it is true that we should not read foreign ideas into the text and that we must treat the literal sense as foundational to all interpretation. No orthodox Christian interpreter disputes that sense. But that is not the whole story. The church fathers did read the creed into the text and were right to do so. But to understand how this could be true, we need to reflect carefully on the nature and method of dogmatic theology and understand it more deeply than modernity has tended to do.

Khaled Anatolios has a lucid discussion of the way Athanasius read Scripture in his polemical work *Against the Arians*.[27] Athanasius deals with one Arian prooftext after another and argues that the Arians are interpreting Scripture in the wrong way. He deals with one group of texts that the Arians interpreted as indicating the origin of the preexistent Christ rather than his being eternal, which included Proverbs 8:22: "He created me as the beginning of his ways for his works." All fourth-century exegetes followed the principle that if Christ is said clearly to be the Wisdom of God (1 Cor. 1:24), then wherever Scripture speaks of Wisdom, it is speaking of Christ. But Proverbs 8:22 seems to say that Wisdom had a beginning. Another group of texts was used by the Arians to argue for the Word's human limitations, indicating a lower level of divinity than that of the Unbegotten God. How does Athanasius respond?

Anatolios points out that Athanasius employs two trinitarian reading strategies. In the first, he reads "the eternal coexistence of the Father and the Son out of the overlapping scriptural identifications of God and Christ."[28] In the second, he says that the christological narrative is twofold, consisting of texts that refer to the divinity and texts that refer to the humanity of Christ. Texts that speak of the limitations of the human Jesus obviously refer to the humanity of Christ, and texts that speak of the power of Christ to create the world obviously refer to the divinity of the preexistent Son. The Arians are guilty of mixing up these two kinds of texts. What we have here is a trinitarian hermeneutic for reading Scripture theologically. Anatolios writes,

> This principle is that the Scriptures are revelatory not only by their reference to external events in history but also by the mutual interrelatedness of biblical texts on a surface linguistic level. In standard allegorical technique, this principle of intertextuality enables one to construct a biblical meaning by connecting together related language from different parts of Scripture, seemingly overstepping the contextual distance between the different usages. The principle of the unity of Scripture is assumed to legitimate the meaningfulness of its intertextual relations. Athanasius's distinctly dogmatic application of this principle is found

27. Anatolios, *Retrieving Nicaea*, 108–22.
28. Anatolios, *Retrieving Nicaea*, 110.

in his assumption that the intertextual patterns of the scriptural naming of God must mirror, in a way accommodated to human understanding, the being of God.[29]

This analysis enables us to understand that Athanasius is not simply disagreeing with Arian exegesis arbitrarily or because it does not fit his own preconceptions. His exegesis of individual passages is controlled by the overall *skopos*, or summary, of Scripture. The Bible as a whole reveals that Christ is both human and divine, and so individual texts of Scripture are assumed to be not contradictory but complementary to each other because the Bible as a whole is the product of a single divine mind. The Bible speaks not only of the incarnate Christ but also of the eternal, preexistent Son of the Father.

Athanasius criticizes the Arians for using the nonscriptural word "Unoriginate" to speak of the Father because the biblical pattern is to speak of Father and Son. Athanasius argues that the word "Unoriginate" designates the difference between God and creatures, but that it should not be applied to the relation between Father and Son.[30] When the Arians ask if there is only one Unoriginate or perhaps two, they are departing from biblically authorized patterns of speech.[31] They hope thereby to prove that the Son is not Unoriginate, but this attempt fails because the Bible itself does not use the term "Unoriginate" but rather uses the term "Son." For Athanasius, the Father and Son are correlative terms, and so they mutually imply each other. If there was a time when the Father did not have a Son, it would mean that he was not at that time Father. This would mean that he became Father, which would imply change in God. To think of God the Father as existing without his Wisdom would similarly be blasphemous. The Wisdom of God, that is, the Son of God, is in biblical terms eternal.

Athanasius also appeals to the direction of the incarnation on the basis of Philippians 2:9–10.[32] This text says that Christ was always God and only at a moment in time descended to take on human flesh: "He was not from a lower state promoted; but rather, existing as God, He took the form of a servant, and in taking it, was not promoted but humbled himself."[33] Athanasius is convinced that the Bible tells us something not only about Christ's incarnation (the economy) but also something about the nature of the being of the God

29. Anatolios, *Retrieving Nicaea*, 111.
30. Athanasius, *Oration* 1, 9.33 (NPNF² 4:325–26).
31. Athanasius, *Oration* 1, 9.31 (NPNF² 4:324–25).
32. Athanasius, *Oration* 1, 11.39 (NPNF² 4:329).
33. Athanasius, *Oration* 1, 11.40 (NPNF² 4:329–30).

who became incarnate (theology). Scripture reveals both together in a pattern of language that coheres together across the canon. This language pattern is divinely inspired and is all the more wondrous because it is more than what any one human author grasped and more than even the sum of the parts of all the perspectives of all the human authors put together. This concept of the whole being greater than the sum of the parts is the reason why contemplation of Scripture is necessary. Exegesis must precede contemplation, but without contemplation, exegesis remains incomplete as knowledge of God. Theology is exegesis plus the contemplation of exegetical results and the expression of the results of that contemplation in the form of doctrines.

One goal of this book is to demonstrate how this premodern approach is in tension with modern methods of theological construction and why it is a superior method. The recovery of the theological method of the pro-Nicene fathers will enable us to preserve the doctrinal substance of the Nicene doctrine as well as the verbal formulae of the creed. Since my goal is to argue that the classical approach to Christian theology is as valid and useful as it ever was, it would be rather inconsistent for me to adopt the modern method that I criticize as deficient and detrimental. Therefore, I intend both to *describe* and to *demonstrate* what I think is a better way to engage in systematic theology. In the rest of this chapter, I will explain how this premodern method of doing theology works. Then in the rest of the book, I will put it into practice. After this introductory chapter, I begin my argument in chapter 2 for the biblical basis of classical theism with a necessarily concise and schematic sketch of the trinitarian classical theism of the orthodox tradition. In so doing, I am setting the stage for the exegetical section in part 2 by summarizing the tradition on this topic, which I take as my starting point in doing exegesis. But is that not putting the cart before the horse? Is that presupposing my conclusion? I think not, and here is why I think this is a valid procedure.

As we have seen above, theology consists of exegesis plus dogmatics; that is, it consists of exegeting Scripture and compiling a list of statements that summarize the exegetical results. These statements gradually coalesce into doctrines. Then we contemplate those doctrines and deduce from them further doctrines, including metaphysical ones. By metaphysical doctrines, I mean doctrines describing God's relationship to the world. For example, that God created the cosmos (that is, the heavens and the earth) by his Word is stated in Genesis 1. When we note that a wide variety of other passages in the Psalms, the Prophets, John 1, Colossians 1, and so forth all say much the same thing, we begin to find it helpful to speak of the doctrine of creation. As we contemplate the totality of what Scripture says about creation, we are justified in identifying the metaphysical doctrine of *creatio ex nihilo* as a deduction from revealed truth.[34] So we begin with revelation, then we move to doctrines, and finally we deduce metaphysical truths from those doctrines. All this seems clear enough, but is this a complete statement of our method? No, it is not, and for a very important reason.[35]

That reason becomes obvious as soon as we ask this question: What theological assumptions or metaphysical doctrines were shaping our thinking as we engaged in the initial work of exegesis? The idea that one can do exegesis of scriptural texts without any presuppositions whatsoever is naive. While it is true that all real scientific scholarship strives for neutrality and objectivity and rejects mere propaganda and subjective twisting of texts to make them mean whatever one wants them to mean, this does not mean that the attainment of neutrality is effortless or natural to the interpreter. All fallen human beings are constantly tempted to read their own biases into any text they interpret. Resisting this temptation requires virtue and grace imparted by the Holy Spirit when we are interpreting Scripture. A further complication arises from the fact that even Spirit-filled, grace-enabled, virtuous interpreters always presuppose many things as they approach the biblical text. As finite creatures, we are not able to doubt everything simultaneously; that is simply beyond our power. Descartes famously tried to do this and could not do it; he found himself unable to doubt that he was thinking about doubting everything. Moreover, we are not even capable of remembering the long list of things that we are taking for granted as we focus on the details of a given problem of interpretation, but this does not mean all is lost. We must remember that, happily, we have more than one shot at the interpretation of a particular passage or the formulation of a given doctrine.

Once we have done our exegesis, formulated our doctrines, and contemplated the implications of those doctrines, it is time to start over again with further exegetical work. A significant component of that second round of exegesis will involve prayerful contemplation of the text in light of the exegesis already done, *and* the relation of that text to other texts *and* to the doctrinal summary statements we have created. At this point, we also carefully consider the metaphysical implications of the doctrines previously formulated because these metaphysical doctrines are supposed to define our own worldview or metaphysical convictions. We may or may not have come to the initial exegesis

34. I will devote the whole of chapter 8 to the doctrine of *creatio ex nihilo*, which I consider to be of central importance to the biblical and orthodox doctrine of God.

35. A great deal of contemporary systematic theology in conservative evangelicalism stops at this point and fails to take the next step. Wayne Grudem's best-selling *Systematic Theology* is an example. The collection of prooftexts in support of doctrinal statements is fine as far as it goes, but it does not go far enough.

of the text with those metaphysical doctrines governing our presuppositions. If we did, well and good. If not, however, this is the time to ask whether our exegesis of the text would be different if we had approached the exegetical task on the basis of the theological metaphysics we have derived from doctrines that summarize wide swaths of exegesis. This is the stage described above when we discussed Athanasius's critique of Arian exegesis. He found their exegetical conclusions to be inadequate because they did not reflect faithfully enough the patterns of biblical speech found in the *skopos* of Scripture as a whole. This kind of contemplative reading of Scripture was fundamental to the doctrine of God that emerged from the pro-Nicene theology in the fourth century.

It is important to stress that the contemplation we are speaking of must be done in the presence of God and in submission to the Spirit's leading. The point is that we are trying to "be transformed by the renewal of your mind," as Paul puts it in Romans 12:2. We are trying to "be filled with the knowledge of his will in all spiritual wisdom and understanding," as he says in Colossians 1:9. We are trying to heed Paul's warning in Colossians 2:8: "See to it that no one takes you captive by philosophy and empty deceit." In short, we are trying to "have the mind of Christ" (1 Cor. 2:16). Theology, therefore, is a lifelong process of constantly starting over.

The work of exegesis is never done once for all and finished. We never leave the exegetical task behind. It is not mere scaffolding that can be dismantled once the builders are finished constructing the edifice of doctrine. (This is one reason, by the way, why the neat and tidy boundaries between the academic disciplines of biblical studies and systematic theology can be so unhelpful.) The prayerful contemplation of Scripture is a spiritual discipline that is used by God to sanctify us and deepen our vision of God's being, which is the ultimate source of all wisdom. How do we ensure that we do not approach the exegetical task with unreformed, worldly metaphysical assumptions? Well it certainly is not by pretending that we have no metaphysical assumptions whatsoever, because that is simply not true. And it is not by figuring out what the right metaphysical assumptions are without consulting Scripture, because that places our metaphysics above Scripture. All our exegesis would then be filtered through the lens of an unreformed metaphysics. So what *can* we do?

The only thing we can do is to recognize that, although we try as hard as possible to have a biblically warranted theology, we are on a journey and in the process of developing one as life unfolds. Each human being enters the stream of history at a specific point and needs to get up to speed with the wisdom discovered so far by the church. This is called getting a theological education. But this is not just a matter of doing a three-year seminary degree; it is a lifelong task. As we approach Holy Scripture, we must have the self-awareness required to adopt a posture of humility about our own personal grasp of the total truth about God and all things in relation to God. This is why we deliberately choose to place ourselves as individuals within the tradition of historic orthodox Christianity as our framework of understanding. Therefore, after conversion, we join a church.

As a confessing Protestant, I believe that the confessions of faith (e.g., Westminster Confession, Savoy Declaration, Heidelberg Catechism, Second London Confession) along with the ecumenical creeds (e.g., Apostles' Creed, Nicene Creed, Definition of Chalcedon) constitute the hard-won fruit of extended contemplation of Scripture by faithful teachers down through the history of the church. I do not exalt them above the Bible, but I certainly regard them as far more likely to be true than the half-baked metaphysics I pick up from the secularized culture around me. And I let these summaries of classical orthodoxy serve as my lens for exegesis. As a result of contemplating Scripture, I may ultimately question a given doctrine contained in the classical tradition. That would be the exception that proves the rule, but it is always possible in theory. The goal is to have our entire system of theology be as accurate and as complete an expression of the revelation of God as possible. We may derive doctrine from general revelation, but in the process of doing theology, those conclusions may need to be refined by special revelation. What I set forth in chapter 2, therefore, is a brief summary of the presuppositions with which I approach the exegesis of the text of Isaiah 40–48, which I offer in chapters 3–6.

Of course, this procedure is sure to elicit strong objections from modernists. Liberal Protestantism and confessional Protestantism are at odds over precisely this issue and have been since the eighteenth century. As noted above, the main Enlightenment critique of classic orthodoxy is that the church was guilty of reading ecclesiastical dogma into the text. The proposed remedy was to approach the text without presupposing the creeds and confessions of the church as the context for exegesis. But we need to see that there is rhetorical sleight of hand going on here. Two separate things are being conflated. On the one hand, it is true to say that the interpreter should not approach the text with the meaning of the text already in mind so that the interpreter is hindered from seeing what the text actually says. Humility and openness to the meaning of the text are necessary for good interpretation. But on the other hand, it is not true to say that the interpreter should approach the text with anti-Christian metaphysical doctrines as presuppositions so that the meaning of the text is shoehorned into the metaphysical system of the interpreter. The modernist method is to do the latter under the guise of doing the former, and this move must be ruled out of order. There is more than one way to read meaning into the text; it can be done by deciding in advance what the text must mean, but it can also be done by deciding in advance what metaphysical doctrines the text is not allowed to contradict. If meaning is truly to arise out of the text, then *the text's own metaphysical implications* must be understood and accepted. Meaning can be obscured by reading the text on the basis of metaphysical doctrines that are foreign to, and incompatible with, the teaching of the text, and this is the basic reason why modern liberal theology is so unorthodox and unbiblical.

Much modern historical-critical interpretation of the Bible smuggles in metaphysical naturalism under the guise of "common sense" or "universal ideas." It also trades persistently on confusion over the meaning of the key term "history." Does history mean "an interpretation of past events on the basis of written sources and artifacts," or does it mean "an interpretation of past events on the basis of written sources and artifacts *assuming that there is no such thing as the supernatural*"? One is never quite sure which meaning is operative in a given context. The statement that Christianity is a historically based religion is true, *but only if the first definition of history is being used*. If the second definition is in view, then the statement means that Christianity is a religion that does not include the supernatural bodily resurrection of Christ from the dead. And that statement is clearly false.

During the past two centuries or so, the philosophical naturalism of modernity has been presupposed, sometimes consciously and sometimes unconsciously, by scholars in the historical-critical stream of biblical interpretation. The reason for this is quite simple. Most biblical scholars, like most of the inhabitants of modern university culture in general, are convinced that Immanuel Kant was correct to conclude that David Hume had demolished once and for all the older metaphysics that was presupposed by scholastic realism both before and after the Reformation. Now if Kant was right about that, it is obvious that some form of post-Kantian constructivism is the only way forward. Scientifically, one must presuppose some kind of philosophical naturalism, and if one wants to advocate for the supernatural, one must redefine it in terms of personal, private, subjective belief. A miracle cannot be knowledge; it can be no more than one's privately held belief (a value, but not a fact). So scholarly study of the Bible must proceed under the constraints of public scientific method—that is, within the constraints of a naturalistic metaphysics. Preaching, on the other hand, can traffic in subjective feelings and beliefs, and doctrine is more closely related to preaching than to scientific biblical exegesis. This is a vicious fact/value dualism, in which scientific exegesis deals with facts, and religious beliefs are merely values. As a result, a wide gulf has opened up between biblical scholars, on the one hand, and theologians and preachers, on the other. This is why I argue in *Interpreting Scripture with the Great Tradition* that hermeneutics must be reformed by the best practices of church preaching, and theological interpretation of Scripture needs to be recovered. Liberal Protestantism perpetuates an ugly dualism between so-called scientific exegesis and preaching and struggles mightily, and with little success, to connect these two solitudes. Its adherents are trying to impose a set of metaphysical doctrines on the Bible that are modern in origin and foreign to biblical theology.

Historical-critical exegesis is part of the liberal project. The liberal project was the response of liberal Christianity to the rise of modernity within Western culture. The liberal project has two wings: historical criticism is the interpretation of the Bible within the metaphysical constraints of naturalism, and doctrinal revisionism is the restating of doctrines within the metaphysical constraints of naturalism. Historical criticism goes back to the pantheist Spinoza, and doctrinal revisionism goes back to the pantheist Schleiermacher. The doctrine of God that undergirds the liberal project is just as much a doctrine as trinitarian classical theism is; it is just a very different doctrine. It is, in fact, a heretical doctrine. Modernist biblical interpretation is not more neutral than orthodox biblical interpretation; it simply begins with a different conception of God and of God's relation to the world. It is actually a different religion, based on pantheism.

In modernist exegesis, the goal is to begin from the metaphysical framework of philosophical naturalism, which is based on a pantheistic doctrine of God. It is here that we see the source of the pressure to move in the direction of relational theism. In confessional orthodox exegesis, the goal is to begin from the metaphysical framework of what I refer to as Christian Platonism,[36] generated by the Nicene doctrine of God, which I refer to as trinitarian classical theism. Although errors can be corrected in the process of doing theology, one's starting point matters. The crucial question is whether a theologian will allow the biblically based metaphysics of the Great Tradition to emerge out of the contemplation of exegesis and doctrines and judge one's starting point. To the extent that those who take the Enlightenment approach to biblical interpretation resist having their metaphysical framework corrected, they are unscientific and biased. Ironically, the same charges that modernists level against historic orthodoxy can be turned back on them and with much greater justification. The greatest failing is not beginning with imperfect

---

36. I define Christian Platonism in *Interpreting Scripture with the Great Tradition*. The specific form of Christian Platonism I defend is a form of "scholastic realism" and can be labeled "Reformed Thomism." I discuss Reformed Thomism in the prologue above.

presuppositions; rather, it is the refusal to allow those imperfect presuppositions to be corrected by the contemplation of the meaning of the text in submission to the Holy Spirit. As the fathers and Reformers would tell you, this is more of a spiritual/moral failing than an honest intellectual mistake.

The truth is that *everyone* approaches the task of exegesis with a conceptual framework derived from some source greater than one's own personal knowledge. The call for "presuppositionless exegesis" is actually a disguised call for acceptance of the majority's presuppositions. Exegesis always occurs in a social context, and in the modern university we see a certain conceptual framework of presuppositions that is taken for granted and seldom laid out explicitly or debated. It is a reliable rule of thumb that the most influential presuppositions are the least debated ones. Those who operate with presuppositions that differ from the consensus of the social matrix in which exegesis occurs tend to stand out as unusual and even odd. They are then described, in the rhetoric of modernity, as approaching the text with "bias" and as, therefore, "unscientific." But theology is not "owned" by the secular university.

Exegesis may occur within the university, but it must resist being deformed by what John Webster calls "the naturalization of *scientia* which has embedded itself deep within the self-understanding of the research university for at least the last two centuries." He goes on to define "naturalization" (what I usually call philosophical naturalism) as follows:

> By "naturalization" is meant the elimination (explicit or tacit) of the category of "creatureliness" in defining the objects, procedures, agents and ends of intellectual inquiry and its institutional forms. Naturalized inquiry concerns itself with the elements of nature and culture, not with their underlying principles, their unity or their capacity to signify a transcendent order of being and causality. Intelligence concerns itself with disparate phenomena, and does not attempt to "reduce" them (that is, to trace them back) to a unifying first cause.[37]

Webster goes on to speak of how it is crucial that theology not succumb to the pressures, subtle and otherwise, "to move away from being a positive science integrally related to a confessional-ecclesial setting, to detach itself from ascetical and religious practices, and to become the historical-cultural science of religious objects and activities."[38] Webster calls for theology to regard itself as a free science and to remember that it rests on God's self-revelation to the saints, not on any sort of cultural prestige derived from a stamp of approval issued by the reigning cultural powers of the present day. His advice is not to

---

37. Webster, "God, Theology, Universities," 166.
38. Webster, "God, Theology, Universities," 166.

withdraw from the public sphere of the university but to resist assimilation to the dominant cultural modes of discourse prevalent there.

Theology is primarily an activity of the redeemed intellect by which the church's speech about God is examined carefully in terms of its accuracy and limits. Its purpose is to prepare us for the rational worship of the Creator and Redeemer and to help us speak truthfully about God and all things in relation to God. As Webster puts it, "Theology is a work of pious intelligence whose foundation and first moving cause is God's loving communication of knowledge of himself to the saints, and whose end is the vision of God."[39] Theology recognizes the authority of God's special revelation in Holy Scripture as its presupposition and its preoccupation. The philosophical naturalism that permeates the modern university setting cannot serve as the presupposition of theology because the God of the Bible cannot be conceived within the conceptual framework of methodological naturalism. God is invisible in such a metaphysical framework. So theology—to the extent that it wishes to speak truly of God—must operate in a different metaphysical framework using different presuppositions.

Where can we get such a conceptual framework? How do we identify such presuppositions? How can we think our way out of the naturalism that is in the very air we breathe in late modernity? Well, the answer is that we must derive our metaphysical description of the situation of the exegete from Scripture itself. But how can we use the *results* of exegesis as the *presupposition* of exegesis? How can exegesis ever get started? The answer is that theology begins with the common confession of the Christian church. This is why exegesis needs the creeds and confessions of the church. Biblical exegetes must be theologians, not secular historians, and they must begin with the classical orthodoxy of the church, because the only alternative is to begin from a set of presuppositions that is hostile to the Bible itself.

When I say that biblical exegetes must be theologians, I mean that they must, at a minimum, understand the history of the development of orthodox doctrine, and they must be aware of its exegetical roots. All exegesis must be done in conversation not only with the text but also with the tradition of interpretation. It is a form of modern hubris to set oneself up as the only one who understands the Bible and to tackle the job alone. This is how sects and cults get started. A responsible interpreter will suppose that the greatest teachers and preachers of the tradition—through whose ministry the Holy Spirit has built up the church that now supports the interpreter's own ministry—should be taken seriously in their exegetical opinions. And

39. Webster, "God, Theology, Universities," 162.

the trinitarian and christological orthodoxy of the councils of the undivided church of the first five centuries, along with the confessions and catechisms of the Reformation, should be regarded as expressing the meaning of the Bible as it has been understood in the church for the past two thousand years. It is not that orthodox doctrine can never be questioned; it is rather that even challenges to and refinements of established doctrines should arise from within the tradition rather than be imposed on it from an entirely foreign context.

The argument of this book will be convincing only if the reader fully appreciates that the view of classical orthodoxy I am proposing really is central to the tradition and really has been embraced by all the major streams of Christianity for most of two millennia. I am arguing that the Nicene doctrine of God consists of joining together a philosophical understanding of God as the simple, immutable, eternal, First Cause of the universe with the biblical understanding of the God who reveals himself in history as Father, Son, and Holy Spirit. Do these two concepts of God really fit together? Do they actually constitute classical orthodoxy? Does it even make sense to join them together? The only way to answer such questions is to contemplate the exegesis of the biblical texts that historic orthodoxy has used to build up its overarching metanarrative or worldview that is enshrined in the church's creeds and confessions and to ask if what we see is harmony and congruence or disharmony and incongruence.

Trinitarian classical theism thus is both the presupposition and the result of responsible exegesis, both the mother and daughter of responsible exegesis. It is legitimate for it to function as the presupposition for exegesis because historic orthodoxy did not just come out of nowhere. It developed over centuries from the exegesis of Holy Scripture and the contemplation of the results of that exegesis by the leading theologians of the Christian tradition. It is not new or untested. It is neither eccentric nor denominationally distinct. It represents what C. S. Lewis, following Richard Baxter, termed "mere Christianity." It underlies the confessional stance of all branches of orthodox Christian East and West, including both Roman Catholic and Protestant. It is biblical in the deepest and most profound sense.

The Argument of This Book

The purpose of this book is to establish congruence between the classical Nicene doctrine of God and the teaching of Holy Scripture. The method is to begin from the perspective of the trinitarian classical theism of historic orthodoxy and to reexamine an important portion of the Bible in some depth (i.e., Isa. 40–48) to show that its message resonates with the history of orthodoxy. Thus chapter 2 sets out a highly compressed summary of the main points of trinitarian classical theism as the conceptual framework for exegesis. Chapters 3–6 then investigate the doctrine of God found in Isaiah 40–48 and shows that Isaiah 40–48 teaches that God is the transcendent Creator and sovereign Lord of history, who alone is to be worshiped. Then in chapter 7, I attempt to demonstrate that the church fathers of the first four centuries, in developing the Nicene doctrine of God, were restating in their cultural situation the doctrine of God taught in Isaiah 40–48. They were not reading Greek metaphysics into the Bible but rather were correcting Greek metaphysics using biblical theology.

Chapter 8 then considers the doctrine of *creatio ex nihilo*, which was central for fourth-century pro-Nicene theologians. Modernist biblical interpretation claims that it is not derived from the exegesis of Scripture. I argue, however, that the fourth-century fathers were right to see it as the teaching of Scripture. Even if it is not explicitly taught in so many words in biblical texts, it can nevertheless be deduced from what those texts say. This is important because *creatio ex nihilo*, properly understood, rules out all forms of pantheism (including panentheism), and this makes the understanding of God that forms the basis of relational theism unacceptable from a biblical perspective. Chapter 8 is meant to model my proposed method of contemplating exegetical results, formulating doctrines, and then deducing metaphysical claims from those doctrines.

Finally, in chapter 9 I offer a reading of modern trends in the doctrine of God from the perspective of the classical tradition. This chapter calls evangelical and confessional Protestants to acknowledge trinitarian classical theism as the faith of the church and to turn away from all forms of relational theology, including the conservative forms of relational theology, such as theistic personalism or social trinitarianism, which might seem like modest compromises with the metaphysical assumptions of the modern world but are actually serious departures from the faith.

This book can be read as a response to the charge made by modernist biblical interpretation that the fathers read extrabiblical metaphysical assumptions derived from Greek philosophy into the text of the Bible and thus developed an erroneous doctrine of God as immutable, impassible, and so forth. By arguing that modernist interpretation begins with a metaphysical naturalism based on a pantheistic doctrine of God, I seek to show that it is actually liberal Protestants who read extrabiblical metaphysical assumptions into the Bible. The goal is to show that the historic tradition of trinitarian classical theism is deeply rooted in the revelation given by God in Holy Scripture and is therefore justifiably taken as the true faith of the Christian church. The liberal project ends in failure because its only possible outcome is the invention of a new religion that is little more than the old paganism in new clothes. All forms of relational theism, therefore, even mildly revisionist ones, should be rejected, and the classical doctrine of God should be celebrated and joyfully confessed by the church.

What Is Trinitarian
Classical Theism?

> Though our lips can only stammer, we yet chant the high things
> of God.
>
> Gregory the Great, *Moralia*[1]

This chapter is an act of remembering the past, that is, of *ressourcement*. Although the act of remembering the trinitarian classical theism of the Great Tradition might not seem very radical, it is actually the first step in fomenting a rebellion against the hegemony of modernity, a revolutionary act directed against the neopagan status quo. The word "radical" comes from the Latin *radix*, meaning "root." Radical change is change of what is basic or fundamental to something. Modernity constitutes a radical change to Western culture because it seeks to expunge the very heart and soul of Western culture, namely Christianity. To remember the Christian soul of our culture is to bring before our minds what is constitutive of our shared memory at its deepest root. As church historian Robert Louis Wilken writes,

> Nothing is more needful today than the survival of Christian culture, because in recent generations this culture has become dangerously thin. At this moment in the Church's history in this country (and in the West more generally) it is less urgent to convince the alternative culture in which we live of the truth of

1. As quoted by Thomas Aquinas, *Summa Theologica*, I, q. 4, art. 1, ad 1 (1:21).

Christ than it is for the Church to tell itself its own story and to nurture its own life, the culture of the city of God, the Christian republic.[2]

The single most important reason why we must remember our own story is to avoid being led astray into the worship of idols (1 John 5:21). By refusing idolatry, the early Christians were able to change the world. But changing the world was not their focus; remaining faithful to the God of Israel who had revealed himself in Jesus Christ was what motivated them. So too our first priority is to remember who God is.

This chapter will summarize trinitarian classical theism by expounding twenty-five theses. The goal here is not to discuss my personal opinions about God or to articulate dazzling new insights into the nature of God. Nor is it to state the current majority opinion about issues relating to the doctrine of God. Rather, the purpose of this chapter is simply to summarize the classical orthodox doctrine of God, which the church has taught consistently for many centuries on the basis of biblical revelation. This chapter will serve to clarify what is meant throughout the book by "classical orthodoxy" or "trinitarian classical theism" or "traditional orthodoxy," all of which are labels that stress various aspects of what is essentially the same thing. We need to understand exactly what we are talking about rather than simply tossing around slogans and buzzwords.

The problem is not merely that more people should get themselves to the library and read up on the subject; it is more complicated than that. When the average modern person reads the standard historical literature on the orthodox doctrine of God or consults the great creeds and confessions of church history, it is very difficult for that person to grasp the meaning and significance of concepts such as impassibility and simplicity. Jumping to conclusions about what is meant leads to a failure to comprehend the tradition. One cause of the difficulty is some metaphysical presuppositions that the average modern person brings to the study of historic orthodoxy, presuppositions that cause one to misunderstand orthodoxy. Metaphysics is not studied today as part of a general education, so people typically hold a set of unexamined metaphysical assumptions picked up informally. This is true even of scholars. We need more critical thinking, but we need the kind that is critical of ourselves and our modern metaphysical presuppositions, not more of the kind that is reflexively critical of tradition.

There is a great deal of confusion over the nature of classical orthodoxy today. Many people, even those with a theological education, assume that it

2. Wilken, "Church as Culture."

is possible to hold to the trinitarian and christological orthodoxy of Nicaea and Chalcedon while at the same time holding some form of the Hellenization thesis. How these two positions are to be reconciled is not exactly clear in the minds of these people. Yet it is not uncommon to find a person who would be horrified to think that anyone would deny the doctrine of the Trinity, yet who also is open to questioning the doctrine of impassibility. There is little awareness of the seriousness of the implications of seeing the teachings of the councils as a mixture of pagan metaphysics and biblical theology.

In particular, many people today do not see the point of the doctrine of simplicity. They do not understand why anyone ever proposed such an idea or what work this doctrine was designed to do. Of course, these are generalizations and do not apply to all theologians. But ignorance that might be excusable in a layperson is often found among pastors and theologians, who just do not know how the classic tradition sees the relationship between the simple, perfect, eternal, immutable God and the God of the Bible, who speaks and acts in history. Such people are vulnerable to attacks on classical theism and the orthodox doctrines of immutability, impassibility, and simplicity because they lack a firm grasp of what is at stake in such matters, and they do not know the history of how the orthodox doctrine of God emerged in the fourth century. They do not know this because most seminaries do a poor job of teaching it, and they have fallen for the shallow argument that such things are unnecessarily complex and irrelevant to our lives today.

As a result of debate with the pagan philosophies of the time, the patristic doctrine of God generated a number of key Christian metaphysical doctrines—such as divine simplicity, *creatio ex nihilo*, and the aseity of God— that enable us to understand the biblical picture of God as the perfect transcendent Creator, who exists necessarily without being in any way dependent on the cosmos he has created. To better understand this, we must address exegetical, theological, and metaphysical questions in close connection with one another. These three types of questions cannot be kept hermetically sealed off from one another in the separate academic disciplines of biblical studies, historical theology, and philosophy.

Why is this the case? The problem lies is our natural tendency to interpret what the Bible says in a way that makes it fit with the antibiblical metaphysics we unconsciously assume to be true. We all tend to do this. If you think about the biblical idea of God and do so reflectively—watching yourself think, so to speak—you can easily catch yourself doing it. For example, you may begin with the genuinely biblical idea that God is personal and then immediately project onto God all sorts of ideas of human personhood, as if God were a person in exactly the same way as we are persons. So it is not as easy as simply reading a verse that mentions a divine attribute and assuming that because we know what it means for a human being to have that attribute, we also know what God is like. We must slow down and contemplate both how God *is like* a human person and how God *is not like* a human person. In this way, we become critical of the metaphysical presuppositions about personhood that we bring to the study of Scripture.

Unfortunately, however, many people today believe that their metaphysical assumptions should not be subjected to critical scrutiny because they suppose them to be "scientific" and "modern." We are subtly conditioned by our education not to be critical of science, which is a form of "scientism." We are often being indoctrinated when we are supposed to be getting an education. This is why many people assume, without giving it five minutes of thought, that whatever is true in the Christian tradition about God obviously could not contradict currently fashionable scientific theories, including the metaphysical doctrines on which modern science is said to be based. But this is to turn science into an idol by absolutizing it. I cannot promise that all orthodox doctrines will be consistent with all modern metaphysical beliefs, but I can promise that orthodox doctrines will be consistent with any modern metaphysical beliefs that are true. Of course, the challenge is to figure out which are true and which are merely currently popular. Doing so will not be easy; one must be prepared to follow a long and complex set of arguments. But difficult is not the same as impossible, and we should be encouraged by the fact that our modern situation is not unique.

Indeed, the knowledge of God is never easy to attain in any age. As we shall see in chapters 3–6, the first readers of the Old Testament had to overcome the mythological beliefs that dominated their own ancient Near Eastern culture in order to absorb the incredible truths that were spoken by the prophets from Moses onward and written down in Holy Scripture. The biblical doctrine of God came to them as a new revelation, not merely as a reiteration of what they already knew from their own culture. In fact, it called into question much of what they thought they knew. It took time to absorb it all and even longer to think through the implications. As the church came perilously close to losing the thread of the biblical concept of God, the early church fathers who battled Arianism in the fourth century had to overcome the conventional philosophical wisdom of their day at many key points in order to preserve and restate the biblical doctrine accurately in their own cultural situation. It took time and a great deal of effort by some of the greatest thinkers in the history of the church to get it right. As the people of God have discovered in every age, reading the Bible is an exercise in having our ideas about God undermined, changed, and refined. We need patience, diligence, humility, and a willingness to become both hearers and doers of the Word if we hope to succeed in remembering the trinitarian classical theism of the Great Tradition, to which we now turn.

■ THESIS 1

Christian theology consists of the doctrine of the church of Jesus Christ derived from Holy Scripture, not from the opinions of mere human beings.

Jaroslav Pelikan offers a classic definition of Christian theology: "What the church of Jesus Christ believes, teaches and confesses on the basis of the Word of God: this is Christian doctrine."[3] First of all, we must bear in mind that the church does not consider the doctrine of God to be merely a matter of the opinion of the smartest people; nor is it determined by majority vote. Either our doctrine is the true teaching of Holy Scripture, and thus a matter of divine revelation, or it is just human opinion. This means that all we say about God must be tested and tried against Holy Scripture, which is the highest and most authoritative source of doctrine in the church of Jesus Christ.

If we speak of a knowledge of God derived from *church tradition*, our conclusions must be compared to the teaching of Scripture and corrected where necessary. All church tradition is subordinate to Scripture, but church tradition is not subordinate to an individual's personal opinion. Church tradition is sometimes confused and diverse and at other times clear and unified. The more unified and clear it is on a given point, the more seriously it must be taken. It is often a mistake to think that we must choose between Scripture and tradition; genuine tradition is actually the history of biblical interpretation. Of course, from time to time there arise doctrinal novelties with no support in Scripture, but those pose little threat to orthodoxy. The real challenge comes from interpretations that place Scripture in contradiction with Scripture, because at least initially such errors can seem more plausible. Tradition must be reformable when, and to the extent that, it leads to contradictory interpretations of Scripture or introduces novelties into the doctrine of God.

If we speak of a knowledge of God derived from *human reasoning or natural science*, our conclusions must also be compared to the teaching of Scripture and corrected where necessary. While we do not believe that Christians are ever required to believe in a contradiction in order to affirm the supreme authority of Holy Scripture, we do admit that we often encounter paradoxes in the discussion of God. As creatures, we often struggle to assimilate what

---

3. Pelikan, *Emergence of the Catholic Tradition*, 1.

we learn from revelation by exegesis. This struggle may be long and arduous, but no other task is as rewarding or as important. We should beware of confusing our inability to follow a complex argument or a current gap in the evidence with a logical contradiction. Humility is essential.

If we speak of a knowledge of God derived from *personal or communal experience*, our conclusions must also be compared to the teaching of Scripture and corrected where necessary. What one feels is ephemeral and controlled by circumstances, presuppositions, and prejudices. Feelings are never more authoritative than logical reasoning and can never supplant tradition. Tradition is far more than the accumulated weight of the personal experience of previous generations. Since even venerable tradition and the conclusions of logical reasoning must be compared to Scripture and brought into harmony with Scripture, how much more do the vague feelings and emotions we derive from our finite, human, personal experience of God. This applies equally to the feelings of individuals and of groups.

▪ THESIS 2

Theology is the study of God and all things in relation to God.

This definition comes from John Webster, but it is classic; he got it from Thomas Aquinas.[4] The theologian's attention should be concentrated relentlessly on God, refusing to be distracted by the world. The goal is to view all reality, including human nature and society, in the context of who and what God is rather than regarding reality as self-existent and autonomous. Theology is in constant danger of losing its focus on God and becoming interested in the world in itself and for its own sake. Liberal Protestantism does this in its unhealthy and nearly exclusive focus on social justice. Christian theology is antimodern insofar as modernity is committed to human autonomy and freedom as the highest goods. As Christians, we believe that our highest good as human beings is to know God and worship him, and we experience this as a given, not as our choice. All else in life must be properly ordered in relation to the worship of the one, true, living God.

Theology begins with the immanent Trinity—that is, with God as he is in himself from all eternity. We know God from his works, from divine actions in the economy: creation, judgment, salvation, prophecy. By reflecting on what God has done, we can know certain truths about God. For example, we can know that every cause is greater than its effect, which means that God

4. Webster, *God and the Works of God*, 3.

is much greater than the world he causes to exist. The primary material for theological reflection is the biblical record of the mighty acts of God in history as interpreted by the prophetic Word and as attested by the New Testament apostles. This is the focus of the discipline of biblical theology. On the basis of God's self-revelation in history, we formulate doctrines both about God and all things in relation to God. Then we review, and correct where necessary, doctrines formulated on the basis of general revelation in order to unify our thoughts about God so that we can organize our knowledge of God, which is the work of systematic theology.

■ THESIS 3

Theology can be divided into two parts: (1) what is taught explicitly in Scripture and (2) what may be deduced from what is taught explicitly in Scripture.

The Westminster Confession of Faith speaks for the entire orthodox tradition on this point:

> The whole counsel of God concerning all things necessary for his own glory, man's salvation, faith and life, is either expressly set down in Scripture, or by good and necessary consequence may be deduced from Scripture: unto which nothing at any time is to be added, whether by new revelations of the Spirit, or traditions of men.[5]

It is important to understand how theology works in the Great Tradition before launching into theological description. The orthodox doctrine of God can be described as a simple restatement of the biblical teaching plus doctrine that goes beyond biblical teaching to assert what is not explicitly taught by the Bible, such as the doctrine of the ὁμοούσιον (*homoousion*, the oneness in being of the Father, Son, and Holy Spirit). This description requires some explanation.

If the Westminster Confession of Faith is correct in teaching that some of the doctrine of God will be a repetition of what is "expressly set down in Scripture" and some will be deduced from what is expressly stated in Scripture, then some of what is meant by trinitarian classical theism will consist of deductions from biblical teaching, and this should *not* be described as going "beyond Scripture" in a pejorative sense. Notice how stringent the

---

5. Westminster Confession of Faith, chap. 1: "Of the Holy Scripture," art. 6 (Dennison, *Reformed Confessions*, 4:235).

requirement is for any doctrinal statement that goes beyond the express teaching of Scripture. It must not merely be *compatible* with the results of biblical exegesis; it must be logically *deduced* from the results of biblical exegesis. A theologian must be competent in logic to be able to tell the difference. Just because something is compatible with biblical teaching does not mean that it must be believed; only what can be drawn out of the biblical teaching as *part of the meaning of the text*, either by restatement of the plain sense or deductions from it, can be required for orthodoxy. That is the standard for anything that is required to be believed for salvation. But we should bear in mind that proper interpretation of one passage of Scripture must not make that passage contradict the plain sense of other passages of Scripture. If this occurs, then the exegesis must be revised, and no deductions from the contradictory sense are admissible as Christian doctrine. To be accepted as pure doctrine, a teaching must be exegetically derived or deduced logically from the plain sense identified in exegesis and not in contradiction to the plain sense of other texts. The study of traditional logic therefore is essential preparation for theologians, along with training in exegetical methods.

There may be other things we believe, which are *adiaphora*—that is, optional for belief according to the opinion of individuals or denominations. But such things should not be considered necessary for salvation, and they should not be included in creeds or confessions of faith unless they are clearly distinguished from essential doctrines.

▓ THESIS 4

Christian theology consists of exegesis, doctrines, and metaphysical implications of doctrine, which form the context for further exegesis.

Christian theology never leaves behind exegesis of Scripture. Exegesis leads to exegetical results being formulated into doctrines, which then generate metaphysical implications about the nature of reality, which in turn create the presuppositions of renewed exegesis. This "hermeneutical spiral" continues indefinitely because the task of thinking through the meaning of Scripture for the Christian life and the mission of the church never ends this side of heaven. There is no such thing as exegesis without presuppositions. So our goal is not to find some way of approaching the text with no presuppositions whatsoever. Instead, our goal is to let the exegetical process challenge and correct our faulty presuppositions as we interpret Scripture. This is why biblical interpretation is always theological and always a spiritual practice that leads to sanctification when done in faith and submission to the Holy Spirit.

The church fathers approached the interpretation of Scripture with faith, believing that the Holy Scriptures are inspired by God and able to make us "wise unto salvation" (1 Tim. 3:15). To read the Bible as the Word of God is to expect to hear God speaking through the text of Scripture, and the spiritual meaning of the text is how we describe the Spirit illumining the text that was inspired by that same Spirit in the first place. Spiritual exegesis, doctrines, and metaphysical implications of doctrines constitute a three-legged stool on which fourth-century pro-Nicene theology built the doctrine of God, symbolized in the Niceno-Constantinopolitan Creed of AD 381. The metaphysics of Nicaea can be described as a "sacramental ontology" or as "Christian Platonism," and this worldview is expressed in the Bible and arises out of biblical interpretation. Reading the Bible in the context of the theological metaphysics of Nicaea is the key to both historic orthodoxy and Christian sanctification.

Although the Nicene doctrine of God is as close to irreformable as any doctrine could ever be, that does not mean that it is sufficient simply to accept and repeat the words in the creed. Instead, each new generation must read Holy Scripture for itself and think through the meaning of how the various texts fit together in order to appropriate for itself the orthodox doctrine of God. We should be extremely suspicious of any claim that the Nicene doctrine of God expressed in the ecumenical creeds of the first five centuries and in the confessions and catechisms of the sixteenth-century Reformation is in need of revision. The burden of proof is on the would-be reformer to show that the church has been wrong for most of its history about the nature and identity of the God we worship. In theory this is possible; in practice it is nearly inconceivable.

■ THESIS 5

God's existence is evident to reason, even though fallen human beings, because of sin, either deny God's existence or refuse to be grateful to him and worship him (Rom. 1:20).

In the wake of Barth's massive influence, the rejection of natural theology became a commonplace in twentieth-century theology. It was an idea that fit well with the spirit of the age, dominated as it was by post-Kantian skepticism about the power of reason to connect us with mind-independent reality. Since roughly 1800, modernity has witnessed a loss of confidence in natural theology (the philosophical proofs for the existence of God) and in natural law (the idea that morality is built into the world as the telos of the nature of creatures). Now in our contemporary situation, confidence has been lost in the laws of nature themselves (the idea of scientific law). In a postmodern culture, there is no reason to believe that natural scientific law will survive any more than natural theology or the natural moral law. Pragmatism is transforming science at a rapid rate into a tool of ideology; the social sciences have been largely corrupted, and the humanities have been degraded into ideological weapons. Even the natural sciences are increasingly infiltrated by neo-Marxists and postmodernists pushing an ideological agenda in which "diversity" is the ironic label for imposed uniformity of thought. Everyone who is concerned for truth and the future of science itself should be alarmed. In this situation, the church has lost confidence in the biblical teaching that it is possible to prove the existence of God and the natural moral law. Hence, even among Christian theologians who think of themselves as orthodox, it has become quite fashionable of late to deny that it is possible to prove the existence of God.

However, for the entire history of the Christian church prior to the twentieth century, it was believed by the mainstream of Christian thought that we can legitimately take for granted that God's existence can be demonstrated. The Great Tradition held that what is known by special revelation is confirmed by reason. Summarizing the tradition on this point, Thomas Oden says,

> To ask whether God exists is to pose a question of fact, not merely of theory. The question is, quite simply: Is this so? To establish a fact is to show the state of things as they are. Fact is distinguished from fancy. In classic Christianity the existence of God is not merely a theory or hypothesis but a necessary axiom of rational minds.[6]

When Barth dismissed natural theology as sub-Christian, he departed rather decisively from the tradition on this point.

In *Five Proofs of the Existence of God*, Edward Feser has summarized the five main arguments for the existence of God in the history of Western thought—namely, those originating from Aristotle, Plotinus, Augustine, Aquinas, and Leibniz. This work is notable as a model of sound reasoning and lucid exposition, and it is a fine summary of the historical proofs for God's existence. Astonishingly, many people today are unaware of much of the contents of this book. He points out that "it is standard Catholic teaching that the God of the Bible and the God which can be known by means of philosophical arguments are one and the same."[7] Feser summarizes the

---

6. Oden, *Classic Christianity*, 81.

7. Feser, *Five Proofs*, 293. See also *Catechism of the Catholic Church*, 20. We could add that it is just as much standard Protestant teaching as Catholic.

arguments succinctly in this passage, although the entire book constitutes an elaboration of these arguments and a refutation of objections to them:

> The Aristotelian proof begins with the fact that there are potentialities that are actualized and argues that we cannot make sense of this unless we affirm the existence of something which can actualize the potential existence of things without itself being actualized, a *purely actualized actualizer*. The Neo-Platonic proof begins with the fact that the things of our experience are composed of parts and argues that such things could not exist unless they have an *absolutely simple or noncomposite cause*. The Augustinian proof begins with the fact that there are abstract objects like universals, propositions, numbers, and possible worlds, and argues that these must exist in a *divine intellect*. The Thomistic proof begins with the real distinction, in each of the things of our experience, between its essence and its existence, and argues that the ultimate cause of such things must be something which is subsistent existence itself. The Rationalist proof begins with the principle of sufficient reason and argues that the ultimate explanation of things can only lie in an absolutely necessary being.[8]

But even though God's existence can be known philosophically, this does not mean that everyone actually knows it.

In Romans 1:20 Paul teaches that human beings can know God from the created order and are therefore culpable for not expressing gratitude to God and for refusing to honor him. As the Reformed scholastic theologian Francis Turretin says,

> The question is not whether this knowledge is perfect and saving (for we confess that after the entrance of sin it was so much obscured as to be rendered altogether insufficient for salvation), but only whether any knowledge of God remains in man sufficient to lead him to believe that God exists and must be religiously worshiped.[9]

Our problem as human beings is not that we do not know that God exists; it is rather that we want to pretend that we do not know it in order to justify our self-centered way of life. Those are two rather different things. Insofar as every human knows intuitively by looking at nature that this world must have a cause, every human knows that there is a God. But by refusing to worship and be thankful to the Creator, fallen human beings incur the righteous wrath of God by which he "gave them up" to their own lusts and to a "debased mind" (Rom. 1:24, 26, 28). So we have a paradox: God's existence is obvious

---

8. Feser, *Five Proofs*, 169. This book should be required reading for every theology student.
9. Turretin, *Institutes of Elenctic Theology*, 1:6.

but not acknowledged, known in one sense but not in another. We know that we are not our own cause, but we refuse to acknowledge the First Cause of all things, and this is both a manifestation of our fallen nature and culpable behavior that incurs God's wrath. Our persistence in such futile thinking is also a sign of being under judgment.

What is needed, of course, is conversion expressed by repentance and faith. After surrendering to the Lord and ceasing their rebellion against his lordship, believers who then look at nature and who apply their minds to the problem of proving God's existence find it to be easily done. "The fear of the LORD is the beginning of wisdom" (Prov. 9:10). Anyone can learn the major proofs for God's existence in a college class, as students do in my course on the doctrine of God. The issues are complicated but not beyond the grasp of the average person who is not closed-minded or afraid of an encounter with the living God. Only a fool denies the existence of God (Pss. 14:1; 53:1), and a fool is someone who is unwise enough to rebel against the Creator, not someone lacking in general intelligence.

■ THESIS 6

God is the First Cause of all that exists but is not himself caused, since existence is part of his own essence (Exod. 3:14).

Thomas Aquinas taught that God's existence is self-evident in itself but not necessarily self-evident to us. It is self-evident in the sense that the predicate is contained in the essence of the subject, as in the sentence "Man is an animal." But not everyone knows the definition of "God," and so God's existence may not be rationally self-evident to some people.[10] Anyone who knows what God is, knows that for God to be God means that his existence is part of his essence and cannot be an accidental predicate. When the Bible proclaims God as creator of the heavens and the earth, it is saying that God is the First Cause of all that exists (Gen. 1:1).

God cannot be self-caused or have a cause external to himself; otherwise, it would be impossible for him to have been the First Cause of all things. Any actualizer that is itself actualized by another is by definition not the *first* actualizer. For God to be the First Cause, he must be the unactualized actualizer. Few would deny that the Bible clearly teaches that God is the creator of all things; can the "Creator" be anything other than the First Cause? It would seem not.

10. Thomas Aquinas, *Summa Theologica*, I, q. 2, art. 1 (1:11).

The biblical doctrine of *creatio ex nihilo* arises from contemplating the meaning of Exodus 3:14 in light of Genesis 1:1 and then deducing the truth about God's relationship to the world from what these verses say. If God causes all things to exist, then God must be eternal; that is, his existence must not be given him from without or attained by effort. In either of those cases, God could not be what Genesis 1:1 says he is—namely, the creator of all that exists. Instead, he would be one more thing in the cosmos with a cause, and the search for the Creator would continue.[11]

When Paul says in Romans 1:20 that the attributes of God have been "clearly perceived, ever since the creation of the world, in the things that have been made," he obviously does not mean to assert that every person admits to knowing that God exists. Instead, in the next few verses he says of the gentiles that their thinking became futile and degenerated into gross idolatry because they refused to worship and give thanks. By the time they sank to the level of worshiping idols, they had suppressed the knowledge of the true God and thus no longer consciously "knew" it (Rom. 1:18).

However, in Exodus 3, when the LORD revealed himself to Moses at Mount Horeb at the burning bush, he identified himself in three ways, each of which employs a form of the Hebrew verb "to be." He revealed himself as "I AM WHO I AM" (*'ehyeh 'ašer 'ehyeh*) and as "I AM" (*'ehyeh*) in verse 14, and in verse 15 he also revealed himself as the LORD (*yhwh*), the God of their forefathers. We need to remember that the context is the divine self-revelation of God as not just another tribal god of a particular nation but as the transcendent Creator of all and sovereign Lord of history. The LORD is God over Egypt and not just over Israel. In the account of the exodus, the LORD humiliates the gods of Egypt as though they were nothing. The traditional exegesis of Exodus 3:14, which sees it as teaching that God's existence is included in God's essence, serves to set the LORD apart as unique and also explains God's use of forms of the verb "to be" in naming himself.[12] This verb is appropriate in naming the one whose essence is unique. Augustine suggests that the great contrast between God and all other things is that they change but he simply is. As he says, "The unchangeableness of God was prepared to suggest itself by this phrase 'I AM WHO I AM.'"[13] For the LORD to say "I AM" is to call attention to the fact that he exists by nature, as opposed to the other gods of the nations,

11. Some modern interpreters deny that Genesis 1:1 teaches *creatio ex nihilo*. I will argue for the traditional interpretation in chap. 8. We will be exploring the exegetical issues involved in Genesis 1:1 and Exodus 3:14 in greater detail in chaps. 3, 4, and 8.

12. Thomas Aquinas, *Summa Theologica*, I, q. 13, art. 11 (1:70).

13. Augustine, *Sermon* 6.4, as quoted in Lienhard, *Exodus, Leviticus, Numbers and Deuteronomy*, 21.

who exist only by *his* (i.e., the LORD's) command and enablement. Since God's existence is part of his essence, his existence is self-evident to anyone who understands the true definition of God. When Richard Dawkins thinks he has refuted Thomas Aquinas by asking, "What caused God?" he simply reveals his utter and serene ignorance of the entire Aristotelian-Thomistic tradition and the fact that he does not know the definition of the word "God."[14]

■ THESIS 7

God has aseity, or independence from creation; while creation is dependent on God, the reverse is not true.

So we can see that God is the uncaused cause or, more precisely, the unactualized actualizer. Change obviously occurs all around us, and all change is the actualization of some potential. For example, an acorn grows into an oak tree. Aristotle was correct in holding that it is something actual that causes potential to be realized. Acorns come from oak trees; they don't just pop into existence randomly. But potential on its own cannot realize itself; what the acorn receives from the oak tree is actualized by nutrition, sunlight, and so forth. We see potential being actualized (that is, change) all around us all the time. Something actual causes all change, but if we trace the causal chain back, we must either have an infinite series of causes or we must come to a First Cause. If there were no First Cause, the chain of causes could never begin, so there must be a First Cause.[15] But if there is a First Cause, that First Cause must be pure actuality in order to be uncaused. Therefore, God must be pure act. This metaphysical proof is not a matter of probability; nor is it a matter of arguing that the universe must have had a cause to get it started. It is a logical deduction that is certain, not merely probable. The starting point of the argument (which comes from Aristotle and is taken up by Aquinas) is not the existence of the universe; rather, it is the existence of change in the world.

14. Dawkins, *God Delusion*, 101; and Feser, *Last Superstition*, 85–86.
15. An objection to this argument is that a certain type of causal chain (called a linear series) can exist even if previous links are broken, even if previous causes have gone out of existence. For example, I can generate a son even if my grandfather has died. That is true. But another type of causal chain (called a hierarchical series) requires the initial cause to be operative in order for any subsequent effect to continue. Think of a boy thrusting a stick into a brook and turning over a rock, which in turn releases sand that temporarily drifts toward the surface, causing the water to become opaque. If the boy stops holding the stick, the water ceases being stirred up. The question is which kind of causal chain is required in order to explain change in the universe. Feser (*Five Proofs*, 19–29) patiently explains why God as First Cause requires the second kind of causal chain. In theology we affirm both divine creation (in the beginning) and also divine providence (which is ongoing).

The point is not that God must have existed "back there" to get things started, as in Deism; rather, it is that God must exist now, or there would be no change occurring now. To evade the logical force of this metaphysical argument, one must hold that all change is an illusion. And there are good arguments against such a position, in addition to its being against all common sense.[16]

This means that God, the unactualized actualizer, is the First Cause of all that exists. All that exists owes its existence to God, but God owes his existence to no one and nothing. Creation, therefore, is dependent (that is, contingent) being, but God is independent (that is, necessary) being, which makes God's being utterly different from created being—different in kind and not merely in degree. It also means that God has aseity (self-existence) and that God is the only being who has it as the First Cause. His aseity makes God unique.

To know what God is, is to know that God must necessarily exist. The exact question being answered in Exodus 3, however, is the relationship of the God of Abraham, Isaac, and Jacob to this one who exists of himself (a se). The answer given in Exodus 3 is that they are one and the same. The God who appeared to Abraham, Isaac, and Jacob is obviously personal; anyone who reads the patriarchal narratives in Genesis 12–50 knows that. But what Exodus 3 tells us is that the personal God of Abraham, Isaac, and Jacob is also the one who exists by virtue of his essence—that is, the one who exists of himself (a se), the only uncreated thing. In the looming contest between the gods of Egypt and "the God of our fathers," the uniqueness of the LORD is stressed in this passage in a mysterious way that invites contemplation, worship, and obedience.

■ THESIS 8

God is eternal, which means that he has neither beginning nor end as all creatures do.

The eternity of God flows logically from the self-existence or aseity of God, which flows naturally from the doctrine that God is the First Cause of all things. The teaching of Exodus 3:14–15, that God's essence is to exist, allows us to deduce that God must be the First Cause of the universe. But the same

---

16. I do not have time here to discuss Eastern religions and their view of the world as an illusion. Even if we were to concede that regarding the world as an illusion is a logically possible response to the Aristotelian-Thomist argument that all change has a cause and that since there is change, there must be a First Cause, this argument could never be used by a Christian, because to regard the world as a mere illusion is to deny the reality of God's creation. Plato's refutation of Parmenides should be studied in this regard.

conclusion is stated directly by Genesis 1:1 "In the beginning God created the heavens and the earth" (*bərē'šît bārā' 'ĕlōhîm 'ēt haššāmayim wə'ēt hā'āreṣ*).[17] God created everything that is. We said above that Christian doctrine consists of the explicit teaching of Scripture plus what may be deduced from the explicit teaching of Scripture. In Genesis 1 we are explicitly taught that God is the First Cause of all things. In Exodus 3 we are given the definition of God's nature as existence, from which we can deduce that God is the First Cause of all things. We thus arrive at the same conclusion—namely, that God is the First Cause of all things in two ways. A doctrine could not possibly have a firmer foundation. God is the First Cause of all things.

Now we also can deduce the eternity of God from the doctrine of God as the First Cause of all things, who has aseity. Why? If God is the First Cause of all things and if all things come into being and are maintained in being by God, then God must not either come into being or pass out of being. Therefore, God must be eternal.

Eternity is not the same as ongoing existence. It is existence that has no beginning or end and thus is atemporal. God is not in time; it is truer to say that time is God's creature. As Boethius wrote, "Eternity is the whole, perfect, and simultaneous possession of endless life."[18] Thus, it is a different kind of existence from creaturely existence, which may have no end if God bestows immortality on a given creature but will nevertheless still have had a beginning. It is also a superior form of existence. Boethius also says, "Therefore, only that which comprehends and possesses the whole plenitude of endless life together, from which no future thing nor any past thing is absent, can justly be called eternal."[19] Creatures possess life but only in a limited measure and for a limited time. Every created thing is a mixture of actuality and potentiality, and therefore it is of the essence of a creature to change. A creature that is dependent on an actualizer to actualize it does not have the same kind of independent existence that God has.

The difference between the existence of God and the existence of the creature is this: divine existence is eternal because it is dependent on nothing but itself, whereas creaturely existence is not eternal because it is dependent on God for its origin and continuation. Even if God bestows immortality on a creature (such as an angel or a resurrected, glorified human being), that creature's existence is still not eternal for two reasons: (1) it had a beginning, and (2) it depends on God for its continuation forever. Only God is eternal in himself.

---

17. In chap. 8 we will extensively discuss exegetical support for understanding *creatio ex nihilo* as the meaning of this text.

18. Boethius, *Consolation of Philosophy*, 115.

19. Boethius, *Consolation of Philosophy*, 115.

■ THESIS 9

As the First Cause of all that exists other than himself, God is immutable.

If God is the First Cause and pure act, then there is no potentiality in God and therefore no change from one state to another. All change is the movement of a thing from one state of being to another, in the process of which some previously unrealized potentiality is actualized. God does not change and cannot change, and this is not a limitation but a perfection. In order for God to be able to change, he would need to have unrealized potentiality. If God had unrealized potentiality, he would be made up of parts and thus on the same level as creatures, needing some outside force to actualize his potentiality. Also, in order for God to change, he would need either to move from a better state to a worse state or from a worse state to a better one. It is difficult to decide which alternative would be more blasphemous! If God changed, then his being would not be unique; it would not be different in kind from created being. If this were true, then either pantheism or polytheism would be true, or it could be that both are true. It is no accident that in an age that rejects the classical metaphysical proofs of God's existence, we see rampant pantheism, panentheism, theistic mutualism, and theistic personalism.

To put this in biblical language, if God is not the Creator, he must be part of what we call the creation. Maybe then pantheism is true, and God is another name for the totality of the cosmos as a whole. Or perhaps God is a person within the universe, a being among beings, in which case God is reduced to the level of a "super angel" or other spiritual entity that exists as part of the cosmos. From this analysis, we can see that theistic personalism reduces God to the level of the gods of polytheism. This is what David Bentley Hart was trying to say with his neologism "monopolytheism."[20] God would be like one of the gods of Mount Olympus or like the biblical Satan. If God is not the Creator of all, there are only two alternative ways he could exist: God can be another name for the cosmos as a whole, or God can be an entity within the cosmos. But if God is the Creator, he must be immutable in being as pure act. Neither the cosmos as a whole nor entities within it are immune from change. So if he is not the Creator, he is not immutable and lacks eternity and aseity (and many other attributes that the Bible ascribes to God, as we shall see).

Modern Western metaphysics is currently preoccupied with what must be the case if philosophical naturalism is true. If philosophical naturalism is true, all that exists would exist within the cosmos; nothing could exist beyond or in addition to the cosmos. If philosophical naturalism is true,

---

20. Hart, *Experience of God*, 127–28.

then "God" must be part of the cosmos. A thing need not be material to be part of the cosmos. Even purely spiritual beings like angels can be part of the cosmos. Quantum mechanics and astrophysics have taught us that the cosmos is a much stranger and more paradoxical place than earlier, crudely materialistic theories have imagined. God can be a person like us, only bigger and stronger, or God can be another name for the cosmos as a whole. But if God is who the classical orthodox tradition says he is, then philosophical naturalism cannot be true, because God would be something that transcends the cosmos, not in the sense of existing as pure energy but in the sense of existing in a different manner from anything we can imagine.[21] Classical theism is biblical because it teaches that God is the transcendent Creator. If God is the First Cause (Creator) of the universe and if God is eternal, self-existent, and immutable, then God transcends the cosmos and cannot be reduced to the level of a creature. His being is unique to himself and beyond all creaturely analogies.

In discussing God's immutability, Karl Barth unfortunately appears to come close to collapsing the immanent Trinity into the economic Trinity. Postulating an unwarranted contradiction between classical orthodoxy and biblical teaching, he stresses that we do not speak of God as "an *immutable* or *immobile* in itself, but of the 'immutable' God in His self-revelation."[22] For Barth, the "living God" of Scripture is to be contrasted with the "pure immobile," which is "death."[23] In a way typical of modern theology, Barth assumes that what the tradition has meant by "immutability" is incompatible with God's actions in history to create, judge, and save. He says that the "Protestant Church, scarcely a hundred years after Luther and Calvin, did not realize that with this *immobile* it was well on the way to receiving and accepting the heathen concept of God, the concept of men who have no hope."[24] But we need to remember that the doctrine of divine immutability goes back to the early church fathers and was taught clearly by Augustine and Thomas Aquinas. It was certainly not an invention of the post-Reformation church.

21. Materialism is the doctrine that only matter exists. Some people think that to imagine beings existing as pure energy would entail transcendent beings, but this is incorrect. Modern physics understands matter and energy as convertible into each other, and so energy is just another form of created being. I use the term "naturalism" to refer to the doctrine that nothing exists other than matter and energy. So in *Star Trek*, for example, when they encounter aliens that exist as pure energy and thus incorporeally, they are encountering entities that are similar to biblical angels but not entities that occupy the same genus as the biblical God, who is beyond matter and energy altogether.

22. Barth, *Church Dogmatics* II/1, 493. Note that he cannot speak of God as immutable without putting the word in scare quotes.

23. Barth, *Church Dogmatics* II/1, 494.

24. Barth, *Church Dogmatics* II/1, 494.

Barth assumes that immutability in God must be a lack of change and that if God is unchanging, then God must be dead. But in fact, the tradition has consistently taught that God is life itself; he is the purely actual actualizer of all else. Something dead cannot impart life to other beings. As the personal God of Abraham, Isaac, and Jacob, God is alive. As the creator of the heavens and the earth, God is the life-giver (John 1:1–4). The Niceno-Constantinopolitan Creed of AD 381 confesses the Holy Spirit to be "the Lord, and life-giver."[25] In the pure actuality of God lies the cause of all the change that occurs in the universe, which means that all life owes its existence, continuation in existence, and future existence to the being of God. Death cannot produce life; only life in itself can be the ultimate cause of all individual living things. God is more than merely the biggest and oldest living thing; God is *life itself*, and therefore to know the only true God is life (John 17:3). He is immutable in that he is not either receiving or losing life as all creatures are doing.

To be immutable because one is purely actual is the complete opposite of being immutable because one is dead. Commenting on this passage in Barth, James Dolezal points out that Barth reads into the tradition something that simply is not there when he claims that the tradition understands divine immutability as God confined by being the pure immobile and thus lacking life. Who has ever said something like this? Barth quotes no historical figure who understood immutability in this way; such creatures are unicorns, who exist only in the imaginations of those convinced that the tradition must have been wrong because they cannot bring themselves to challenge modernity head on. Barth's unspoken assumption here seems to be that the being of God is merely different from ours in degree, can be spoken of univocally, and therefore can be said to change. If we must change in order to be alive, then God must have to change in order to be alive. Such assumptions drastically depart from the classical orthodox tradition. God is immutable because he is perfect in every possible way; God is not merely alive as a creature is alive but is in himself life itself.

■ THESIS 10

As pure act, God is simple.

Apart from immutability and impassibility, the doctrine of divine simplicity is possibly the most misunderstood attribute of God in modernity. This doctrine is affirmed by Athanasius, the Cappadocian fathers, Augustine, Anselm, Thomas Aquinas, and by Reformed orthodoxy, including such figures as John

---

25. "The Constantinopolitan Creed" in Leith, *Creeds of the Churches*, 33.

Owen, Francis Turretin, and Stephen Charnock.[26] But one would not know how central it is in the tradition from the dismissive attitude taken toward it by many modern theologians.

The doctrine of divine simplicity says that God is not composed of parts. As Tyler Wittman points out, for Thomas Aquinas, the doctrine of divine simplicity functions primarily as a negative assertion and does not tells us "how God is."[27] Thomas utilizes this concept to express what the Bible teaches when it presents God as utterly different from creation. As Wittman puts it, "Only the denial of all such composition maintains the insight into God's divinity that there is nothing more absolute or fundamental than God."[28] As pure act, God is perfect and not subject to change. The key idea to grasp is that God does not have attributes in the manner of creatures, for whom attributes are accidental predicates. A creature can acquire or lose accidental predicates over time. But God is not even *in* time! God simply is each of his attributes, and all his attributes are ultimately identical with his being. God does not have wisdom; he is wisdom itself, which is to say that wisdom is his essence considered from a particular creaturely vantage point. What we know as wisdom in creatures is what it is only because in some small way it reflects the wisdom that God is.

When we speak of divine simplicity, we are asserting that God is not composed of parts and that all his attributes are words we use to describe his immutable, eternal, self-existent, fully actual being. When we speak of God's attributes as his perfections, or when we speak of God's nature as perfect, we are not engaging in modern "perfect-being theology." Modern perfect-being theology begins with a human concept of what we think divinity ideally should be and then projects this idea onto God. As John Webster points out, it often sees itself as being in conversation with the classical tradition, and it spends a great deal of time arguing about how we should conceive of perfection with regard to God. But, Webster reminds us, there is a huge difference between "spelling out the logic of *a god* and indicating the particular perfection of the God manifest in Jesus Christ and in the Spirit's presence."[29] Classical

---

26. For a fine overview of the historical background of divine simplicity, see Duby, *Divine Simplicity*, 7–25. For an excellent refutation of recent criticisms of divine simplicity from analytic philosophy of religion, see Dolezal, *God without Parts*. For a good discussion of recent departures from the orthodox doctrine of divine simplicity by evangelical theologians, see Dolezal's *All That Is in God*, 37–58. For a discussion of the function of divine simplicity in the key period of the fourth century, see Ayres, *Nicaea and Its Legacy*, 278–80. For a detailed treatment of the Cappadocian refusal to surrender the concept of simplicity in order to secure the Nicene doctrine of the Trinity, see Radde-Gallwitz, *Transformation of Divine Simplicity*.

27. Wittman, *God and Creation*, 41–42.

28. Wittman, *God and Creation*, 43.

29. Webster, *Confessing God*, 89, italics original.

theism does not start with the *idea* of God; it starts with God's revelation of himself in creation, conscience, and most importantly, Holy Scripture. So we do not know what God is until God reveals himself. Theology is a matter of considering the meaning of facts, not of creating opinions about what God would be like if, hypothetically, there were a God. What we mean when we speak from a classical theist perspective of God's perfect being is that God is Pure Act and includes all perfection in himself, and that is a deduction from revelation known by exegesis. God is not getting better as time goes along, because he is not contained within time; time is his creature.

Divine simplicity expresses the perfection of the fully actual God. He is what he is, and what he is is perfect. All his attributes express the fullness of the divine being from one perspective or another. They are multiple from our creaturely perspective but one in God himself. God is each of his attributes; each are identical with his existence. Thomas Aquinas says, "Since in God there is no potentiality, . . . it follows that in Him essence does not differ from existence." For Thomas, "God is not only his own essence . . . but also His own existence."[30] Thomas goes on to explain that God is not a member of a genus, and there are no accidents in God.[31] Herman Bavinck treats the simplicity of God as part of what it means for God to be one. He points out that Scripture does not just attribute truth, life, righteousness, and so forth to God in a high degree; rather, Scripture sees God as being true, alive, righteous, and so forth in an absolutely perfect way. For this reason, he argues, "every attribute of God is identical with his essence."[32] God is absolute truth, wisdom, life, and so forth, and to the extent that creatures share in these attributes by being wise or alive, for example, they have these attributes relatively and by participation in the infinite and perfect being of the Creator. Simplicity names the difference in the way God has attributes from the way creatures have them.

▪ THESIS 11

God is transcendent, which means that he is not a being within the universe but the sovereign Lord of all that exists.

This attribute of God traces a thread that runs through the preceding five attributes and emphasizes how each of them differentiates God from his creation. God is the simple, immutable, eternal, self-existent, First Cause of the universe. We see the creator-creature distinction in all the attributes of God, and

30. Thomas Aquinas, *Summa Theologica*, I, q. 3, art. 3 (1:17).
31. Thomas Aquinas, *Summa Theologica*, I, q. 3, art. 4 (1:17–18).
32. Bavinck, *Reformed Dogmatics*, 2:173.

transcendence serves as a pointer to the crucial truth that God must never be confused with God's creation. The distinction between God and creation is one of kind, not merely of degree. In all human religion, except what derives from the Old Testament, there is no real concept of the transcendence of God. There are instead a thousand ways of conceiving of God, all of which are variations on two themes: one in which the being of God is differentiated from created being only by grades of purity, and one in which the gods are superhuman beings who exist as finite entities within the cosmos—in other words, pantheism and polytheism. All the ancient Near Eastern mythologies surrounding ancient Israel—Egyptian, Mesopotamian, and Canaanite—were polytheistic. The fact that the deity is thought of as invisible is not a reliable marker of transcendence, and neither is the affirmation of one ultimate principle behind the plurality of the cosmos. It is striking that no ancient Near Eastern or Greco-Roman mythology ever taught the concept of *creatio ex nihilo*. That concept is as foreign to Neoplatonism as it is to Babylonian so-called creation myths. They are not actually "creation" myths at all; they seem to assume that matter is eternal or at least that its origin (if it has one) is unknown and unknowable. The gods bring order out of chaos, which suggests that both the gods and the chaos fit into the cosmos somehow. This idea is precisely what the Bible says is not true of God, according to historic Christian orthodoxy.

As the simple, immutable, eternal, self-existent, First Cause of the universe, God transcends the universe. This means that God is not a part of the universe, not on the same ontological plane as the universe, and not in any way limited by the universe or dependent on it. On the other hand, transcendence does not mean that God is so remote and detached that he lacks the ability to interact with his universe, and it does not mean that God is in any way locked out of his creation. Quite the contrary; it means that God is able to act as the ultimate cause of all things in regular ways (described scientifically in the laws of nature) and in unusual ways (called miracles). God's transcendence is often described in Scripture by means of the closely related idea of his sovereign lordship over creation, which can also be expressed as divine immanence.

God's transcendence means that he is not limited by time or space. All points on the time line are equally and simultaneously present to God, and all places are equally and simultaneously present to him. God is timeless in the sense that he is not within time nor constrained by time, although he is capable of acting in time since he is the First Cause and creator of all things. God is also immaterial, not in the sense of being cut off from the material and uninvolved in the material realm, but in the sense of not being limited by space. All space is immediately present to God, and all points in the time line are equally present to him.

Like the other attributes of God, transcendence is a perfection, not a limitation. Immutability does not mean God cannot speak and act in history, simplicity does not mean God does not choose to create, and transcendence does not mean God is locked out of his creation. As the creator of all that exists other than himself, God is the sovereign Lord of history and the only one worthy of worship.

■ THESIS 12

The language we use for God is analogical rather than either univocal or equivocal.

If God is transcendent, how can a mere finite creature speak of such a God? How can we speak of the one who transcends space and time and who cannot be contained within the cosmos, which is his creation? How can creaturely language express the transcendent nature of the Creator without compromising the creator-creature distinction?

When we speak of God as holy or as loving or wrathful or merciful, we employ analogical language to speak of God in creaturely terms. As creatures, we have no other way to speak of God, because we have no experience of what it is to be divine. All human language about God is analogical, by which we mean that it is neither univocal nor equivocal.[33] Let us take the example of calling God "Father." When Scripture calls God "Father," it means that there is a comparison between a human father and God. But comparison is not identity; God is not like a human father in every possible respect. To speak of God in a *univocal* way would mean that every aspect of what "father" means in human terms would apply to God. So if I am a father and God is a father, we are alike. If God has a son and I have a son, I might wonder who is God's wife? After all, a human father cannot have a son by himself. But here we run into a problem; God has no wife. So maybe God being a father is not anything like a man being a father, and so maybe our language is *equivocal* in the sense that there are no valid points of comparison whatsoever. But if that were true, then using the term "Father" to speak of God as in "Our Heavenly Father" would actually be using a term devoid of meaning. The only way our language about God can be meaningful without reducing God to the level of a creature, then, is if it is *analogical*. In analogical language, one or more than one specific point or points of comparison between God and creaturely reality are valid, but there are always far more differences than similarities. God loves

33. Thomas Aquinas, *Summa Theologica*, I, q. 13, esp. art. 10 (1:69).

and cares for his creation and is thus like a human father in certain respects. But in many more respects, God and human fathers are incomparable.

The Reformed scholastic theologian Francis Turretin writes,

> The communicable attributes are not predicated of God and creatures univocally because there is not the same relation as in things simply univocal agreeing in name and definition. Nor are they predicated equivocally because there is not a totally diverse relation, as in things merely equivocal agreeing only in name. They are predicated analogically, by analogy both of similitude and of attribution. . . . God alone is said to be good (Matt. 19:17), i.e. originally, independently, essentially; but concerning creatures only secondarily, accidentally and participatively."[34]

The Great Tradition does not collapse the creator-creature distinction; nor does it accept the complete and total separation between God and creation that makes creation arbitrary, chaotic, and impossible to understand rationally.

Analogical language is the language of trinitarian classical theism, but there is one more point that must be clarified. Strictly speaking, we do not define God by reference to the creature, because the direction of the analogy goes the other way: we define the creature by reference to God. Thus, if part of the definition of a human being is that a human being has the ability to reason, we must not imagine God reasoning in exactly the same way as human beings do. And we must not think of God as being like us in this way. Rather, we should think of humans as in some small way sharing in the rationality that is in God perfectly. We can have rationality in only a creaturely manner and not in a divine manner. We must be careful not to think of reason in God as a faculty, and we must not think of God reasoning in a sequential manner to increase his knowledge by the actualization of some potential for knowledge in his being.

This is not easy to grasp, but divine simplicity is important in theology precisely *because* it is very difficult to conceive clearly. It functions as "an apophatic qualifier."[35] That is, it functions as a reminder that God is more than we could ever grasp. God is incomprehensible to the creature in the way in which he has his attributes. That is not, of course, to say that God cannot be known by the creature, because we can know God truly without comprehending God fully. If we define knowledge as full comprehension, then in order to know God, either we would need to become God, or God would need to be thought of as a mere creature. To think that we could achieve the former is arrogant pride, and the latter approach is idolatry.

---

34. Turretin, *Institutes of Elenctic Theology*, III.6.4 (1:190).
35. Gavrilyuk, *Suffering of the Impassible God*, 60–63.

◼ THESIS 13

God is omnipotent, which means that his act fulfills his nature perfectly in all things.

The Apostles' Creed, the oldest and most authoritative creed in the church, begins with the phrase "I believe in God the Father Almighty." In this description of God, we find two emphases joined in a paradoxical fashion. On the one hand, the personal nature of God as Father is stressed. God is not just another name for nature, and God is not merely a force or energy field on which the rest of the material world depends. God is our Father, as Jesus taught us in the Lord's Prayer (Matt. 6:9). But in addition, we find that God is also "Almighty," which means that his power is unlimited by anything external to himself. God's will cannot be frustrated, and nothing in all creation is as powerful as he is. But the word "Almighty" means more than just that God is *somewhat* more powerful than the next most powerful being; it means that the power of any being whatsoever in the universe, great as it might be, must necessarily have a limit of some kind, whereas God's power has no limit whatsoever. Thus any rebellion against God by any creature or combination of creatures is doomed to failure.

Thomas Aquinas reminds us that we must beware of falling into the trap of conceiving of God's power as a passive potency, because this is incompatible with understanding God as perfect. We must also understand that while God is active power, he is not passive power, which Thomas defines as "the principle of being acted upon by something else."[36]

God cannot do what is a contradiction in terms. For example, God cannot make $2 + 2 = 5$. But if anyone thinks that this constitutes a limitation on God's power, one is just being a sophist. When a student hands in a math test with the answer 5 to the question "How much is $2 + 2$?" it is a fault or mistake. For God to make a mistake would not be a perfection but an imperfection. But if the objector persists and demands that God actually be able to make the correct answer to this question "5," it would entail God ceasing to be Truth. The equation $2 + 2 = 4$ is truth, and all truth is true because it corresponds to universals created by God and resident in the mind of God. And what God creates is reflective of his own surpassingly perfect being and therefore true. A society that views as a defect God's inability to lie or deceive or do what is evil or contradictory is a society that has lost it purchase on the truth. "Let God be true though every one were a liar" (Rom. 3:4).

36. Thomas Aquinas, *Summa Theologica*, I, q. 25, art. 1 (1:136).

▩ THESIS 14

God is omnipresent in the sense that all things are present to him, and "in him all things hold together" (Col. 1:17).

That God does not occupy one particular space as we creatures do is not a limitation but rather divine freedom to be universally present to all of creation. David wrote,

> Where shall I go from your Spirit?
>   Or where shall I flee from your presence?
> If I ascend to the heavens, you are there!
>   If I make my bed in Sheol, you are there!
> If I take the wings of the morning
>   and dwell in the uttermost parts of the sea,
> even there your hand shall lead me,
>   and your right hand shall hold me. (Ps. 139:7–10)

Whence comes this confidence that God is everywhere? It comes from a knowledge of God as creator of the heavens and the earth. As Creator, God is not part of the cosmos. We find it difficult to come up with human language to describe what it would mean for God to be everywhere simultaneously without thinking of God as part of the cosmos. But that is *our* problem, not his, and we should neither be surprised nor dismayed at how hard it is for creatures of space and time to describe God.

In Colossians 1:15–17 Paul declares that all things were created by and through Christ, and then he says that "in him [Christ] all things hold together" (v. 17). Paul makes a similar statement in Acts 17, where he quotes a Greek poet as saying "In him we live and move and have our being" (Acts 17:28). What is Paul getting at here? Is this biblical panentheism? No, Paul is here speaking of the divine immanence, the continuous presence of God to his creation, which participates in God and receives its being from him. God is continually causing the creation to exist. The creation is not autonomous or independent; it depends for its being on God, who not only created it in the past but also upholds it in the present. We should not think of God as remote or even absent from the world. Instead, we should think of God as perpetually and universally present to his creation, so that creation's dependence on God is constant and total.

▩ THESIS 15

God is omniscient, which means that he knows all things—past, present, and future—in one eternal act.

Besides being omnipotent and omnipresent, God is also omniscient. The force of the prefix "omni" in all three cases is not that God is *more* powerful or *more* dispersed or *more* knowledgeable than creatures, as if the point were a comparison of degree. Instead, the force is that of a superlative: God is powerful, present, and knowledgeable in a way that is different from how any creature or extension of a creature could ever be. For a creature to be omniscient, the creature would need to be outside time and space and able to comprehend all truth simultaneously and totally. Doing this would require the creature to transcend creation, which is impossible.

I sometimes startle my students by saying that "God does not have foreknowledge; . . . [long pause] . . . he just has knowledge." They are startled because at first it appears that I am saying that God does not know the future. But they soon realize that I mean that God is not located at one spot in space and is not fixed at one point on the time line so that successive points on the time line are still future to him. Rather, God is equally present in every place at every time, and in the same way, God is equally present to every point in time. Or, better, all times are simultaneously present to him. So he cannot have foreknowledge, because nothing is future to him. The concept of "futurity" is a concept that applies only to creatures, that is, to beings who have an origin at one point in time, who currently occupy a certain point in time, and for whom all future times are yet to come. To be in time is to be limited; to be free of time is a perfection.

Thomas Aquinas says that God does not know things the way creatures know things, and this is a very important point to remember. We need to engage in the act of knowledge and pass from a state of potency to actuality in knowing individually existing things, but God does not engage in such an act. The act by which God knows all things is unified, perfect, eternal, and fully actual because God is unified, perfect, eternal, and fully actual. God's knowledge is of himself, in whom are found all things as ideas.[37]

■ THESIS 16

God's transcendence does not prevent him from acting in history to speak, judge, and save.

From Genesis to Revelation, the Bible presents God as acting in history as judge of the entire world and the savior of his people. The Bible itself is the record of God's self-revelation to his people through the prophets of the Old Testament and, supremely, in Jesus Christ, as witnessed to by the New Testament apostles. "The Word became flesh" (John 1:14). The startling message

---

37. Thomas Aquinas, *Summa Theologica*, I, q. 14, art. 6 (1:76).

proclaimed by the apostles and church fathers to the Greco-Roman world was that the God of the Jews and Christians is the God of the philosophers—that is, simple, immutable, eternal, self-existent, and First Cause of the universe—and that this one has spoken through the prophets and become incarnate in Jesus Christ.

What is startling about this is that at least some of those who heard this message could understand the concept of an immutable First Cause, but they could not imagine thinking of such a being as personal or as speaking to us. They could also easily imagine the concept of a god speaking, acting, and doing miracles, but no one had ever suggested that the gods of the Greek and Roman pantheon were simple or immutable or eternal or self-existent or the first cause of all things.[38] They could understand both senses of the word "God" (*theos*), but they could not grasp how anyone could believe that both senses could be combined into one concept of God. This message was new, paradoxical, and threatened to overthrow their entire worldview.

But central to the message preached by the early church was precisely this point: the simple, immutable, eternal, self-existent, First Cause of the universe has spoken through the prophets and become incarnate in Jesus Christ. The early church did not first invent a theory sufficient to explain how such a thing could happen and then argue that it had happened. Instead, they discovered that it had happened, and then they had to figure out how to proclaim it and clarify exactly what they were saying and not saying in doing so. That such a being could speak and act in history is precisely what makes the Christian doctrine of God unique and absolutely devastating to anyone who wants to domesticate God or imagine God in ways that make God less than the sovereign Lord of heaven and earth. To confess belief in "God the Father Almighty" is to declare that only this one is legitimately to be worshiped and that all people everywhere must bow before him.

▓ THESIS 17

God is holy, just, and wrathful, but God is also loving, merciful, and gracious.

Many Christians approach the Bible naively and fall into the trap of taking for granted that God is basically like us, only greater. This is a natural failing

---

38. Although the Greek and Roman gods were thought of as having immortal life, they were not eternal, for they were also often thought of as having a beginning. Many were the children of parent gods. As was explained above in the exposition of thesis 8, the biblical concept of God is that he is unique in being outside time and having no beginning or end. The God of Genesis 1 and Exodus 3 has no beginning and thus transcends time.

and reflects our dilemma in thinking about God. As Calvin said, "Man's nature, so to speak, is a perpetual factory of idols"[39]; idolatry comes easily to us in our fallen condition. Avoiding idolatry requires conscious effort, and sound teaching is of great importance as we make this effort.

If asked to describe God, most modern people would probably say that he is loving, merciful, and gracious. And if the argument were made that God's love, mercy, and grace presuppose the reality of God's holiness, justice, and wrath, most people would find it hard to disagree that we should believe all that Scripture reveals about these six attributes. All of them can be derived from multiple passages of Scriptures, and all of them are actually themes of Scripture that can be traced throughout the canon. Although it does require effort to think of holiness and love together, justice and mercy together, and wrath and grace together, it can be done. So far, so good.

However, what is most puzzling to many people, including both simple believers and learned philosophers and theologians, is how God can be holy, just, wrathful, loving, merciful, and gracious while at the same time also being immutable and impassible. What it boils down to is the question of how God can have these attributes while also being the transcendent Creator, that is, the simple, immutable, eternal, self-existent, First Cause of the universe. Can the immutable God love us? Does God have emotions as we do?

In *Remythologizing Theology*, Kevin Vanhoozer draws on the work of Thomas Dixon to make some key terminological distinctions that we can use to answer this important question. According to Vanhoozer, Dixon shows that the word "emotions" is a modern term that was not used for the divine attributes by patristic, medieval, and Reformation theologians.[40] For the premoderns, God has "affections," not passions. The Westminster Confession of Faith, for example, says that God is "without body, parts or passions."[41] For premoderns, the word "passions" referred to things like rage or jealously, which involved being acted upon by outside forces. Vanhoozer writes, "Augustine viewed passions as involuntary movements of the man's lower animal soul that bypass both mind and will."[42] So it is not hard to understand why classical theologians would refuse to countenance the idea of God having passions. Affections, on the other hand, are voluntary movements of the rational soul, and so it is easy to see why the tradition could view divine mercy, love, and so forth as affections.[43]

39. Calvin, *Institutes*, I.xi.8 (1:108)

40. Vanhoozer, *Remythologizing Theology*, 403.

41. Westminster Confession of Faith, chap. 2: "Of God and the Holy Trinity," art. 1 (Dennison, *Reformed Confessions*, 4:236–37).

42. Vanhoozer, *Remythologizing Theology*, 400.

43. Vanhoozer, *Remythologizing Theology*, 401–3.

The word "emotions" was not used in classical orthodoxy to describe divine attributes. In the nineteenth century this word began to be used "for all those feelings that were neither [physical] sensations nor intellectual states."[44] A materialistic interpretation of emotion as the action of the brain and nerves on other parts of the body became dominant. So emotions, in the context of modernity, are understood as involuntary and irrational forces originating in the physical dimension of the human being, not in the soul. It is impossible and irresponsible even to consider attributing emotions in this sense to God. God does not have a body and is not subject to irrational forces that are beyond his conscious control. Such ideas are blasphemous.

Even when we speak of God having affections, we are speaking analogically. When we speak of divine love, mercy, wrath, and so forth, we are talking about God's self-determination in history as an expression of his fully actual, perfect nature. He does not have experiences in time because he is not in time, and he does not undergo change. When we speak analogically of God being, for example, angry, we are saying something about the perfect attitude of God toward sin, but we should not imagine him being angry as we would be angry. The point of the analogy is extremely narrow, and the dissimilarities almost overwhelm the point of similarity in this case.

▦ THESIS 18

The immutable First Cause of all things, who speaks and acts, is a paradox, not a contradiction; this is a mystery, which is what the major paradoxes of the faith are called.

The discussion above stresses the creator-creature distinction and the mysterious nature of divine being. One of the hallmarks of modernity is impatience with mystery. But there can be no true knowledge of the Christian God without recognizing the boundaries of rational comprehension and where mystery prevents full understanding of the divine nature.

The early church fathers preached the gospel in a Greco-Roman culture in which most people were polytheists and a few educated people held to a kind of philosophical monotheism. The Stoics were pantheists, and most Platonists believed in some sort of immaterial first cause of the universe. Christians who wanted to describe the God of the Bible faced a dilemma. If they emphasized only the personal nature of God, then their pagan audience would see the Christian God as being similar to the gods of the Greek and

---

44. Dixon, *From Passions to Emotions*, 23. See also Vanhoozer, *Remythologizing Theology*, 403.

Roman pantheon, which were basically exalted humans or personifications of the forces of nature. In fact, it was commonly believed that some humans became gods after death. These gods were limited, even though they were much more powerful than the average human, and they shared in the character flaws of humans. To Jews and Christians, they looked like fallen angels but not at all like the God of Scripture, the LORD God of Israel.

On the other hand, pantheism was also definitely incompatible with the biblical God, who is the creator of the cosmos, not simply another name for it. And many of the philosophical concepts of God, such as Aristotle's Unmoved Mover or Plato's Form of the Good, were completely impersonal and incapable of creating, judging, and saving. If the fathers emphasized the personal side of biblical teaching about God, they risked the philosophers concluding (quite rightly) that the philosophical god was behind and greater than the God of the Jews and Christians. But if they identified the God of the Bible with the god of the philosophers, they risked making him seem impersonal. What could they do?

The church fathers rightly refused both horns of the dilemma. They saw quite clearly that neither the metaphysically absolute nor the personal side of the biblical God could be compromised if they were to be true to biblical revelation. The God of Abraham, Isaac, and Jacob was also the God who humiliated the gods of Egypt, because he also was the God of Genesis 1, the creator of the heavens and the earth, that is, of all that exists (including the fallen angelic beings posing as the gods of the nations). So the early church proclaimed that the God of the Bible was all that the god of the philosophers was in terms of being the simple, eternal, immutable, self-existent, First Cause of all that is. At the same time, they also proclaimed that this God has spoken through the prophets and become incarnate in Jesus Christ. The God who is simple, eternal, immutable, self-existent, and the First Cause of all that exists has encountered us in Jesus Christ.

▪ THESIS 19

God is incomprehensible to the creature; although we can have true knowledge of God, we can never have comprehensive knowledge of God, which means that we can know God without comprehending God.

The church fathers never explained fully and rationally how the immutable God could create. Augustine struggled with the question and made some progress toward a rational explanation. However, he also repeatedly emphasized that God is beyond creaturely comprehension: "For if thou comprehend, He is not God."[45] But rather than viewing this incomprehensibility of God as a "bug," they saw it as a "feature."

If you really want to say that the one true God is different both from the superhuman gods of popular polytheism and from the ultimate principle behind the universe, then is it not to be expected that such a one is going to be incomprehensible? In addition, is not the fact that the gods of polytheism and the philosophical god are both, in different ways, comprehensible proof that they are not really the true God? How could anything capable of being metaphysically absolute be less than eternal, simple, immutable, self-existent, and perfect? But how could human reason demonstrate that such a God could reveal himself to humans? The Christian answer is revelation; we could never have imagined such a thing. We believe it because it happened.

The church fathers preached that the true God has revealed himself through the Hebrew prophets and that special revelation is necessary if we are going to know him truly. Philosophy finds its fulfillment only in prophecy. So the Christian doctrine of God, unlike the god of Aristotle, is not a rational theory cooked up by the human mind as the solution to certain philosophical problems. God is a fact, not a theory. God's self-revelation in the prophets from Moses to Christ makes it necessary to say what Christian theology says about God. We are not devising a theory; we are defining a confession. This God has spoken. On the basis of what he has revealed, we now know what we never could have known otherwise. For this reason, all the results of philosophical reflection on general revelation in nature, conscience, and human nature must be subject to correction and completion by special revelation discovered by exegesis of Holy Scripture.

■ THESIS 20

The God of the Bible is more than the god of the philosophers but not less.

When we speak of the god of the philosophers, we mean the First Cause of the universe, which may be known by reason. It is possible, as we saw above (thesis 5), for human beings to know that God exists apart from special revelation. There we saw that the primary reason for believing this teaching is that the Bible tells us that it is so. Only "the fool says in his heart, 'There is no God'" (Pss. 14:1; 53:1). "The fear of the LORD is the beginning of wisdom" (Prov. 9:10). And we saw that Paul in Romans 1 argues that the gentiles are culpable for suppressing the knowledge of God they already had when they

---

45. Augustine, *Sermon LXVII*, sec. 5 (*NPNF¹* 6:459).

became idolaters. But we also saw that fallen human beings usually deny and suppress their knowledge of God because of sin, and thus many people do not know God even though it would be possible to demonstrate by reason the necessity of his existence.

Here and there a very few philosophers have managed to overcome the obstacles put up by their own sinfulness and have broken through to the point of affirming the existence of God as the First Cause of the universe. The Platonic tradition stands out as a rarity in the ancient world in this respect. But even the philosophers who affirmed the existence of God did not necessarily *worship* God. Augustine severely chastised the Platonic philosophers of his day as inconsistent and blameworthy for continuing to worship idols; they clearly knew better but were afraid of the people and therefore conformed to popular religious practices.[46]

The church fathers also were well aware that the Platonic philosophers were able to affirm that God exists but still lacked any way of connecting the soul with God. Justin Martyr describes his journey through the various schools of ancient philosophy and how he found the Platonists to be the best. But he says he was greatly disappointed because Platonic philosophy offered no way to get to God. Only after he heard the gospel of how Jesus Christ fulfilled the Old Testament prophecies and died for our sins to bring us to the Father was he able to complete his philosophical quest.[47]

■ THESIS 21

The created order bears the imprint of the divine Logos, and humans are created in the image of God, which means that the human mind can apprehend the order and structure in the creation, which is the basis of natural theology, natural moral law, and scientific laws.

The God of trinitarian classical theism is the transcendent Creator of the heavens and the earth, which is a Hebraic way of saying "the entire creation." Our entire metaphysics is shaped decisively by this understanding of God. Instead of reality being a chaotic mess that is incomprehensible and unpredictable, the universe is indeed characterized by order and structure in a way that is one (*uni*verse) and not many. There is one God, and because the one true God has created, we can speak of *creation* and not of matter and energy

---

46. Augustine, *City of God* 8.13 (I/6, 257–58).

47. Justin Martyr gives an account of his philosophic quest and conversion in chaps. 2–8 of his *Dialogue with Trypho* (ANF 1:195–98). I will discuss this account more extensively in chaps. 7 and 8.

interacting randomly. Universals are ideas in the mind of God that are the patterns for the things that exist in the universe. Things have natures, which makes their behavior predictable and rationally comprehensible. Because of this order and structure, the human mind, which itself is created in the image of the Creator, is capable of studying, understanding, and ruling over nature.

For this reason, natural theology is possible. We can know that God exists, and when believers do philosophy with the reason endowed by the Creator and without the confusing effects of sin clouding their vision, "the heavens declare the glory of God" (Ps. 19:1). The wisdom traditions of Israel, as found in Scripture, show that the knowledge of God is natural to those who are not in rebellion against him.

For this reason, the natural moral law can also be discerned. Some things are right, and others are wrong, and knowledge of which is which is available to those who seek it. From the nature of things, we can discern the telos of those things. What enables a thing to move toward its telos is understood to be good, while what inhibits a thing from moving toward its telos is understood to be evil. An entire system of ethics can be derived from a true philosophical knowledge of things in the world, including human beings themselves.

For this reason, the laws of science exist and wait to be discovered by human beings. The world is not booming, buzzing, random confusion but an orderly world waiting to be understood by a human mind that combines the experimental method with the universals that permit the knowledge of mathematics. Science is possible because nature is created and because humans are made in the image of the Creator.

■ THESIS 22

The transcendent Creator of the universe has revealed himself to Israel and climactically in Jesus Christ, which is the First Mystery of God.

There are three great mysteries of God. The first is that the simple, immutable, eternal, self-existent First Cause of the universe has spoken through the prophets and revealed himself in the history of Israel. Why Israel? Why in the time of Abraham, Isaac, and Jacob? No possible answer can be given to such questions. The contingency of special revelation is not something that humans can reduce to a rational explanation. In the first article of the Apostles' Creed, we confess our faith in God the Father Almighty; in the second article, our faith in God the Son, Jesus Christ; and in the third article, our faith in God the Holy Spirit. The central, second article is the longest and contains all the active verbs. Here we touch history with a mention of Pontius Pilate and the

Virgin Mary. The Creator of all things has come to us in Jesus Christ in a historical revelation, and this is the heart of our faith.

But Christianity is not designed to lead us to a God who fits inside our minds; it is designed to lead us to the God who actually exists and who is truly God. The goal is not rational comprehension but rational worship. That the transcendent Creator of the heavens and the earth has revealed himself to Israel and supremely in Jesus Christ, the God-Man, is a mystery that drives us to worship, not merely to a series of logical propositions that we can explain. This is the First Mystery of God.

■ THESIS 23

The Nicene doctrine of the Trinity expresses the unity of the Father, the Son, and the Spirit—three persons (hypostases) but one being (ousia), which is the Second Mystery of God.

The second great mystery of God is expressed in the most important creed of the church, the Niceno-Constantinopolitan Creed of AD 381. It is the mystery of the Holy Trinity. The simple God is three persons and one being. God is one in respect of being, but three *hypostases*. Theologians wrestle with the question of how *ousia* is related to *hypostasis*. We can say that they are not identical; in referring to these two words, we do not merely repeat ourselves. But as for specifying exactly how they can be distinguished, we find ourselves unable to articulate the exact nature of the difference.

The confession of the church is that the central mystery of the faith is a paradox, not a contradiction, because there *is* a difference, but the exact nature of that difference is covered like a veil blocking the profane out of the holy of holies. Our eyes are too impure to see into the nature of God, and our minds could not comprehend what we saw if we could see. And *per impossible*, even if we could see and comprehend, we would still be unable to utter in merely human speech what we saw and comprehended. This is the Second Mystery of God.

■ THESIS 24

The Second Person of the Trinity, the Son, has assumed a human nature into a hypostatic union with himself in the incarnation, which is the Third Mystery of God.

The Third Mystery of God is addressed in the Definition of Chalcedon (AD 451). Here we find that Jesus Christ is the God-Man, one person in two natures, fully God and fully man. Does Chalcedon explain how this can be so? No, it has a different purpose. The purpose of the Chalcedonian Definition is to define our confession, not to define the God-Man. What does Holy Scripture require us to say about Jesus Christ? It requires us to affirm that he is fully God and fully man. It does not permit us to blend the natures or to divide the person. It ensures that we confess the totality of biblical revelation about Jesus Christ, but it never presumes to explain the "how" of the hypostatic union.

The eternally preexistent Son, the Second Person of the Holy Trinity, assumed into union with himself a human nature that was created by a miracle in the womb of the virgin. He derives true manhood from his mother, but the power of the Holy Spirit overshadowing the virgin—like the Spirit hovering over the primal waters of Genesis 1:2—results in a creative act of God such that the holy one born of her is rightly called holy, the Son of God (Luke 1:35). This is the Third Mystery of God.

▓ THESIS 25

The purpose of theology is neither to dissolve nor to explain the mysteries of the faith; rather, the purpose of theology is to define what the church believes, teaches, and confesses about these mysteries to enable contemplation and worship of God while avoiding heresy.

This brings us to the end of our description of trinitarian classical theism, the faith of the Christian church based on the inspired Scriptures of the Old and New Testaments. It should be noted that thesis 25 is an elaboration of thesis 1, which is appropriate, because the goal of theology is to progress in wisdom continuously. The purpose of Christian theology is to aid and support the Christian who faces the demand "Christian, say what you believe." For we must obey the command to be witnesses to our Lord Jesus Christ, as he gave it in the Great Commission (Matt. 28:18–20). We confess our faith in the ecumenical creeds of the first five centuries, and we joyfully affirm the three mysteries of God. We do not pretend that our knowledge is comprehensive, nor do we presume to understand all things. But we know *whom* we have believed (2 Tim. 1:12), and to know him is life eternal (John 17:3). To do theology is to be "lost in wonder, love and praise"[48] and to confess with the great saints and theologians of the church that "though our lips can only stammer, we yet chant the high things of God."[49]

48. Wesley, "Love Divine."
49. Gregory the Great, *Moralia*, as quoted by Thomas Aquinas in *Summa Theologica*, I, q. 4, art. 1, ad 1 (1:21).

Part Two

The Biblical Roots of Trinitarian Classical Theism

Three

Interpreting Isaiah 40–48 Theologically

It is easy for the critics to draw a picture which is a caricature of the Isaiah whom the Church for centuries believed to be the real Isaiah and to contrast him, as an impossible visionary, with their very human Isaiah who was a man of his age, vitally concerned with the immediate problems of his contemporaries. But it is important to remember that while such a conception of the prophet and of his role in Bible history must effectually destroy the unity of Isaiah, it must also go far beyond this. It must also destroy the entire fabric of Messianic prophecy.

Oswald T. Allis[1]

As we saw in chapter 1, the biblical teaching that God has acted in history to redeem the world seems to many modern people to contradict the classical theist emphasis on the immutability and impassibility of God. We also saw that the orthodox doctrine of God is often challenged by pitting biblical theology against what is described as Greek metaphysics. In one sense, this is an exegetical problem, but it also reveals just how intertwined exegesis is with dogma, metaphysics, and spirituality. This chapter considers what it means to read Isaiah theologically. I argue that what makes a reading theological, as opposed to what modern higher critics mean by "a historical reading," is

1. Allis, *Unity of Isaiah*, third unnumbered page of the preface.

primarily a matter of two issues: determining the proper context in which the text should be read and understanding the nature of the text as revelation.

To address the question of context and the question of revelation, we must consider issues that require us to affirm certain metaphysical doctrines and reject others. The trinitarian classical theism described in chapter 2 is the conceptual framework in which we must think through the issues of canon, inspiration, predictive prophecy, miracles, and the relationship of the biblical text to the pagan religions of the cultures in which God spoke through the prophets. All these questions are part of the general question of how revelation comes through history.

Interpreting Scripture in Its Proper Context

Isaiah 40–48 are central chapters in the book of Isaiah, and they make use of themes that are central to the Bible as a whole, such as creation and exodus. By focusing on this significant portion of the book of Isaiah, I hope to show, first, that trinitarian classical theism is a restatement of the plain sense of the text, that is, of what the text explicitly says plus what can be deduced from its explicit meaning. And second, I also hope to show that trinitarian classical theism not only arises out of the text but also enables us to penetrate more deeply into the *res* of the text, that is, the subject matter of the text, which is God. The goal is to show that trinitarian classical theism and an important section of a central biblical book are not merely compatible but are actually mutually illuminating. Reading the text of Isaiah 40–48 using trinitarian classical theism as our metaphysical framework allows us to perceive a depth of meaning in the text that otherwise is obscure, namely, the doctrine of God as the transcendent Creator and sovereign Lord of history, who alone is worthy to be worshiped.

Modern doctrines of God that abandon classical theism in favor of theistic mutualism represent not only a departure from the plain sense of Scripture but also a reversion to the pagan mythology that the biblical writers knew and decisively rejected. That a rationalization of sexual immorality and perversion often accompanies modern revisionist biblical interpretation and revisionist theology is no accident but is rather what one would expect if modern theology, as I claim, is reverting to pagan mythology. This conclusion will become apparent only at the end of this chapter, so the reader is asked to be patient as we go step by step through the argument.

An important implication of the Bible's being the inspired and authoritative Word of God is that its message is not just for the first generation of readers who encountered it. Theological interpretation operates with this conviction, which is precisely what motivated reading communities to preserve, transmit, and ultimately canonize these writings. The meaning of Scripture is deep and profound. Since the ultimate Author of the Bible is God himself, the Bible is inspired in a way that enables it to function as a message to the faithful people of God in every century. This was part of God's plan from all eternity and led him in his providence to cause the Scriptures to be written through the specific human authors he chose and prepared for this task (e.g., Jer. 1:5; Acts 9:15).

As we meditate on what Isaiah wrote in his situation in the late eighth and early seventh centuries (ca. 740–680 BC) to the exiles in the mid-sixth century (586–515 BC), we must remember that the first hearers/readers of these poems were actually not the exiles but rather Isaiah's contemporaries and all those who lived between 740 and 586 BC.[2] Many contemporary biblical scholars reject the idea that biblical prophecy is predictive of the distant future. For example, R. W. L. Moberly writes,

> Prophetic speech is predictive, but it is predictive in relation to the near future, to the circumstances that impinge on the lives of the prophet's contemporaries. On such an understanding, the notion that Isaiah should be predicting events to do with Jesus, events that lie centuries in the future, becomes difficult—not that it is inconceivable, but that it is out of place. A future that is contingent in relation to response to the prophetic message is not a future that is sure to be realized regardless of contemporary response.[3]

There are two highly questionable claims embedded in this passage.

First, not all prophecy deals with the near future. Moberly and modern critical scholars in general can only make such an assertion after having first defined all long-term prediction out of existence. One way they do this is by denying traditional views of the date and authorship of various books, thus—conveniently for their theories—making many parts of the Old Testament after the fact. The other way they do this is by refusing to see how many prophecies have a double fulfillment, with a near fulfillment that does not negate the longer-term fulfillment. We see the former approach in their dating Isaiah 40–55 to the time of the exile, right after the decree of Cyrus predicted in Isaiah 44:28. We see the second strategy in their refusing to see a

2. I am assuming an early date and unified authorship for the book of Isaiah, and I will say more about those issues below. But this point is still valid even if one assumes a late date and multiple authors. If, as the church has taught for 2,000 years, the book of Isaiah has a messianic meaning, then it must have a meaning for the New Testament era and not merely for the preexilic, exilic, and postexilic communities.

3. Moberly, *Old Testament Theology*, 147.

long-term fulfillment in the Immanuel prophecy of Isaiah 7:14, even though Matthew the evangelist does. Moberly is trying to put Isaiah into a conceptual box, but the text simply does not fit within this little box. Isaiah 6, the call of the prophet, is one example of how Moberly's view of prophecy does not do justice to the text of Scripture. Having volunteered to deliver the message of judgment to Israel, Isaiah asks in verse 10 how long he is to preach it. He receives the answer "until the cities lie waste . . . and the LORD removes people far away" (Isa. 6:11–12). In other words, Isaiah begins his ministry knowing that the exile is inevitable, even though it was over a century in the future. Yet he is to declare the fact that the exile is coming to *his* generation, not just to the people who would actually experience the exile a century later.

Second, the contingency of the future, which we experience on a creaturely level, does not affect God's ability to know and predict it. Moberly claims that the future must be contingent and so therefore future outcomes cannot, in principle, be promised by God. Why not? Moberly's theological assumption seems to be that the future is "open" and that both God and creatures operate within time and on the same plane. This view is a form of theistic personalism, which thinks of God as a being among beings, and this understanding of God is incompatible with classical theism. In classical orthodoxy, God and creatures operate on different levels. God is outside time and completely sovereign over time. Human free will does not challenge or negate divine sovereignty; they are compatible. This theological issue affects not only one's view of predictive prophecy but also the possibility of inspiration as well. This is a paradox, not a contradiction.[4]

The alleged contradiction between human free will and divine foreknowledge raised by Moberly's statement is a perfect example of how, in attempting to be "modern," modern biblical scholars unwittingly revert to the pagan perspective that the fathers were at pains to oppose. In book 5 of the *City of God*, Augustine argues against Cicero's contention that "if we take foreknowledge of future events, the will's choice is eliminated; if we take the will's choice, foreknowledge of future events is eliminated."[5] Cicero was writing against the Stoics, and in an attempt to uphold human free will, he was trying to show that divination is not valid. His argument, however, would also rule out predictive prophecy in the Christian Scriptures, which is something Augustine is eager to highlight, and which he views as highly significant. Therefore, Augustine argues that human free will is not incompatible with

---

4. Because of the massive importance of this issue for hermeneutics, I spent chap. 2 of *Interpreting Scripture with the Great Tradition* discussing it.
5. Augustine, *City of God* 5.9 (I/6, 154).

divine foreknowledge and seeks to distinguish between the Christian world-view and pagan determinism:

> Over against these audacious, sacrilegious, and ungodly assertions, we say both that God knows all things before they happen and that it is by our own free will that we do whatever we feel and know we would not do unless we willed to do it. We do not, however, say that all things happen by fate; rather we deny that anything happens by fate. For we have shown that the word "fate," as it is commonly used, that is, in reference to the position of the stars when a person is conceived or born, means nothing, since there is nothing there for it to assert. As to an order of causes, where the will of God mostly prevails, we neither deny it nor do we call it by the name "fate." . . . Moreover, even if there is a fixed order of all causes for God, it does not follow that, as a consequence, nothing depends on the choice of our will. In fact, our wills are included in the order of causes that is fixed for God and contained in his foreknowledge.[6]

Cicero, the Stoics, the astrologers, and the diviners worked with a metaphysics that viewed all things (including the gods) as part of one cosmic order and that therefore all interactions between them occurred on the same plane of reality. Augustine, however, worked with a theological metaphysics derived from the Bible, which viewed God as transcending this cosmos of which humans are a part and regarded God's will as the "cause of causes." God orders all things by virtue of being the creator of the natures of creatures, including their wills. In such a metaphysical system, human free will is creaturely free will, which means that human free will is free in that we are free to will whatever we want. What we want depends on our nature. Making ourselves want the right thing, however, is not easy, for we cannot create ourselves ex nihilo; we are stuck with the nature with which we were created. As the transcendent Creator, God on the other hand has an absolutely free will with respect to creation, because he can create ex nihilo. God creates us, our natures, and our wills.

The metaphysics of God's relation to creation is highly relevant to ortho-dox theological interpretation of Scripture. The metaphysics of modernity has more in common with the metaphysics of pagan Greece and Rome than with the theological metaphysics of Christian orthodoxy. Biblical interpretation needs to work self-consciously within the theological metaphysics of Nicaea and reject the pagan metaphysics of both ancient and modern philosophical naturalism.

Those who claim that Isaiah's message about what would happen to the exiles over a century later would be irrelevant to his contemporaries must

6. Augustine, *City of God* 5.9 (I/6, 154–55).

assume that his contemporaries had no concern about the future of Israel in God's eschatological plan, which seems highly implausible. Jeremiah also spoke to his contemporaries, prior to 586 BC, about what would happen to the exiles approximately a century later (Jer. 30:1–33:26). Both prophets gave exactly the same message; namely, that the LORD would restore the nation and honor the Davidic covenant after the exile. Many Israelites were intensely interested in this topic.

Calling "irrelevant" this message about the future just because it concerns a future generation is somewhat like saying that the message about the second coming of Christ is irrelevant to us unless we know for sure that it is going to happen in our lifetime. Since the New Testament era, many generations of believers have found this doctrine meaningful, because they know that it applies to them *no matter how much time passes between their death and the actual occurrence of this event*. As Christians, we hope for the resurrection of all the saints, no matter when they died. So too, the future of Israel in God's redemptive plan would define the meaningfulness of the lives of those who lived in anticipation of God's future work of exodus, just as God's past work of creation defines the meaning of our lives in the present. The beginning and ending of the story give history its meaning, and so the beginning and ending of the world give our lives meaning.

In addition to these considerations, Isaiah's message of hope in chapter 40 was also relevant to Isaiah's contemporaries because it concerned the nature of their God. Isaiah's message was obviously also relevant to the exiles in Babylon a century and a half after he wrote it *because it was about the same God*. The message was also highly relevant for the New Testament apostles, who quoted Isaiah extensively throughout their writings and structured their interpretation of the meaning of Jesus's death and resurrection using Isaiah's schema of the twofold coming of the messiah as both suffering servant and anointed conqueror. And it was also relevant to the fourth-century church fathers embroiled in the Arian controversy, who saw in it a prediction of a divine messiah, and to Thomas Aquinas as he wrote his classic exposition of the doctrine of God in his *Summa Theologica*. The message of Isaiah 40–48 remained relevant and edifying to the Protestant Reformers, the Puritans, evangelicals, and Christians down to the present day because in all these different centuries they worshiped the same God.

The ongoing relevance of the message of the text is made possible by the inspiration of Holy Scripture. Because Scripture is inspired, meaning is not limited to what the original human author consciously intended to say to the original human readers as reconstructed by contemporary scholars through a kind of literary archaeology. Meaning arises in the process of God using the literal meaning of the text to speak to his people in all centuries of church history. For this reason, the meaning of the text cannot be reduced to what it had to say to any one of these audiences alone but includes the meaning or meanings that all of them discerned, even though some of these audiences perceived more and deeper meaning than others did. The virtue of hermeneutical humility enables us to understand that we do not read the Bible with a "God's-eye view." Like all the previous readers of the Bible, we read it from within the limitations of our own historical situation, using our best metaphysical presuppositions—that is, the ones we think correspond as closely as possible to reality. We should not presume that *our* analysis (unlike that of previous readers in previous centuries) exhausts all the meaning that is contained in the text. It seems undeniable that I will understand the text of Isaiah more deeply after the second coming of Christ than I do now. Meaning is consistent and unified (that is, objective), but it is not always perceived subjectively in its totality by any particular reader at any one point in the history of redemption.

If divine authorial intent is the determining factor for what meaning actually inheres in the text, then even though the meaning we discern as we read contemplatively is only part of the total meaning, it may nonetheless be the full and complete meaning that the divine author intends *us* to receive here and now. The doctrine of the sufficiency of Scripture, which is an implication of the doctrine of providence, was articulated in Protestant scholastic theology in order to express the idea that this meaning is all that we need in order to live the Christian life faithfully in our situation (2 Tim. 3:16–17).[7]

In interpreting Scripture, the first step is to read the words on the page carefully: "What does it say?" Much could be said about reading with care and attention to detail. Speed reading is not helpful here; the goal is slow, meditative reading. We need to slow down enough to notice things that one might otherwise overlook. There are grammatical, stylistic, structural, and other aspects to slow reading, but fundamentally it involves observing what is there in the text. What does the text say? That is the first step.

The second step is to ask "What does it mean?" When we ask what it means, we must realize that the single most important thing to do in reading any text well is to consider the context. There are, of course, many potential contexts for any given text. The more hypothetical and subjective a proposed context is, the less reliable it is in identifying the authoritative meaning of the text. Scholarly reconstruction of the historical situation in which the text was written and first read may be of some help, but it will bear more authority if

7. Muller, *Post-Reformation Reformed Dogmatics*, 2:318–22.

the historical situation is known from the biblical text itself and less authority if it is a speculative, extrabiblical reconstruction. So although the historical context is important, it is not necessarily solely determinative for meaning, particularly if the reconstructed historical situation is more speculative.[8]

The literary context, on the other hand, is potentially more objective because it is right there in the text and not the hypothesis of the interpreter. Each text is embedded permanently within a literary body of work (the canon), and nothing can change that basic fact. Of course, the exact *significance* of the placement of the text within a section, book, or testament is up for discussion and needs to be analyzed. There is always room for discussion about which aspects of canonical context bear most critically on a particular text. But at least the starting point is objectively known; we start with the canon. If we want to read the Bible theologically, the canonical context, including the historical information provided in the Bible itself, is absolutely crucial and ultimately authoritative. In the case of Isaiah 40–48, there are three concentric circles of canonical context, all of which must be taken into consideration in answering the question "What does it mean?"

The Book of Isaiah as Context

The first canonical context of Isaiah 40–48 is the book of Isaiah itself. The book of Isaiah is a unified scroll, translated into English in sixty-six chapters, that presents itself under the following heading:

> The vision of Isaiah the son of Amoz, which he saw concerning Judah and Jerusalem in the days of Uzziah, Jotham, Ahaz, and Hezekiah, kings of Judah. (Isa. 1:1)

There is no need to assume that the oracles are in chronological, rather than thematic, order, and there is no need to read texts intended as metaphorical

---

8. The degree of certainty assigned to various historical background information can vary widely. Some points are virtually certain, while others are purely subjective guesswork, and still others fall somewhere between these extremes. So when someone asks whether I value history for biblical interpretation, I find it a hard question to answer. It all depends on what historical background is being proposed as important, how we know it, and how certain the evidence is. For example, if someone suggests interpreting Jesus against the background of the history of biblical Israel, this is obviously a good idea. However, if someone proposes interpreting Jesus as a kind of cynic philosopher, I cannot take that idea very seriously. Between these extremes, I think it is extremely important to interpret Jesus in the context of Second Temple divisions within Judaism—groups such as the Pharisees, Sadducees, Zealots, and Essenes—even though our knowledge of the history of these groups is far from complete. In sum, such a question must be decided on a case-by-case basis.

in a literal way, in order to take the book of Isaiah for what it is: a collection of prophetic oracles and poems (with a few prose sections scattered in here and there), which express Isaiah's attempts to communicate to his hearers and readers the vision he received from the LORD. The book of Isaiah presents itself as a unified work from one prophet, unlike the scroll containing the book of the Twelve, which presents itself as the work of twelve different prophets, or the Psalter, which presents itself as a collection of works by various authors (some named and some anonymous) organized into five books. Isaiah is a single book with a named author, which strongly implies that it has a coherent theme and message.

I remain unconvinced by the modern historical-critical view of Isaiah as a collection of writings by multiple authors patched together over three or four centuries by a succession of scribes who felt free to add to, subtract from, rearrange, and rewrite the sense of a sacred text purporting to be based on revelation given by the LORD to his prophet in the eighth century BC.[9] The older idea of two or three "Isaiahs" was problematic enough, but that view seems relatively conservative today. Contemporary historical-critical scholarship on Isaiah posits many redactors and moves sections of text around so freely that not even most of chapters 1–39 can be said to come from Isaiah of Jerusalem. When one reads the historical-critical commentaries, one finds that all too often the answer to any apparent contradiction or inconsistency in the text is to get out scissors and paste, rather than to patiently reflect on the meaning and structure of the details of the text as it stands. The biggest single problem with giving oneself permission to consider emendations and interpolations is that as soon as we find something difficult to understand, we tend to hurry past what is meant to be contemplated patiently, with the result that we miss the hidden treasure. It gives us permission to be superficial and confuses scholarly sophistication with the invention of creative theories about what *might* have been the case or guesses about what *might* have been meant. A summary of the results from a century of this sort of thing makes for dry and boring reading. It is a little like going to a performance of Handel's *Messiah* and having to listen to the tenor display his virtuosity by hitting increasingly higher notes instead of simply singing the aria as written. It is ultimately a form of narcissism. If the scroll as it stands has any sort of internal coherence, the sense of a unified message remains hidden from impatient critics who assume too quickly that there is no sense to be made of a paradoxical juxtaposition of statements in the text. They seem to think

9. For an excellent defense of the traditional dating and authorship of the book of Isaiah, see Allis, *Unity of Isaiah*.

that their job is to rescue the text from itself, rather than to understand it. Thus they patronize the Word of God.

If modern critics had been given the task of creating, preserving, and transmitting the text of Isaiah during the period from the eighth to the second centuries BC, I have no doubt that they would have treated it like "Wiki-Prophecy," a community product. However, it was not modern critics but ancient religious Jews, who revered these texts as communications from their God, who undertook the work. Therefore, it seems quite likely to me that the text of Isaiah that we see in the Great Isaiah Scroll of Qumran (1QIsaᵃ), which dates from no later than 125 BC,[10] is basically the same book that came from Isaiah himself or else from a close and like-minded disciple, who sometime in the mid-seventh century BC arranged Isaiah's writings and/or transcribed oral speeches into the shape in which they appear in the present book of Isaiah.

No manuscript or archaeological evidence exists for shorter versions of Isaiah or of portions of Isaiah circulating separately (such as a scroll containing only chapters 1–39, for example).[11] All the divisions, insertions, recensions, interpolations, theories of multiple authorship, and so forth are merely conjured up from the fertile imaginations of the critics. Most of these views are based on the subjective opinion that the text we have in front of us does not "hang together properly" or "appear coherent." In reality, a great deal of the theory has evolved because of a rejection of the metaphysical possibility of predictive prophecy. Regarding the view that the second part of the book of Isaiah was written by unknown persons 150 years after Isaiah of Jerusalem, John Oswalt says, "This hypothesis is necessitated by an inability to accept the claims of the book, not by independent data."[12]

My theory is that the book is the product of a single mind (certainly at the divine level, but also at the human level) and can be understood in a way that makes sense of the parts in terms of the whole. If it is not the product of a single mind, it looks as if it were, and we have no objective proof that it is not. Even if it turned out not to be the product of a single human mind, it is nonetheless the product of a single divine mind by virtue of inspiration operating through a combination of providence and miracle. So we should begin our investigation of the book with the assumption that it makes sense, even if our ability to make sense of it is imperfect. We should read with charity

10. Vanderkam and Flint, *Meaning of the Dead Sea Scrolls*, 131.

11. This contrasts with the Psalms, in which are numerous indications of prior collections being joined together. For example, the end of Psalm 72 says, "The prayers of David, the son of Jesse, are ended."

12. See Oswalt, *Book of Isaiah: Chapters 40–66*, 5. He quotes R. N. Whybray and R. F. Melugin in support of this assertion. We could add Oswald T. Allis to that list as well.

and humility rather than suspicion, because this is, after all, sacred Scripture. This assumption of coherence, however, will ultimately be justified or not depending on how successfully we can make sense of the book in its present form as a unified work with a message that can be discerned by careful study.[13] The theory can be tested by experiment, but baseless speculation does not count as counterevidence.

Regardless of one's views on dating and authorship, theological interpretation of Isaiah 40–48 requires us to read and interpret the book as it stands if Isaiah is to be of use to us theologically. The elephant in the room is the issue of authority; if one speculatively reconstructs the book into what is, for all intents and purposes, a *different* book with a different message, then one is not basing one's interpretation on the canonical book that Christians and Jews over two millennia have regarded as inspired. Anyone who wishes to reconstruct a different book is of course free to do so. No "Grand Inquisitor" threatens to censor anyone, and publishers appear eager to publish all sorts of theories and speculation. But simply *preferring* a hypothetical reconstruction of the book of Isaiah to the canonical one does not give the reconstruction authority equal to the canonical book of Isaiah as far as the Christian church is concerned. And I fail to see how preferring a reconstructed version of Isaiah could be construed as accepting in any meaningful sense the doctrine of the authority of Holy Scripture. After all, how could the authority of shifting, changing historical reconstructions that never stand still for very long ever be sufficient for theological purposes, let alone for preaching the Word in the context of Christian worship? If one generation is required to believe something that contradicts what previous generations believed, in what sense can both interpretations be said to be based on the authority of God?[14] While the question of truth, as David Steinmetz once remarked, can

13. I am at work on a multivolume theological commentary on the book of Isaiah for the International Theological Commentary series. One of my goals is to lay out the case for the thesis that the book of Isaiah is a unified theological work that expresses a coherent view of God. The best commentary expounding the theological perspective of the book of Isaiah is that of Motyer, *Prophecy of Isaiah*.

14. For example, if biblical interpretation requires one generation to believe that Isaiah 53 is a prophecy of Jesus Christ and then a few generations later scholars determine that Isaiah 53 is not a prophecy of Jesus Christ, is the church supposed to believe contradictory things simultaneously or change its preaching and contradict itself? This problem is especially intense when we read sentences that begin, "We used to view this passage in this way, but modern research shows. . . ." This sentence can mean that people in previous centuries had no reason to doubt the old interpretation, but now we do, and interpretations held in good faith are overturned by "new research." How is this compatible with the Bible functioning authoritatively in the church? It seems to me to be far more likely that the theological message of the Bible can be discerned all through the history of the church by interpreters who pay close attention to the canonical context

"endlessly be deferred"[15] in the university seminar, ministers who stand before a congregation to preach the Word of the Lord must be convinced that they are preaching something that precedes them and that they are standing under its authority. This is why the church confesses that the sixty-six books of the Old and New Testaments, in the original languages, constitute the inspired Bible that is our authority in all matters of faith and practice.[16]

In sum, we can say that the book of Isaiah presents itself as a unified book that has been arranged in deliberate ways, either by Isaiah himself or a disciple/editor compiling his material, in order to convey a distinct theological message. In a complex work of this size, there are many crosscurrents, tensions, and paradoxes, but that sort of complexity is to be expected and is also true of a polyphonic novel like Dostoevsky's *Brothers Karamazov* or a great work of philosophy such as Plato's *Republic*. I suggest that the central theme of Isaiah 40–48 is that *the God of Israel is the transcendent Creator and the sovereign Lord of history, and this one alone is to be worshiped*. The theme of the book as a whole is that God is the Holy One of Israel, and the theme of chapters 40–48 supports and elaborates on that overall theme.

Below is a possible way to outline Isaiah with the nature of God as the theme of the book.

    I. The Holy One of Israel (chaps. 1–6)

        A. Introduction: The case against God's people; the current, ideal, and future Jerusalem; the allegory of the vineyard (chaps. 1–5)

        B. The Holy One of Israel: The prophetic calling of Isaiah and the problem of the book of Isaiah as summarized in the phrase "the Holy One of Israel" (chap. 6)

    II. The messianic king (chaps. 7–12)

        A. The fall of the house of David: The crisis of 735 BC and the Immanuel prophecy (chaps. 7–8)

        B. The introduction of the messiah: The future Davidic king and his kingdom (chaps. 9–12)

---

of texts and read them in submission to the illumination of the Holy Spirit. If my interpretation of a text in Isaiah is utterly novel and contradicts the tradition, the reasonable course of action for my readers is to regard my interpretation with great suspicion. It is always theoretically possible that the majority tradition has been wrong, especially when a strong minority interpretation has been held alongside the majority interpretation for many centuries. But to the extent that an interpretation is *unprecedented*, it is to that extent unlikely to be true.

15. Steinmetz, "Superiority of Pre-critical Exegesis," 14.

16. Westminster Confession of Faith, chap. 1: "Of the Holy Scripture," art. 2 (Dennison, *Reformed Confessions*, 4:234–35).

III. The sovereign Lord of history (chaps. 13–39)

    A. The oracles against the nations: Three cycles of oracles, which include Israel and Judah, and eschatological hope (chaps. 13–27)

    B. Lament as a philosophy of history: Lament as a third way beyond despair and utopianism; how to wait patiently for the salvation of the LORD (chaps. 28–35)

    C. The historical background to the prophecy of Isaiah: The crisis of Sennacherib's invasion of 701 BC and the introduction of the Babylonian threat (chaps. 36–39)

IV. The suffering servant (chaps. 40–53)

    A. The good news of deliverance: The predicted return from exile and the nature of God as the transcendent Creator (chap. 40)

    B. The lesser deliverance through the lesser servant: The LORD as the sovereign Lord of history and the prediction of the decree of Cyrus, which solves the immediate political problem (chaps. 41–48)

    C. The greater deliverance through the greater servant: The work of the suffering servant, who solves the sin problem (chaps. 49–53)

V. The anointed world conqueror (chaps. 54–66)

    A. The invitation to believe: First Israel and then the nations are called to put their trust in the suffering servant, who has atoned for sin and conquered death (chaps. 54–58)

    B. Songs of the anointed one: Four songs corresponding to the four servant songs, which fill in the other side of the portrait of the messiah as world conqueror (chaps. 59–63)

    C. The new heavens and new earth: Eschatological visions of the judgment of the earth and the climax of history (chaps. 64–66)

The book of Isaiah thus portrays God in five panels or portraits as the Holy One of Israel, the messianic king, the sovereign Lord of history, the suffering servant, and the anointed world conqueror. The last two panels consist of two distinct but complementary portraits of the messianic king described in the second panel. They arise from Isaiah's meditations in his old age on *how* the messianic king might come, given the unholiness of the people. Both portraits must be true, but how this is possible is not explained. What Isaiah did see clearly was that God himself is the final answer to Israel's problem, which is its unholiness. The opacity of this book arises from God's being portrayed as acting in history as a human figure. No explanation is given as to how this can be. Thus there exists in the book of Isaiah an ineradicable layer of mystery, because Isaiah's subject is not merely history or Israel or religion; the *res*, or subject matter, of the book is God.

The Old Testament as Context

The second canonical context of Isaiah 40–48 is the Old Testament, including particularly the Law of Moses. The Prophets all presuppose the Law, because their task, as presented in the writings of the Prophets themselves, is to call Israel back to the covenant made at Sinai, in which Israel took on the responsibility of obeying the law. So Isaiah should be read not as calling Israel to a new, novel doctrine of who and what God is but rather as calling Israel back to the doctrine of God embedded in the Law of Moses.

In discussing the relation of the Prophets to the Law, John Calvin says that the Prophets derived their doctrine from the Law "like streams from a fountain; for they placed it before them as their rule, so that they may be justly held and declared to be its interpreters, who utter nothing but what is connected with the Law."[17] Calvin goes on to say that the Law consists of three parts: "First, the doctrine of life; secondly, threatenings and promises; thirdly, the covenant of grace, which, being founded on Christ, contains within itself all the special promises."[18] He views the Prophets as expanding on the doctrine found in the Law, explaining more fully the Law as summarized in the Ten Commandments, applying the Law of Moses to their own times, and expressing "more clearly what Moses says more obscurely about Christ and his grace."[19] Can we legitimately read the Prophets this way in view of modern historical-critical scholarship?

It surely makes a difference to our interpretation of Isaiah whether we view it as presupposing the text of the Law of Moses, especially Genesis 1–3 and Exodus 1–15. Did Isaiah know, for example, Genesis 1:1–3 and Exodus 3:14–15? These are two crucially important biblical texts for determining the meaning of creation and the relation of God to the world, and Isaiah 40 contains both creation language and exodus imagery. Could Isaiah presume that his immediate hearers/readers would know these texts when he preached using creation and exodus themes? Could he assume, at least, that his disciples would know them? When he uses exodus imagery in Isaiah 40:3–5, could he expect his hearers/readers to know about the event in Israel's history to which he is alluding? Could he expect them to know the account of it in the book of Exodus? If we value human authorial intent as fundamental to the meaning

17. Calvin, *Isaiah*, 1:xxvi.
18. Calvin, *Isaiah*, 1:xxvi.
19. Calvin, *Isaiah*, 1:xxvi.

of the text, our interpretation of Isaiah cannot get off the ground without answers to these basic questions. According to the canonical order of books, both in the Hebrew Bible and in the Christian Old Testament, one would think that the answer to all these questions would be in the affirmative. One would certainly think that whoever arranged the canonical order as it stands would expect future readers (like us) to read Isaiah in light of Genesis and Exodus.[20]

But according to the reconstruction of the Old Testament writings undertaken by historical criticism in the last two centuries, the order found in our Bible is the wrong order for interpretation. The thesis of Julius Wellhausen's seminal work of 1878, A Prolegomena to the History of Ancient Israel, is as follows:

> In the following pages it is proposed to discuss the place in history of the "law of Moses"; more precisely, the question to be considered is whether that law is the starting point for the history of ancient Israel, or not rather for that of Judaism, i.e. of the religious communion which survived the destruction of the nation by the Assyrians and Chaldeans.[21]

Wellhausen regarded the Prophets as the true founders of the religion of Israel, which was later codified into the Law of Moses during the exile and brought back from Babylon by Ezra in 458 BC. Today some historical critics, known as the minimalists, go even further. They believe that the entire Old Testament narrative of Israel's history up to the exile is a creative fiction that was invented in the exilic period.[22]

Mark S. Smith is a leading Old Testament scholar who works specifically on the doctrine of God in the Hebrew Scriptures. His Memoirs of God is a good example of contemporary liberal scholarship on this issue.[23] In chapters 1 and 2, he lays out the reconstructed history of Israel that represents a middle position in contemporary historical-critical scholarship. It is not as

20. This comment would seem to hold true regardless of whether we are thinking of the Jewish canonical order or the Christian one. Seitz (Elder Testament, 22n1) sees the relationship of the Law and the Prophets as basic to the structure of the canon, with the Writings as peripheral. The heart of the canon is the relationship of the Prophets to the Law.

21. Wellhausen, Prolegomena, 1.

22. Whitelam, Invention of Ancient Israel. See also Block, Israel. Also see chap. 2 of Dever, What Did the Biblical Writers Know?, 23–52. In that chapter Dever critiques the current revisionist school and links it to postmodern ideology. Whitelam's anti-Zionist agenda of detaching the Jews from their historical association with the land is facilitated by the postmodernist revisionism described by Dever. We should not be naive about how such ideological dynamics may be at work in modern historical criticism generally and not merely at its most extreme fringes evident in this example.

23. See M. Smith, Memoirs of God.

extreme as the minimalist position, but it also departs significantly from the traditional conservative approach, even in its mid-twentieth-century moderate form represented by John Bright's *History of Israel*.[24] Rather than believing what the Bible says only when it is confirmed by outside archaeological or textual evidence, Bright and others committed the "sin" of treating the Bible as true until proven false. For Bright, the exodus traditions as well as the patriarchal traditions in Genesis 12–50 are historical, as are the depictions of Israel in the books of Joshua and Judges, although legendary bits are mixed in with historical kernels of truth. This approach might be broadly identified as part of the "Biblical Theology movement" and is closely associated with mid-twentieth-century neoorthodoxy. Smith notes that since the 1970s, this approach has been under attack. For Smith, the history of Israel begins with the first extrabiblical reference to Israel in the victory stela of Pharaoh Merneptah from 1208 BC, which refers to his victory over Israel. Smith does not regard anything prior to the monarchy as historical. He also sees the original religion of Israel as polytheistic, based on the frequent criticism of Israel's idolatry by the Prophets. The history of Israel's doctrine of God evolved from the polytheism of its early period to a high philosophical monotheism in the period of the exile. The Torah is a composite work, with the priestly material originating in the exile, and it is precisely this priestly material plus the priestly redaction that makes the Torah monotheistic. Just as Wellhausen said, the Prophets founded the religion of Judaism and, so far as Smith is concerned, the religion of preexilic Israel was essentially a product of its pagan environment.

My purpose here is limited; I cannot enter into a detailed discussion of which parts of the Old Testament are historical and why. My goal here is simply to bring to light something that Smith points out with regard to the issue of the context for reading the Prophets. He recommends Ahlström's *History of Ancient Palestine* as "the best single-volume work available in English" on the history of Israel. Then on the basis of what he takes to be the consensus of the best scholarship, he observes the following about the historical outline he is summarizing in chapters 1 and 2: "The resulting picture hardly looks like the Bible's own outline of Israel's history."[25] Here we see the heart of the problem. The Bible as it stands—the canon—is simply not authoritative for Smith. It is actually deceptive, and if we naively allow it to be the context in which we interpret individual texts (such as Isa. 40–48),

24. Bright, *History of Israel*. See also Provan, Long, and Longman, *Biblical History of Israel*, which takes a moderate position as well.

25. M. Smith, *Memoirs of God*, 15.

then we will inevitably get them wrong, because we will fail to see them in their true context. Their true context was unknown to the Christian church prior to the Enlightenment—really, prior to the nineteenth century—and so an interpreter like Calvin could not possibly have understood the true meaning of the Old Testament texts. He was interpreting them in the wrong context. Think about what that means for historic Christian orthodoxy and for the content of Christian faith.

Owen Palmer Robertson makes clear some of what is at stake here when he argues that, if we understand the Prophets to have been making the point that the exile resulted from Israel's disobedience to a covenant that had never actually been entered into by their ancestors, then their whole explanation for the exile is only a "pretense." Furthermore, it would mean that God had not actually given the nation adequate warning through the Prophets. Finally, it would mean that God was essentially no different from the other gods of the other nations in that he did not bring Israel into being and did not predict its punishment in advance. Robertson presses home the point that, in such a case, why should we in the twenty-first century put our faith in such a God?[26] Why indeed? The question of the proper context for the interpretation of the book of Isaiah cannot be separated from that of the historical-critical reconstruction of the Old Testament and the reconstruction of history itself. Should the ever-shifting, hypothetical, reconstructed historical context be permitted to replace the canonical context as the primary context that is determinative of the meaning of the text? Would meaning not become permanently unstable in such a case? Is this not a clear instance of how modern rationalism leads directly to postmodern relativism?

There are, of course, great disputes about what sources were used and the antiquity of each source. Some of the J and E materials are thought by some to date back to the centuries before Isaiah. Deuteronomy, however, is seen as originating in the seventh century BC. But just because a scroll that may have contained Deuteronomy only (or the Law as a whole) was found in the temple in the time of Josiah (621 BC), this does not prove that it had been written only a few months or years before that point. That is pure speculation. But even if Deuteronomy in its present form were late (seventh century BC), this would not necessarily mean that there was no core of legal material that went back to Moses and had been known throughout the intervening centuries (i.e., 1400–700 BC). In fact, I think the most likely scenario is that most of what we know today as the Pentateuch originated in the period of Israel's exodus wanderings, even though it shows signs of being lightly edited in subsequent

---

26. Robertson, *Christ of the Prophets*, 85.

centuries.[27] The way the canon is put together seems to indicate that this is the way the final editors intended it to be read, and this point is crucial.

After all, if someone finds it impossible to believe that Isaiah and Moses were inspired by God and if that person finds it incredible that the editors of the final form of the Hebrew Scriptures were inspired, it seems equally unbelievable for this person to attribute infallibility to the higher critics whose theories are currently fashionable in the early twenty-first century. Either we regard the canonical Scriptures of the Hebrew Bible to be the infallible Word of God, or else biblical authority will not be salvageable. And that means that higher criticism cannot be regarded as neutral or unbiased insofar as it contains within itself an antisupernaturalist presupposition that dissolves the faith in the acids of rationalism—a rationalism, it should be noted, that ends in postmodern relativism and irrationalism.

To sum up, in interpreting Isaiah 40–48, I will regard this material as stemming ultimately from God and secondarily from the single mind of Isaiah himself, and I will regard Isaiah as working out his thought on the basis of a thorough knowledge of the Law of Moses and, in particular, of Genesis 1–3 and Exodus 1–15. It can be argued that this is a theological approach that treats the Isaianic text not as a mere set of historical sources but as an inspired text suitable for theological interpretation. The real issue is not a dispute over this or that historical detail. The real issue is the authority of the Old Testament canon in its historic form as the proper context for the interpretation of texts in the Old Testament writings. A truly theological interpretation of Scripture can hardly ignore the issue of biblical authority.

The Bible as Context

The third canonical context of Isaiah 40–48 is the Bible as a whole, including the New Testament. The Bible is a unified work with one inspired Author and one overarching theme, namely, "God's glory in salvation through judgment."[28] As we read Isaiah, our problem is to establish what it means, that is, what it means *now* in the present *to us*. Exegesis that is content to remain at the level of what the original human author meant to convey to the original human readers in the original situation as reconstructed by modern scholars who assume philosophical naturalism as their metaphysical framework for exegesis is simply not theologically responsible. It is the approach of secular historians, and secular historians are not qualified to tell the Christian church

---

27. For a defense of this view, see Garrett, *Rethinking Genesis.*
28. This is the thesis of Hamilton's excellent book *God's Glory in Salvation through Judgment.*

what it ought to believe and not believe. Such an approach also places the text at the mercy of those who desire to twist its meaning into a shape that fits the modern worldview, even if this means leaving behind the true meaning of the text. In this respect, it is less objective than the traditional theological interpretation practiced throughout church history.

If all one looks at is the Isaianic scholarship of the past century, my approach may seem eccentric, but if you look at the entire history of the church over the past two thousand years, it is well within the mainstream Christian tradition of commentary on Isaiah. However, among contemporary Isaiah scholarship, it is a minority report and is not even universally accepted among those today who claim to be doing theological interpretation of Scripture. For example, a recent commentary by Paul Kim on Isaiah, subtitled *A Literary and Theological Commentary*, never once mentions the New Testament use of Isaiah, so far as I can tell. In the section on Isaiah 53, Kim raises the question of the servant's identity, and he mentions several possibilities, including individuals such as Moses; Cyrus as the new Moses; the prophet Deutero-Isaiah in the legacy of Jeremiah; a Davidic king such as Hezekiah, Josiah, or Jehoiachin; Zerubbabel; and collectives such as Jacob-Israel or a steadfast minority within the nation. But he shows no awareness of the New Testament, which just happens to offer an interesting interpretation of its own![29] I find this studied avoidance of the New Testament highly curious. It might be supposed that this is a Jewish commentary on Isaiah, but this is unlikely since Professor Kim teaches at Methodist Theological School in Ohio. But even a commentary written by an orthodox Jew, one would think, would need to mention the Christian interpretation of the suffering servant, even if only to refute it. This book does not even do that.

The problem is as follows: If the purpose of a commentary on Holy Scripture is to say what the text means, how can one come to any conclusion on Isaiah 53 without considering the way in which the New Testament writers interpret Jesus as the fulfilment of these prophecies?[30] Were they right, or were they wrong, and why? Regardless of whether one thinks the New Testament authors correctly interpreted Isaiah 53 or misinterpreted it, it seems reasonable to expect the interpreter to say *something* about it one way or the other. Even if the New Testament writers were wrong, they were pretty influential. The only reason I can see for why Professor Kim would feel that it is unnecessary to address this issue is because he does not believe that the

29. Kim, *Reading Isaiah*.

30. According to Hill and Walton (*Survey of the Old Testament*, 745), the New Testament quotes Isaiah 53 a total of thirty-eight times.

purpose of a commentary is to say what the text *means to us in the present*. But the problem with viewing the purpose of a commentary in this way is that it leaves the reader free to regard the text as a dead artifact from the past, which had meaning to the people of its own day but is basically foreign and irrelevant to us. Many modern historical critics are uninterested in the history of interpretation because they approach the text as secular historians do a text from an ancient culture, even though this text claims to be the Word of the LORD.[31] This prejudges the text by refusing even to consider *its own claim* to be the Word of God (Isa. 1:1) and therefore relevant to people of every age.

Such interpreters begin the interpretive task knowing in advance that whatever the text might mean, it definitely does not mean what it claims to mean. The kind of modern historical criticism that focuses on what the text meant back then and does not consider what the text means to us here and now is actually a biased and prejudiced approach. It is also unscientific, because it refuses to shape the method to the nature of the thing being studied in order truly to understand the object of study. Instead it presumes to impose modern prejudices upon the text, thus refusing to let the text speak for itself. It doesn't even afford the text the dignity of being *false* in its claims, let alone true.

In order to study Isaiah 40–48 in its proper canonical context—that is, to take the text seriously as what it purports to be: a section of the book of Isaiah situated in the Old Testament as part of the two-Testament Christian Bible—one must view it from two angles. On the one hand, the passage harks back to the Law of Moses, calls Israel to cease its apostasy, and urges it to return to the covenant and obey the Law. The text also stipulates what will happen if this does not occur. On the other hand, the passage points forward beyond itself to a future fulfillment: how God plans to keep his eternal covenant with David despite having to judge Israel for disobedience. We shall see that this future orientation is not imposed from the outside arbitrarily by later writers but arises out of the text of Isaiah itself.

How then should we interpret Isaiah 40–48? We should interpret it within its proper context, and the most important context for theological interpretation is the canonical context. This approach involves interpreting these chapters as part of a unified book of Isaiah that looks back to the Law of Moses and forward to the coming of a Davidic messiah, who is both a suffering servant and an anointed conqueror.

31. It allows what Krister Stendahl ("Biblical Theology, Contemporary") calls the descriptive task—"What *did* it mean?"—to overwhelm the theological task. Once the question "What *did* it mean?" is completely divided from the question "What *does* it mean?" bringing them back together is very difficult.

To summarize the argument so far, the most important issue in the interpretation of the book of Isaiah is whether it is actually *a book* in the sense of a unified work that means something as a whole. In the history of Jewish and Christian interpretation from the Second Temple period to the Enlightenment, the book of Isaiah was regarded as a unified literary composition with a unified message. Arguments were possible over exactly how that message should be framed, and contemplation of the text yielded different insights, depending on the historical context in which that contemplation occurred. Obviously, the apostles saw the meaning of Isaiah 53 more clearly in light of the death and resurrection of Jesus. So the New Testament account of what Isaiah means is regarded by Messianic Jews and Christians as an advance on the understanding of Isaiah in the intertestamental period, although as a matter of historical fact, the Jews who wrote the New Testament were themselves very much a part of Second Temple Judaism. Rabbinic Judaism later disagreed with the apostles but then had nearly as much trouble as the higher critics of the Enlightenment era in making sense of what Isaiah as a book *does* mean. In any case, such disagreements were primarily between Jews and other Jews, and only later did gentiles join the debate. When they did join the debate, they did so on both sides of the issue of whether Jesus is the Messiah. Today Messianic Jews (who have much in common with the Essenes and Qumran sectarians in the Second Temple period) together with orthodox Christians affirm a messianic interpretation of Isaiah, while rabbinic Jews (who have much in common with the Pharisees of the Second Temple period) together with historical critics reject a messianic interpretation of Isaiah. The cast of characters may change in different centuries, but the fundamental issues at stake remain constant.

Dissolving Isaiah's Message in the Acids of Modernity

The real break in the tradition of Isaiah interpretation occurs in the Enlightenment,[32] which comes to its climax in Kant's rejection of classical metaphysics on the basis of the skeptical arguments of David Hume. At that point, the Christian Platonism that had been generated by the Nicene doctrine of God, which had undergirded hermeneutics for over a millennium, was decisively undermined as far as many European intellectuals were concerned. After Kant, a new metaphysics arose. The attributes of God began to be transferred to the material cosmos. The material universe was regarded as fundamentally

---

32. Childs, *Struggle to Understand Isaiah*, 301.

unknowable by human beings in the way that God had previously been regarded as unknowable. The material universe was now also regarded as eternal and as having aseity, whereas before it had been God who was seen as eternal and as self-existent.

The Enlightenment myth of the cosmos as a giant machine gradually gave way to the newer nineteenth-century myth of the cosmos as a living organism. This enabled modernists to think of the universe as self-moved, which allowed them to dispense with the concept of God as First Mover. Once again, an attribute of God was transferred to the universe. As a result of this shift to thinking of the cosmos as self-moved, the notion of history underwent a crucial change. History began to be thought of in terms previously reserved for the deities of the various polytheistic religions that personified and deified the forces of nature. History came to be regarded as an "immanent power" that moves people and nations and engenders novelty. If the cosmos is alive and if it moves itself eternally, then all that exists must have come into being by powers immanent to nature. Darwinian evolution is more the implication than the source of this understanding of the nature of the universe.

How is "God" to be understood when the cosmos has taken on most of God's attributes and has become capable of performing divine acts? The options for understanding the nature of God were basically pantheism, polytheism, and various combinations of these two fundamental options. (Panentheism is best understood as a variation of pantheism.) Divine transcendence was ruled out as a fairy tale believed only by primitive people, who lacked scientific sophistication. The classical theist understanding of God was not so much refuted as rejected and left behind by scholars eager to make nice with the spirit of the age. Unfortunately, the spirit of the age was into nature worship, which is a reversion to pre-Christian paganism. Today it is often called "progressivism," which is ironic, since such a worldview renders progress an incoherent idea.

When the Christian belief in the existence of a transcendent Creator is denied, a vacuum is created in theology. When people no longer believe in the God of classical theism, certain old questions require new answers. The universe is here, and we are here, but why? Human beings demand an explanation of the origin of the cosmos and of humanity, because without an explanation, our lives seem to be meaningless, and humans cannot survive without meaning any more than they can survive without food and water. This is why humans are relentlessly religious beings. Everywhere one looks, in history and throughout the various cultures of the world, human beings worship something in some way, even if the object of their worship is the cosmos itself or even humanity itself. The quest for meaning is universal, and some sort of religious or quasi-religious answers are necessary if meaning is to be found.

The liberal project began in earnest in the nineteenth century. It stemmed from the thought of two pantheists: Baruch Spinoza and Friedrich Schleiermacher. From Spinoza came the historical-critical approach to the Bible, and from Schleiermacher came revisionist theology. The astonishing variety of concepts of God that we see in twentieth-century academic theology must *necessarily* arise in such a situation; this diversity is not simply a result of confusion. Within the context of philosophical naturalism, pantheism and polytheism actually presuppose one another. One embodies and explains unity, and the other embodies and explains diversity; any coherent worldview must account for both unity and diversity. Pantheism and polytheism do not need to be seen as contradictory; they are not so much rival conceptions of metaphysics as complementary components of a mythological worldview. How they fit together was a matter of discussion and debate throughout the nineteenth and twentieth centuries.

We see this in the way that Hegel hypostasizes history. For him, history is a force of nature that does things.[33] This is not fundamentally different from pagans hypostasizing forces of nature like the sun or lightning or fire or water. Of course, one is never quite sure what Hegel means by "history," just as one puzzles over what exactly Marx meant by the "materialist concept of history," in which he supposed matter to be the driving force of all historical change.[34] They do not seem to mean literal personal agency by a being who orchestrates the outcomes of the interplay of matter and energy over time, and yet they talk freely of direction and purpose. They seem, somehow, to be talking about something the universe itself does. Yet the universe is just the random interplay of matter and energy; how can it have any sort of purpose? What is this *Geist* of which Hegel speaks? Who enacted these "iron laws" that Marx thinks he has discovered? Observing a series of chance events followed by a particular outcome and then identifying that outcome as the "reason" why those chance events occurred is nonsense.[35] Purpose requires intention, which is a function of mind. Without this, one is just projecting human mental states on impersonal blind forces. It is like saying that cancer is trying to kill you.

---

33. Hegel (*Hegel's Philosophy of Right*, 216–17) writes, "The history of mind is its own act. Mind is only what it does, and its act is to make itself the object of its own consciousness. . . . History is mind clothing itself with the form of events or the immediate actuality of nature. The stages of its development are therefore presented as immediate natural principles."

34. Marx, "*German Ideology*," 171.

35. All this is implicit in accepting David Hume's destruction of classical metaphysical accounts of causation.

No, it isn't. It is just cells dividing; it does not have your demise "in mind," because cancer does not have a mind. When we anthropomorphize in this way, we can easily fall into mythological thinking. The universe doesn't care what fairy tales you dream up about what it means or intends, because it doesn't care about anything at all. It doesn't care, because it doesn't think. It just is.

The fundamental limit that must not be questioned in nineteenth-century metaphysics is that whatever sort of historical explanation one proposes, that explanation must arise from *within* the cosmos itself rather than come from outside the cosmos in a way that affects the cosmos sovereignly. The psalmist, on the other hand, sees the created order as upheld, directed, and moved by the Creator:

> O Lord, how manifold are all your works!
> > In wisdom you have made them all;
> > the earth is full of your creatures.
>
> . . . .
>
> These all look to you,
> > to give them their food in due season.
> When you give it to them, they gather it up;
> > when you open your hand, they are filled with good things.
> When you hide your face, they are dismayed;
> > when you take away their breath, they die
> > and return to their dust. (Ps. 104:24, 27–29)

The biblical understanding of God is that he is not remote and isolated from nature; rather, he is intimately related to his creation in the preservation and government of it. From a classical theist perspective, which is the theological context from which modern science originated in the late Middle Ages, a scientific explanation is the identification of the secondary cause through which God works to uphold creation. Biology explains that food grows by photosynthesis, and metaphysics explains that God created the chemical and physical entities with the kinds of natures that make photosynthesis possible. So God can rightly be said by the psalmist to be the cause of the feeding of creatures as described here without denying the secondary causes described scientifically by biology. There is no contradiction between different levels of causation. God is the First Cause of the universe, but he works through secondary causes most of the time. In cases where he works in unusual rather than the usual ways, we call his action a miracle. But it is all divine action, regardless of whether it is by providence or miracle.

What qualifies as a scientific explanation in the context of modern naturalistic metaphysics, however, is quite different. The only explanation modernists regard as scientific involves an immanent power of some kind that is inherent in the cosmos, as opposed to the operation of a transcendent being who is causing the system to operate from the outside. If one speaks of god at all in such a context, the definition of god would have to be some sort of pantheistic or polytheistic idea. I suggest that this definition of "scientific" is actually identical to what scholars of the ancient Near East mean by "mythological." I will say more about this issue below.

The modern myth of the universe as a giant self-sustaining perpetual-motion machine took hold of the Western mind in the eighteenth century, and those of the nineteenth century moved this world picture from a strictly mechanical one to a more organic one. But the continuity is actually much greater than the discontinuity in this move, because in both versions of the myth, the cosmos is seen as a unified whole. There is nothing beyond or above it; the cosmos depends on nothing beyond itself. The eighteenth-century myth of the cosmos as machine says that the cosmos has aseity, is eternal, and contains all that is real. But a crucial feature of the coherence of this world picture is added in the nineteenth century: self-motion. The mechanism of the Enlightenment, in which the laws of nature operate like a giant machine, required Deism. A machine needs a builder. All machines originate in the mind of a maker and need to be started by a person; someone must flip the switch to turn it on. Even if the machine is now operating everlastingly without outside interference, it needed someone or something to get it going. So philosophical naturalism could never be complete as long as a creator had to be presupposed, even if that creator was merely the "Great Architect of the Universe," the "Great Clockmaker," who brought the universe into being, wound it up, and then let it run on its own. A remnant of transcendence remained, and the Western philosophical mind chafed at this vestige of classical theism.

Enter the theory of evolution. The point of Darwinism was not that it was such a great scientific theory as such; rather, it was a scientific theory that met the metaphysical need of the hour. As C. S. Lewis put it, "The attraction of Darwinism was that it gave to a pre-existing myth the scientific reassurances it required. If no evidence for evolution had been forthcoming, it would have been necessary to invent it."[36] The theory of natural selection purported to explain how change occurs "naturally," that is, without outside interference from a transcendent Creator. Prior to Darwin, the problem was how to explain complex biological organisms like human beings without reference to a Designer. Darwin's suggestion was to view all life on planet Earth as the

---

36. Lewis, "World's Last Night," 74.

product of random changes in organisms plus the survival of the fittest.[37] Darwin's theory supposedly enabled the metaphysical system of philosophical naturalism to become a more complete explanation for the world and for human beings. This in turn enabled philosophers to drop the Deist God as unnecessary, which was another important step in the de-Christianization of the West and the reversion to ancient mythology. Only one residual biblical element remained: the continuing belief in progress in history, a kind of secularized providence. Secular progressivism seemed to reign supreme.

The problem, however, is that nothing in Darwin's theory actually explains why there is something rather than nothing. Nor does his theory provide any basis for the meaning of life or value, and without some criteria for value, there can be no such thing as progress. Progress requires a goal, and a goal presupposes some standard of value to distinguish it from other possible outcomes. Darwinism was developed both by humanistic-minded progressivists in North America, who fought for the rights of the working class, and by Nazi theorists in Germany, who used it to undergird their theories of racial superiority. Nothing in Darwin's theory itself made one use of it more appropriate than the other. The idea of progress is reduced to the level of a vague ideology that functions as a fig leaf covering the raw will to power. Suddenly Hitler and Stalin look less like exceptions and more like prototypes of the future of modernity, which inevitably degenerates into the totalitarian imposition of the will to power by the strong over the weak. Whether the strong have in mind the welfare of the weak is irrelevant. The theory neither justifies nor invalidates the benevolent or malevolent rule of the strong. The will to power simply fills the vacuum of meaning created by Darwinism.

Darwin's theory replaced the function of a transcendent Creator as First Cause with forces immanent to the cosmos, but in so doing, the whole idea of progress was undermined, and history can no longer be viewed as linear progress toward a goal. Only a transcendent Creator can define the goal of history. Without a transcendent Creator, the only alternative is to revert to the default position of the fallen human race, namely, a cyclical view of history. Matter and energy eternally combine and disintegrate randomly according to the blind, purposeless laws of physics, moving things around in an endless cycle of organization, chaos, and destruction. There can be no progress, no history, and no meaning in such a metaphysical system. The myth of progress is dying today and is being replaced by a revived pagan mythology that has

---

37. As many have pointed out, the idea of the survival of the fittest is a tautology with no predictive power. The "fittest" beings are simply those organisms that, for whatever reason, happen to have survived.

no concept of progress. This is a major reason why contemporary biblical studies, as an academic discipline, is in crisis.

As an academic discipline (insofar as it can legitimately be seen as a unified "discipline"), modern biblical studies emerged out of the matrix of the evolutionary metaphysics of the nineteenth century at a time when the myth of progress still reigned supreme. We can see this in the way the Old Testament was understood by scholars of that period. The canonical ordering of the Old Testament was completely revised. The Prophets came first; the Law of Moses was an exilic creation. The history of Israel as presented in the Bible was seen as largely fictional, and the biblical text was reduced to a collection of historical sources to be utilized in the construction of a "scientific history" in which everything evolved progressively from primitive to sophisticated, from simple to complex, and from amoral to ethical. Israel's religion emerged out of Canaanite paganism and slowly evolved from polytheism to monotheism.[38] The idea of monotheism had to be explained naturalistically, without recourse to supernatural revelation, and the result was a kind of "monopolytheism."[39] It was defined in philosophical terms rather than in terms of the biblical idea of Israel's God as the unique, transcendent Creator of the cosmos. Historical-critical biblical scholars were guided by the dominant metaphysical system of the nineteenth century in which the cosmos, including religion, is an ongoing process in which things progress toward the present by means of powers immanent in the cosmos itself.[40] Having married the progressive spirit of the modern age in the nineteenth century, contemporary biblical studies now finds itself widowed in the postmodern era. Hegelian metaphysics provides no defense against the onslaughts of the postmodern deconstruction of metanarratives.

I suggest that whatever theological interpretation of Scripture may be, we can know with certainty that it is *not* the study of the biblical text on the basis of these two assumptions: (1) the cosmos is eternal, self-existent, and self-moving, and (2) religion emerges over time as a result of immanent forces operating within the cosmos itself. Why not? Because this is the pagan mythological worldview of the culture in which the Bible was written and against which the Prophets spoke the revealed truth enshrined in Scripture. John Oswalt makes this clear in *The Bible among the Myths.*

38. On this point, see two books by M. Smith, *Origins of Biblical Monotheism* and *Early History of God.*

39. This term was discussed in chapter 2. It comes from Hart, *Experience of God,* 127–28.

40. Darwin was clear that his theory of natural selection was designed to explain everything about human beings, including ethics and religious beliefs, not just our physical bodies. See his *Descent of Man,* 244–54, esp. chap. 3 on the mental powers of man, including language, memory, imagination, self-consciousness, belief in God, and sense of beauty.

The Old Testament and Ancient Near Eastern Mythology

In his work, Oswalt identifies the key difference between the ancient Near Eastern worldview of the nations around Israel in Egypt, Canaan, and Mesopotamia and the worldview of the biblical writers. This difference is rooted in the uniquely biblical concept of God as transcending the cosmos. Scholars today know that the ancient Near East was dominated by mythological thinking, which can be seen in the stories inscribed on thousands of tablets recovered by archaeologists. We have many ancient myths from a variety of centuries and nations, all of which share certain fundamental worldview perspectives. Oswalt describes the central core of mythological thinking as the idea of "continuity," which, he says, is "the idea that all things that exist are part of each other."[41] When he says "all things," he specifically means nature, humanity, and the divine. Each of these three fundamental categories exist within the circle symbolizing the cosmos as a whole, and each one flows into and affects the others. There is "a community of essence" among them in the sense that each partakes of the other two.

Such a concept of reality is widespread in the world, not just in the ancient Near East. Westerners are being parochial when they take the creator-creature distinction for granted as the obvious truth about the nature of reality. I do not mean to say that the Christian understanding of God as the transcendent Creator is not true; of course it is true. But this view is the exception to the rule in world history; it is the view only of religions that have grown out of the Old Testament. For most of history, most of humanity has gravitated toward mythological thinking centered on the idea of continuity. That a longstanding, widespread tradition of Jewish-Christian theology describing a transcendent Creator even exists in the world is a tribute to the uniqueness and power of the theology of the Old Testament. The idea of a transcendent Creator could not possibly have evolved out of the pagan mythology of the ancient Near East; rather, it stands in total and complete contradiction to its environment. It repudiates continuity-thinking as false metaphysics and condemns mythological religion as false religion. It is not a higher form of the same thing; it is an alternative worldview.

What are the main tenets of ancient Near Eastern mythology, according to Oswalt? First, only the present is real in mythological thinking. Past and future are not really important. Time is not moving in a specific direction in a linear fashion toward a goal. Reality is timeless and is actualized in the cult. There is no progress.

41. Oswalt, *Bible among the Myths*, 48.

Second is an obsession with fertility and potency. This is seen in temple prostitution, for example, which figures so prominently in many pagan religions. It is really a form of sympathetic magic in which the worshiper tries to get the gods to imitate what is done in the ritual so that the land will be blessed with crops and the flocks will bear young.

Third is a denial of boundaries. Paganism is characterized by incest, bestiality, and homosexuality, all of which transgress boundaries. The mythical stories of the gods regularly feature promiscuity, violence, and other transgressive behavior. If all reality is one, then to separate things into divisions and put up fences is to act against reality. Genesis 1 is unique among ancient Near Eastern writings in depicting a transcendent God, who is not a part of the cosmos, separating one thing from another and drawing boundaries in the creation. Humanity is created as male and female, a complementary binary that is basic to all human relations. Biblical religion is about order and a structured creation, which is why it can be studied scientifically, whereas mythological thought sees all reality as ultimately one and therefore sees boundaries as arbitrary and meaningless.

This leads directly into a fourth point of contrast: mythological thought sees reality as basically chaotic and violent, whereas biblical theology sees it as basically peaceful and ordered. The difference is because in mythological thought, the world is eternal matter and energy in aimless flux, whereas in biblical theology, the world has a beginning and a goal toward which it is moving. Mythology is all about gods emerging from the primal chaos and imposing order through violent conflict. Strictly speaking, the Enuma Elish, which is often loosely termed a "Babylonian creation myth," is not really about creation at all. It is an etiological story that provides a rationale for the then-current sociopolitical regime by purporting to explain how Marduk brought order out of chaos by defeating the monster Tiamat.[42] Strictly speaking, it is a story about the rearrangement of eternal matter into its current configuration, not a creation story.

Finally, there is a fifth point of contrast between myth and biblical theology: the Bible proclaims the existence of a transcendent Creator who stands apart from and above the cosmos, which is his creation. Myths tell stories about the gods, but they never mention the LORD, even though it leaves unexplained who created the gods. They just pretend that the LORD does not exist and simply ignore the question of where all reality came from in the first place, which is a question that cannot be answered without appeal to him. The gods of the myths are not creators, and mythology is not about creation.

42. See the text of this myth in Pritchard, *Ancient Near East*, 28–35.

What Oswalt summarizes here is not particularly new or unique; he is simply summing up the scholarly consensus from the last century or so of study of ancient Near Eastern religions. The picture of pagan myth described here can be derived from the Bible itself, but it has been confirmed by archaeological and historical study of the ancient Near East.[43] But if the differences are as stark as Oswalt claims, of what possible value for the interpretation of Scripture could the study of the historical background of the Bible be? Oswalt seeks to articulate and expose the stark differences between the teaching of Scripture and the worldview of the cultures around Israel, and he does a good job of doing so. But the degree of difference he identifies leads to criticism from the historical critics, because Oswalt seems to imply that the Bible fell from heaven and is totally unrelated to its cultural environment. Critics claim that such a view is ahistorical and that, since biblical revelation comes to us in history, Oswalt's emphasis on the discontinuity of revelation and historical situation is itself unbiblical. Now there is something to this criticism, but we need to be careful to consider what assumptions are driving the critics who make it. If the objection reflects the view that the religion of Israel is nothing more than an evolved version of its cultural context and, therefore, not fundamentally different from the paganism out of which it evolved, then we must reject the view as incompatible with the concept of inspiration and as incapable of understanding what the Bible is saying. On the other hand, there is a perfectly legitimate sense in which the claim that we should interpret the Bible in its historical context is appropriate and even critically important to good theological interpretation. Interpreting the biblical text as speaking directly to its original culture and historical situation does not require us to reduce the meaning of the biblical text to nothing more than what a person of that culture and historical period might have been able to conceive.

The key is to understand something that John Currid emphasizes.[44] Like Oswalt, Currid is concerned with the problem of how the Old Testament relates to the ancient Near Eastern culture out of which it emerged. He notes that Israel, like other nations, made use of polemical writing in the form of stories and expressions in order to criticize theological beliefs of other religions and to assert the truth of their own doctrines. He writes,

> The primary purpose of polemical theology is to demonstrate emphatically and graphically the distinctions between the worldview of the Hebrews and

43. For example, see the texts recovered in the early twentieth century from the ancient city of Ugarit as described in Coogan and M. Smith, *Stories from Ancient Canaan*. These texts give insight into the religious background of Canaan in early Israelite history.

44. See Currid, *Against the Gods*.

the beliefs and practices of the rest of the ancient Near East. It helps to show that Hebrew thought is not a mere mouthpiece of other ancient Near Eastern cultures.[45]

Currid is thus able to show that the historical background of a biblical text is important for interpreting it without importing into his exegesis the unspoken presupposition that the text cannot possibly be expected to say anything novel or anything not explicable in terms of previously known thoughts or ideas in the general culture of that historical period.

For example, Currid notes that the way the book of Exodus describes Yahweh's presence on Sinai as accompanied by thunder from the clouds is similar to the Ugaritic literature's description of the storm-god Baal. As Currid points out, many scholars see the biblical writers as drawing on the figure of Baal as a source for how they portray God. For example, Michael Coogan writes, "The character of the god of Israel is thus a composite; while Yahweh is primarily an El figure, many of the images and formulae that distinguish him from El are adopted from the theology of Baal."[46] In response, Currid points out that a parallel does not prove dependence but could be explained in other ways. It is possible to see the biblical writer as polemicizing against Baal worship by claiming that Yahweh is the true God and Baal is only a pretender. The polemical character of 1 Kings 18 makes this rather obvious, in my opinion. In 1 Kings 17:1 the LORD's prophet tells King Ahab that Yahweh will cause the rain to be withheld, which results in famine in Samaria (1 Kings 18:2). In chapter 18 we have the great contest on Mount Carmel: when the prophets of Baal are unable to get Baal to send fire, Yahweh sends fire to consume the sacrifice in response to Elijah's prayer. Then in verses 41–46 of chapter 18, the LORD sends rain, which Elijah announces in advance to Ahab. The message could not be clearer. Yahweh is in control of the rain and the fire; Baal is impotent before Yahweh. When Yahweh tells his prophet that he is going to do something, it happens. Baal does not control nature; he just pretends to be able to do so. Even though Baal may be capable of a few parlor tricks here and there with his superhuman but still limited powers, the true sovereign Lord of nature is the LORD, the God of Israel. All the references to Yahweh riding on the clouds (e.g., Ps. 104:3; Isa. 19:1) and doing other things that Baal is said to do should be interpreted in light of this polemical motif.

There is an incomplete and quite defective knowledge of God among all peoples in all parts of the earth, which is derived from general revelation but

---

45. Currid, *Against the Gods*, 25–26. In his book, Currid provides a series of convincing examples of polemical theology in the Old Testament.

46. Coogan, *Stories from Ancient Canaan*, 20, as quoted by Currid, *Against the Gods*, 31.

then twisted by the lies and deception of the false gods who invented pagan religions and gave the mythologies to humans. These false gods are actually fallen spiritual beings who mislead the human race into worshiping them instead of the one who alone is worthy to be worshiped—that is, the LORD, the creator of all things, including these fallen spiritual entities who pose as the gods of mythology.[47] We need to understand the Old Testament as a polemical correction of false religion and as God's revelation of the truth, not to people who know nothing about God, but rather to people whose faulty knowledge needs correction and completion.

Mythology, Modernity, and Reading the Old Testament as Revelation

This chapter has attempted to lay a foundation for a theological reading of Isaiah 40–48 that treats the canonical context of the book of Isaiah, the Old Testament, and the Bible as a whole—as interpreted by the Great Tradition of Christian orthodoxy—as of decisive importance for determining its meaning. Such a theological reading does not detach the biblical text from its historical context, but it does steadfastly resist the reduction of the meaning of the text to a mere repetition of what the culture already knew prior to the writing of the biblical text. In this way, it attempts to take seriously the doctrine of the inspiration of Scripture as having some actual value for determining the meaning of the text. Reading the Old Testament theologically means reading it as revelation.

Divine authorial intent is finally decisive for the meaning of the text. Although divine authorial intent will never contradict human authorial intent and grows out of it in some logical fashion, it would be wrong to think that divine authorial intent could never go beyond conscious human authorial intent. The human authorial intent should be understood to be the literal sense of the text, and the divine authorial intent that goes beyond conscious human intent should be understood as the extended literal sense of the text. The two are often identical, but sometimes divine authorial intent—as in messianic typology, for example—goes beyond what the human author consciously understood himself to be doing. This is the crucial difference between inspired writing and noninspired writing.[48] If one cannot clearly specify the difference between inspired and noninspired writing, then one's doctrine of inspiration is functionally meaningless.

---

47. The best recent book on this important point is Heiser, *Unseen Realm*.

48. For more on authorial intent, see my *Interpreting Scripture with the Great Tradition*, esp. chap. 6.

Comparing the cultural situation in which the Old Testament was written (ancient Near Eastern mythology) with the contemporary cultural situation in which we seek to interpret it today (modernity), it is apparent that their understandings of the nature of God and how God relates to the world have more in common with each other than either has with the teaching of the Old Testament itself. Often in reading scholarly works on the Old Testament, one finds the author assuming that modern readers have one set of metaphysical doctrines that are assumed to be true, while the text is situated in a prescientific culture that had very different answers to basic worldview questions such as "Who am I?" "Where am I?" "What is wrong with the world?" and "What is the solution?"[49] This frames the interpretive situation in an inadequate way.

In fact, such basic worldview questions may be answered using either mythology or metaphysics, depending on the culture. One set of answers can be couched in mythological terms and naturally yields a mythological account of the world, while another set of answers is more naturally expressed in metaphysical terms. Both the ancient Near Eastern cultures and the Greco-Roman culture of the Second Temple period were based on mythology, and their mythologies are actually quite similar in many ways. Both are based on the fundamental idea of continuity. The rise of Greek philosophy, on the other hand, was unique in Greek culture and was based on a conviction, absent from all mythological systems, that the world is governed by *logos*, that is, by a rational principle at the heart of all things, which makes the world a unified cosmos knowable by human reason. A culture that sees *logos* as fundamentally determinative of reality will inevitably develop a metaphysical account of reality and will also, inevitably, develop natural science. A mythological culture, on the other hand, will never develop either metaphysics or natural science on its own. But it is crucial to see that such a culture still answers the same worldview questions; it just has different answers and gives those answers in different forms.

Let us compare how the mythological culture of the ancient Near East and the metaphysical culture of the Greco-Roman world answered the basic questions of human existence. First are the answers of the ancient Near Eastern mythological worldview.

---

49. Walsh and Middleton (*Transforming Vision*, 35) introduced me to the idea of using these particular questions to analyze a worldview. However, Leslie Stevenson articulated four very similar questions about a decade earlier in his *Seven Theories of Human Nature*. This book was later revised and published as Stevenson and Haberman, *Ten Theories of Human Nature*. A book of readings to accompany this book was published in 2000 as Stevenson, *Study of Human Nature*. Walsh and Middleton updated their book as Middleton and Walsh, *Truth Is Stranger Than It Used to Be*.

"**Where am I?**"—I am in a world that is fundamentally chaotic, so the order and structure that enables human civilization to flourish is fragile.

"**Who am I?**"—I am a human being created by the gods for their use and born to serve the kings who represent the gods.

"**What is wrong?**"—The chaos at the heart of all reality constantly threatens to overwhelm us with a loss of fertility of crops and flocks or out-of-control forces of nature, such as floods or volcanoes.

"**What is the solution?**"—I must offer sacrifices to the gods, engage in magical rituals, and submit to the rule of the king so as to maintain the order of the world.

The rise of Greek philosophy resulted in different answers being given to these basic questions. Metaphysics instead of mythology was used by the philosophers to answer the worldview questions.

"**Where am I?**"—I am in a universe governed by a principle of reason called the *logos*, which is mysterious but real.

"**Who am I?**"—I am a rational animal with the ability to reason logically.

"**What is wrong?**"—The irrational forces both within me and in nature threaten to overcome reason and subvert my ability to control both myself and the world around me.

"**What is the solution?**"—Education and philosophy will solve these problems.

The Greek answer to the final question, however, was found to be inadequate even by those most committed to philosophy themselves. For one thing, education in antiquity was limited to a small elite of those with leisure. But more important, even those who knew the right thing to do, sometimes found it impossible to do it. This fatal flaw in human nature, coupled with the suspicion that the cosmos was really an unstable blend of *logos* and chaos, fueled the growth of Greek tragedy. Greek philosophy was never able to transcend tragedy.

For this reason, Greek philosophy remained incomplete and was fulfilled only in Christianity. The Christians agreed with the Greek philosophers in viewing nature as rational and as knowable by us as rational creatures; for Christians, this was true because of the doctrine of creation (Gen. 1; John 1). But Christians also had a solution to the problem of how to live so as to do the right thing. With its doctrines of Christology, sin and redemption, and the power of the Holy Spirit, Christianity offered a solution to the problem identified by Greek philosophy. On the one hand, it was only natural for Christianity to join with philosophy in rejecting and seeking to overcome mythology. But on the other hand, philosophy could not remain unaltered by its assimilation into Christianity. Even Platonism, the highest and best of philosophies, had to become *Christian* Platonism by accepting Jesus Christ as the incarnation of God, Messiah of Israel, and Lord of creation and by accepting the creator-creature distinction based on the doctrine of God as the transcendent Creator.

In an attempt to know the text from the inside, as it were, it seems evident that proper interpretation of the biblical text involves cultivating a deep empathy with the worldview embodied in the text. The historical-critical approach, however, often fails spectacularly in this task because it is too highly invested in the metaphysical assumptions deemed "scientific" and "modern" and thus beyond question in the contemporary academy. In one of the great ironies of intellectual history, this commitment to "modern" "scientific" methodology often leads the modern scholar to side with the ancient mythological worldview that the Old Testament seeks to refute and overcome. Historical criticism becomes an exercise in reading the text against itself.

The mythological worldview of the cultures around ancient Israel, against which the biblical writers vigorously polemicized, viewed the world as eternal matter under the constant threat of chaos. Only the actions of the gods held back the forces of chaos symbolized by the sea and by various mythological monsters.[50] Their founding narratives (myths) were stories in which various gods emerged out of the watery chaos and fought great battles against the monstrous threats to order and thereby established the social and natural structure that made civilized life possible. They held to a polytheism in which the various gods were all ultimately part of nature itself. They had no concept of an eternal immutable Creator of all things who designed the cosmos, upheld it in being, and governed it by his providence, which is to say that they had no real concept of a transcendent Creator.

The Old Testament, on the other hand, is the record of the revelation to Israel by the LORD, the God of Israel, of his nature and of the doctrine of creation. Because Yahweh is the transcendent Creator of the cosmos, he is also the sovereign Lord of history, and therefore he alone is to be worshiped. Such a concept of God did not arise, and could not have arisen, as an extension of the pantheism and polytheism of ancient Near Eastern mythology.

---

50. See Day, *God's Conflict*. Note that this mythological context is Canaanite, and so a Babylonian provenance for the Old Testament text is not required in order to see it as reacting against mythology.

It contradicts everything that ancient mythology holds as foundational. It requires those who believe this revelation to worship differently, live differently, and hold to a completely different theology. It implies a totally different set of metaphysical doctrines. It requires the rejection of "cleverly devised myths" (2 Pet. 1:16) in favor of the revelation that culminates in Jesus Christ.

Since the Enlightenment, modern historical-critical study of the Bible has embraced the materialism, nominalism, and mechanism rejected by the church fathers as they developed a Christian Platonist metaphysics on the basis of Nicene trinitarianism. Instead of the theological metaphysics of Nicaea, Enlightenment-inspired historical critics ended up embracing the myth of the cosmos as a machine set up by a distant, impersonal God who allowed it to run by itself. In the nineteenth century, this myth morphed into an organic one in which the cosmos began to be viewed as a living organism that moves itself because it is alive and evolves on its own by laws immanent in the universe so that from chaos comes order, structure, and beauty.

The idea of progress was a holdover from the older Christian metaphysics, but in the era of postmodernism, it has become increasingly clear that modern mythological thinking has no real basis for believing in progress. There is no criterion of value by which progress can be measured and no reason to think that eternally evolving matter and energy with no beginning and no end has any telos whatsoever, apart from whatever telos human beings arbitrarily choose to give it. Progress becomes just a fancy term for what is really the will to power of the strong. Those who have the strength to face it know that life and the world are meaningless; nihilism is the hidden truth of modernity. Plato loses to Nietzsche.

"Modern metaphysics" is thus better understood as a rejection of metaphysics insofar as it is actually a reversion to ancient mythology. Therefore, we can readily understand why postmodernist theorists are so resolutely antimetaphysical. Of course, in one sense it is true that everyone has metaphysical views, even if they are mostly just denials of traditional doctrines. Thus nominalism is a metaphysical view just as much as realism is in that sense. But at a deeper level, it is not incorrect to say that postmodernists—that is, extremely consistent late modernists—are really postmetaphysical. In describing Derrida's deconstruction of language, Stephen Hicks says that for Derrida, "Language connects only with more language, never with a non-linguistic reality."[51] For Hicks, this is the ruthless implementation of postmodern antirealist metaphysics that flows from Kantianism.[52] I believe he is correct in this

51. Hicks, *Explaining Postmodernism*, 175.
52. Hicks, *Explaining Postmodernism*, 82.

interpretation of the history of nineteenth- and twentieth-century thought. What the postmodernists of the later twentieth century will tell you, if you listen to them carefully, is that they want us to turn our backs on the project began by Thales some twenty-six centuries ago in Greece, which is the attempt to comprehend the *logos* of the cosmos, the rational principle that explains why the world is as it is. This is a rejection of science and metaphysics. They also want us to turn our backs on another project begun thirty-five centuries ago by Moses in the desert, which is the attempt to comprehend the world as the creation of a transcendent God. This is a rejection of biblical theology. Once these two things—metaphysics and transcendence—are gone, what is left? Nothing but mythology.

The theological metaphysics of the Great Tradition arose out of the creative clash of biblical revelation and Greek philosophy during the Second Temple period and the patristic era. It flourished on the basis of the fundamental idea that the *Logos* of the cosmos is the divine Son by whom the Father created all things and in whom are hidden all wisdom and knowledge. Metaphysics requires Christology in order to survive in the long term, and when a culture rejects Jesus Christ, as Western modernity has done, it condemns itself to losing metaphysics, science, and logic. It first loses natural theology, then the natural moral law, and finally even the scientific laws of nature. In so doing, it embraces nihilism. This is the history of Western modernity so far and its fate.

Christian theology is exegesis leading to the formulation of doctrines based on the plain sense of the biblical text and metaphysical doctrines deduced from these exegetical results, which then become the basis for further exegetical work. In a spiral of understanding, theology seeks to penetrate deeper into the mystery of God. Although theology can never be complete, it can always grow, deepen, and become more fruitful in stimulating wisdom. This is our goal in the chapters that follow.

God as the Transcendent Creator (Isa. 40)

In the beginning, God created the heavens and the earth.

Genesis 1:1

God said to Moses, "I AM WHO I AM."
And he said, "Say to the people of Israel, I AM has sent me to you."

Exodus 3:14

When we read chapter 40 of the book of Isaiah in the context of the book as a whole, it is clear this this chapter plays a pivotal role in conveying the main message of the book. Most commentators focus on the fact that this chapter differs significantly from the prose section that immediately precedes it in chapters 36–39 and on its role in introducing the second part of the book. We see a shift in the intended audience in chapter 40 in that it is addressed to people for whom the exile is a present, ongoing reality.

> Comfort, comfort my people, says your God.
> Speak tenderly to Jerusalem,
>   and cry to her
> that her warfare is ended,
>   that her iniquity is pardoned,
> that she has received from the LORD's hand
>   double for all her sins. (Isa. 40:1–2)

123

The destruction of Jerusalem and the temple, which had been predicted at various points in chapters 1–39, is now spoken of as having taken place, and the prophet's message in chapter 40 is that the exile is not going to last forever. This was not something to be taken for granted. The prophet's message is that, unlike Samaria, Jerusalem will be rebuilt. Unlike those taken into captivity by the Assyrians in 722 BC, the exiles from Judah who are now in Babylon will return to their own country. Unlike the northern tribes that rebelled against the house of David under Jeroboam, the surviving remnant of Judah will continue to exist as a people. This is extremely good news. The message of Isaiah 40 is that the coming disaster of exile should not be interpreted as meaning either that the LORD is finished with the people of Judah or that he has revoked the eternal covenants he made with Abraham and David.

All this is true and important. But one crucial matter is often overlooked in interpreting this chapter and the ones immediately following it. The section from chapters 40–48 constitutes an *argument* for the prophet's message of hope. After all, it was asking a lot of the discouraged exiles sitting in Babylon—bereft of land, temple, sacrifices, and king—to have hope. The words of Psalm 137 undoubtedly express what they were feeling:

> By the waters of Babylon,
>   there we sat down and wept,
>   when we remembered Zion.
> . . . .
> How shall we sing the LORD's song
>   in a foreign land? (Ps. 137:1, 4)

It is one thing to speak of hope; it is quite another to inspire hope in a conquered, discouraged, and depressed people. Their question is valid: "*How* shall we sing the LORD's song in a foreign land?" How do we worship our God in the land of another god, especially since our presence here apparently is a testimony to the defeat of our God in battle? On what basis would it be reasonable to sing the LORD's song when it appears that either he has abandoned us or else he has failed to protect us. Either way, why bother?

A Theological Hope

Isaiah's message is one of hope, but he is not merely an advocate of the power of positive thinking. His message is not "Cheer up, things could be worse." Instead, he is saying that something is going to happen that will change their circumstances, and it is realistic for them to put their trust in God's Word.

It is a matter not just of their having faith but of there being something real in which to put their faith. In other words, the message of Isaiah 40 is based on something solid, something concrete, something real. There is a reason to have hope, and that reason is the nature of God. The God who sends the prophet with this message of hope is a God who is real and who is the kind of God who can act in history to save his people. Verse 9 is the key verse of the chapter: "Behold your God!"

We miss the point of this chapter if we fail to see that it is about God rather than about human religious experience. Isaiah's message is not fundamentally political or ethical or even religious in the sense of ritual and cult; his message is primarily theological. Hope is possible because *God* says so, because *this* God says so, and because this God is *a certain kind* of being. It is the nature of God that is the basis of everything else, and this is true of the book of Isaiah as a whole. It is one of the most profound meditations on the nature and being of God ever written.

Of course, on one level, the book of Isaiah is about many things—Jerusalem, idolatry, the judgment of the nations, atonement for sin, the Messiah, eschatological hope, the meaning of history, and more—but at the bottom of it all is the doctrine of God. The LORD, the God of Israel, is the transcendent Creator and sovereign Lord of history, who alone is to be worshiped. The reality of that One is the heart of Isaiah's message. This doctrine of God is the unifying factor that makes all the other themes of the book of Isaiah hold together harmoniously. It is God's uniqueness that makes idolatry so horrible. It is God's holiness that makes his wrath so dangerous. It is God's transcendence that makes him able to accomplish his will in history. It is God's power that makes the pagan empires mere putty in his hand. The view of God underlying all the poetry and prose in Isaiah is what makes it a *book* and not merely a collection of disparate texts written from differing viewpoints with various perspectives. Unity of authorship is the small miracle; unity of theme is the greater miracle. To understand the latter is to make the former seem completely plausible.

This is why Isaiah 40 is such an important text for us as we think about whether the Christian church today should abandon the trinitarian classical theism of the past millennium and a half and embrace some form of the new, twenty-first-century relational theism, such as theistic mutualism or social trinitarianism. Isaiah 40–48 is *an argument for a certain view of God*, one that the exiles in Babylon needed to accept as true if they were going to find a hope that could sustain them in exile. But it seems equally clear that we as Christians in the twenty-first century also need hope that can sustain us in "exile." As Christendom unravels and the Christian culture built by believers over many centuries here in the West disintegrates, the church will increasingly experience a kind of exile and lament over the fall of institutions and traditions that have sustained life for centuries. The sense of a collapsing culture was expressed by W. B. Yeats in 1919 in his poem "The Second Coming":

> Turning and turning in the widening gyre
> The falcon cannot hear the falconer;
> Things fall apart; the centre cannot hold;
> Mere anarchy is loosed upon the world,
> The blood-dimmed tide is loosed, and everywhere
> The ceremony of innocence is drowned;
> The best lack all conviction, while the worst
> Are full of passionate intensity.[1]

As our Jerusalem turns into a Babylon, we need to hear the same message that Isaiah preached to the exiles in chapters 40–48. But it is crucial to understand that the point of Isaiah 40–48 is not merely that the LORD has done something or will do something in history; it is also about what the God who does such things as exodus and creation must be like in order to be able to do them. It focuses on what the actions of God in history reveal about the being or essence of God.

If we read Isaiah 40 carefully, paying attention to the intertextual echoes that permeate the text, we note two prominent themes in this chapter: exodus and creation. That is not to say that these two themes exhaust the meaning of the text, but certainly these two themes are pervasive. It should be noted at the outset that these two themes are both works of God that reveal the nature of God. Rather than diverting us from the theme of the book of Isaiah and of Isaiah 40–48, these themes take us to the heart of what Isaiah means by "God." The nature of God is known from his works. If we ask "Which God are we talking about?" the short answer is "The God of exodus and creation."

The Meaning of the Exodus in the Ancient Near Eastern Context

First, then, we look at verses 3–5.

> A voice cries:
> "In the wilderness prepare the way of the LORD;
>   make straight in the desert a highway for our God.
> Every valley shall be lifted up,
>   and every mountain and hill be made low;

---

1. Yeats, "Second Coming," lines 1–8.

> the uneven ground shall become level,
>> and the rough places a plain.
> And the glory of the LORD shall be revealed,
>> and all flesh shall see it together,
>> for the mouth of the LORD has spoken." (Isa. 40:3–5)

Here we see a proclamation of a new exodus, this time from Babylon. Michael Heiser argues rather convincingly that this is one of several divine-council scenes in the book of Isaiah.[2] He suggests that the Bible from Genesis to Revelation assumes a perspective on reality that is encapsulated by the phrase found in the Lord's Prayer, "as in heaven, so on earth" (Matt. 6:9–15).[3] Jesus taught his disciples to pray to the Father, "Your kingdom come, your will be done on earth as it is in heaven" (Matt. 6:10). Heiser points out that the Bible assumes that reality has a spiritual realm (heaven) and a material realm (earth) and that there are hints throughout the Bible of parallels and two-way interaction between the two realms of creation. The material realm of the cosmos is dependent on and integrally related to the spiritual realm, both of which are equally real in the Bible and in Christian Platonism. The material realm is not autonomous, but in fact depends on and participates in the spiritual reality of heaven. The earthly holy of holies was a model or picture of the heavenly throne room into which the ascended Jesus Christ entered after his death and resurrection. According to Hebrews 9:24, the earthly things "made with hands" (like the tabernacle and temple) are copies of heavenly realities, referred to there as "true things."

One reason I use the term "Christian Platonism" when I could just as easily use something less controversial, such as "Nicene metaphysics" or even "the philosophical implications of the Christian doctrine of creation," is because Platonism is so reprehensible to the modern mind. I am trying to jolt us into reconsidering our shallow belief in modern philosophical naturalism, without implying that the only alternative is mythology. In the previous chapter, I showed that modernity, having rejected the transcendent Creator of classical Christian orthodoxy, is lapsing back into the mythological way of thinking that characterized the ancient Near Eastern culture within which God revealed himself to Israel and the Old Testament literature was written. I stressed the stark contrasts that can be drawn between the worldview of the Old Testament and the worldview of the mythology of Egypt, Canaan, and Mesopotamia. But there is more to this story than contrast and contradiction.

2. Heiser, *Unseen Realm*, 352.
3. Heiser, *Unseen Realm*, 38.

Not every aspect of ancient Near Eastern religion and the mythology on which is rests is wrong. Given the intensity of the biblical polemic against Baal worship, for example, I know that this may be hard for some to accept. But truth is found alongside error in non-Christian religions because the Enemy knows that a lie containing a mixture of truth and falsehood is far more powerful and much more likely to deceive than one containing nothing but falsehood. If we think of the mythology of the ancient Near East as the religion taught to humans by the fallen angelic beings that are worshiped in those religions, we will be adopting the view of the biblical writers themselves.

I realize that it is difficult for people who have lived their lives immersed in scientific materialism to think of the gods of pagan religions as real spiritual entities who can reveal themselves to humans and impart supernatural knowledge. But the doctrine of angels is as biblical as any other part of divine revelation and has formed part of Jewish and Christian orthodoxy for approximately 3,500 years, so it is not exactly a novelty. If we can get past our modern prejudices long enough to consider the role of fallen angelic beings in pagan religion, we can make significant progress in penetrating the mind of the biblical writers and understanding how they view reality. Even if you are skeptical, I urge you to suspend disbelief temporarily and try to understand how the Old Testament writers think by looking at pagan mythology as they do; that is, as religious views foisted on humanity by evil, fallen angels who are seeking to divert worship to themselves and away from Yahweh the Creator as part of their rebellion against heaven and their war against the LORD. Once you begin to look at it this way, the idea that they would mix truth and error into their stories makes perfect sense.

In both the Old and New Testaments, the Bible assumes that reality has two levels, the material and the spiritual, rather than just one as both ancient and modern materialism would have it. In this respect, the Bible is more in agreement with mythological worldviews than with either ancient or modern materialism. Both the Bible and the ancient Near Eastern (that is, Mesopotamian, Canaanite, and Egyptian) mythological worldviews agree that materialism is not true, but this does not mean that the Bible is just another ancient mythology. It is actually a polemical corrective of ancient mythology, an alternative set of answers to the basic worldview questions. The biggest difference is that the mythologies of the ancient Near East are silent about where the original chaos came from. They all begin the story at the same point as Genesis 1:2, that is, with water and chaos. This makes Genesis 1:1 the single most revolutionary sentence in the entire history of the world, because it dares to go beyond the eternal formless matter out of which the current configuration of the universe was shaped to what preceded that formless void. (Even the modern "big bang theory" does not do that.) And Genesis 1:1 purports to define the nature of the reality that was there: that reality was personal, transcendent, sovereign, and the creator of all that exists. The God of Israel is before all things and over all things.

When the New Testament wishes to explain the relationship of Christ to the Father, it identifies Christ with the Creator. Paul writes,

> He is the image of the invisible God, the firstborn of all creation. For by him all things were created, in heaven and on earth, visible and invisible, whether thrones or dominions or rulers or authorities—all things were created through him and for him. And he is before all things, and in him all things hold together. (Col. 1:15–17)

Paul specifies that the category of all created things includes both visible and invisible things. God is creator not only of the visible material universe (earth) but also of the invisible spiritual realm (heaven). Paul is a typical Second Temple Jew in that he believes in the existence of angels and heaven. However, the term "angels" is not really adequate to describe what he is talking about here. His terminology—thrones (θρόνοι, *thronoi*), dominions (κυριότητες, *kyriotētes*), rulers (ἀρχαί, *archai*), authorities (ἐξουσίαι, *exousiai*)—indicates beings with ruling/governing functions in the cosmos rather than mere messengers, which is what the English word "angel" means. The Hebrew *mal'āk* and the Greek ἄγγελος (*angelos*), which is used to translate *mal'āk* in the Septuagint, both have the meaning we typically associate with the English word "angel," namely, "messenger." But the beings Paul is referring to here in Colossians 1 are higher in the hierarchy than angels and, apparently, different enough from one another to warrant the use of various terms for them. In Ephesians 6, Paul also uses the terms "rulers" (ἀρχάς), "authorities" (ἐξουσίας), "cosmic powers over this present darkness" (κοσμοκράτορας τοῦ σκότους τούτου, *kosmokratoras tou skotous toutou*), and "spiritual forces of evil in the heavenly places" (πνευματικὰ τῆς πονηρίας ἐν τοῖς ἐπουρανίοις, *pneumatika tēs ponērias en tois epouraniois*, Eph. 6:12). He also mentions a person he calls "the devil" (τοῦ διαβόλου, *tou diabolou*, Eph. 6:11). Apparently there are different levels of spiritual entities in the cosmos, some fallen and some unfallen, which have various ruling functions in the administration of the cosmos. Christ, however, is not just another one of these; he is identified with the Creator as one with the Father in dignity and power. The Letter to the Hebrews spends considerable time arguing for the uniqueness of Christ in contrast to these angelic beings (Heb. 1:5–14).

So the New Testament pictures a spiritual dimension of reality inhabited by spiritual beings with ruling functions. Where did it get this metaphysical framework? We need to be careful with our answer here. It is tempting to say that it reeks of pagan mythology and regard it as a case of borrowing pagan religious ideas that we need to demythologize, excise, or at least politely ignore. But I would suggest that the New Testament simply continues the Old Testament worldview and that both Testaments teach that the pagan gods are real spiritual beings who are in rebellion against Yahweh and who have taught all sorts of misleading religious ideas to gullible humans in order to promote false religion that diverts attention to themselves and away from the true Creator. Like ancient Near Eastern mythology before it, Greco-Roman mythology is false in many ways, but this does not prove that it is false in every respect. As noted above, we must sift through the rubble to filter out truth from error. For Paul, it is true that worshiping idols is stupid (1 Cor. 8:4), but it is also true that the gods behind the idols are real and that joining in idolatry can be a serious case of demon worship (1 Cor. 10:20). This is the same view of idolatry and the gods that Isaiah has in Isaiah 44.

My point is simply this: the biblical writers, in this case Isaiah, do not regard the existence of spiritual entities who interact with humanity as an aspect of pagan mythology we need to reject. Isaiah would agree that these entities do exist. They are capable of mischief, and they seek to mislead and deceive people into false worship and immorality. Most problematic of all, they seek to corrupt true religion and draw people away from a focus on Yahweh, the transcendent Creator and sovereign Lord of history, who alone is to be worshiped. The metaphysics that arises from sound biblical exegesis recognizes all this and understands the polemical nature of the Bible's teaching about the relationship of these spiritual beings to God.

With the term "Christian Platonism," I am signaling that the metaphysics that grew out of biblical revelation, that is, trinitarian classical theism, is a complex set of doctrines and not merely a manifestation of either ancient Near Eastern mythology or rationalistic Greek philosophy, even though it does owe a debt to both of these ways of thinking. In chapter 1, I stressed the difference between the orthodox doctrine of God and the relational theisms of the last two centuries. In chapter 3, I stressed the difference between the orthodox doctrine of God and the pagan mythologies of the ancient Near East. Here I am pointing out that the orthodox doctrine of God has some points of overlap with the metaphysics that developed in the Platonist tradition and also some points of overlap with the mythologies of the ancient Near East. It is too simplistic to reject absolutely everything about mythology, and Christians who fall for this oversimplification often end up as materialists with no discernible Christian faith left. It is also too simplistic to reject metaphysics altogether, because those who fall into this trap often end up in skepticism and relativism with no real answer to nihilism.

It is easy to say that biblical orthodoxy does not completely reject either mythology or metaphysics; it is far more difficult to express accurately exactly what about either of these approaches to reality the Bible agrees with and exactly what it rejects. But discussing the divine-council idea is a promising place to start.

Heiser points to the library of clay tablets discovered at Ugarit in 1929. These tablets contain a great deal of information about ancient Canaanite religion, much of which seems to have been influenced by the religion of Syrian and Phoenician cities like Ugarit, Tyre, and Sidon to the north of biblical Israel.[4] The Elijah Cycle in 1 Kings 17–22 describes the fierce war waged by the prophet Elijah against the importation of Baal worship into Israel by the Omri dynasty, especially by Ahab's queen Jezebel, who was the daughter of the king of Sidon (1 Kings 16:31). The cities of Sidon and Tyre were founded by the Phoenicians, who likely were part of the migration/invasion launched by the "Sea Peoples" in the twelfth century BC.[5] The Phoenicians overwhelmed and destroyed the power of Canaanite cities such as Ugarit (or Ras Shamra), but they adopted a great deal of the religion of the culture they conquered, which is why we find that Ahab, after taking Jezebel for his wife, is said to have served Baal and worshiped him: "Ahab erected an altar for Baal in the house of Baal, which he built in Samaria" (1 Kings 16:32). Ahab and Jezebel are portrayed as pushing Baal worship on the people of Israel, and Elijah fights back in the name of the Mosaic covenant, which mandates the worship of the LORD alone.

What was Baal worship all about? One thing we learn from the archaeological findings at Ugarit is that Canaanite religion held that a divine council existed in which the high god was El, and Baal was a sort of coruler through whom El ruled. Various other messenger gods (mal'ākim) participated in this council. El's offspring included the warrior Rashpu, the sun-goddess Shapshu, and the moon-god Yarikh but also the warrior goddesses Anat and Astarte, both of whom are mentioned in the Bible.[6] The consort of Baal was the biblical

---

4. Note, however, that these cities were within the boundaries of the land promised to the children of Israel and identified in the allocation of the land in Joshua 13:1–7. The LORD intended for these centers of Baal worship to be rooted out, and because this did not happen, Baal worship was a source of great problems for Israel for centuries thereafter.

5. M. Smith, "Ugarit and the Ugaritians," 150.

6. M. Smith, "Ugarit and the Ugaritians," 152. Some might think that gender bending is "modern" and "progressive," but it is actually a revival of pagan religious ideas that are more than 3,000 years old.

Asherah, and the council met on a mountain in a lush garden where there was an abundant water supply. The name of this place means "north" (*Tsapanu*), and of course the area of Syria is north of Israel. Council meetings were held in the "tents of El" or "El's tent shrine," whence divine decrees were issued.[7] By now any knowledgeable reader of the Bible is probably wondering what is going on with all the parallels to the Bible in this ancient Canaanite religion.

We must determine where the Bible agrees with Canaanite religious ideas and where it disagrees. How exactly does the prophetic critique of Canaanite religion work in the Old Testament? After all, it was not in the name of ecumenical fellowship that Elijah cut off the heads of the 450 prophets of Baal. Obviously, the book of Kings presents the biblical prophets as locked in a life-and-death struggle against a pernicious false religion famous for, among other things, a predilection for child sacrifice. This war between biblical Mosaic religion and Canaanite idolatry went on throughout Israel's history. In his famous temple sermon just before the exile, Jeremiah accuses the people of Jerusalem of burning their sons and daughters in the fire in the Valley of Hinnom, which is just outside the walls of the preexilic city and visible from the temple mount (Jer. 7:1–8:3). The kings and people of Judah practiced child sacrifice to Molech within sight of God's holy temple, in the doors of which Jeremiah is standing as he speaks. The point the reader is supposed to get is how this makes the coming destruction of Jerusalem both utterly inevitable and also completely just.

Heiser argues that the Old Testament portrays the LORD as having a divine council, which is identical to his royal household, and having divine council meetings in which decrees are issued. We see this sort of thing in Job 1–2, where the satan (*hassatan*, the accuser) attends a divine council meeting. We see it in the description of Eden in Genesis 2 as a well-watered garden where God met with Adam and Eve, and Eve was not surprised to encounter one of the great spiritual beings in the form of the serpent, which spoke to her. Heiser contends that even though God (as omnipotent) does not *need* a council, he chooses to use one. He argues that "the biblical version of the divine council at the divine abode includes a human presence," because "Yahweh desires a kingdom rule on this new Earth that he has created, and that rule will be shared with humans."[8]

Thus the biblical critique of ancient Canaanite religion does not consist of denying the existence of other "gods," nor does it reject the existence of a supernatural realm parallel to our realm in which divine beings do things that

---

7. Heiser, *Unseen Realm*, 46.
8. Heiser, *Unseen Realm*, 47.

affect this world. The Bible is neither antisupernatural nor skeptical about the reality of the beings worshiped through pagan idolatry. Isaiah knows full well that the piece of wood or metal used to represent the god is not the spiritual being who is being worshiped, and his mockery of the idolater in Isaiah 44 is not based merely on the idea that the pagan idolater is stupid for worshiping a piece of the same tree he just used to cook his meal (Isa. 44:14–16). But even allowing for the fact that the pagan worshiper is actually worshiping a real spiritual entity that is imaged by the idol, the worshiper is still foolish because that spiritual entity, just like the piece of wood or metal, is merely a creature and not the one true God. It is absolutely crucial to understand Isaiah on this point; it is a key to understanding his concept of God. He is not skeptical about the existence of the pagan gods, but he insists that they not be worshiped.

It is in this cultural context that Isaiah 40:3–5 uses exodus language. The exodus, as described in Exodus 1–15, is the founding event of Israel's history because it marks the miraculous act of God by which he brought a band of slaves up from Egypt and began the process of turning them into a nation. But at its heart, the exodus was a contest of strength between Yahweh and the gods of Egypt. The key to understanding this account is to refrain from demythologizing it in the name of modernist prejudices against the supernatural, because if we do that, we will miss the main point of the story, and we will not be able to understand what it is meant to teach us about the nature of God. This will become evident as we go along.

Foundational to the narrative is the mysterious encounter described in Exodus 3, in which the Lord calls Moses and commissions him to go to Pharaoh and demand that he liberate Israel so that Israel can go out and worship the Lord. Moses sees a burning bush that does not burn up, and the angel of the Lord (*mal'ak yhwh*) appears to him in the flame (Exod. 3:2). And then we are told that "God called to him out of the bush" (*wayyar' yhwh kî sār lir'ôt wayyiqrā' 'ēlāyw 'ĕlōhîm*, 3:4). Already we have a mystery to deal with in that the one who is referred to here as "the angel of the Lord" (*mal'ak yhwh*) is also referred to as "the Lord" (*yhwh*) and as God (*'ĕlōhîm*). In addition, the God who speaks in this passage is revealed to be the God of Abraham, the God of Isaac, and the God of Jacob. We are confronted with the fact that "the angel of the Lord" is equated with the Lord who is the God of the patriarchs. But it gets even more convoluted when Moses asks a perfectly reasonable question concerning God's name:

> If I come to the people of Israel and say to them, "The God of your fathers has sent me to you," and they ask me, "What is his name?" what shall I say to them? (Exod. 3:13)

No doubt Moses is also wondering what he is going to say to Pharaoh, for surely the subject of the name of this God that Moses speaks of is bound to come up when Moses makes his demand of Pharaoh. In the ancient Near Eastern cultural context, names were closely bound up with identity, nature, and character. The name of the god may tell you how powerful he is and certainly will tell you what he is like. What name does God give himself?

In a way, Exodus 3:14–15 reveals the divine nature, but in another way the text conceals the divine nature, and this is as it should be. Even after the name is given, it remains mysterious. The God who is speaking here is not a being among beings in the universe; this God is not another one in the pantheon like El or Baal or Re or any other god known in the ancient Near East. This God is fundamentally unknowable and therefore highly mysterious. The phrases "I AM WHO I AM" (’ehyeh ’ăšer ’ehyeh), "I AM" (’ehyeh), and "the LORD" (yhwh, Yahweh) are all forms of the Hebrew verb "to be" (hāyâ). This God simply is. The reader is invited to contemplate this name because its very mysteriousness signals depth of meaning at which one can only guess initially. Commentators such as Thomas Aquinas have noted that this One does not come to be or pass out of being or change in being; this One simply is.[9] A possible translation is "He who is."[10] In Genesis 12–50, the God of Abraham, Isaac, and Jacob reveals himself as real. That is step one. In Exodus 3, this God reveals himself mysteriously as the God who exists by nature, that is, who exists necessarily. This idea suggests his qualitative distinction from all beings in the cosmos. Then in Exodus 4–14, this God is revealed as so much more powerful than the gods of the greatest empire in the world of that time; he is merely toying with them in the context of the ten plagues and the Red Sea crossing. Yahweh is more powerful than all the gods of Egypt put together, but the degree to which his power exceeds their power is not clarified. He wins, but how close was the contest? Did he just barely pull out a victory at the last minute by a close margin? Is Yahweh greater by degree? Or is he different in kind? The mysterious name must have been pondered by Moses for a long time. What does it mean?

Although Moses is traditionally regarded as the author and/or compiler of the Pentateuch, I do not think that he necessarily composed every part of Genesis from scratch and left it in its final form. He personally witnessed the events described in Exodus–Deuteronomy, but Genesis describes what was ancient history even for Moses. He was learned in the wisdom of Egypt, and he undoubtedly had access to records, mythological writings, and chronicles of ancient Near Eastern civilization going back millennia. He must have read

9. Thomas Aquinas, *Summa Theologica*, I, q. 9, art. 1 (1:38).
10. Thomas Aquinas, *Summa Theologica*, I, q. 13, art. 11 (1:70).

mythology, utilized various traditions of the patriarchs, and at the same time reshaped all of them in light of the powerful self-revelation of Yahweh in the exodus. So why not regard Genesis 1:1—the most powerful and dramatic opening sentence of any piece of writing in the history of world literature—as the result of Moses's Spirit-directed meditation on the meaning of Yahweh's crushing of the power of Egypt's gods? Simply put, Yahweh does not relate to the gods of the nations as El does, as the first among equals or the strongest of the lot. Rather, Yahweh is their creator. Other things come into being, exist for a while, and then pass away. Some come into existence and remain. But Yahweh's existence is part of his nature; he cannot not be because he is. Only Yahweh has neither a beginning nor an end to his existence. He is the transcendent Creator. Should we not interpret Exodus 3:14–15 in light of Genesis 1:1 and vice versa? Would Isaiah not have read these texts in this way?[11]

If Isaiah does indeed follow this line of thought, then the structure of Isaiah 40 makes perfect sense.

1. The prophet reports the words of the God of Israel, who speaks comfort to the exiles, whose situation is parallel to that of their ancestors in slavery in Egypt.

2. The prophet reports further that a voice he heard in the divine council proclaimed a new exodus, an eschatological revelation of the glory of the LORD that will be even greater than the first exodus.

3. The prophet replies to the voice and asks for further elaboration of what he should cry in view of the fact that "all flesh is grass" and withers and fades away, whereas the Word of the LORD is eternal (Isa. 40:6–8).

4. The prophet is told to go up to a high mountain and speak in the name of Zion, that is, of Jerusalem, and say to the cities of Judah, "Behold your God!" (Isa. 40:9). The mountain motif is found both in Canaanite mythology and also in the biblical tradition, because the theological message of the Old Testament is that Yahweh the transcendent Creator rules on the earth, rather than being confined to the heavens. This strongly implies that Baal and El are mere usurpers who pretend to rule

---

11. The interpretation of Isaiah and the Old Testament in general being advanced here does not require a Babylonian, and therefore exilic, background. It is compatible with the belief that both the Pentateuch and Isaiah were written before the exile within an Israelite-Canaanite context. Any Mesopotamian elements in the text might be instances of Mesopotamian thought having influenced Egyptian or Canaanite thought, or they could be later glosses by an editor seeking to clarify and bring up to date the meaning of the text in the exilic situation. In neither case is it necessary to assume that the sum and substance of the Pentateuch is not Mosaic in origin or that the Law of Moses was not available to Isaiah.

the earth but in fact are not the real rulers. They exist, it is true, but they do not occupy the offices they pretend to hold, insofar as they attempt to portray themselves as worthy of receiving worship.

5. The rest of the chapter (vv. 10–31) extolls "the LORD God [who] comes with might, and his arm rules for him" (Isa. 40:10). The rest of the chapter scrolls through the attributes of the transcendent Creator, who redeemed Israel from slavery in Egypt and who also can save the exiles in Babylon. The emphasis is thus on the nature of the One who is said by the prophet to be bringing salvation to the people of God.

God's infinite immensity is beyond our comprehension:

> Who has measured the waters in the hollow of his hand
>   and marked off the heavens with a span,
> enclosed the dust of the earth in a measure
>   and weighed the mountains in scales
>   and the hills in a balance? (Isa. 40:12)

God cannot be comprehended by the finite human mind. His mind is so much greater than our finite human minds that we need to say that, compared to us, the LORD is all-knowing:

> Who has measured the Spirit of the LORD,
>   or what man shows him his counsel?
> Whom did he consult,
>   and who made him understand?
> Who taught him the path of justice,
>   and taught him knowledge,
>   and showed him the way of understanding? (Isa. 40:13–14)

God knows all things and is perfect in his justice. He does not need us to teach him.

God is also the Lord of the nations, which are nothing in comparison to him.

> Behold, the nations are like a drop from a bucket,
>   and are accounted as the dust on the scales;
>   behold, he takes up the coastlands like fine dust.
> Lebanon would not suffice for fuel,
>   nor are its beasts enough for a burnt offering.
> All the nations are as nothing before him,
>   they are accounted by him as less than nothing and emptiness.
>   (Isa. 40:15–17)

God is the Lord of the nations; Egypt and Babylon are subject to his will. He is responsible for their rise and fall, and they cannot frustrate his will.

God is also the living God, in contrast to idols, which are mere inanimate objects and, therefore, incapable of being adequate images for him.

> To whom then will you liken God,
>   or what likeness compare with him?
> An idol! A craftsman casts it,
>   and a goldsmith overlays it with gold
>   and casts for it silver chains.
> He who is too impoverished for an offering
>   chooses wood that will not rot;
> he seeks out a skillful craftsman
>   to set up an idol that will not move. (Isa. 40:18–20)

Here we see not only the contrast between the living God and the dead idol. Ancient peoples did not imagine that they were worshiping the wooden or metal image; they intended to worship the spiritual entity behind the idol. This is why the widespread occult "opening of the mouth ritual" was used in the dedication of a new idol.[12] Both Yahweh and the false gods of the nations were real. This point is made clear in Exodus 7:8–14, when Moses and Aaron are before Pharaoh. Aaron throws down his staff, and it becomes a serpent. The wise men, sorcerers, and magicians of Egypt do the same miracle by their secret arts (Exod. 7:11). They actually have supernatural power, as Aaron does, but in the end, the narrative makes clear that the power of the LORD is far greater.

The contrast that Isaiah 40:18–20 intends for us to grasp is between the living God who creates humans to image him and the false gods who require humans to create idols to image them. The superior power of Yahweh emanates from his nature as the creator of all that exists, other than himself. As the eternal One, he is uncreated.

God is also the sovereign Lord of history, who controls all that happens on earth from his throne in heaven.

> Do you not know? Do you not hear?
>   Has it not been told you from the beginning?
>   Have you not understood from the foundations of the earth?
> It is he who sits above the circle of the earth,
>   and its inhabitants are like grasshoppers;
> who stretches out the heavens like a curtain,
>   and spreads them like a tent to dwell in;

12. Heiser, *Unseen Realm*, 35.

> who brings princes to nothing,
>   and makes the rulers of the earth as emptiness.
>
> Scarcely are they planted, scarcely sown,
>   scarcely has their stem taken root in the earth,
> when he blows on them, and they wither,
>   and the tempest carries them off like stubble. (Isa. 40:21–24)

God is in control of history, which means that history is linear and moving toward a goal God has determined. This is intensely relevant to Jews caught up in the affairs of great empires and historical forces beyond their control.

God is in control because he is the creator of the heavens and the earth.

> To whom then will you compare me,
>   that I should be like him? says the Holy One.
> Lift up your eyes on high and see:
>   who created these?
> He who brings out their host by number,
>   calling them all by name;
> by the greatness of his might
>   and because he is strong in power,
>   not one is missing. (Isa. 40:25–26)

Notice how the power and sovereignty of God are rooted by the prophet in the fact that God is the creator of all things.

God is therefore the savior of his people who put their hope in him. He is Lord because he is the Creator, and he can be the savior of his people because he is the sovereign Creator.

> Why do you say, O Jacob,
>   and speak, O Israel,
> "My way is hidden from the LORD,
>   and my right is disregarded by my God"?
> Have you not known? Have you not heard?
> The LORD is the everlasting God,
>   the Creator of the ends of the earth.
> He does not faint or grow weary;
>   his understanding is unsearchable.
> He gives power to the faint,
>   and to him who has no might he increases strength.
> Even youths shall faint and be weary,
>   and young men shall fall exhausted;

> but they who wait for the LORD shall renew their strength;
>   they shall mount up with wings like eagles;
> they shall run and not be weary;
>   they shall walk and not faint. (Isa. 40:27–31)

Here the prophet quotes the complaint of the exiles who feel that the LORD is absent and that he has abandoned them: "My way is hidden from the LORD, and my right is disregarded by my God" (40:27). They were tempted to give up, and the purpose of this entire chapter is to encourage them not to do so and to call them to faith in Yahweh, the transcendent Creator and sovereign Lord of history. The purpose of all these rhetorical questions is similar to the use of rhetorical questions in the book of Job; they serve to direct attention to the transcendence of God. They indicate that we need to put our faith and trust in God, even though his being is so far above ours and so different from ours that we could never hope to comprehend his essence. The very unknowableness of God makes him utterly different from the gods of the nations, who are mere creatures.

This chapter teaches that God is eternal, infinite, omnipotent, omniscient, alive, and yet also faithful, gracious, and gentle. God can be trusted because of his nature. He is both willing and able to save. Just as we saw in chapter 2 when we considered the Westminster Confession, the philosophical attributes of God (eternity, infinity, omnipotence, etc.) are mixed in with the personal attributes (faithful, gracious, gentle, etc.). God is both the metaphysically absolute First Cause of all things and also the One who speaks and acts in history in order to judge the world and save his people. Isaiah 40 reviews and summarizes the nature of the God who proclaims hope and comfort for the captives in Babylon, and it introduces the argument that Isaiah is about to launch to explain why the exiles should believe in this God and trust him. I suggest that the argument Isaiah presents here is based on an interpretation of the meaning of Exodus 1–15 in the light of Genesis 1. Isaiah is presenting the LORD as capable of saving Israel and keeping the Davidic covenant because he has created the heavens and the earth out of nothing.

The Meaning of Creation in the Ancient Near Eastern Context

Now we must consider in more depth the meaning of Isaiah's concept of creation by comparing it to ideas found in its ancient Near Eastern context. There is no inherent conflict between interpreting Isaiah 40 in its canonical context and considering the historical context from which the text emerged. The purpose of examining the historical context of the biblical writings is not to make the ancient Near Eastern context the limit for what the text is allowed to say. For example, it will not do to argue that since the Babylonians (or Egyptians or Canaanites for that matter) had no concept of *creatio ex nihilo*, therefore the concept could not be in Genesis 1:1 or in Genesis 1:1 as interpreted by Isaiah in Isaiah 40. The concept is in the text because of divine revelation, which is sufficient to account for sheer novelty as a polemical correction of pagan mythology.

Even among evangelicals, there is a strong tendency today to assert that the traditional teaching of Genesis 1:1 is mistaken in seeing the concept of *creatio ex nihilo* in the text. For example, Iain Provan poses the question of whether Genesis 1:2 describes the result of one of the creative acts of God introduced in verse 1 or if it describes what was there before the work of creation began. He denies that *creatio ex nihilo* is the right way to think of the meaning of verse 1 and claims that, in the mind of the author, Genesis 1:2 describes "realities that existed (however they got there) before the creative acts of God that produced the habitable world as we know it."[13] But so far as I am aware, no one has ever denied that verses 3 and following describe the work God did in shaping the formless matter (*tōhû wābōhû*) of verse 2 into the present form of the cosmos. Saying that much, in and of itself, need not require us to deny that Genesis 1:1 affirms *creatio ex nihilo*. Provan's statement that Genesis 1:2 describes the state of affairs that existed prior to the shaping and filling work of 1:3–31 does not prove that the material world described as "without form and void" was made up of eternal matter. The idea of eternal matter has to be read into the text just as surely as the idea of *creatio ex nihilo* does; the question is which idea accords best with the phrasing of Genesis 1:1? Provan might answer that the question is left open. If Genesis 1:1 were not part of the text, then I could agree. But it is there, and it means *something*. I think it very unlikely that it means that the matter God went to work on in verse 3 was eternal like God and not the result of his creative work, which means that *creatio ex nihilo* is more likely to be the meaning.[14]

Provan acknowledges that Genesis 1 can be contrasted with the Babylonian creation myth Enuma Elish, in which the forming and shaping of the chaos takes the form of a battle between the god Markuk and the dragon sea-goddess

13. Provan, *Discovering Genesis*, 63.

14. I come back to the exegesis of Genesis 1 in chap. 8 below, where I discuss the scriptural basis for the doctrine of *creatio ex nihilo* more generally, including Genesis 1 and several other texts. The main point I wish to make here is that my theological reading of Genesis 1 is rooted in the relationship between the Old Testament and ancient Near Eastern mythology that I am developing in this chapter. In chap. 8 I will present other arguments in addition to the ones discussed here for reading Genesis 1:1 as teaching *creatio ex nihilo*.

Tiamat, and he rightly notes that there is no sign of conflict in Genesis 1. But he neglects to ask the burning question "*Why* is there an absence of conflict in Genesis 1?"

As we contemplate the text, one plausible move is to interpret Genesis 1:1 as affirming that God brought the formless matter itself into existence and is, therefore, totally sovereign over it. It cannot resist his will precisely because it is his creature. By "creature" I do not mean an eternally existing thing of less power than Yahweh; I mean something Yahweh brought into existence out of nothing. It may be formless and shapeless, but it is not rebellious or resistant to the will of the Creator. It is just waiting for the next step. Genesis differs from all ancient Near Eastern myths of origin because the false gods who deceived the nations with these myths were not capable of *creatio ex nihilo*, since they themselves were mere creatures of the transcendent Creator. So they chose to pretend that (1) there is no transcendent Creator and that (2) the material cosmos is itself eternal. Thus they misled human beings into worshiping the creature (that is, them) rather than the Creator (Rom. 1:25). The humans who followed these "cleverly devised myths" (1 Pet. 1:16) became "futile in their thinking and their foolish hearts were darkened" (Rom. 1:21). The absence of conflict in Genesis makes it distinct from ancient Near Eastern myths precisely because Genesis 1:1 teaches that all that exists came into existence by the agency of the Word of God.

As we saw above, Exodus 3 stresses the uniqueness of the LORD, and Genesis 1 shows an implication of this uniqueness: unlike the gods of the nations, the LORD in his being is distinct from all created beings and is also the source of the existence of all created beings. The gods of the nations are real, and they do have some power, but compared to the LORD, they are as nothing. Strictly speaking, then, we should not refer to ancient Near Eastern myths as "creation stories." They are stories about the reshaping of preexisting matter rather than creation stories. Only Genesis is actually a creation story, because only in Genesis does God create everything (the heavens and the earth) out of nothing. The doctrine of creation, it seems, is unique to the Old Testament.

Isaiah's extensive use of creation language all through Isaiah 40 is intended to tell the exiles that they can trust the LORD, because the LORD is the Creator. This is the point of our discussion of Genesis 1. The nature of the LORD as described in Isaiah 40 is the crucial foundation of Isaiah's argument in the seven chapters that follow, showing why the exiles can safely put their trust in this God to bring about a new exodus through which the Davidic covenant will be fulfilled and all the promises of God will be kept. What makes the doctrine of *creatio ex nihilo* so utterly foundational to biblical faith is that it is a statement about the uniqueness of God and a statement about the relationship of God to the world. In fact, these two things cannot be separated from each other. Alter the nature of the relationship between God and the world, and you unwittingly alter the nature of the being of God. The Bible does not lay out for us a metaphysically dense description of either the nature of God or the relationship of God to the world. There is further work of contemplation and deduction for theologians to do in order to work out the implications of the God-world relationship and, in particular, to think through how philosophical and scientific theories must be revised in order to bring them into harmony with the special revelation in Scripture. There is a contemplative task (deepening insight), a speculative task (deducing implications of biblical teaching), and a polemical task (correcting false philosophies). Theology cannot safely neglect any of these tasks.

There is one other point regarding the issue of why Genesis 1 reflects an absence of struggle between God and chaos when all the other Near Eastern myths contain an account of such struggle. The Old Testament does portray God as being at war against mythological creatures of chaos such as Leviathan and Rahab. According to Genesis 1:21, God created the great sea creatures and pronounced them good along with everything else. There is no hint of rebellion, conflict, or war. However, consider Psalm 74:

> But God has been my king from long ago,
> working salvation in the midst of the earth.
> You split open the sea [yām] by your strength;
> You broke the heads of the sea monsters [tannînîm] in the waters.
> You crushed the heads of Leviathan [liwyātān];
> you gave him as food to the desert dwelling creatures.
> You split open spring and wadi.
> You dried up ever-flowing rivers.
> Yours is the day, yours is the night also.
> You established light and the sun.
> You defined all the boundaries of the earth;
> Summer and winter—you formed them. (Ps. 74:12–17 LEB)

Note the mention of mythological monsters of chaos and their association with the sea. Anyone familiar with the Canaanite mythology of Ugarit will recognize that the biblical writer seems to be using language identical to its description of the monsters of chaos that Baal overcame, such as the sea monsters and Leviathan.[15] There is also language that evokes Genesis 1,

15. See the discussion of the Canaanite background of this mythological language in Day, *God's Conflict*, chap. 1.

such as God dividing the waters, establishing light and the sun, and defining the boundaries of the earth as well as forming summer and winter. Yet we have noted above that this kind of struggle to overcome chaos is absent from Genesis 1. What is going on here? Is Psalm 74 in conflict with Genesis 1?

The idea of giving the crushed head of Leviathan as food to the desert-dwelling creatures makes no sense until we start thinking like an ancient Israelite and recognize that this psalm is talking about the opening of the Red Sea in Exodus 15.[16] The psalmist is linking the exodus event to the creation account in just the way we would expect if Israel's understanding was that the absolute power of the transcendent Creator was on display during the exodus as Yahweh defeated the gods of Egypt. This is the background against which we must understand the mixing of creation language with exodus language in Isaiah 40. The Old Testament moves the struggle between God and chaos away from the beginning (creation) to history after the fall (redemption). God does not struggle to create order out of chaos in Genesis 1–2; he merely creates effortlessly by his Word, and the result is all good and harmonious. However, after the fall into sin in Genesis 3, which is part of history and therefore not part of the original creation, God enters into a war between the Seed of the Serpent and the Seed of the Woman. It is in the struggle to overcome sin that we see Yahweh portrayed as a warrior, and it is in the context of Yahweh's struggle to redeem his fallen creation in history that we see him crushing the forces of chaos that rise up against his sovereign rule.

The difference between the Old Testament and ancient Near Eastern mythology could hardly be starker. The same supernatural worldview is presupposed, the same mythological creatures are involved, and the same pagan gods play a role. But the difference in the Old Testament is the presence of a transcendent Creator, Yahweh, who is not a part of the cosmos but the self-existent, eternal, unchanging First Cause of all that exists. Yahweh strides onto the scene and explains what the pagan gods conveniently "forgot" to share with humans: Yahweh is the only true God, who alone is to be worshiped. Israel's worship is directed to him and to him alone as the one who creates, redeems, and judges all the earth.

Conclusion: Two Approaches to Old Testament Interpretation

In this chapter, we have explored the meaning of Isaiah 40, and we have seen that it proclaims comfort and hope beyond the judgment of exile. It presents

---

16. For an excellent discussion of the background of this psalm, see Heiser, *Unseen Realm*, 152–54.

the future hope in terms of a new exodus, and it bases the legitimacy of such hope squarely on the nature of the LORD, the God of Israel. The LORD is described as the God who brought Israel out of slavery in Egypt, and he is described as being capable of doing that because of his unique nature. The LORD is not like other gods; he is the transcendent Creator of all that exists. He calmly sits in the heavens, directing history by his decree toward its appointed goal. God is able to sustain his people because he is eternal, all-powerful, all-knowing, and immense, and he will bring salvation because he is faithful, gracious, and gentle.

There are two fundamentally incompatible approaches to the exegesis of the Old Testament: the progressive-evolutionary approach and the polemical-corrective approach. The former approach originated in modern historical criticism—starting in the Enlightenment, gathering steaming in the nineteenth century, and becoming dominant in the academy in the twentieth century. Although many of the "assured results of higher criticism" have been left behind as criticism has developed, most of the historical-critical guild retains a kind of loose unity on the level of metaphysics. Philosophical naturalism is assumed so universally that it is seldom discussed explicitly. Historical criticism is a branch of the liberal project that aims to reinterpret the Bible in the context of modern metaphysical assumptions, especially the rejection of the classical metaphysics of trinitarian classical theism in the post-Kantian constructivist situation. Central to modern metaphysics is the loss of true divine transcendence. The cosmos is the starting point and the limiting condition for all descriptions of reality.

In modernity, if God is to be spoken of at all, he must be conceived in either pantheistic or polytheistic terms or in some combination of the two. It is pressure from modern metaphysics that drives biblical interpreters to reject the traditional *creatio ex nihilo* interpretation of Genesis 1 and leads to an ancient Near Eastern mythological interpretation of Genesis 1, in which eternally existing matter and energy are rearranged by the "God" or "gods" to produce the order we experience in our world today. God can be identified as the soul of the universe (pantheism) or as a powerful person working with eternal matter and doing the best he can to shape and direct it (theistic personalism), but God cannot be thought of within modernity as the transcendent Creator. In this chapter and in this book as a whole, I contend that Isaiah's argument for why the exiles can trust this God succeeds only if God *is* the transcendent Creator. The proof of this is not merely the exegesis of a few verses with difficult grammar, such as Genesis 1:1 and Exodus 3:14–15, but rather the entire structure and progression of thought of a major section of the book of Isaiah understood within its canonical context.

The best approach to the exegesis of the Old Testament is the polemical-corrective approach. This is how the text has been read throughout the history of the church, and it is founded on the doctrine of the inspiration and authority of Holy Scripture. This approach sees the special revelation given by God to his prophets and recorded in the Old Testament as intended to correct the lies, misunderstandings, and gaps in the religious systems of the cultures surrounding Israel. In this view of the Old Testament, the emphasis is on Scripture's role in sanctifying the reader and shaping the mind of God's people. As finite creatures surrounded by the mysteries of creation, creatures who are fundamentally oriented toward God but corrupted by our sinful natures, we need illumination to acquire truth. We were made for truth, but we are subject to error because we tend to suppress the truth about God that we know intuitively and are easily misled by "cleverly devised myths" and by mistakes in our own reasoning.

As we study the Old Testament text, we should observe the difference between the LORD, the God of Israel, and the gods of the nations worshiped through idols. We are instructed by the text of Scripture on the nature and being of the one true God, and Scripture is designed by the divine author to lift our minds up from error and darkness in order to behold the light of his glorious countenance. The proper posture to assume in relation to the text of Holy Scripture is one of prayerful, careful contemplation of God in his self-revelation. As we contemplate the depth of meaning in the text, our minds are prepared to speculate in the most reverent sense of that term—that is, to deduce by good and necessary consequence the metaphysical implications of the biblical revelation of God known through exegesis. This is what it means for theology to "study God." Then we are in a position to evaluate, and correct where necessary, the philosophical and scientific theories of our day. This is what it means to study "all things in relation to God."

What have we learned so far? We have learned something of who God is and how he relates to the world. He is the Creator, and as such he is transcendent. As the transcendent Creator, he is totally trustworthy and able to keep his covenant. We have laid a fair amount of groundwork for further study of Isaiah 41–48, but in the next two chapters we must examine these chapters in depth and, in so doing, flesh out Isaiah's argument for the reliability of Israel's God.

God as the Sovereign Lord of History (Isa. 41–48)

> Thus says the LORD to his anointed, to Cyrus,
>
> . . . .
>
> "I will go before you
>   and level the exalted places,
>
> . . . .
>
> that you may know that it is I, the LORD,
>   the God of Israel, who call you by your name.
> For the sake of my servant Jacob,
>   and Israel my chosen,
> I call you by your name."
>
> Isaiah 45:1–4

In the previous chapter we saw that Isaiah 40 presents God as the transcendent Creator who can be trusted, even by a people languishing in exile, to redeem his people and bring about a new and greater exodus in the future. In this chapter, we will concentrate on what it means for God to be the sovereign Lord of history as that idea is unfolded in Isaiah 41–48 and especially in the central poem containing the Cyrus prophecy (44:24–28). Using a polemical-corrective approach to the theology of the Old Testament, we observe that Isaiah presumes the basic outline of the ancient Near Eastern mythological worldview as his starting point and then brings to bear on it the special revelation he received from the LORD God of Israel as a corrective to the mythological concept of the divine and of the relationship of God to the world. He attacks the view of God presupposed in the cultures around Israel and asserts not only the uniqueness of the God of Israel but also the sovereignty of the LORD over the historical process, which is being guided by him alone to the goal of a new creation in which the glory of the LORD fills the earth and his kingdom of peace and justice is established. In the process, Isaiah says something entirely new and utterly astonishing for the context in which he is writing.

The discussion will proceed in three stages. First, we will look at Isaiah's proclamation of divine redemption in these chapters. In support of his argument that the LORD is unique among all the other gods of the nations, Isaiah presents as "exhibit A" the LORD's work in creating Israel, and on this basis, he explains how the LORD has promised to use Israel in the future to bless the world. Specifically, the LORD will use a pagan king as his instrument to Rescue Israel from exile in Babylon.

Second, we will examine the Cyrus Prophecy (44:24–28) in some detail, as well as the other allusions to Cyrus in chapters 41–48, seeking to understand how the references to Cyrus function rhetorically and logically within these chapters. We will see that the idea of predictive prophecy is integral to the meaning and structure of the text as it stands.

Third, we will consider the metaphysical implications of the idea of predictive prophecy for our understanding of history. I will suggest that what is articulated here is something utterly different from anything to be found in the ancient Near Eastern cultural context from which the book of Isaiah emerged. Our familiarity with the linear concept of history, which has done so much to shape our culture and which we often take for granted, can hinder us from grasping just how radical and new this idea was in the first millennium BC. I will conclude by suggesting that if we reject the concept of predictive prophecy, as many biblical scholars do today, we will lose the linear concept of history and the idea of progress in history.

Isaiah's Message of Divine Redemption

One key to unlocking the meaning of the oracles in chapters 41–48 is to understand that they constitute a body of work containing insight received from the LORD by his prophet for the benefit of his people in generations to come. From the outset of his ministry, Isaiah knew that there would be no mass revival in his day in which the people of Israel would turn to the LORD in order to prevent the exile from occurring. We learn this in the context of his call to be a prophet in chapter 6, when he asks how long he is to proclaim the unrelenting message of judgment:

> Then I said, "How long, O Lord?"
> And he said:
> "Until cities lie waste
>   without inhabitant,
> and houses without people,
>   and the land is a desolate waste,
> and the LORD removes people far away,
>   and the forsaken places are many in the midst of the land."
>   (Isa. 6:11–12)

So preventing the exile is not the goal of Isaiah's prophetic ministry. He knows from the beginning of his ministry that those who respond positively to his preaching will be few in number and that the impending disaster of exile will not and cannot be averted. In view of this kind of call to prophesy, it seems too facile to say that Isaiah is concerned *primarily* with speaking to his own generation. He *is* concerned to speak to his own generation, but he knows that his own generation will reject his message, and therefore he also knows that the ultimate purpose of his preaching is that future generations will understand that the exile was not an accident or evidence of the inability of the LORD to save his people, but rather, that it was the LORD's righteous judgment on Israel. Therefore, Isaiah sees his role as being primarily a witness to future generations, at least in chapters 40–66, but also throughout the book.

If one believes that God is in control of history, it is possible to face the disappointment of seeing the failure of God's people in one's own time without losing hope altogether. Believing in a transcendent Creator who is in charge of history makes it possible to live without seeing salvation in one's own day while still being confident that God will nonetheless ultimately act to save his people. Actually, we express this kind of hope every time we attend a Christian funeral. A funeral helps the bereaved accept that a death has really occurred, yet in a Christian funeral, this truth is paired with the complementary truth that because of our hope in the resurrection of the body, death will not have the last word. It seems reasonable to think that Isaiah wrote the second half of his book late in his career, after his public ministry had been curtailed, probably due to the rising influence of the evil Manasseh as coruler with the elderly Hezekiah from 697 BC onward and then as sole king of Judah after 687 BC. At that point in Isaiah's career, the extreme evil of Manasseh's reign (idolatry, human sacrifice, disregard for the covenant, corruption of the temple, etc.) would have started to become apparent. It would be natural for the aged prophet to anticipate the nearness of his own death and to cast his mind toward the future. Rabbinic tradition says that Manasseh had Isaiah executed.[1] Therefore, it makes perfect sense to assume that Isaiah wrote chapters 40–66 for the sake of future generations and not just for the benefit of his own contemporaries. Once we grasp the crucial insight that Isaiah is writing for both his contemporaries and for posterity, it is possible to make much more sense of what is written in chapters 41–48 and how it speaks to us in our day, because we can see its relevance to all generations.

As we discussed in chapter 3 above, Isaiah 40 is the introduction to the second half of Isaiah (chaps. 40–66). The theme of the second half of the book is comfort to the exiles and hope in the eschatological redemption of the world by the LORD. Isaiah 40–66 contains the fruit of Isaiah's meditation on the problem created by the twin facts of the holiness of the LORD and the unholiness of his people. Isaiah refers to God as "the Holy One of Israel" twenty-six times, and the title occurs outside the book of Isaiah only a handful of times. It sums up the central problem that preoccupies Isaiah: how an unholy nation like Israel can possibly survive, given the fact that the LORD is holy. This conundrum permeates Isaiah 6, which describes Isaiah's call, and it runs through the entire book of Isaiah. The title "the Holy One of Israel" is evenly distributed throughout the book of Isaiah, occurring thirteen times in chapters 1–39 and thirteen times in chapters 40–66, thus providing a unifying focus to the book.[2]

The second half of Isaiah has two main sections in addition to the introductory chapter. The first section (chaps. 41–53) is dominated by the figure of the suffering servant, while the second section (chaps. 54–66) is dominated by the figure of the anointed conqueror. There are four Servant Songs (42:1–9; 49:1–13; 50:4–9; 52:13–53:12)[3] and four songs of the anointed conqueror (59:15b–21; 61:1–9; 61:10–62:12; 63:1–6).[4] The first section (chaps. 41–53) is pervaded by

1. Beyer, *Encountering the Book of Isaiah*, 26.

2. Oswalt, *Holy One of Israel*, 41.

3. Identifying these four passages as the Servant Songs has been a staple of Isaiah commentaries since the work of Bernhard Duhm in the late nineteenth century. He saw them as separate poems later inserted into the text, and many interpreters have sought to understand them in isolation from their context. However, this method is inadequate, since the goal is the interpretation of the book of Isaiah as it stands, and the theme of the "servant of the LORD" runs throughout chapters 41–53.

4. Motyer (*Prophecy of Isaiah*) deserves the credit for identifying these four poems and elucidating their importance in parallel to the Servant Songs (see esp. the very useful chart on p. 15 of his work). Although the historical-critical scholarship of the twentieth century for the most part tended to divide chapters 40–55 from 56–66 and to view the former as exilic and the latter as postexilic, I see a different division as fundamental. In so doing, I stress the two figures of the suffering servant and the anointed conqueror, and I put the emphasis on literary

an increasing sense of tension and mystery as first the lesser servant (who turns out to be Cyrus) is revealed, and then the greater servant (whose identity is never made clear) is described. The second section (chaps. 54–66) begins with a cry of hope for the salvation of Israel (chap. 54) and continues with an urgent call to faith (chap. 55) that corresponds to the first half of the book of Acts and the mission of proclaiming salvation to the house of Israel. Chapter 56 corresponds to the second half of the book of Acts and calls for the inclusion of foreigners in the covenant.[5] The theme of the entire section in chapters 54–66 is the call to repentance and faith in view of the coming eschatological revelation of a second messianic figure, which comes to a climax in chapter 63 in the description of an anointed world conqueror who, in contrast to the suffering servant of chapter 53, fulfills the warlike function of the messianic king by subduing the nations and bringing judgment to the whole earth.

The first section (chaps. 41–53) can also be divided into two subsections: chapters 41–48 and chapters 49–53. In chapters 41–48, Isaiah is concerned to assure his contemporaries, the exiles, and all who will believe his message in the future that because of the nature of the God in whom they believe, their hope is not in vain. Once again, the nature of God is the key. This section predicts the return of the exiles to Jerusalem and the rebuilding of the city and temple in the relatively near future. This miraculous and unanticipated action of the LORD demonstrates that he is in charge of history in two ways.

First, the LORD shows that the pagan empires are like putty in his hands as he makes use of the Babylonians to bring down judgment on his people, just as he previously used the Assyrians to judge Samaria in 722 BC. After he uses the Babylonians to bring judgment on Judah (in 586 BC), he will then cast them aside and replace them with the Persians, whom he will use to restore the exiles to Jerusalem (through the decree of Cyrus in 538 BC). Isaiah presents the LORD as being in total control of the rise and fall of the Assyrian, Babylonian, and Persian empires. This use of pagan empires to restore the political fortunes of the people of God can be called the lesser (political) deliverance through the lesser servant (Cyrus). The ministry of the suffering servant, by which the much more serious problem of sin is dealt with, is described in chapters 49–53 and can be called the greater (spiritual) deliverance through the greater servant (the mysterious figure described in chapter 53). In Isaiah's theology there is a parallel between the political deliverance

---

analysis rather than historical speculation. I think the pressure exerted by the canonical form of the text itself should be decisive here.

5. The relationship of the book of Acts to these chapters is a fascinating question but unfortunately one I cannot go into here. I plan to address it in the commentary on Isaiah that I am in the process of writing.

(the return from exile) and the spiritual deliverance (atonement for sin), and there is also a parallel between Cyrus, who is called the LORD's "anointed" (Isa. 45:1), and the suffering servant of chapter 53. The LORD is so great and mighty that the political problem of exile is a minor issue for him; the sin problem is much more profound because of the holiness of the LORD. In an ironic twist, the great conqueror Cyrus turns out to be the lesser servant, and the suffering one turns out to be the greater servant by far. Thus we see that God is at work in the affairs of history to accomplish redemption according to his sovereign plan and that his work is seldom comprehended by us humans from our limited point of view.

The second way in which Isaiah shows that the LORD is in charge of history is by means of predictive prophecy. God does not just *do* these things; he predicts that he is going to do them before they happen, just to eliminate the possibility that it is an accident or coincidence. In chapter 45 the LORD says,

> Who told this long ago?
>> Who declared it of old?
> Was it not I, the LORD?
>> And there is no other god besides me,
> a righteous God and a Savior;
>> there is none besides me. (Isa. 45:21)

Isaiah is not just spinning events in a favorable manner to put God in the best light *ex post facto*; he is predicting the future in order to show that God is sovereign over history even when, from the perspective of the exiles, it is impossible to see how that could be so.

That the decree of Cyrus is predicted and that Cyrus is named is not a minor detail in the text but the point of the whole argument and should be understood to have had great significance for Isaiah's understanding of the nature of God. If the text were written after the fact, Isaiah's claims about the nature of God would lose all their force. It is theoretically possible that it is a fake prophecy; that is, a description made to look like a prediction but actually written after the fact. But if that were the case, it would have lacked credibility in the eyes of readers in the sixth century BC and thus been unsuccessful in its intended effect. Which is worse: worshiping an idol god who cannot tell the future or worshiping a pretend deity who gives fake "prophecies"? How exactly does a God who must have his "prophecies" written after the occurrence of an event differ from a god who must be worshiped through an idol created by the hands of the worshipers? In both cases, such a "God" is not the transcendent Creator, who moves history by his will to its already-determined goal. What this means is that if we treat the Cyrus prophecy as a "prophecy" after the fact, we eviscerate the substance of the whole argument of Isaiah 41–48 by destroying the contrast between the LORD and the gods of the nations. It is difficult to imagine how such a piece of writing, with such an obviously invalid argument, could have been regarded as inspired and worthy of inclusion in the canon of Scripture. Reverence for the book of Isaiah as sacred Scripture is inseparable from its message about Yahweh as the sovereign Lord of history demonstrated by predictive prophecy.

As the history of Isaiah studies unfolded between the middle of the nineteenth century and the end of the twentieth century, philosophical naturalist metaphysics gradually tightened its grip on the discipline of biblical studies. It is often instructive to look at the trajectory of scholarly opinion over a period of several decades or centuries, rather than evaluating one scholarly work at a time in isolation. Biblical scholars do not work in isolation from wider intellectual and cultural trends, and since they tend not to discuss critically the metaphysical foundations of their approach, they often are not aware of how metaphysical doctrines are either presupposed unconsciously in their work or of how such presuppositions act as filters that prevent them from reading the text on its own terms.

Often scholars conceive of their situation as mediators in a two-sided debate: the text is placed in its ancient Near Eastern context within a supernatural, mythological worldview while the scholar's own disciplinary context is regarded as modern and naturalistic. It is common for biblical scholars to view themselves as being "above the fray" and as charged with the responsibility of serving as a mediator between these two worldviews. I suggest, however, that a better way to think of our situation is to view it as a three-sided debate: (1) the text comes to us from an ancient Near Eastern mythological context, (2) the modern academy operates within a modern naturalistic framework, and (3) the orthodox tradition of Christian interpretation stands over against both of these other worldviews in different ways. Scholars, instead of naively imagining themselves to be "neutral" or "above the fray," should be realistic enough to realize that it is necessary to choose a side and be honest about their deepest commitments and starting point. Then from that starting point of honesty and transparency, they can accept the responsibility to be as fair as possible to the other points of view. However, if one wishes to have metaphysical beliefs that grow out of the exegesis of the text, one cannot totally identify with either the ancient mythological worldview or the philosophical naturalism that dominates the late modern academy.

In this book, I come from the historic trinitarian classical theist perspective, and I seek to identify the different ways in which the text of Isaiah at times agrees with and at other points critiques its ancient mythological context and also challenges and supports modern metaphysics in different ways. The text resists reduction to either worldview. I am highly suspicious of interpretations that turn Isaiah into either a precursor of modern metaphysics or simply another instance of ancient Near Eastern mythology. I believe that the text should exercise a corrective-polemical function vis-à-vis both ancient mythology and modern naturalistic metaphysics. I also believe that the classical orthodox tradition has always recognized this insight implicitly if not explicitly, insofar as it has always waged a two-front war against reductionistic materialism and unrestrained mythology.

In chapters 49–53, Isaiah presents the greater deliverance through the greater servant. Since the problem encapsulated in the phrase "the Holy One of Israel" is primarily sin rather than politics, the solution to the political problem of exile is, for the LORD, a rather easy problem to solve. He just arranges things by his universal providence for the desired outcome to be achieved. A pagan emperor, namely Cyrus, can be employed for this salvific purpose as easily as a pagan emperor can be used as an instrument of judgment. But even a godly and relatively good king like David is a flawed human being, as 2 Samuel demonstrates with painful clarity and Psalm 51 confirms explicitly. Thus even David (and if David, then surely any human king in his line of descendants as well) would himself need the redemption that consists of atonement for sin and the change of nature that would be required for the problem of sin to be dealt with properly.

Through his interactions with King Ahaz in the crisis of 735 BC, Isaiah came to realize that the possibility of a human king like David or Hezekiah rising up to be the messianic king and usher in the messianic kingdom described in chapters 9 and 11 was just not feasible, because a flawed human king could at best solve only the political problem, and the problem goes much deeper than that. This is the context of Isaiah 7. The problem encapsulated in the phrase "the Holy One of Israel" is really a problem of the sinfulness and corruption of the human heart, and the social expressions of sin—strife, greed, exploitation, sexual immorality, and so forth—are merely manifestations of the deeper problem of the unregenerate, corrupt heart within us. Idolatry is the root of all sin, and political arrangements cannot eradicate it or compensate for it. So cleansing from sin and atonement for sin must be accomplished, and Israel cannot do this for itself. If the history of Israel from the exodus to the exile demonstrates anything, it makes this crystal clear. Therefore, the only hope Isaiah can see is for God to do for Israel what Israel cannot do for itself, which is to say that God must do for the human race what humans cannot do for themselves.

From chapter 40 onward, we note that Israel is mostly passive, and God is the main actor in pushing the plot along. Even though Israel is addressed as God's servant (Isa. 41:8), the LORD soon begins to speak to an individual figure as the servant, whose task is to save Israel (Isa. 49:5–7). In a sense, the servant is both Israel and an individual who arises out of Israel to perform a work that Israel as a whole has failed to do. This person is identical to the messiah, but Isaiah's conception of the messiah is not of a one-dimensional warrior-king.

In many passages in chapters 1–39, we see the LORD waiting for Israel, lamenting Israel's lack of response, and pointing out Israel's failures. But in chapters 40–66 the LORD acts, and Israel is the recipient of the LORD's gracious redemption. For example, we hear the LORD speaking as follows:

> But now thus says the LORD,
> he who created you, O Jacob,
>   he who formed you, O Israel:
> "Fear not, for I have redeemed you;
>   I have called you by name, you are mine.
> When you pass through the waters, I will be with you;
>   and through the rivers, they shall not overwhelm you;
> when you walk through the fire you shall not be burned,
>   and the flame shall not consume you.
> For I am the LORD your God,
>   the Holy One of Israel, your Savior." (Isa. 43:1–3a)

Here we see the LORD identifying himself as the redeemer of Israel. In the second Servant Song, we hear the following:

> Thus says the LORD,
>   the Redeemer of Israel and his Holy One,
> to one deeply despised, abhorred by the nation,
>   the servant of rulers:
> "Kings shall see and arise;
>   princes, and they shall prostrate themselves;
> because of the LORD, who is faithful,
>   the Holy One of Israel, who has chosen you." (Isa. 49:7)

The LORD is at work redeeming Israel through his servant on both the personal-spiritual and the public-political levels. In Isaiah 53 we read of substitutionary atonement for sin:

> Surely he has borne our griefs
>   and carried our sorrows;

> yet we esteemed him stricken,
>> smitten by God, and afflicted.
> But he was pierced for our transgressions;
>> he was crushed for our iniquities;
> upon him was the chastisement that brought us peace,
>> and with his wounds we are healed.
> All we like sheep have gone astray;
>> we have turned—every one—to his own way;
> and the LORD has laid on him
>> the iniquity of us all. (Isa. 53:4–6)

And later in the book we read of the restoration and glorification of Zion:

> For Zion's sake I will not keep silent,
>> and for Jerusalem's sake I will not be quiet,
> until her righteousness goes forth as brightness,
>> and her salvation as a burning torch.
> The nations shall see your righteousness,
>> and all the kings your glory,
> and you shall be called by a new name
>> that the mouth of the LORD will give.
> You shall be a crown of beauty in the hand of the LORD,
>> and a royal diadem in the hand of your God. (Isa. 62:1–3)

In these passages, which are representative of the sections from which they are drawn, we see God declaring that he will do for his people what his people have proved incapable of doing for themselves. The LORD will redeem them on a personal-spiritual level by bringing about atonement for sin, and the LORD will redeem them on a public-political level by restoring the exiles to Jerusalem and making the salvation of God's people shine out from Zion to all the earth like "a burning torch" (Isa. 62:1).

In the second half of the book (chaps. 40–66), the subsection we are focused on (chaps. 41–48) deals with the lesser deliverance (the political) by the lesser servant (Cyrus), and it only hints at the eschatological fullness of the political deliverance while pointing to the down payment on that eschatological fullness in the form of the return to Jerusalem and the rebuilding of city and temple in the sixth century BC. The return to Jerusalem will not lead to the restoration of the Davidic kingship; no Davidic king will rule in Israel between the exile and the time of Jesus. But it will create the necessary conditions for the preservation of David's line, which is essential for the eventual emergence of the messianic king, who will be the greater servant and who will accomplish the greater deliverance (from sin).

The importance of the lesser deliverance by the lesser servant is secondary to the greater deliverance by the greater servant, but it is important precisely as a means to allow the greater deliverance to occur. The return from exile is not unimportant, but neither is it the main thing. It is a means to an end. Political deliverance is always penultimate, but in this case its importance is magnified because it constitutes a part of the providential activity of God in the long, involved process of delivering his people and redeeming the world through them. For this reason, the theological focus in our discussion of chapters 40–48 is not the man Cyrus or the political significance of his decree, and it is not the physical fact of the return from exile by a motley band of exiles. Rather, it is the nature of the God who is playing the long game and whose plans far exceed the significance of these rather minor events in the backwaters of the Persian Empire. God is the kind of God who subsumes all the events surrounding the exile and return under his sovereignty, and they all fit together in his overall plan for his fallen creation. So the main message of chapters 40–48 is the nature of the God who promises to do all this. This God is the sovereign Lord of history.

The Cyrus Prophecy

Cyrus the Great is mentioned twenty-three times in the Bible. The name occurs three times in 2 Chronicles 36:22–23, where it says that "the LORD stirred up the spirit of Cyrus" to issue his decree allowing the Jews to return home. Cyrus is mentioned fifteen times in four of the ten chapters in Ezra. As in Chronicles, Ezra 1:1 says that "the LORD stirred up the spirit of Cyrus" to issue his decree. The name occurs three times in the book of Daniel, who is said to have served in Babylon until the first year of King Cyrus, a period of sixty-nine years (Dan. 1:21). In addition to these references to Cyrus, he is named twice in Isaiah (44:28; 45:1) and probably alluded to in several other places in that section, as we will discuss in detail below.

At the center of the section Isaiah 41–48, we have what Oswald T. Allis calls "the prophetical poem celebrating the transcendence of the Lord God of Israel."[6] The name "Cyrus" is found twice in this section: at the climax of the poem in 44:28 and again in the following verse (Isa. 45:1), which begins another poem (45:1–7) in which Cyrus is addressed by the LORD and called "my anointed." Some scholars have speculated that the name Cyrus was inserted first into the margin and later into the text by a scribe who lived after

6. Allis, *Unity of Isaiah*, 62.

538 BC and knew the name of the king who issued the decree.[7] But there are three major problems with this theory. First, it has no manuscript evidence to support it; that is, there are no variant readings in manuscripts that are missing the name or have it in the margins. All known manuscripts have the name in the text. Second, the poem in 44:24–28 would not make sense without the name, because as we shall see, the poem builds up to a climax of revealing the name. Third, and this is an extension of the first two issues combined, the block of material from chapters 41–48 as a whole is built around the theme of God using a pagan king to accomplish his will, and there are several allusions to Cyrus that are best understood with the name of Cyrus being at the center of the section. The irony (and implicit rebuke to God's people) of God having to use a pagan king to bring about the conditions for the emergence of the messianic king of Israel should not be overlooked. Cyrus's name is not incidental but central to this section.

The first allusion to Cyrus occurs in 41:2–5, where he is introduced as "one from the east whom victory meets at every step" (41:2). The LORD, verse 2 states, has "stirred up" this "one from the east." Victory is said to meet him at every step, but the text specifically states that the LORD has "performed and done this" (v. 4). The identity of the LORD is elaborated: "I, the LORD, the first, and with the last; I am he" (Isa. 41:4). A distant echo of Exodus 3:14–15 can be detected in this description of God. Twice more in this section the LORD is said to be "the first and the last" (44:6; 48:12). This is a theme that runs throughout the section and seems to identify the LORD as in some way above or not contained within history. The LORD transcends history and therefore relates to history differently than creatures do. He is simultaneously before historical events and at the end of the historical process, which enables him to be in control of history. This thought would have been extremely comforting to the faithful minority under the shadow of national judgment and to the Israelites in exile, as well as to any of the people of God who experience the temptation to despair at the apparent hopelessness of the historical situation they face. This same comfort is relevant to persecuted Christians in any age of uncertainty or decline because we worship exactly the same God described here. When chapters 41–48 are read as a whole, the identity of this reference in 41:4 is crystal clear.

The reason for withholding the name is dramatic; it is a literary technique used to create a sense of mystery and heighten interest. The next allusion to Cyrus is in 41:25, where we read the following:

7. Beyer (*Encountering the Book of Isaiah*, 157) discusses this possibility while rejecting it himself.

> I stirred up one from the north, and he has come,
>> from the rising of the sun, and he shall call upon my name;
> he shall trample on rulers as on mortar,
>> as the potter treads clay. (Isa. 41:25)

Here we see further emphasis on Yahweh's initiative in causing Cyrus to arise and come from the north (the traditional direction from which Israel's enemies came) to "call upon my name." There is no indication in Isaiah or elsewhere in the Old Testament that Cyrus was a genuine believer in the LORD. However, that did not stop him from couching his decree in terms of a response to the God of Israel. In Ezra we read,

> In the first year of Cyrus king of Persia, that the word of the LORD by the mouth of Jeremiah might be fulfilled, the LORD stirred up the spirit of Cyrus king of Persia, so that he made a proclamation throughout all his kingdom and also put it in writing:

> "Thus says Cyrus king of Persia: The LORD, the God of heaven, has given me all the kingdoms of the earth, and he has charged me to build him a house at Jerusalem, which is in Judah. Whoever is among you of all his people, may his God be with him, and let him go up to Jerusalem, which is in Judah, and rebuild the house of the LORD, the God of Israel—he is the God who is in Jerusalem. And let each survivor, in whatever place he sojourns, be assisted by the men of his place with silver and gold, with goods and with beasts, besides freewill offerings for the house of God that is in Jerusalem." (Ezra 1:1–4, underlining added)

In the underlined text, Cyrus calls on the name of the LORD. This decree may simply be politely worded in speaking of the God of Israel, and it may even imply that the LORD is only the God of Jerusalem rather than God of the whole earth. Nevertheless, Isaiah's assertion that Cyrus would call on the name of the LORD is shown to have come true literally, according to the record of Cyrus's decree in Ezra. Isaiah goes on in chapter 41,

> Who declared it from the beginning, that we might know,
>> and beforehand, that we might say, "He is right"?
> There was none who declared it, none who proclaimed,
>> none who heard your words. (Isa. 41:26)

Here Isaiah is speaking to God with the expectation that his hearers/readers will agree with his insight when they see the predicted events come to pass. Isaiah is saying that God declares ahead of time what is going to happen, and when people see come to pass the good news that he has foretold, they say "He is right." In the verses following this passage, Isaiah compares the idol gods to the LORD and calls them "a delusion" and their images "empty wind" (Isa. 41:29). When the LORD says that we should be comforted because deliverance is coming, it is totally different from when the false gods of the nations make promises they cannot keep, because all that the LORD decrees comes to pass.

If this section was written after 538 BC, when the decree of Cyrus was issued, then it loses all its logical and rhetorical power.[8] It demonstrates, in fact, that the opposite of what it teaches is true. As John Oswalt puts it, if Isaiah 41–48 was written after 538 BC, then

> his God Yahweh cannot tell the future any more than the gods can, but he wishes his hearers to believe that Yahweh can. In order to prove this point, the prophet tries to get his readers to believe that it was really Isaiah of Jerusalem who said these things, all the while knowing this was not true. He even goes so far as to alter some of the earlier writings (e.g., ch. 13 with its reference to Babylon), or to insert some of his own (chs. 34–35), in order to make those writings correspond more closely to his own work.[9]

If this were the case, it is difficult to understand why the book of Isaiah was ever accepted as canonical Scripture. If the fraud was known, it surely would have discredited the book. If the fraud was not known, then we must suppose that a book was accepted as inspired with a ticking time bomb in the middle of it, set to go off at a later time when the deception was discovered. How this could accord with a theory of divine providence and canon formation is difficult to imagine.

Cyrus is likely alluded to again in chapter 43:

> Thus says the LORD,
>   your Redeemer, the Holy One of Israel:
> "For your sake I send to Babylon
>   and bring them all down as fugitives,
>   even the Chaldeans, in the ships in which they rejoice.
> I am the LORD, your Holy One,
>   the Creator of Israel, your King." (Isa. 43:14–15)

In this passage Babylon is mentioned explicitly for the first time in chapters 40–66. The LORD promises that once they have served their purpose as

---

8. This, however, is the most widespread view among historical critics today. Goldingay and Payne (*Isaiah 40–55*, 2:14) mention C. C. Torrey and P. R. Davies as two examples.

9. Oswalt, *Book of Isaiah: Chapters 40–66*, 5–6.

executors of God's wrath on Israel, they too will be punished. The Abraha-
mic Covenant of Genesis 12:1–3 is still in force, and so those who dishonor
Abraham's descendants must be cursed by God. The reference to the LORD
as the Creator of Israel in verse 15 reminds us of the miraculous birth of
Isaac, who was created by God not quite out of nothing but out of two elderly people whose reproductive capabilities were unquestionably extinct.
In that respect, the creation of Israel is at least analogous to the *creatio ex
nihilo* of Genesis 1:1. Interestingly, these verses are immediately followed by
a series of verses that use exodus language about parting the sea, making a
path in the mighty waters, and extinguishing chariot and horse, army and
warrior (Isa. 43:16–17). So we again see the union of creation language and
exodus language, just as we saw in chapter 40. The return from Babylon is
a new exodus, and God uses Cyrus to judge Babylon as God used Moses to
judge Egypt.

This brings us to Isaiah 44:24–28, where the name of Cyrus is revealed.
Allis's treatment of what he calls "a prophetical poem celebrating the transcendence of the Lord God of Israel" is unparalleled in the literature on
Isaiah for its power and depth of theological insight.[10] In what follows, I will
summarize and interact with the main points of his analysis, but readers are
urged to study this book by Allis as an indispensable guide to understanding
the book of Isaiah.

Allis argues convincingly that this poem is structured to build to a climax
in which the name of Cyrus, which has been hinted at but not stated so far
in chapters 40–44, is ultimately revealed in the final line. The poem runs
from Isaiah 44:24–28 and in the Hebrew consists of an introduction plus
nine relative clauses that are correctly translated in the English Standard
Version as beginning with "who" in recognition of the fact that they all
refer to the LORD and describe him. The nature of God is thus the theme of
the poem. These nine relative clauses are arranged in three stanzas of three
lines each. The first stanza has one clause per line; the second stanza has
two clauses joined by a conjunction in each line; and the third stanza has
three clauses in the first line, a shorter second line with two clauses, and a
final line with four clauses. The pattern is three single-clause lines (stanza 1)
followed by three double-clause lines (stanza 2). Then stanza 3 begins with
the next logical step, a triple-clause line in line 1, but there is a variation
in line 2 (two clauses) and a further variation in line 3 (four clauses). The
final line is obviously designed to draw attention to itself and begins with
the name of Cyrus.

---

10. Allis, *Unity of Isaiah*, chap. 5.

The whole poem (Isa. 44:24–28) can be laid out as follows, using the wording of the ESV:

Introduction: Thus says the LORD, your Redeemer, who formed you from the womb:

Main Statement: "I am the LORD"

Descriptions of the LORD:

stanza 1

line 1: who made all things

line 2: who alone stretched out the heavens

line 3: who spread out the earth by myself

stanza 2

line 4: who frustrates the signs of liars
and makes fools of diviners

line 5: who turns wise men back
and makes their knowledge foolish

line 6: who confirms the word of his servant
and fulfills the counsel of his messengers

stanza 3

line 7: who says of Jerusalem, "She shall be inhabited,"
and of the cities of Judah, "They shall be built,"
and I will raise up their ruins

line 8: who says to the deep, "Be dry;
I will dry up your rivers"

line 9: who says of Cyrus, "He is my shepherd,
and he shall fulfill all my purpose";
saying of Jerusalem, "She shall be built,"
and of the temple, "Your foundation shall be laid."

Allis lays out the structure in two tables, which I have adapted. The first one (his diagram II) shows how we would expect the third stanza to develop, based on the pattern begun in the first two stanzas. The second table (his diagram I) is the actual pattern followed in the third stanza of the poem.[11]

---

11. Allis, *Unity of Isaiah*, 68–69.

Anticipated Clause Pattern

Stanza 1 (three lines)	1		
	1		
	1		
Stanza 2 (three lines)	1	1	
	1	1	
	1	1	
Stanza 3 (three lines)	1	1	1
	1	1	1
	1	1	1

Actual Clause Pattern

Stanza 1 (three lines)	1			
	1			
	1			
Stanza 2 (three lines)	1	1		
	1	1		
	1	1		
Stanza 3 (three lines)	1	1	1	
	1	1		
	1	1	1	1

Instead of the expected pattern of one clause in the three lines of stanza 1, two clauses in the three lines of stanza 2, and three clauses in the three lines of stanza 3, we get a variation at the end that draws attention to the final line, in which uniquely four clauses appear, which makes it the longest line in the poem as well as being situated at the end. The poetic devices of climax, length, and uniqueness all point to the last line as the most important line of the nine.

This does not mean, however, that the poem is primarily about Cyrus. Clearly the poem is about the LORD, and the main statement is that he is the LORD. The main statement of the poem evokes the revelation of the divine name in Exodus 3:14–15 by using the phrase "I AM" and then giving the divine name "Yahweh." The following nine relative clauses, correctly translated as beginning with "who," all describe who this one is; they articulate various implications of the main statement "I am the LORD."

In these nine relative clauses the themes of creation (lines 1–3) and new exodus (lines 7–9) are prominent, just as they are in chapter 40. In between, in the second stanza, is a contrast between the LORD, whose word spoken by his servants and messengers is fulfilled, and the pagan gods, whose servants, the diviners and wise men, are made to look foolish. This motif recalls the conflict between Moses and Aaron and the magicians of Egypt (Exod. 7:8–13). The climax of the poem is the revelation of the name of the pagan king by whom God will fulfill his promise of comfort first given in chapter 40.

Klaus Baltzer suggests that the reference in Isaiah 44:27 to "the deep" and "your rivers" may have in mind the Canaanite myth of El having his seat "at the source of the two rivers, amid the springs of the depths," and the background may be the struggle between Baal and Yamm (the sea god) in the Ugaritic tradition.[12] However, I think it is better to understand this imagery in a canonical context, noting that the Hebrew word in Isaiah 44:27 translated by the ESV as "to the deep" (*laṣṣûlâ*) is the same word that is translated as "into the depths" in Exodus 15:5 (*bimṣôlōt*). The root word in both cases is "deep" (*ṣûlâ*). Exodus 15:1–18 is the Song of Moses, which celebrates Yahweh's mighty victory over Pharaoh at the Red Sea. So the background of the imagery of verse 27 is the exodus.[13] Yet the exodus victory itself is spoken of in terms that pagan mythology used to describe the gods' victory over watery chaos. The difference is that in the Old Testament, the battle between God and chaos occurs in *history* after the fall, not in creation. It is a battle against the rebellious fallen powers within the frame of history, that is, from Genesis 3 onward, not a struggle in primeval time against the eternal chaos that confronts the gods. That the struggle occurs within history means that it can and will be resolved within history, which is the basis of the Old Testament hope that the eschatological future will be like the original good creation in being totally good.

But if the imagery in the third stanza is exodus language, does that mean that Baltzer's suggestion of a Canaanite mythological background is completely wrong? Not necessarily. Baltzer quotes Otto Kaiser's suggestion that there is also an Egyptian provenance for the mythological struggle of the gods against the sea. He claims that the background to the myth is the storms that blow up from the sea at the beginning of winter against the Mediterranean coast from Egypt to Syria. Whereas in Ugarit the god who subdues the sea is Baal, in Egypt it is Seth.[14] Irrespective of the validity of the geographical explanation for the origin of the myth, the idea of the gods subduing the forces of chaos is a widespread theme across all ancient Near Eastern mythology,

12. Baltzer, *Deutero-Isaiah*, 218.

13. There is no need to appeal to a Mesopotamian mythological provenance for the imagery here in what is often supposed to be "Deutero-Isaiah."

14. Baltzer, *Deutero-Isaiah*, 218. Baltzer notes that Kaiser is working with texts from the Egyptian Book of the Dead 108.14–43, as well as the Typhon myth according to Apollodorus.

and so to find Exodus 15 using it to affirm Yahweh's power over the gods of Egypt is utterly unsurprising. In the ten plagues, Yahweh demonstrated his power over nature in a way that the gods of Egypt were unable to prevent.

This is a clear example of the kind of polemical-corrective approach to biblical theology that I discussed in chapter 3. Just as Exodus 1–14 presupposes the doctrine of the transcendent Creator as the one who is in control of the spiritual entities claiming divine status despite their being only Yahweh's creatures, so here we see that Yahweh is the one who controls kings like Cyrus despite their typical (for kings) pretensions of omnipotence. The mockery of the liars, diviners, and foolish wise men in verse 25 is contrasted with the fulfillment of the word of Yahweh's servants (like Isaiah), and this mockery is situated right in between the proclamation of Yahweh as Creator in stanza 1 and the proclamation of Yahweh as redeemer and sovereign Lord of history in stanza 3.

The first clause of the third stanza identifies Cyrus by name and describes him as "my shepherd" (rō'î), a title applied to the Israelite king in Jeremiah 22 and Ezekiel 34.[15] Baltzer calls attention to the connection of the shepherd imagery to the Davidic dynasty and notes how shocking it must have been for readers of this text to hear this image applied to a foreign ruler. This is true, but the authority of the Israelite king is a derived authority; both Davidic kings and foreign rulers shepherd God's people under the ultimate authority of the LORD.[16] The second clause asserts of Cyrus that "he shall fulfill my purpose." The third and fourth clauses express God's purpose for Cyrus: to decree that Jerusalem be built and the foundation of the temple be laid. What is omitted here, however, is highly significant; there is no mention of a restored Davidic monarchy. God's use of Cyrus is not a replacement for his use of the Davidic monarchy; it is something else in addition to his use of the Davidic monarchy. The LORD is now working through a pagan king in this one instance. In Isaiah 40–53 Cyrus as the lesser deliverer is paired with the suffering servant as the greater deliverer. The anointed world conqueror is the fulfillment of all that was typologically foreshadowed in the Davidic kingship, but it represents a separate development from the atoning work of the suffering servant in Isaiah 40–66, and how the two strands of messianic hope are related to one another is left hanging mysteriously by the prophet.

It is shocking that the LORD would use Cyrus to restore his people to Jerusalem, but it is not the most shocking thing Isaiah has to say in the second half

15. Allis, *Unity of Isaiah*, 54.
16. Baltzer, *Deutero-Isaiah*, 219.

of the book. Rather than being scandalized that God would stoop to using a pagan king to accomplish his purposes, the reader is supposed to understand that this is a sign of God's sovereignty over history, which entails his being in charge of not just Israel but the pagan empires as well. The point is that Yahweh is not merely the tribal deity of the Hebrews but the sovereign Lord of heaven and earth. This message is the same as that of Exodus 1–15, which is why new exodus language is joined with creation language throughout Isaiah 40–48 to make this point. Isaiah's vision goes far beyond merely restoring a remnant of the Jews to their homeland and the rebuilding of the temple; it is cosmic in scope and almost beyond comprehension or description. Isaiah struggles to express what he has seen and heard in the divine council (Isa. 40).

Immediately following this poem, in 45:1–8 Cyrus is held up as proof of God's providential control of history and his unique sovereignty over all the earth. In verse 1 Cyrus is addressed by the LORD, "Thus says the LORD to his anointed [*limšîḥô*], to Cyrus." God uses a form of the Hebrew word *māšîaḥ* (messiah, anointed one). This is surprising, for we are not accustomed to hearing a messianic title applied to a foreign king. However, the word is used in a wide variety of contexts in the Old Testament. Kings, priests, and prophets are all anointed for specific tasks. Even evil kings of Judah like Manasseh would have been anointed. Cyrus is anointed for a specific task by the LORD. However, there is more than that going on here. Cyrus is a type of Christ in that he executes judgment on Israel's enemies (Babylon) and liberates his people from bondage in a new exodus. All this can be true without us needing to suppose that Cyrus was a closet believer in the LORD or that he became a Jew or came under the covenant. All we need to suppose is that there is a parallel between the lesser servant who brings the lesser deliverance and the greater servant who brings the greater deliverance.

As Christians, we understand that Jesus is the Christ (Greek for "anointed one") in the sense of being the suffering servant who dies to atone for the sins of his people and rises again to live forever. But Jesus is also the anointed conqueror of Isaiah 59–63 in his second coming. Cyrus foreshadows Jesus not in his first coming but in his second coming. When the Jews of Jesus's day rejected him as messiah because he did not fit their mold of a Maccabean warrior messiah, they were wrong but not entirely wrong. Jesus was not a suffering messiah *instead of* being a warrior messiah; rather, he had to be a suffering messiah *before* he could be the warrior messiah. So the fact that Cyrus does not suffer and die for the sins of the world is not reason enough to deny that he foreshadows, in a partial but still meaningful way, the coming messiah. He simply models one facet of the messiah's multifaceted mission. The exact nature of the relationship between the two portraits of the divine messiah (suffering servant and anointed conqueror) is never clarified in the book of Isaiah, and the ambiguity creates an air of mystery that hangs over the second half of the book. But Isaiah's faith is in Yahweh as the sovereign Lord of history, who can and will bring about wonderful things in his good time according to his unfathomable plan.

We have several more allusions to Cyrus in the rest of this section. In 45:4 the LORD says that he calls Cyrus by name even "though you do not know me." It is not necessary for pagan kings to acknowledge the LORD as lord in order for the LORD to make use of them for his purposes. In 45:13 the LORD uses Cyrus as an example, saying,

> "I have stirred him up in righteousness,
>   and I will make all his ways level;
> he shall build my city
>   and set my exiles free,
> not for price or reward,"
>   says the LORD of hosts.

Then, in 46:11 he alludes to Cyrus in saying,

> Remember this and stand firm,
>   recall it to mind, you transgressors,
>   remember the former things of old;
> for I am God, and there is no other;
>   I am God, and there is none like me,
> declaring the end from the beginning
>   and from ancient times things not yet done,
> saying, "My counsel shall stand,
>   and I will accomplish all my purpose,"
> calling a bird of prey from the east,
>   the man of my counsel from a far country.
> I have spoken, and I will bring it to pass;
>   I have purposed, and I will do it. (Isa. 46:8–11)

Cyrus is the "bird of prey from the east" who is used by God to accomplish his purpose. One final allusion occurs in 48:14.

> "Assemble, all of you, and listen!
>   Who among them has declared these things?
> The LORD loves him;
>   he shall perform his purpose on Babylon,
>   and his arm shall be against the Chaldeans.

> I, even I, have spoken and called him;
>> I have brought him, and he will prosper in his way.
> Draw near to me, hear this:
>> from the beginning I have not spoken in secret,
>> from the time it came to be I have been there."
> And now the Lord GOD has sent me, and his Spirit. (Isa. 48:14–16)

Cyrus is used by the LORD to execute judgment on Babylon. This section (Isa. 40–48) then ends with a call to the exiles:

> Go out from Babylon, flee from Chaldea,
>> declare this with a shout of joy, proclaim it,
> send it out to the end of the earth;
>> say, "The LORD has redeemed his servant Jacob!"
> They did not thirst when he led them through the deserts;
>> he made water flow for them from the rock;
>> he split the rock and the water gushed out. (Isa. 48:20–21)

The exiles can respond to this call because of what God has done through Cyrus.

It is hard to deny that the prophet has Cyrus on his mind all through chapters 41–48, with allusions to Cyrus in chapters 41 and 43, the explicit naming of Cyrus in chapters 44 and 45, and further allusions to Cyrus in chapters 45, 46, and 48. Cyrus and Babylon rival the servant for prominence in these chapters and function to reassure the prophet's audience that the mysterious redemptive work that God intends to perform through his servant can and will be successful because God is the sovereign Lord of history, which is proved by his prediction of, and use of, Cyrus as his chosen instrument to publicly deliver his people from captivity in Babylon and restore them to Jerusalem after the punishment of the exile is compete.

Predictive Prophecy and the Philosophy of History

The revisionist doctrines of God we discussed in chapter 1 all presuppose the impossibility of predictive prophecy because the god they describe is, himself, a part of the historical process and not transcendent over it. In contemporary historical-critical scholarship, the question of revelation is troubled. In fact, it would not be an overstatement to say that the concept of revelation has been largely elided in liberal biblical scholarship, even though some liberal scholars, such as Mark S. Smith, continue to use the word. But what Smith means by "revelation" is quite different from what it meant to the church fathers, medieval schoolmen, Protestant Reformers, modern evangelicals, and all those upholding Nicene trinitarian orthodoxy from all branches of Christianity.

Smith uses the term "revelation" as a follower of Schleiermacher would do. For Smith, "revelation" is human experience expressed in metaphors to construct ideas of God that reflect our experience of the world. For example, he claims that the polytheistic concept of God as head of a divine family changed in the situation of the Assyrian threat in the seventh century BC and the exile. Summarizing this process, he writes of changes in Israelite society, "The family no longer functioned as the sole or primary mode of social identification, . . . and correspondingly the Israelite god could be seen as the individual deity responsible for the operation of the universe."[17] My point is not whether this particular argument makes sense; rather, I wish to highlight the method that Smith uses to understand "revelation." In no sense is revelation for him a matter of humans receiving information (truth) from God about reality. Rather, it is a matter of projecting metaphors drawn from human experience onto the divine. Feuerbach's critique of religion as projection seems to apply to this approach quite clearly; he says,

> In the divine omniscience man merely fulfils his own desire to know everything or objectifies the faculty of the human mind to be everywhere at once. . . . In other words, God is nothing other than the future immortal man, differentiated from man as he exists at present in the body and flesh, and conceived of as an independent being.[18]

As an atheist, Feuerbach would say that the seventh-century Israelite writers were simply projecting their own experience onto a mythical cosmic figure they called "God" and thus were giving expression to their aspirations. Naturally, Feuerbach would say, there is no reason to think that such a being exists in reality. I would reply to Feuerbach that it is not the biblical writers doing this but rather the modern critics.

Later Smith says that the monotheism we see reflected in Exodus is really a later imaginative construct imposed back onto Israel's mythic origins as an act of "memory" rather than history.[19] He criticizes those who insist that truth must be historical, saying that they are guilty of an "idolatry of history."[20]

---

17. M. Smith, *Memoirs of God*, 154.
18. Feuerbach, *Lectures on the Essence of Religion*, 274.
19. M. Smith, *Memoirs of God*, 167.
20. M. Smith, *Memoirs of God*, 164.

Smith admits that some basic biblical events stand on biblical claims that they actually occurred, but the only example he can come up with is one that, conveniently, lies outside his scholarly field—namely, the resurrection of Jesus from the dead. He then attacks a number of straw men and posits several false dichotomies by claiming that it is not true that the Bible stands or falls as revelation "depending on whether or not every single fact recorded in the Bible was historically true."[21] But surely there is a fair bit of middle ground between "every single fact" and the entire history of Israel being fictional! Smith also argues that biblical books giving parallel accounts of the same events must mean that they are not giving history, but surely this does not follow. Having several witnesses in court describe a car accident from different perspectives does not mean that the accident never happened. Smith seems to think that we must accept the biblical accounts of events as memory rather than history if we don't have "exact transcripts of events."[22] Surely the real issue is being obscured here: What do the texts themselves claim about the historical events they recount? Sometimes the Bible tells stories, such as the parables of Jesus, the historicity of which is clearly incidental to their meaning and truth. At other times the Bible tells us of historical events that reveal God's saving acts in the world, acts on which our faith is based, as in 1 Corinthians 15:1–11, where Paul makes it clear that our whole faith is based on the historical fact of Jesus's resurrection. I do not think it unreasonable to suppose that certain stories in the Old Testament might be more like the parables than the Gospels' resurrection accounts. But that does not mean that *all* Old Testament stories that include miracles can or should be shoehorned into that category.

We do not get to decide which accounts are which based on the dictates of modern metaphysics; that is a matter for exegesis. What do the texts themselves claim? The text of Isaiah 41–48 clearly seems to claim that God is going to do something in the future to save his people that is analogous to (though greater than) the exodus event, which created Israel as a nation. If we think that the new exodus will occur in history but the old exodus did not, does the message still make sense? And if the new exodus will happen only in the subjective religious experience of the community and not in history, is this hope an adequate expression of the plain sense of the words of Isaiah 41–48? The texts we have examined in Isaiah 44:24–28, for example, say something that does not fit within the narrow confines of the philosophical naturalism of modern metaphysics. We are faced with a choice: Which is to be our final authority, the Bible or modernity? Smith would like to have it both ways, but

21. M. Smith, *Memoirs of God*, 164.
22. M. Smith, *Memoirs of God*, 164.

this is just not feasible. I predict that Smith's quixotic quest to have both a liberal theology of experience and an evolutionary historical-critical approach to the Old Testament will be left behind as the field of biblical studies continues to secularize. If revelation is just a projection of human experience onto the sky, the future belongs to the minimalists and to Feuerbachian atheism. Or maybe pantheism is the future. It is telling that in the final two pages of his book, Smith admits that the evolutionary approach by which Israel went from pagan polytheism to "a cosmic theology of a single deity" continues in the modern period as "traditional trinitarian monotheism moved into a world theology that tries to address the Christian Deity vis-à-vis other religious views of reality and divinity."[23] He asserts that different world religions "take alternative routes up the sides of the mountain that will eventually meet at the top."[24] No doubt modern religious experience (or at least the religious experience of left-leaning Western academics shaped by the ethos of the late-modern university) will require a "new" doctrine of God. But will it really be new, or would Elijah recognize it instantly?

The modern Western faith in never-ending progress is touchingly naive. Since we no longer believe in a transcendent Creator or an eschatological goal for history, the concept of exactly what constitutes progress becomes increasingly blurry to Western eyes. Darwinian evolution explains only change, and change is not the same as progress. Progress is not part of the theory of evolution; it must be added from the outside as an extra. But in late modern theology, there is nothing outside naturalistic metaphysics. All our experience is inside the cosmos, not outside it. If our doctrine of God is simply a projection of our experience of the world, then it is either nothing real at all or else a reflection of the cosmos, like an image in the mirror.

As the West slides back into the pagan mythological worldview from which it was dragged kicking and screaming by the Old Testament prophets, something of inestimable value is being lost. Something precious is dying and should be lamented. And the loss is both the church's loss and the general culture's loss. I suggest that the secularization of eschatology is impossible over the long term; if we refuse predictive prophecy and futurist eschatology, then we forfeit all notions of progress in history. In fact, technically, we lose the very concept of history itself, insofar as it is distinguished from a description of purposeless flux or cycles of chaos and order. Secular history must inevitably dissolve into mythology. If Isaiah is right in what he argues in these chapters about the nature of God, the most important thing we will lose is hope.

23. M. Smith, *Memoirs of God*, 171.
24. M. Smith, *Memoirs of God*, 171.

One could argue that the anomie of modern Western culture is a result of the breakdown of the theological metaphysics of Nicene Christianity due to what Walter Lippman terms "the acids of modernity."[25] In the late nineteenth century, Émile Durkheim introduced the theory of anomie to describe a feature of modern life in which a general listlessness and aimlessness results from the breakdown of standards of behavior and the disintegration of cultural norms.[26] The twentieth century has witnessed the steady increase of these conditions as cultural anomie has spread from initially being confined to the leisured classes to affecting the broad middle classes of society and now even taking root among the working classes. The sexual revolution of the 1960s was the "democratization of anomie" as the general sense of a loss of truth and moral realism spread through the youth movement to society in general and produced "the generation of '68." The social media revolution of the early 2000s accelerates the spread of lethargy and aimlessness among young people.

This sense of purposelessness—epitomized in casual, meaningless sex and routine drug abuse—is the natural, predictable, and inevitable result of believing in philosophical naturalism. The materialism of the Enlightenment and the developments in the nineteenth century—by which the myth of the world as a machine gave way to the myth of the world as a living organism—represent the loss of the Christian worldview due to the rejection of Christian metaphysics. Philosophical naturalism rejects (1) a transcendent God (natural theology), (2) the idea of an objectively existing telos in nature as the basis of the moral law (natural law), (3) metaphysical realism by which things have natures that cause them to act in ways consistent with their natures (natural science), and (4) a linear concept of history, which is required for the idea of progress (history). Belief in these four things lifted the West out of mythology in the first place, and so rejecting them must inevitably result in plunging the West back into the mythological worldview that characterized Greco-Roman and ancient Near Eastern cultures.

It is ironic that philosophical naturalism so often presents itself to the public as "scientific" materialism since it actually leads back to mythology. Science functions as a kind of "secularized mythology" in our society, and scientists in white lab coats serve as the priesthood, scrutinizing the "entrails" of matter in order to tell us what we must believe and do. Darwinism is a myth, and if the purpose of a myth is to give life meaning, Darwinism is a pernicious myth, because it sucks meaning out of life. The rejection of the trinitarian classical theism of Christian orthodoxy in the late-modern West

25. Lippman, *Preface to Morals*, 8.
26. Durkheim, *Division of Labor*.

entails the loss of any real basis for believing in the concept of history or progress. These two concepts are mutually dependent; without one, you do not really have the other.

History as linear requires a beginning (creation) and a terminus (eschatology). If there was no beginning, there will never be an end, which means that the cosmos is eternal. But if there is no end point, then there is no basis for judging whether we are getting nearer to or further from the goal. Without a goal, we do not know how to judge whether we are making progress. If we are all free as individuals to invent or choose our own goals, then we have as many end points as we have agents of free will. In that case, no one can say whether the goal I have chosen is better or worse than the one you have chosen. So it becomes impossible to work together toward the common good. Hyperindividualism and the breakdown of the family (not to mention the village and the nation) are inevitable in such a situation. Society can tolerate quite a lot of individualism, but eventually the process goes too far—as in the Weimar Republic in Germany—and the public starts looking for a "strong man" who can make the trains run on time. Thus Nietzsche's *Übermensch* is called forth. It is too simplistic to think that the dictator imposes his will on the masses by violence; one need only watch newsreel footage of the crowds adoring Adolf Hitler and throwing themselves at his feet to know that it is the post-Christian masses who call out for someone to be their "god" when they no longer believe in the God of the Bible.

History as linear requires a Mind that transcends the whole of creation and has a goal in mind for creation. So the requirements for predictive prophecy are actually identical to the requirements for a linear concept of history as opposed to a cyclical one. In chapter 2 of *Interpreting Scripture with the Great Tradition*, I identified a loss of understanding the doctrine of providence and a loss of understanding different levels of causation (both metaphysical issues) as the reasons why modern people have difficulty accepting the idea of the inspiration of Scripture. For those who think that human free will is as absolute as God's will and who see choice as a zero-sum game in which the more God has, the less we have, and the more we have, the less God has, the whole idea of predictive prophecy is problematic, because it seems to be incompatible with free will. Of course, it is not incompatible with limited creaturely free will, which is the only kind creatures could possibly have. But it is incompatible with the grandiose concept of absolute free will that modern people imagine themselves to have. A certain humility is required in order to believe in the Christian God, because it entails remembering which side of the creator-creature distinction we are on. The first two rules of good theology are that (1) there is a God, and (2) it isn't me. In order to have history, we need to accept the Lord of history. Trying to have history without the transcendent Creator is like trying to disbelieve in cake while eating it too.

Isaiah 41–48 is an argument for why the exiles in Babylon—and, by extension, all those who wait for the redemption of the world—should have hope. The argument is not based on the marvels of human ingenuity or the potential of a new politics or anything that ever has or ever could emerge from the matrix of a fallen creation. The argument is based on the nature of the God who has revealed himself to Israel. "Behold your God!" says the prophet (Isa. 40:9). "I am the Lord" says the Lord (Isa. 44:24). The argument is not that we should believe in the concept of the divine or in the gods in general; rather, it is that hope is possible, based on the reality of this particular God, this kind of God. This God is not like the idols, and he is not like the gods of Egypt, Canaan, or Mesopotamia. He is not limited, immoral, or narcissistic. This God is the transcendent Creator, the sovereign Lord of history, and the One who alone is worthy of our worship. We will explore this theme further in the next chapter.

God as the One Who Alone
Is to Be Worshiped (Isa. 41–48)

> You shall have no other gods before me.
>
> Exodus 20:3

> Hear, O Israel: The LORD our God, the LORD is one.
>
> Deuteronomy 6:4

The argument so far is that trinitarian classical theism is at the heart of the historic tradition of Christian orthodoxy. The classic Christian doctrine of God holds that the God who revealed himself to Israel, and ultimately in Jesus Christ, is the simple, immutable, eternal, self-existent, First Cause of the universe. How this can be so is a mystery confessed by faith; we believe it because it happened. We do not have an overarching theory to explain how it could happen; we just know it did happen. The apostolic testimony is as follows:

> That which was from the beginning, which we have heard, which we have seen with our eyes, which we looked upon and have touched with our hands, concerning the word of life—the life was made manifest, and we have seen it, and testify to it and proclaim to you the eternal life, which was with the Father and was made manifest to us. (1 John 1:1–2)

The apostles never questioned the existence of the God of Israel and would have been horrified to be accused of abandoning monotheism by including Jesus Christ within the definition of the God of Israel. One of the reasons we need a *doctrine* of God, rather than simply repeating what the Bible says about God, is in order to understand how and why they were right in understanding themselves to be monotheists even as they developed the doctrine of the Trinity.

If the God of creation (the transcendent Creator) and the exodus (the sovereign Lord of history) described by Isaiah is also the Father of our Lord Jesus Christ proclaimed in the New Testament as well as the simple, immutable, eternal, self-existent, First Cause of the universe known to the best of the philosophers, then we need a way of understanding how these various descriptions cohere. One point where many of these themes intersect is the concept of monotheism.

In this chapter, we take up the question of the meaning of monotheism. In our contemporary situation, the concept of monotheism displays evidence of serious confusion, and this chapter addresses that problem. Monotheism is a word most people use and assume they know what it means—that is, until one starts asking detailed questions about it. If there is only one true God, does that mean that all the gods of the pagan nations around Israel did not exist? Why does the Old Testament talk as if they do exist? If the "gods of the nations" are nothing more than wood and metal, how exactly did they lead the nations astray? And why does the Old Testament emphasize so strongly the duty to *worship* only the Lord, rather than the duty to believe that only the Lord exists (Exod. 20:3–6)? Why do prophets like Isaiah emphasize the uniqueness rather than the sole existence of the Lord? What is meant by Yahweh judging the rebellious gods? Where did the worship of false gods come from in the first place; that is, what is the origin of pagan religion? Did Israel's religion evolve out of Canaanite polytheism, or was monotheism revealed by God at the beginning of Israel's existence? Does the New Testament change the meaning of monotheism from what was taught in the Old Testament? Is monotheism compatible with the doctrine of the Trinity? How does biblical monotheism relate to philosophical monotheism? Are they identical? If not, how do they differ? Should we speak of biblical henotheism rather than biblical monotheism? Many other questions could be added to these, but this list suffices to make clear the scope of the problem. I answer most of these questions in this chapter, but we must proceed one step at a time. This chapter builds on chapters 3–5 and continues our investigation of Isaiah 41–48.

The Meaning of the Term ʾĔlōhîm

Most people are aware that the Old Testament, including the book of Isaiah, uses several different words for "God" and that English translations reflect that fact as best they can. The most commonly used Hebrew word for God is *'ĕlōhîm*. In Psalm 82 we read the following:

> God [*'ĕlōhîm*] has taken his place in the divine council;
>   in the midst of the gods [*'ĕlōhîm*] he holds judgment. (Ps. 82:1)

Someone who has not studied Hebrew might be surprised to learn that the Hebrew word translated "God" in line 1 and translated "gods" in line 2 is the same word and the same form of the word. Although the Hebrew word *'ĕlōhîm* is plural in form, its meaning can be either singular or plural depending on context. It is like the English word "sheep." If I say that "I found the biggest sheep in my flock stuck in a bog yesterday," I am referring to a single sheep. If I say "Wolves killed three of my sheep last week," I am using the word with its plural meaning. The context of the sentence enables you to know this. But if I said "My sheep got tired walking up the hill," you could not be sure whether I intended the singular or plural meaning—that is, unless you knew from a previous sentence in the story that yesterday I took one of my sheep, which was sick, to the vet who lives just up the hill from me.

The grammar of a sentence might give you a clue about which meaning is intended. If I said "My sheep stands still," the form of the verb tells you that "sheep" is singular; otherwise I would say "stand," not "stands." And if I said "Those sheep ran away," you would know "sheep" is plural because "those" is a plural form. If only one sheep were meant, I would have said "*That* sheep."

From the Hebrew grammar, it is clear that the first *'ĕlōhîm* in Psalm 82:1 is singular. The verb translated "has taken" requires a singular subject. But the second *'ĕlōhîm* is plural since you cannot be in the midst of just one. The translators (correctly) capitalize the first occurrence, "God," which is singular, because when the meaning is singular, it is usually speaking about Yahweh, the God of Israel. But the translators (correctly) do not capitalize the second occurrence, which is plural, because when it is plural, it is usually referring to the gods of the pagan nations around Israel.

So if *'ĕlōhîm* means "god," and the Old Testament is talking about "gods" (plural), we immediately have a question about monotheism. Who are these "gods"? Some commentators try to argue that Psalm 82 is talking about human rulers who are being judged by God for unjust actions, but this does not work. These beings (gods) are compared to "men" in verses 6–7: "You are gods, sons of the Most High, all of you; nevertheless, like men you shall die." They are being threatened with death, that is, with being judged and given the fate that characterizes humanity, which is death. This will happen, it says, *as if* they were men. So they cannot be human rulers. Michael Heiser argues that they are sons of God and that "the sons of God are divine beings under the authority of the God of Israel."[1] Heiser interprets passages like Job 1–2 and Psalm 89:5–7 as revealing the existence of a divine council of *ʾĕlōhîm*, who assist God in ruling the universe and meet with him, the head of this council, to discuss issues and hear rulings from Yahweh.[2] Psalm 89 reads,

> Let the heavens praise your wonders, O LORD,
>   your faithfulness in the assembly of the holy ones!
> For who in the skies can be compared to the LORD?
>   Who among the heavenly beings [*bᵊnê ʾĕlōhîm*] is like the LORD,
> a God greatly to be feared in the council of the holy ones,
>   and awesome above all who are around him? (Ps. 89:5–7)

The English Standard Version translates *bᵊnê ʾĕlōhîm* in verse 6 as "heavenly beings," but it gives a footnote saying that the Hebrew can be translated "the sons of God" or "the sons of might." Here is one of those situations where no possible translation is perfect. If I tell you that this verse is talking about angels, you will probably not think that I am denying monotheism. But if I argue for the meaning "sons of God" or "gods," you may think that I am denying monotheism. I prefer the literal translation, "sons of God."[3] So who are these beings?

The divine council is made up of a number of hierarchically arranged spiritual entities that have ruling functions in the universe and so are not mere angels. Angels do exist, of course, but there are more beings in the unseen realm than just angels. Both the Hebrew word *malʾāk* and the Greek word ἄγγελος (*angelos*), from which we get the English word "angel," mean "messenger." Angels are lower-level functionaries with important roles, but they are not usually described as ruling or governing. Their name reflects their function, and we usually find them delivering messages and carrying out commissions for God. As we discussed in chapter 4 above, Paul in Ephesians 6:12 speaks of "rulers" (κυριότητες, *kyriotētes*), "authorities" (ἐξουσίαι, *exousiai*), "the cosmic powers over this present darkness" (κοσμοκράτορας τοῦ σκότους τούτου, *kosmokratoras tou skotous toutou*), and "the spiritual forces of evil in the heavenly places" (πνευματικὰ τῆς πονηρίας ἐν τοῖς ἐπουρανίοις, *pneumatika tēs ponērias en tois epouraniois*). These are in addition to "the

---

1. Heiser, *Unseen Realm*, 27.
2. Heiser, *Unseen Realm*, 29.
3. Because the ESV usually tries to be as literal as possible, I would have expected it to favor the translation "sons of God." However, it is a difficult phrase with many meanings, so it is a judgment call.

devil" (τοῦ διαβόλου, *tou diabolou*), to whom he refers in 6:11. Throughout the Bible, we see a range of terms, which are hard to systematize, used to refer to a variety of spiritual entities who exercise various kinds of functions, including carrying out commissions, delivering messages, fighting as part of the heavenly army, governing aspects of creation, and ruling in various ways. Biblical monotheism does not deny the existence of these beings, and they all are called *'ĕlōhîm* throughout the Old Testament.

Interestingly, Christian theology has typically used the term "angel" as an umbrella term for all of these entities that exist in the spiritual realm, both fallen and unfallen beings. The fallen angels usually tend to be called "demons," which again functions as a broad category. But the terminology of the Hebrew Bible does not correspond to this use of the words "angel" and "demon." In Hebrew, the word "demons" (*šēdîm*) is not used frequently and is not used of all fallen spiritual entities. It is, however, sometimes used when a particularly pejorative meaning is intended (e.g., Deut. 32:17; Ps. 106:37). But the pagan deities behind the idols used to represent them in paganism are often just referred to as *'ĕlōhîm* rather than *šēdîm*, which could indicate that while all *šēdîm* are fallen *'ĕlōhîm*, not all fallen *'ĕlōhîm* are *šēdîm*.[4] And we have already seen that Paul uses a variety of terms for ruling spiritual entities besides the term "angel," a word he also knows and uses (2 Cor. 11:14; Gal. 1:8; 4:14). Some or all of the ruling entities to which Paul refers are fallen; that is, they are in rebellion against God and threats to us. If Paul were to write in Hebrew, he would undoubtedly call them *'ĕlōhîm*, following Old Testament precedent.

Judging from the way it is employed in the Old Testament, the Hebrew word *'ĕlōhîm* appears to have a wide variety of possible meanings. Heiser has a fascinatingly diverse list of entities that are designated as *'ĕlōhîm* by the Hebrew Bible.[5] It is, of course, used of (1) Yahweh, the God of Israel, thousands of times. It is also used of (2) the members of Yahweh's council, as we saw in Psalms 82:1, 6–7 and 89:5–7. It is used for (3) the gods and goddesses of other nations in 1 Kings 11:33. It refers to (4) demons (*šēdîm*) in Deuteronomy 32:17. It is used for (5) the deceased Samuel conjured up by the witch of Endor in 1 Samuel 28:13. It is used (6) interchangeably with the angel of the LORD in Exodus 3:4. Apparently, from the perspective of the biblical writers, the word *'ĕlōhîm* can be used of any entity in the unseen realm, ranging from Yahweh himself down to demons and the spirits of dead humans in Sheol. All

---

4. I do not have time to discuss the convoluted question of the origin of the *šēdîm*. See Heiser, *Unseen Realm*, 33–34, 107, 280n7, 340nn9 and 10.

5. Heiser, *Unseen Realm*, 30.

of what we would think of fitting under the categories of angels and demons would fit within the semantic range of the word 'ĕlōhîm. Therefore, when a biblical writer uses the word 'ĕlōhîm, we must determine what is meant by examining the grammar and the context. All that we can presume from the use of the word itself is that it refers to rational beings who are part of the unseen spiritual realm and not living human beings. Obviously, the other 'ĕlōhîm are not on the same level as Yahweh, and they are not members of the same class as Yahweh merely by virtue of being in the category of spiritual beings. They have a wide variety of ranks from very high (next to Yahweh) to very low (shades in Sheol). Thus we are left with the counterintuitive conclusion that the existence of other 'ĕlōhîm is not a contradiction of biblical monotheism.

However, the Old Testament does go out of its way to assert the uniqueness of Yahweh. We should bear in mind that the word "unique" is an absolute, not a comparative. Despite the incorrect way this word is often used today, it does not mean "relatively different" or "quite different." To say that something is "relatively unique" is nonsense. It either is or is not unique, and many things can be very unusual without being utterly and completely one of a kind, which is what unique means. For example, the psalmist stresses the uniqueness of God when he says, "For you, O LORD, are most high over all the earth; you are exalted far above all gods ['ĕlōhîm]" (Ps. 97:9). Isaiah 40–48 is emphatic on this point.

> "You are my witnesses," declares the LORD,
> "and my servant whom I have chosen,
> that you may know and believe me
> and understand that I am he.
> Before me no god ['ēl] was formed,
> nor shall there be any after me.
> I, I am the LORD,
> and besides me there is no savior." (Isa. 43:10–11)

We also read in the next chapter,

> Thus says the LORD, the King of Israel
> and his Redeemer, the LORD of hosts:
> "I am the first and I am the last;
> besides me there is no god.
> Who is like me? Let him proclaim it.
> Let him declare and set it before me,
> since I appointed an ancient people.
> Let them declare what is to come, and what will happen." (Isa. 44:6–7)

Isaiah declares the uniqueness of Israel's God. So Yahweh is an *'ĕlōhîm*, but he is a unique *'ĕlōhîm*, the only one of his kind and different from all the rest. Now we are ready to consider the meaning of monotheism in the Old Testament.

The Meaning of Biblical Monotheism

What does biblical monotheism mean? I offer the following definition as a starting point.

> *Transcendent monotheism*: This is the view that God is the transcendent Creator of all things. We see this view in the Bible, beginning in the Old Testament and continuing in the New Testament. It is also the view of the Nicene fathers and the trinitarian classical theism of the Great Tradition. This view is compatible with the existence of many levels and kinds of spiritual beings in addition to the LORD; what they all have in common is that they were all created by the transcendent Creator God, who is Yahweh, the God of Israel.

So that we can be as clear as possible about what is and is not being said here, let me offer some related definitions.

> *Pantheistic monotheism without polytheism*: This is the view that there is only one God and this God is identical with the totality of all that exists. It can also be termed "philosophical monotheism." We see this view in the writings of Baruch Spinoza.
>
> *Pantheistic monotheism with polytheism*: This is the view that God is identical with all things but that certain forces of nature may be personified and regarded as gods. We see this view in Hinduism. We also see Augustine in *The City of God* criticizing some of the Platonist philosophers of his day for taking this position, as evidenced by their willingness to participate in the polytheistic paganism of their day, even though they professed a philosophical monotheism.[6]
>
> *Polytheism*: This is a view found in many areas of the world, in which there are many gods and even sometimes a "high god," but all reality is not identified with God in an abstract manner. However, in many mythological cultures, such as the ancient Near Eastern ones surrounding Israel, the human, nature, and the divine all connect and interact

6. Augustine, *City of God* 8.13 (I/6, 257–58).

with each other, which brings them close to pantheistic monotheism with polytheism.

Theistic personalism: This is the view that God is a person like us but different in degree. Many of the attributes of classical theism may be assigned to this type of God, but usually not simplicity, immutability, or impassibility. This view is like polytheism, but instead of a pantheon of gods, only one "high" God is worshiped, and only this one God is thought to exist. This view has made great inroads in modernity among evangelicals today.

Theistic mutualism: This is the view that God and the world coexist in a two-way relationship in which each affects the other for good or ill. This view is a type of post-Christian, neopaganism that is not the same as ancient mythological worldviews, but it shares one key point in common with them that makes it more like mythology than the biblical doctrine of God—namely, the rejection of transcendence. The soft version of this view, in which God sovereignly allows creation to cause change in him although he is not forced to do so, is increasingly popular among evangelical theologians, including conservative Reformed ones.

Elective monolatry: This is the view that there are many gods but that only one God is to be worshiped by our group. This is often held by polytheists who believe that their people or tribe should worship a certain god but that other tribes or nations should worship their own gods. This view was common in the Roman Empire of the New Testament period. It is really a subset of polytheism and not as close to ethical monolatry as the terminology might suggest.

Ethical monolatry: This is the view that there are many gods, but only one God is to be worshiped by anyone. This is the view of the Old Testament writings and of the Jews of the New Testament period. They held it to be morally wrong for anyone to worship any god but Yahweh, which of course made them seem extreme and arrogant to polytheists of all kinds. This view may be held without an accompanying belief in transcendent monotheism, but in that case, it lacks any solid theoretical foundation and can appear arbitrary.

In order to understand Isaiah 41–48 properly, we must see that ethical monolatry is compatible with transcendent monotheism, because pagan religions worship *'ĕlōhîm* who are not Yahweh and are not worthy of worship. In fact, transcendent monotheism provides an ontological basis for ethical monolatry. While it is true that ethical monolatry is incompatible with scientific materialism, so is transcendent monotheism. Isaiah's belief in a transcendent Creator rules out the possibility of any sort of pantheism, panentheism, theistic personalism, or theistic mutualism, because all of these doctrines view the divine as part of the cosmos rather than before and above the cosmos. It does not, however, rule out belief in many kinds of *'ĕlōhîm* in addition to Yahweh.

Isaiah 41–48 teaches that only Yahweh is to be worshiped, not because Yahweh is the only *'ĕlōhîm* that exists, but rather because Yahweh is the only *'ĕlōhîm* who is worthy of worship. As the transcendent Creator, he is unique, and only the transcendent Creator should be worshiped. The other *'ĕlōhîm*, at least the unfallen ones, may be respected in the way that accomplished human beings or occupants of high office should be respected with the honor that is rightfully due to their accomplishments or station. But worship is not to be directed toward creatures, no matter how high and lofty they may be in comparison to human beings. These conceptual clarifications highlight how Isaiah's polemic against idolatry is quite different from scientific materialism, which denies the existence of all gods, and also quite different from pantheistic monotheism without polytheism, which denies the existence of the gods while maintaining the essential deity of nature as a whole.

The force of the assertion in Deuteronomy 6:5 that "the Lord is one" is that the Lord is unique. He is the only member of a class of one; the Lord is not an instance of a class of beings differing from one another by degree. The Lord is simply one of a kind, unique. Biblical monotheism is thus the conviction that Yahweh is unique among the *'ĕlōhîm*, and he alone is worthy to be worshiped, because he alone is the transcendent Creator.

Isaiah's Polemic against Idolatry

Isaiah's polemic against idolatry is a major theme of the entire book of Isaiah, and some of the classic texts are found in the oracles contained in chapters 41–48. Isaiah 41:21–29 is one such passage. The chapter begins with a six-stanza poem (vv. 1–7), in which we read that Yahweh is the one "who stirred up one from the east" (v. 2), the first reference to Cyrus. The poem ends with a description of the nations responding to the rise and fall of empires by turning to idols; they are said to seek certainty by literally nailing their idols down (v. 7)! Verse 8 begins with an adversative: "But you, Israel, my servant, Jacob whom I have chosen," and the passage goes on to talk about how God chose the offspring of Abraham from the ends of the earth and fashioned them into a people. God makes his people to image him just as a craftsman makes an idol to image the god. The next section stresses that Israel should not fear because "the LORD your God" (*Yahweh 'Ĕlōhîm*) will help them.

> Fear not, you worm Jacob,
> > you men of Israel!
> I am the one who helps you, declares the LORD;
> > your Redeemer is the Holy One of Israel. (Isa. 41:14)

The emphasis is on the power of the LORD to sustain and strengthen amid historical upheavals, in contrast to the powerlessness of the idols. The section from verses 17–20 contains echoes of the LORD's provision of water in the desert for the children of Israel after the exodus, and once again creation language is joined to exodus language:

> I will put in the wilderness the cedar,
> > the acacia, the myrtle, and the olive.
> I will set in the desert the cypress,
> > the plane and the pine together,
> that they may see and know,
> > may consider and understand together,
> that the hand of the LORD has done this,
> > the Holy One of Israel has created it. (Isa. 41:19–20)

This brings us to the section on the futility of idols (41:21–29).

The LORD is the speaker in this entire section, and he draws a stark contrast between himself and the gods represented by idols.

> Set forth your case, says the LORD;
> > bring your proofs, says the King of Jacob.
> Let them bring them, and tell us
> > what is to happen.
> Tell us the former things, what they are,
> > that we may consider them,
> that we may know their outcome;
> > or declare to us the things to come.
> Tell us what is to come hereafter,
> > that we may know that you are gods;
> do good, or do harm,
> > that we may be dismayed and terrified.
> Behold, you are nothing,
> > and your work is less than nothing;
> > an abomination is he who chooses you. (Isa. 41:21–24)

Here the LORD challenges the gods to make a case for why they should be worshiped. Isaiah is saying that the LORD is speaking through him and saying that the people of Israel are not being rational in being tempted to worship other gods. Remember that throughout Isaiah's prophetic ministry, from 740 through 680 BC, there was no letup in the continuous idolatry in Israel; not even Hezekiah's best efforts could suffice to eradicate it. In fact, with the rise of Manasseh toward the end of Isaiah's life, it appeared that things were set to degenerate even further.

In verse 21 the LORD challenges the gods to set forth their case and bring their proofs. The proofs of their worthiness to be worshiped include telling the former things and the things to come. The former things would include the origin of the cosmos; where did we all come from? In Genesis, biblical revelation declares these things, but the ancient Near Eastern myths of the nations around Israel never explain the true origins of the world. The gods provide self-glorifying narratives about how they are responsible for the stability of the current order, but they do not say whence the original chaos came. They also cannot tell the future, and this is not just a statement about the idols themselves but also about the spiritual beings that the idols represent. The gods do not know the future; only Yahweh does. Only the transcendent Creator knows the past and the future.

In verses 25–29 we read,

> I stirred up one from the north, and he has come,
>> from the rising of the sun, and he shall call upon my name;
> he shall trample on rulers as on mortar,
>> as the potter treads clay.
> Who declared it from the beginning, that we might know,
>> and beforehand, that we might say, "He is right"?
> There was none who declared it, none who proclaimed,
>> none who heard your words.
> I was the first to say to Zion, "Behold, here they are!"
>> and I give to Jerusalem a herald of good news.
> But when I look, there is no one;
>> among these there is no counselor
>> who, when I ask, gives an answer.
> Behold, they are all a delusion;
>> their works are nothing;
>> their metal images are empty wind. (Isa. 41:25–29)

In contrast to the gods, the LORD has acted in history by raising up Cyrus to deliver the people from exile. Of course, this has not happened yet; this is an example of "the prophetic perfect":[7] the prophets' tendency to write oracles in the past tense to emphasize the certainty of what will happen in the future. It is as certain as if it has already happened. This oracle is intended to preserve the knowledge in Israel so that when the deliverance comes, everyone will understand that this is no fluke or coincidence but the predicted act of the sovereign Lord of history guiding events along according to his timetable and in accordance with his plan. In contrast, the supposedly triumphant gods of the nations may enjoy a victory for a short time, but they did not predict it, and they cannot control the LORD's reversal of it.

When Isaiah 41:29 says "They are all a delusion," we should not be too quick to interpret this from within a set of modern antisupernaturalist metaphysical assumptions. The verse is not saying that the gods do not exist; it is saying that they are useless when it comes to doing the things only Yahweh can do. They do not know the origin of the cosmos because they did not exist when Yahweh spoke it (including them) into existence. And they do not know the future because they are limited creatures, unlike Yahweh, who is omniscient. We need not deny the existence of such limited, weak creatures in order to secure Yahweh's glory. Neither is the existence of humans required in order for Yahweh to be considered God. The mocking tone of the oracle often escapes the modern reader; Yahweh through his prophet is putting the gods in their place. They prance around, preening and pretending to be wise in front of the human beings whom they can dominate and strike with fear. They are like bullies who panic when the big brother shows up and intimidates them. As long as they are talking to humans, they sound tough, but when Yahweh shows up, their weakness is apparent, and their pathetic bragging no longer seems intimidating. That is the tone of these oracles. The exiles should feel comforted, not because the gods of Babylon do not exist, but rather because compared to the transcendent Creator, such gods are mere creatures and con artists pretending to be something they are not. The nature of the delusion is their claim to be greater than Yahweh and worthy of worship. They are deluded, and so are their pagan followers; the children of Yahweh should know better, and this is the truth of which the prophet is reminding them.

The next passage we need to examine is the declaration of the uniqueness of the LORD found in chapter 43. There we read as follows:

7. Commenting on Isaiah 9:2, Oswalt (*Book of Isaiah: Chapters 1–39*, 242) notes that this is an example of a "prophetic perfect." Motyer (*Prophecy of Isaiah*, 98) comments on Isaiah 9:1–7 as follows: "For it belonged to the prophetic consciousness of men like Isaiah to cast themselves forward in time and then look back on the mighty acts of God, saying to us: 'Look forward to it, it is certain, he has already done it!'" Motyer (*Prophecy of Isaiah*, 317) refers to Isaiah 41:25 as a "perfect of certainty."

> "You are my witnesses," declares the LORD,
>   "and my servant whom I have chosen,
> that you may know and believe me
>   and understand that I am he.
> Before me no god was formed,
>   nor shall there be any after me.
> I, I am the LORD,
>   and besides me there is no savior.
> I declared and saved and proclaimed,
>   when there was no strange god among you;
>   and you are my witnesses," declares the LORD, "and I am God.
> Also henceforth I am he;
>   there is none who can deliver from my hand;
>   I work, and who can turn it back?" (Isa. 43:10–13)

Here the LORD says that no god was formed before him, which seems to refer to his role as Creator as depicted in Genesis: "In the beginning God created the heavens and the earth" (Gen. 1:1). Also, no god could ever come into existence that would be like him because Yahweh includes existence as part of his essence: "I AM" (Exod. 3:14). In Isaiah 43:12, Yahweh says "I declared," "I saved," and "I proclaimed." Again, the emphasis is on how Yahweh speaks and acts in history. Israel is called as a witness, for the people who are descended from Abraham witnessed the action of Yahweh firsthand and heard him speak. They know that he is the one true God. And because of all this, we can be confident that no one can foil his purposes in history: "I work, and who can turn it back?" (43:13).

These four verses are at the heart of this chapter of twenty-eight verses, and they are framed by yet more creation language and more exodus language. At the beginning of Isaiah 43, the LORD draws attention again to the fact that he created Israel. In fact, he created Israel twice over. He created Israel in that he created the entirety of the world, including Israel, but he also created Israel as a nation by delivering them from slavery in Egypt, or as he puts it in verse 3: "I give Egypt as your ransom, Cush and Seba in exchange for you. Because you are precious in my eyes, and honored, and I love you" (Isa. 43:3–4a). Then later in the chapter we see more of the new exodus language:

> Thus says the LORD,
>   who makes a way in the sea,
>   a path in the mighty waters,
> who brings forth chariot and horse,
>   army and warrior;

> they lie down, they cannot rise,
>   they are extinguished, quenched like a wick. (Isa. 43:16–17)

But then, surprisingly, he says, "Remember not the former things, nor consider the things of old" (Isa. 43:18). Why not remember the exodus? Because something greater than the exodus is going to occur.

> Behold I am doing a new thing;
>   now it springs forth, do you not perceive it?
> I will make a way in the wilderness
>   and rivers in the desert. (Isa. 43:19)

The LORD is going to deliver his people again, and it will be an even greater thing than the original exodus. It will involve blotting out their transgressions and remembering their sins no more (43:25). There is just a hint here of the greater deliverance through the greater servant, Christ (chaps. 49–53), which will come after and through the lesser deliverance through the lesser servant, Cyrus (chaps. 41–48). Israel is the object of the LORD's attention and the recipient of his revelation. Therefore, Israel is uniquely positioned, called, and commissioned to be a witness to the uniqueness of the LORD.

In chapter 44 we come to the high point of the section, and we find two themes juxtaposed in this chapter: the folly of idolatry and the ability of the LORD to save his people by acting sovereignly in history. The chapter unfolds as follows: in verses 1–8 the LORD declares his intention to redeem his people; in verses 9–20 we have a section on the folly of the idolater; verses 21–23 return to the theme of the first five verses, namely, the redemption of Israel; in verses 24–28 we have the poem describing the LORD as the redeemer, culminating in the revelation of the name of Cyrus. So we have four main sections: the first and third sections focus on the promise of redemption first announced in chapter 40, the second section declares the folly of trusting in the idol gods, and the fourth section focuses on the nature of the LORD, the God of Israel, the redeemer of his people. The section thus contrasts Yahweh with the gods of the nations, and the difference between them is night and day. Although the people of Judah will go into captivity in Babylon, they will be redeemed by the mighty hand of the LORD; in this mighty act of God in history, the vast incalculable difference between Yahweh and the false gods of the pagan empires will be revealed clearly for all who are able to see—that is, for those who observe these events after having been prepared to understand them by the prophetic word. The difference between Yahweh and the false gods is that he saves and redeems his people, while they are helpless to prevent him from doing so. Their conquest of Jerusalem and enslavement of the people of Judah are revealed to be something permitted by Yahweh for his purpose and not a sign of their victory over him. They are his instruments, and to worship them is foolish, for Yahweh controls history.

I do not have space here to comment on every verse in this rich and powerful chapter, but I must point out the contrast drawn between the idols (44:9–20) and the LORD (44:24–28). The original readers of Isaiah 44:9–20 would have recognized that the pagans do not really consider the wooden and metal idols to be the actual gods they worship. Throughout the ancient Near East, idols were ubiquitous and were universally considered to be images of the gods. The actual gods were spiritual entities who could assume bodily form but did not dwell in their temples all the time. The idol was there to image the god and remind the worshiper of the god's appearance. The worship offered (e.g., sacrifices) was not offered so much to the idol as through the idol to the god.

When modern readers read Isaiah 44:9–20, it is easy to read it from a materialistic worldview and assume that the prophet is saying "How stupid they are to think that the idols are real gods when we all know that they are just wood and metal." The problem is that this interpretation is half right and half wrong. It is right in that we correctly read the prophet as mocking the pagan idol maker as stupid and self-deceived and as worshiping a lie. But if we think that the reason the pagan is stupid is that everyone knows there is no such thing as a real "god," we impose modern antisupernaturalist presuppositions on the text and misinterpret what it means. The prophet and his Jewish readers of the seventh century BC would have been thinking something similar but not identical. They would have agreed with the pagan that the god was a real spiritual entity who was merely imaged or represented by the idol. But they would also have believed that the god was a mere creature of Yahweh with certain powers appropriate to his level of ability as created, but in the end the god is just a creature. The god is just as much a creature as the piece of wood is! This is what makes the worship of the pagan gods pathetic and stupid. To worship these fallen angels, these spiritual entities posing as true gods, is to worship the creature rather than the Creator, and that is ridiculous. It is, in fact, just as ridiculous as worshiping a piece of wood. In 44:17, when the pagan prays to the idol, anyone reading this story in its original cultural context would understand that Isaiah is taunting the pagan by deliberately distorting what he is doing; the pagan is really praying to the god *through* the idol. Yet what we have here is a disagreement about the worthiness of the god, and from Isaiah's perspective, it makes no difference whether you are praying to wood or to the kind of god who can be imaged by wood; one is as bad as the other. In both cases, you are praying to a created thing, and that is stupid. Isaiah is not trying to make good little materialists out of his readers; rather, he is trying to convince them that Yahweh is different from the gods, and therefore it is not stupid for them to put their trust in Yahweh. Yahweh is not like the idols or the entities they represent.

In the Ten Commandments, the first two commandments are related but distinct from each other (Exod. 20; Deut. 5). First, Israel is commanded to have no other gods before the LORD. This is a matter of *who* is worshiped. Second, Israel is commanded not to make any graven image. This is a matter of *how* to worship. The point is that worshiping false gods is worshiping creatures that may be imaged by material idols. Israel is to worship the Creator, who cannot be imaged by any created thing. The closest to an image of the one, true, and living God that exists among created things is the human being. As living, rational creatures, we were made to image our Creator, and this makes the human being unique in all creation. Therefore, to make an idol in the shape of a bull or snake or goat is an abomination. And to worship using such a thing is an abomination. But although the idol itself is bad, what it represents is also problematic. Israel is forbidden to worship the spiritual beings who inhabit the unseen realm and who may inspire awe in humans but are nevertheless merely creatures like them and not like the transcendent Creator.

In the poem of Yahweh's transcendence, this contrast between Yahweh and the idol gods is highlighted. Isaiah 44:9–20 describes the idol gods, and verses 24–28 describe Yahweh. I analyzed this poem in chapter 5 above, so I will restrict my comments here to pointing out a few comparisons to the idol gods. We saw that the poem has nine lines, each beginning with the relative pronoun "who" and each describing the nature of Yahweh, who is identified at the beginning of the poem as "your Redeemer." In the first three lines, we see the theme of the LORD as the creator of the heavens and the earth. In the last three lines, we see the theme of the LORD as the redeemer who engineers a new exodus, enabling his people to return to the city of Jerusalem to rebuild the temple. In the middle three lines, we see the theme of the LORD making fools out of the wise men and diviners of the pagan nations by confirming the word of his messengers, the prophets. To a degree that might make the modern liberal Christian quite uncomfortable, the prophet here makes the contrast between the LORD and the idol gods depend completely on the ability of the LORD to act in history and fulfill the predictions he has made through his prophet. The biblical God is different from the pagan gods, not in that he exists and they do not, but rather in that he speaks and acts in history and they do not, because they lack his power and his knowledge of the future. In short, he is the sovereign, transcendent Creator, and they are just creatures.

In Isaiah 45 the LORD elaborates on how he plans to use Cyrus as his instrument (vv. 1–3) to benefit his people (v. 4). Again he says, "I am the LORD, and there is no other, besides me there is no God" (v. 5). The futility of the idols and their inability to save is stressed (vv. 15–16), and the ability of the LORD to save is stressed (v. 17). The identity of the LORD as Creator is reiterated (v. 18). The theme of there being no God like the LORD is sounded once again:

> Assemble yourselves and come;
>> draw near together,
>> you survivors of the nations!
> They have no knowledge
>> who carry about their wooden idols,
> and keep on praying to a god
>> that cannot save.
> Declare and present your case;
>> let them take counsel together!
> Who told this long ago?
>> Who declared it of old?
> Was it not I, the LORD?
>> And there is no other god besides me,
> a righteous God and a Savior;
>> there is none besides me.
>
> Turn to me and be saved,
>> all the ends of the earth!
>> For I am God, and there is no other. (Isa. 45:20–22)

Once again we see the theme that the LORD is the one true God because he alone tells the future. He is no mere wooden idol but a living savior. This passage ends with an altar call worthy of a Billy Graham crusade: "Turn to me and be saved, all the ends of the earth!" Why should all people of earth turn to him? Because he is God (El) and there is no other. Here we can see the foundations being laid for the fulfillment of the promises to Abraham, in which the LORD promises that the whole earth will be blessed through the seed of Abraham (Gen. 12:1–3).

The next two chapters (Isa. 46–47) continue with the same themes but focus on Babylon and its gods. In the ancient Near Eastern culture, the gods of each nation were closely identified with the king and military power of the nation. The basic idea was that each nation "belonged to" its god or gods. Originally the gods had organized and ruled the nations directly and openly, receiving worship themselves from humans. But in later days they "handed down kingship" to designated human rulers and faded into the background, letting themselves be represented by idols. This increased the sense of awe and mystery surrounding their being and allowed them to manipulate matters from behind the curtain, so to speak. Modern people have a hard time thinking their way into empathy for such a worldview, but we should practice doing so, because the same mentality exists in the New Testament and in the church fathers. Augustine's *City of God*, especially the first ten books refuting paganism, is a relatively late expression of a worldview that runs continuously from before the first books of the Old Testament were written up to the beginning of the modern period. In this worldview, the gods of the nations are real, and the affairs of peoples and nations are affected by the spiritual realm that in various ways overlaps with the visible world of politics and armies.

In Isaiah 46, we see a brutal attack on Bel and Nebo, the chief gods of Babylon. Bel was originally the god of the city of Nippur but was later understood to be an expression of Marduk, and Nebo was his son. The chief rhetorical strategy of the chapter revolves around the contrast between the Babylonians having to carry their gods around in their religious ceremonies, on the one hand, and the fact that Yahweh has carried Israel and taken its people from slavery in Egypt. The whole literary strategy is one of role reversal. Bel and Nebo go into captivity (v. 2) while Israel is saved out of their clutches.

The center of the chapter is verse 5:

> To whom will you liken me and make me equal,
>   and compare me, that we may be alike?

The Lord is the living God, who is all-powerful and active and speaking in history, whereas the idols are limp, useless, and need to be carried around by their human subjects. Repeated for emphasis is the theme that God's ability to predict the future is what makes him superior to the pagan gods:

> Remember this and stand firm,
>   recall it to mind, you transgressors,
>   remember the former things of old;
> for I am God, and there is no other;
>   I am God, and there is none like me,
> declaring the end from the beginning
>   and from ancient times things not yet done,
> saying, "My counsel shall stand,
>   and I will accomplish all my purpose,"

> calling a bird of prey from the east,
>   the man of my counsel from a far country.
> I have spoken, and I will bring it to pass;
>   I have purposed, and I will do it. (Isa. 46:8–11)

The reader may wonder why there is so much repetition in these chapters, but we should bear a couple of points in mind. First, this is a collection of oracles that may have been written at different times and never delivered orally, or oracles that were first delivered orally and later written down and collected. Second, we are meant to ask why something is so important that it must be repeated so many times. What we have in the book of Isaiah in general is a collection of oracles arranged by topic and theme—arranged either by Isaiah or by a close associate who functioned as editor, or perhaps some of each, with the disciple/editor putting the finishing touches on the work as a whole. This section, Isaiah 40–48, has a definite theme and presents a series of coherent thoughts about God, but it consists of occasional pieces put together thematically and in some cases chronologically. It is more like the *Norton Anthology of English Literature* than Stephen Charnock's *The Existence and Attributes of God*. But this does not mean that there is no sustained, coherent theological message; it just means that we must read it, aware of what it is, and not expect it to be something else.

The theme is God as the transcendent Creator and sovereign Lord of history, the one who alone is to be worshiped; this theme has three interconnected and interdependent thoughts joined to form a portrayal of the nature of Israel's God. Poetic presentation of God's nature is a highly appropriate form for biblical revelation to take because poetry is a highly precise use of language that fosters a sense of mystery even as it reveals. Poetic language pushes language to the limit of its ability to convey a sense of who and what God is and implies more than it states. This is necessary because human language about God is always analogical, which means that it makes comparisons in which there are some points of similarity and yet always more points of dissimilarity. I believe that the concept of analogy—used without a great deal of theoretical discussion by the fourth-century Nicene fathers, developed precisely by Thomas Aquinas, and then utilized by both Roman Catholic and Protestant scholastics—has its roots in the poetry of the Old Testament, particularly the Psalter and Isaiah.

If it is true that the roots of the use of analogical language in theology are in Isaiah, and if the essence of analogy is comparison between two things that are both alike in some way and unalike in other ways, then we should contemplate that one of the most sustained and important comparisons in

Isaiah 40–48 is between Yahweh and the gods of the pagan empires. The goal in analogical thinking is to establish a valid point of comparison between some aspect of creation and the Creator in order to say something true about God. The only way humans can talk about God is by utilizing analogies from our human experience of creation; we have no other means to talk about God. We know that all human or creaturely ways of describing God must inevitably fall short of conveying what God is, yet the only alternative is silence, and silence would be the only proper way to proceed except for the miracle of inspiration, by which prophets were moved (carried along) by the Holy Spirit to speak the words God wanted spoken (2 Pet. 1:21).

As we contemplate the idea of the prophet making an analogy between the gods of the nations and the God of Israel, we see that certain aspects of pagan religion are good and true. This might seem like a surprising conclusion, but it follows logically. (It also means that our secular materialism hinders our ability to perceive spiritual truth, but surely we know that by this point!) One right aspect of pagan religion is the sense of dependence that humans have on a power that is higher than us. It is noteworthy that even in this post-Enlightenment, so-called secular age the first step in the Twelve-Step program of Alcoholics Anonymous is the recognition of a higher power on whose help we depend. Contemporary secular humanism advocates personal autonomy and individual will, but humans are social creatures with many limitations. To depend on ourselves is a recipe for despair. Religious faith is natural and good for humans.

The question we all must answer, however, is in whom or what should our faith be placed? Isaiah is addressing that question. When a nation in the ancient Near East fell in war to a stronger nation, the assumption was that the victorious nation's god(s) had triumphed over the losing nation's god(s). If the people of Israel came to the conclusion that the destruction of Jerusalem implied the defeat of Yahweh, then they could be plunged into despair and nihilism, or they could be converted to the worship of the supposedly victorious gods of Babylon. In chapter 46 Isaiah is trying to head off both possibilities by comparing the gods of Babylon with the God of Israel. He wants to stress the inadequacy of the gods of Babylon, and his rhetorical weapon of choice is mockery and scorn, coupled with an argument from the mighty acts of the LORD in Israel's past and his prediction of the LORD's future mighty acts. Isaiah is assuming one key feature that the false gods of Babylon and the God of Israel have in common: both are possible objects of faith for the people of Israel, but only one is sufficient to redeem and save.

Isaiah 47 follows with a prediction of the coming humiliation of Babylon. The pride of Babylon was legendary in the ancient world. In fact,

Babylon was more than a mere city; Babylon was a symbol of human pride and of the rebellion of pagan gods against Yahweh. In chapter 47, notice the stress on enchantments and sorceries (vv. 9, 12) and astrology (v. 13). Pagan religion, military ambition, and political domination were all bound up together in Babylon. Later in Scripture, Babylon appears in this symbolic role as a way of speaking of the world system organized in opposition to God (Rev. 18). Here in Isaiah 47, God speaks directly to the Babylonians and says that he allowed them to conquer his people only because he was angry with them for their sins (vv. 5–7). Babylon represents anti-God forces that always like to attack God's people, and in this one instance God withheld his protection from his people. But that does not excuse Babylon for its cruelty in taking the people of Judah into captivity after destroying Jerusalem and the temple. So God pronounces judgment on Babylon (47:8–15).

Isaiah 48 reviews the main themes of this section (chaps. 41–48) and explains clearly why this prophecy is being given through the prophet in advance of the events it describes.

> The former things I declared of old;
> > they went out from my mouth, and I announced them;
> > then suddenly I did them, and they came to pass.
> Because I know that you are obstinate,
> > and your neck is an iron sinew
> > and your forehead brass,
> I declared them to you from of old,
> > before they came to pass I announced them to you,
> lest you should say, "My idol did them,
> > my carved image and my metal image commanded them."
> > (Isa. 48:3–5)

Because God has predicted the exile through the mouth of his prophet a century in advance, the people can know that he is the one true God. In this chapter, the message of chapter 40 is reiterated:

> Go out from Babylon, flee from Chaldea,
> > declare this with a shout of joy, proclaim it,
> send it out to the end of the earth;
> > say, "The LORD has redeemed his servant Jacob!" (Isa. 48:20)

The upshot of all the talk of Yahweh's superiority to the gods of Babylon is that the exiles should therefore get out of there and come home!

The God of Judgment and Grace and the Shape of the Canon

As we bring this chapter to a close, we should discuss an issue we have touched on in previous chapters, but it requires further elaboration at this point. Based on the biblical monotheism we see in Isaiah 40–48, the polemic against idolatry displays both the wrath of God revealed against all false worship and the grace of God in preserving the believing remnant so that his promises to Abraham and David might be fulfilled. The nature of God determines the deepest structure of Scripture, and what we see in microcosm in Isaiah 40–48, we see in the macrocosm of the Bible as a whole. Allow me to explain.

In chapter 3, we considered the historical-critical restructuring of Israel's history in order to determine the Old Testament context in which Isaiah 40–48 should be interpreted. We concluded that it is important and right to take the ancient Near Eastern cultural context into account when interpreting texts of Scripture, but it is not necessary to do so by assuming an evolutionary metaphysics and viewing Israel's religion as evolving from polytheism to monotheism, as scholars such as Mark S. Smith do. Instead, I used the work of John Oswalt and John Currid to develop an approach that views the Old Testament as revealed polemical correction of pagan religious ideas. I also suggested that by adopting philosophical naturalism—including the concept of the cosmos as an eternal, self-existent, living organism with the power of self-motion—Western modernity was rejecting the doctrine of a transcendent Creator and regressing into the mythological worldview of the ancient Near East. Given that no idea is dearer to the hearts of modernity's children than that of progress, this is an ironic and astonishing conclusion. What I am saying is that the idea of progress is dead in post-Christian late modernity (that is, in so-called postmodernity). This is not a popular message today, but it is true.

Now that we have worked our way through Isaiah 40–48, we can see that that the message of these chapters is a call to believe in the transcendent Creator, who is the sovereign Lord of history and the one who alone is worthy to be worshiped. We can see that Isaiah has mustered every rhetorical weapon in his arsenal to fight against the mythological worldview of the ancient Near East, in which the gods of the pagan empires draw worship to themselves in every possible way they can. In Isaiah 6, the prophet is given access to the divine council and overhears the divine plan to allow his people to be punished by the destruction of Jerusalem and exile. He is not commissioned to preach to Israel for the purpose of giving time to repent, for that time is already past. Instead, he is commissioned to preach to those who are destined for exile so that when the events actually occur, the people will understand what is happening and why it is happening. The goal is that the people of Israel will comprehend that the pagan gods have not triumphed over Yahweh and that Yahweh has not permanently abandoned his people but will keep his eternal covenant made with Abraham and David. Even though the Mosaic covenant ends in unfaithfulness and in the land spewing them out, God will still ensure that blessing comes to the nations through the descendants of Abraham and by means of a Davidic king. This is Isaiah's message, and at the heart of this message is his argument that we can believe all these wonderful things despite the agony and suffering of the exile because of who and what God is. The nature of the LORD is the basis for our hope. This is what Isaiah 40–48 is all about.

In chapter 3 above, we investigated what a theological interpretation of Isaiah would look like. I believe that the basic canonical shape of the Old Testament—Pentateuch, Prophets, Psalms—is divinely inspired and based on the nature of the holy God who redeems his people. I do not think that the difference between the so-called Jewish canon and the so-called Christian canon is of fundamental importance on this issue. In Luke 24:44 Jesus speaks of the Law of Moses, the Prophets, and the Psalms. Christians have historically preferred the Old Testament to end with the Prophets so that the essentially unfinished character of the collection is stressed. But if the canon ends with the Writings, at the head of which is the Psalter, I don't believe this means that the essentially unfinished character of the Old Testament is denied, given the messianic, eschatological, and prophetic character of the Psalter. The bigger issue is that the Law comes first and the Prophets second. The sequence is law followed by gospel, judgment followed by salvation, holiness followed by grace. The prophets speak to Israel about the failure of the law, and their message culminates in the hope of a messianic king who will bring the kingdom of God to earth. This messianic hope is at the heart of the Psalter and can be discerned throughout the Writings as well. When understood messianically, Chronicles points forward to the messiah as surely as the Psalter does, so having the Old Testament end with Chronicles (as the Jewish canon does) rather than Malachi is equally a messianic ending.

However, if the historical-critical inversion of the Prophets and the Law of Moses is allowed to stand, then both the Jewish and the Christian canons are fundamentally altered. The meaning of the Prophets changes drastically, and their charging Israel with unfaithfulness to the covenant becomes un-historical. It basically inverts the law and gospel sequence to gospel first, with law seen as a decline from gospel. The triumph of the historical-critical method in Germany in the nineteenth century led to two great heresies in twentieth-century theology. First, the Law was viewed as a decline from the higher ethical religion of the Prophets. Higher criticism tended to lionize the social-justice emphasis of the Prophets and, in a way very unlike Psalm 19, viewed the laws on holiness as legalism. Second, it led to a downgrading of the Old Testament in general as less than Christian, which was a factor that weakened the church's resistance to Nazism and anti-Semitism. Overall, we can see a Gnostic tendency to liberate Christian theology from history and turn it into a culture religion of the post-Christian Western elites. It seems strange that something called "the historical method" would lead to detaching religion from history, but the inversion of the Law-Prophets sequence advocated by historical-critical scholarship in the nineteenth and twentieth centuries did just that.

The traditional canonical orderings—both Jewish and Christian—are designed to induce the reader to read the sacred writings in a certain order. First the Law of Moses is read, which ends with the warnings of Deuteronomy against apostasy. Then the Former Prophets document the failure of the people of Israel to keep the Law and remain loyal to the covenant. The Latter Prophets then predict the coming exile and offer the messianic hope beyond exile. The present shape of the Psalter is prophetic, messianic, and eschatological. The other Writings fit into the overall canon in several different ways without disturbing the fundamental sequence of Law and prophecy, which includes both condemnation and hope of redemption.

The sequence of law and gospel is fundamental to the New Testament as well as to the Old Testament and grows out of the understanding of the Old Testament presented here. If the problem of sin is obscured, the message of grace is likewise obscured. The biblical canon's shape means that we have not obeyed God's command, and therefore God must do something by his grace to ensure that obedience is rendered, atonement is made, and redemption is accomplished. This is the meaning of the gospel. It is also the message of the book of Isaiah. The historical-critical inversion of the Law and Prophets disturbs the fundamental theological meaning of the Hebrew Bible/Old Testament and therefore must be rejected. Also, the destruction of the unity of the book of Isaiah destroys the message of the book, which takes great pains to wrestle, as energetically as any piece of literature ever written, with the problem of God's holy nature and God's relationship to sinful human beings, the problem of the Holy One of Israel.

If my argument in chapter 3 above is correct—that modernity is reverting to a mythological worldview—then it should come as no surprise that evolutionary metaphysics causes a change in the doctrine of God from God as transcendent Creator to various types of pantheism and theistic personalism. What we are witnessing today, therefore, is actually the post-Christian West choosing the pagan gods of nature worship and polytheism over the transcendent Creator, the LORD, the God of Israel. These gods are not holy, nor are they creators. The roots of trinitarian classical theism are found in Isaiah 40–48, in the book of Isaiah generally, in the Old Testament, and in the full canon of Scripture as a two-Testament book, with Jesus Christ as its leading theme. In the next chapter, we turn to the patristic age and the crucial fourth century to see just how clearly the ancient Nicene doctrine of God followed the pattern of "sound words" (2 Tim. 1:13) found in Scripture.

Part Three

Trinitarian Classical Theism in History

The Biblical Character of
Pro-Nicene Theology

No theory of the development of doctrine which attempts to save
the classical doctrines without accounting for the unanimous conviction of the Christian tradition that they are the teaching of
Scripture can overcome the marginalization of the doctrines which
is so evident in the contemporary western church and theology.

David S. Yeago[1]

A central purpose of this book is to argue that the classically orthodox doctrine of God, which the church has believed and taught for over 1,500 years,
is the true teaching of Holy Scripture. In chapters 3–6, we saw that the Bible
reveals the transcendent Creator, who is the sovereign Lord of history and
the One who alone is to be worshiped. In this chapter, we compare the biblical teaching of Isaiah 40–48 with the trinitarian classical theism of the Great
Tradition to show that the roots of classical orthodoxy are in fact biblical.

The classically orthodox doctrine of God crystalized in the fourth century
with the Niceno-Constantinopolitan Creed of AD 381. We usually associate
this creed with the doctrine of the Trinity, but it is actually the doctrine of the
Trinity stated in the context of the classical theist understanding of God. One
of my concerns in this book is to show that the doctrine of the Trinity cannot
be extricated from classical theism without falling back into mythological

1. Yeago, "New Testament and the Nicene Dogma," 153.

thinking. The specific goal of this chapter is to show that the pro-Nicene theology of the fourth century is deeply rooted in the biblical understanding of God that we examined in part 2. To put it more simply, the goal is to show the biblical character of fourth-century pro-Nicene theology.

We saw that Isaiah 40–48 contains an extended argument for why the exiles should put their trust in Yahweh's promise given through his prophet that the exile is not the end of God's promises to Abraham and David. The prophet portrays God as able to keep his promises because of who he is, and his nature is summarized in the themes of transcendence, sovereignty, and monotheism. The nature of God is the basis for the hope of the exiles that salvation will ultimately come through judgment, rather than judgment being the final word. In this chapter, I will discuss how patristic theology treats these three key themes in Isaianic theology: divine transcendence, divine sovereignty over history, and divine uniqueness as the only one worthy of worship. My purpose is to show that fourth-century, pro-Nicene theology is deeply and profoundly Isaianic, both structurally and materially. In other words, it is biblical.

In pursuit of this goal, I will employ three strategies. First, I will highlight a tradition stretching from Moses and Isaiah to the New Testament apostles and on to the fourth-century fathers, all of them participating in one extended conversation based on certain shared convictions. Second, I want to show that the Arian controversy was primarily an exegetical debate rather than a matter of importing Greek metaphysical ideas into Christian theology. Third, I want to identify some major similarities between the way in which the fathers engaged their culture and the way in which the biblical writers engaged their cultural situation. Each of these three strategies will come to the fore at various points throughout the chapter, but the chapter will be structured around the three divine characteristics mentioned above: transcendence, sovereignty, and monotheism. I will relate fourth-century, pro-Nicene theology to each of the themes discussed above in chapters 4, 5, and 6. But before turning to the theme of divine transcendence in the fourth century, I need to make some preliminary comments about the early church fathers and Greek philosophy.

Greek Philosophy in the New Testament and the Church Fathers

My goal in this chapter is to show that the early church fathers went about doing theology in much the same way the New Testament apostles did theology. So how did the fathers do theology? They exegeted biblical texts, formulated doctrines based on these exegetical results, deduced metaphysical implications from those doctrines, and then used the metaphysical ideas as their philosophical framework for doing further exegesis. Along the way, the metaphysical implications of biblical doctrines led them to critique and correct ideas in their surrounding culture, thus making them suitable for use in Christian theology. As Robert Louis Wilken puts it,

> One observes again and again that Christian thinking, while working within patterns of thought and conceptions rooted in Greco-Roman culture, transformed them so profoundly that in the end something quite new came into being.[2]

One major difference between the cultural situation of the fourth-century fathers and that of the biblical writers was the existence in the patristic era of Greek philosophical schools such as Epicureanism, Stoicism, and Platonism, which made truth claims unlike the ones found in ancient Near Eastern and Greco-Roman mythological writers. Whereas the Old Testament writers had to deal only with mythology, the New Testament writers and the fathers had to deal with both mythology and metaphysics. The church fathers found some things to admire and some things to correct in Greek philosophy, but they did *not* seek to integrate biblical patterns of thought into larger frameworks defined by the philosophers. That is what modern revisionist theologians do in the liberal project. The early church fathers were engaged in a project that is superficially similar but actually quite different. Just as theologians do today, they engaged their culture, but they were interested in integrating the valid bits and pieces from that culture into an essentially biblical framework instead of trying to salvage what they could from the Bible and fitting it into an alien metaphysics.

The fathers were doing something more akin to what we observed the authors of the Old Testament writings doing. The fathers were determined to integrate what was salvageable from Greek philosophy into a Christian worldview built on the basis of biblical exegesis because they wanted to assimilate all human culture into a biblical framework, which is what one would expect from people who believe that God is the transcendent Creator. This approach is similar to what Isaiah does by asserting that Yahweh "is riding on a swift cloud" (Isa. 19:1; cf. Ps. 104:3). Isaiah draws from Canaanite mythology and uses the idea of Baal, the storm god, riding on the clouds to assert that it is really Yahweh rather than Baal who controls the forces of nature.[3] In the biblical worldview, Yahweh is the creator of everything, including Baal, so the idea that Baal controls the weather is addressed by using the polemical-corrective approach that characterized Israel's theology.

2. Wilken, *Spirit of Early Christian Thought*, xvii.
3. Currid, *Against the Gods*, 108.

In much the same way, the fathers accepted the Platonic concept of universals as the basis for the logical order discernable in creation, but through scholastic realism, they relocated them from a hard-to-define Platonic "third realm" into the mind of God.[4] They saw the Greek concept of the logos as appropriate for use in theology because, like the Platonist tradition, they saw creation as ordered and structured by God rather than as basically chaotic, the view of the ancient Near Eastern and Greco-Roman mythologies. The author of the Enuma Elish would never in a thousand years have thought of saying that some sort of principle of reason was behind the original chaos, controlling and organizing it. In ancient Near Eastern mythology, the chaos needs to be tamed through violent struggle precisely because it *lacks* reason and order; only the gods can impose structure, and even they can do it only by force. At least that is the lie the gods told humans in founding pagan religions. It is a lie that is corrected in the first chapter of John's Gospel, which presupposes the truth of Genesis 1 as the foundation of its thought.

But even though the fathers agreed with the Greek philosophers in viewing the cosmos as rational and orderly over against the pagan myths, and although they further agreed with the Greek philosophers in viewing this as the result of the existence and work of the logos, they nevertheless insisted that the philosophers were wrong in viewing the logos as an impersonal principle or entity immanent in the cosmos. For the Stoics, the logos was conceptualized as fire (which came precariously close to relapsing into mythology), but what they meant, apparently, was an immanent principle of reason inhering naturally in the cosmos, making the cosmos a *cosmos* rather than a meaningless flux.[5] The fathers had two highly important corrections to make to this picture on the basis of Scripture.

As the Prologue to John's Gospel reveals, the logos turns out to be the Son of God, who became flesh in the person of Jesus Christ. John 1:1–14 says two crucial things about the logos. First, it says that the logos transcends the cosmos.

> In the beginning was the Word [λόγος, *logos*], and the Word was with God, and the Word was God. He was in the beginning with God. All things were made through him, and without him was not any thing made that was made. (John 1:1–3)

John identifies the Word as being with God (θεός, *theos*) "in the beginning" ('Εν ἀρχῇ, *En archē*), just as Genesis 1 identifies God (*'ĕlōhîm*) as being in the

---

4. Feser, *Five Proofs*, 107–8.
5. See Copleston's (*Greece and Rome*, 132–38) discussion of Stoic cosmology.

beginning (*bərē'šît*). As we saw in Isaiah 40, the doctrine of creation is closely bound up with divine transcendence. God is in control precisely because God precedes creation as its creator, and thus the creation as his creature is totally subject to his will.

The rest of Genesis 1 clearly shows that God creates the cosmos with order, structure, and beauty out of the initial chaos of unformed matter described in Genesis 1:2. The ancient Near Eastern myths took the chaos as eternal and uncontrolled until some god or other came along to tame its wildness. Genesis 1 says that this story is false; that is not the way it really happened. In reality, God created all things good in the sense that they were ordered, structured, and beautiful. The rebellious gods came after that original good creation and are simply rebels against it rather than originators of anything. Even the gods themselves were originally created good as part of the good creation, but they rebelled, just as human beings did in the garden of Eden. The gods bring order only when it suits their purposes; they are equally capable of stirring up chaos, violence, and disorder when that suits their purposes (which it often does). The Genesis account and the ancient Near Eastern mythological accounts are completely different narratives, and both cannot be true regarding the issue of origins and the role of the gods. In fact, much of the Old Testament is focused on getting the people of Israel to stop worshiping the false gods and put their trust in Yahweh alone.

The author of the Gospel of John employs a Greek philosophical term (λόγος) to describe the organizing, structuring, shaping Word spoken by Yahweh the Creator in Genesis 1:3 and following. "Yes," John says in effect, "you could call it λόγος. But you must understand that it is not part of the creation itself, but rather it is actually the transcendent Creator who brought matter into being and then shaped that unformed matter into a rationally ordered cosmos: the Word was God" (John 1:1). The Stoic idea of λόγος is fundamentally transformed from an immanent principle of the cosmos into an expression of the transcendent being of the Creator God.

Second, John makes clear that the λόγος was personal and, in fact, became a man. A few verses down in this chapter we read,

> And the Word became flesh [λόγος ἐγένετο σάρξ, *logos egeneto sarx*] and dwelt among us, and we have seen his glory [δόξαν, *doxan*], glory as of the only Son from the Father, full of grace and truth. (John 1:14)

The astonished witness of the apostles is that the Word took on flesh and lived among us in the person of Jesus the Christ. They do not propose to explain how this is possible; they simply report their eyewitness testimony that it happened. Peter says they were "eyewitnesses of his majesty" (2 Pet. 1:16). John says that his message concerns "that which was from the beginning, which we have heard, which we have seen with our eyes, which we looked upon and have touched with our hands" (1 John 1:1). The Gospel writers stress that the same Jesus who had been living, walking, teaching, and doing miracles with them was seen by many witnesses as having been raised from the dead (Matt. 28; Mark 16; Luke 24).

The term λόγος was taken over by the apostles and used to express something new with respect to Greek metaphysics and Greco-Roman mythology. Early Christian theology imitated the apostles in using the term λόγος and other terms, such as ὁμοούσιον (*homoousion*). Such terms were taken over from Greek philosophy and used to say something that Greek philosophy never in its wildest dreams could ever have imagined—that Jesus Christ, the Word of the Father, is the transcendent Creator. It is simply inaccurate to dismiss the fathers as craven conformists seeking to modify biblical doctrine to fit into the overall metaphysical framework determined by Greek philosophy. It is more accurate to see the situation as, in Robert Wilken's apt words, "the Christianization of Hellenism."[6]

How did the claim gain credence in the first place that the fathers were merely cultural conformists reading Aristotle into the Bible? It may have seemed plausible in the nineteenth century because of unacknowledged yet influential metaphysical assumptions held generally in the culture and assumed by Christian theologians after Hume and Kant. As part of their attempt to reconfigure Christian doctrines to make them fit within the constraints of the nominalism, materialism, and mechanism of modern metaphysics, liberal Protestants such as Albrecht Ritschl and Adolf von Harnack attempted to detach Christian theology from what they called "Greek metaphysics," which they viewed as a distortion of the simple biblical (mostly ethical) message. In place of the biblical gospel of sin and salvation, by which we gain eternal life through faith in the atoning death of Christ, they wanted to substitute the "social gospel" of government programs to alleviate poverty in the here and now. Salvation became a this-worldly matter because this world is all there is.

Adolf von Harnack popularized the "Hellenization thesis" in the late nineteenth century,[7] but some left-wing evangelicals, such as Brian McLaren, were

---

6. Wilken, *Spirit of Early Christian Thought*, xvi.

7. See Harnack's lectures from 1900 titled *What Is Christianity?*, esp. lecture 12. He deplores the fact that "Christendom became more and more penetrated by the Greek and philosophical idea that true religion is first and foremost 'doctrine,' and doctrine, too that is coextensive with the whole range of knowledge" (211). Then he writes, "It takes the form, not of a Christian product in Greek dress, but of a Greek product in Christian dress." And just in case you did not

still "discovering" this thesis in the early twenty-first century.[8] Paul Gavrilyuk calls this "the theory of theology's fall into Hellenistic philosophy" and demonstrates that it deserves to be given a decent burial as a theory that, upon closer inspection, cannot possibly be true.[9] In biblical studies it is rare for a theory to be refuted so decisively, but this one simply *cannot* be true for two reasons. First, it understates the complexity of Greek philosophy, and second, it oversimplifies the problem of biblical interpretation to the point of misrepresenting both. Gavrilyuk shows that Greek thought contains several different views of God and of the possibility of God changing or suffering. Greek metaphysics contains contradictory positions on such issues, so taking one view out of several means that one is just as much non-Greek as Greek, no matter which view one takes! He also points out that the Bible does not have just one view on this issue either. We find Scripture declaring that God does not change (e.g., Ps. 102:26; Mal. 3:6; Heb. 1:11–12; James 1:17) and that God does change his mind (e.g., Gen. 6:5–7; Exod. 32:12–14; Ps. 106:45). Thus Scripture requires interpretation. To say that the doctrine of God's immutability is Greek rather than biblical is a gross oversimplification at best and highly distorting of fourth-century theology at worst. In fact, Michael Haykin, following Jaroslav Pelikan's critique of Adolf von Harnack, points out that it is actually "various heretical systems opposed by the Fathers that reveal the deepest impress of Hellenization."[10] This is a valid and important insight, as we shall see in the next section.

---

get the point, he presses it home like a dagger pointed at the heart of orthodoxy: "In its external form as a whole this Church is nothing more than a continuation of the history of Greek religion under the alien influence of Christianity, parallel to the many other alien influences which have affected it. We might also describe it as the natural product of the union between Hellenism, itself already in a state of oriental decay, and Christian teaching. . . . In this sense it is a natural religion" (Harnack, *What Is Christianity?*, 221).

8. The title of McLaren's 2010 book says what he wants instead of classical orthodoxy, namely, *A New Kind of Christianity*. Like Harnack, McLaren thoroughly despises the old Christianity of the past 2,000 years and wants to bring it "up to date," which is to say he wants to join in the liberal project, using historical criticism to "reinterpret" the Bible and support his doctrinal revisionism (such as his denial of the doctrine of original sin and many other basic doctrines). In chapter 4, he claims that the "overarching story line of the Bible" has been misunderstood for 2,000 years and is merely the Greco-Roman narrative imposed on the Jewish Bible. His deference to philosophical naturalism is all too apparent in his insistence that we abandon what he terms "dualism." He writes, "The Greco-Roman mind was habitually dualistic, in the sense that an enlightened or philosophic mind would always see the world divided in two, the profane physical world of matter, stuff, and change on the low side and the sacred metaphysical world of ideals, ideas, spirit and changelessness on the high side" (McLaren, *New Kind of Christianity*, 38–39).

9. Gavrilyuk, *Suffering of the Impassible God*, chap. 1.

10. Haykin, *Rediscovering the Church Fathers*, 160.

Divine Transcendence and the Arian Controversy

In chapter 4, we looked at the first major theme in the doctrine of God found in Isaiah 40–48, which is that the LORD is the transcendent Creator. The pro-Nicene theology that emerged in the fourth century as the consensus doctrine of God in the Christian church was not a result of the imposition of Greek metaphysical ideas onto the Bible, as if Aristotle was preferred over Moses, Isaiah, and Paul. Rather, on the crucial issue of divine transcendence, Aristotle was *corrected* on the basis of Moses, Isaiah, and Paul.[11] Just like Old Testament theology, the theology of the early church fathers was polemical-corrective in nature. We can see this in the debate that began with a flare-up between Bishop Alexander of Alexandria and the priest Arius over the issue of the relationship of the Son to the Father and extended through the fourth century.

This debate was at the heart of the long struggle for the definition of the doctrine of the Trinity, a struggle extending from the Council of Nicaea in AD 325 to the Council of Constantinople in AD 381. What follows here is not a history of this complex period of doctrinal controversy, nor is it a comprehensive discussion of the many and various views of the various players. My goal is to focus on one theme and to show that the doctrine of divine transcendence was assumed by all Christians on all sides of the debate and that the argument was over how to do justice to the being of the Son, given the transcendence of God. It turns out to be the heretical Arian view that comes closest to Neoplatonism, and it is precisely its failure to protect true divine transcendence that was one factor in turning many fence-sitting bishops against Arianism and the neo-Arianism of Asterius and Eunomius.

It would be wrong to think that the Christian church did not believe in the doctrine of the Trinity prior to the fourth century. Khaled Anatolios offers a list of what all sides took for granted as already established when the great trinitarian controversy began. He says that there were three major areas of agreement on fundamental theology, three important doctrines held in common, and at least four negative boundaries that all agreed must not be transgressed.[12]

The three areas of fundamental theology or methodology were as follows:

1. All agreed on the biblical canon of inspired Scripture as the "prime source of divine revelation."

---

11. Moltmann's project is built on a faulty foundation because he simplistically equates the use of Aristotelian concepts with the *uncritical* use of such concepts, as when he writes smugly, "Aristotle's God cannot love" (*Crucified God*, 222), as if no one from Athanasius to Aquinas had noticed that fact. It is possible to read Moltmann's whole theological project as an exercise in deconstruction, which uses the cross against Christianity.

12. Anatolios, *Retrieving Nicaea*, 36–38.

2. All agreed that the apostolic tradition is the normative interpreter of Scripture and so held the office of bishop in high regard.

3. All saw the necessity of applying reason to what is held by faith—not to undermine it or judge it, but to understand it.[13]

There were also three major doctrinal affirmations held in common. First and foremost was the doctrine of the Trinity itself. Crucially, all would agree that the Father, Son, and Holy Spirit are to be worshiped. Second, all were agreed that God had created the world out of nothing, and thus the world is neither coexistent with God nor eternal. Third, everyone affirmed the lordship of Jesus Christ, including his biblical titles—such as Lord, Wisdom, Word, Light, and Life—and his preexistence. It was generally agreed that the preexistent Christ was creator of the world and that he became human to save the world.[14]

As to negative boundaries recognized by all parties as limiting discussion, it was agreed that Manichaeism was heretical and out of bounds. The world is not governed by two equal forces, one good and the other evil; instead, the one true God is the sovereign creator of all. Another no-go zone was all forms of Gnostic emanationism, in which the universe is the natural overflow of divine being. A third boundary was the teaching attributed (rightly or wrongly) to Paul of Samosata that Jesus was a mere man who had been adopted by the Father. Fourth, the whole idea of Sabellianism (or modalism) was shunned. This referred to any teaching that "undermined the real differentiation between Father, Son and Spirit."[15] After reading this list of extensive and substantial agreements, one could be forgiven for thinking that whatever differences remained must have been relatively minor. But that would be a mistake, for the ensuing debate threatened to divide the church into two different religions.

What sparked that debate? We know that early in the fourth century an Egyptian presbyter named Arius began to criticize the preaching of his bishop, Alexander of Alexandria, on the relationship of the Father and the Son. Alexander strongly emphasized the eternal generation of the Son from the Father, as Origen had taught, but Arius emphasized the uniqueness and singularity of the one unbegotten and unoriginated God.[16] Despite our talk of God as Trinity, the reality for Arius is that we can speak only of the Father as truly God without qualification. The three *hypostases* (ὑποστάσες) of the Trinity are unequal; the Son's divinity is real, but it is a result of the will of the

13. Anatolios, *Retrieving Nicaea*, 36.
14. Anatolios, *Retrieving Nicaea*, 36–38.
15. Anatolios, *Retrieving Nicaea*, 38.
16. Anatolios, *Retrieving Nicaea*, 17.

Father, not a matter of substance. The Son, Arius insisted, is divine because the Father makes him divine. The Son is changeable by nature and does not know the Father's essence. The Son's divine status is a matter of God's will, not a result of a common nature or essence. The issue that sparked the debate was the nature of the relationship between Father and Son.

Khaled Anatolios makes an important contribution to our understanding of this ensuing debate, which lasted the whole fourth century—with Arius, Asterius, Eusebius of Caesarea, and Eunomius on one side and Athanasius, the Cappadocians, and Augustine on the other side. Anatolios frames the main point at issue as whether the Father-Son relationship is primarily a matter of will or a matter of substance. The Creed of Nicaea in AD 325 affirmed the doctrine of the ὁμοούσιον, that is, the sameness of the Father and the Son in being. Critics of Nicaea attacked it as implying some form of Sabellianism or at least as not sufficiently guarding against Sabellianism. They preferred expressing the relatedness of Father and Son in some way other than by identifying them as one in being. At the risk of oversimplification, one could characterize fifty years of intense, complicated theological debate as the pro-Nicene fathers trying to find a formula that would work to rule out all forms of subordinationism and affirm the full equality in divinity of the Father and the Son without using substance language and failing to find any such formula. In the end, the Cappadocians found various strategies for understanding ὁμοούσιον in ways that ruled out Sabellianism and the implications of Sabellianism. Therefore, the Council of Constantinople reaffirmed the Nicene ὁμοούσιον, and the rest, as they say, is history.

By focusing on the issue of unity of being versus unity of will, Anatolios offers an important insight into the heart of the dispute. As we will see below, this is an important way of characterizing the difference between the Nicene and non-Nicene theologies. However, Lewis Ayres adds some important perspective when he points out that there was not just one theology of Nicaea versus one heretical doctrine. Rather, he argues that in the period of 360–390, a set of theologies appeared that were compatible with, though not identical to, each other and supported the Nicene ὁμοούσιον.[17] He shows that Christian orthodoxy is not threatened by pluralism in pro-Nicene theologies but is actually strengthened by it.[18]

All pro-Nicene theologies accepted the idea that the reality of God's transcendence makes it impossible for the human mind to comprehend God, which means that finding the perfect terminology was secondary to respecting

17. Ayres, *Nicaea and Its Legacy*, 6.
18. Ayres, *Nicaea and Its Legacy*, 98–100.

certain boundaries and affirming certain central truths. There is no one correct set of terms to use of the Triune God, because there is no single, comprehensive definition of God available to us creatures. One of the chief reasons for the emergence of consensus between 360 and 390 was the recognition by pro-Nicenes that some of the critics of Nicaea were critical of it because they were truly subordinationist in their view of the Son, while others were using language similar to the subordinationists (image, similarity in being) to mean something akin to what the pro-Nicenes meant. For example, if your reasons for using the term ὁμοιούσιον (similar being) instead of ὁμοούσιον (same being) are (1) that the latter word is not a biblical term and (2) that the Son is in all ways like the Father except in being begotten, whereas the Father is unbegotten, then the pro-Nicene theologians would eventually come to accept that you do not mean by ὁμοιούσιον what the true subordinationists mean. The true subordinationists would say that the Son is inferior to the Father in being or "other in being" or *heteroousios* (ἑτεροούσιος), that the Son does not comprehend the Father, and that he has divinity only by the will of the Father as opposed to having it in his own being. The recognition that more than one set of terminology can be used to express an orthodox position was critical to the coming together of the church around the Nicene formula.

Below is the AD 325 text of the Nicene Creed, which is an expansion of the baptismal creed we know today as the Apostles' Creed:

> We believe in one God, the Father Almighty, Maker of all things, seen and unseen; and in one Lord Jesus Christ, the Son of God, begotten as only begotten of the Father, that is, of the being of the Father [ἐκ τῆς οὐσίας τοῦ πατρός, *ek tēs ousias tou patros*], God of God, Light of Light, true God of true God, begotten not made, consubstantial [ὁμοούσιον] with the Father through whom all things came into existence, both things in heaven and things on earth; who for us men and for our salvation came down and was incarnate and became man, suffered and rose again the third day, ascended into the heavens, and is coming to judge the living and the dead.
>
> And in the Holy Spirit.
>
> But those who say "there was a time when he did not exist," and "before being begotten he did not exist," and that he came into being from non-existence, or who allege that the Son of God is from another hypostasis or ousia [ἐξ ἑτέρας ὑποστάσεως ἢ οὐσίας, *ex heteras hypostaseōs ē ousias*] or is alterable or changeable, these the Catholic and Apostolic Church condemns.[19]

19. This is the text given by Ayres, *Nicaea and Its Legacy*, 19. He takes it from Hanson, *Search for the Christian Doctrine of God*, 163. The text is widely available online in both Greek and various English translations.

In this creed of Nicaea, the word οὐσία is used in three ways. First, the description of the Son as "only begotten" is followed by the phrase "that is, of the οὐσίας of the Father." Second, Father and Son are then described as ὁμοούσιον. Third, those who say that the Son is of another οὐσία than the Father are condemned.

Controversy continued both before and after AD 325 over the use of the term ὁμοούσιον to describe the relationship of the Father to the Son. It is very important to understand what the objections were to the use of this word.[20] In the second century certain Gnostic writers had used it to mean emanation in the Neoplatonic sense. In the fourth century, some Gnostics were using it to refer to a semimaterialist division of being by which the world was produced. Anyone who has read part 2 of this book will immediately recognize what was at stake here: the Gnostics were teaching mythology, and the danger of mythology is the failure to recognize the existence of a transcendent Creator. In mythology—whether it be ancient Near Eastern, Greco-Roman, or modern mythology—the gods are all part of the eternal cosmos, and their being is continuous with that of nature, different only in degree not in kind.

Were the Nicene fathers really being tempted to embrace such ideas? Of course not. But they made one of the most daring moves in all of human intellectual history as part of thinking through how best to express the doctrine of the Trinity without violating monotheism. They shifted the use of the word ὁμοούσιον from the God-world relation to the Father-Son relation. This enabled them to affirm the continuity in being of the Father, Son, and Spirit as one God, while differentiating the being of the transcendent Triune Creator from all else in existence. The continuity in being between the gods and nature in mythology is appropriately attributed to the Father-Son relation but not to the God-world relation, because the Son is fully divine and uncreated, whereas the world is not divine and is created. The doctrine of *creatio ex nihilo* is absolutely critical here, just as it was for Isaiah, because it marks off the absolute distinction between the eternal, self-existent, necessary being of God and the temporal, dependent, contingent being of creation. The Son is part of God, not a creature.

In his *Orations against the Arians*, Athanasius does not argue for the doctrine of *creatio ex nihilo* but uses it as the foundation for everything he says about the Son. Anatolios points out (as noted above) that the doctrine that God created all things out of nothing was one of the bedrock assumptions held in common by all sides in the fourth-century debates over the status of

---

20. For a good discussion of the controversy, see Ayres, *Nicaea and Its Legacy*, 92–98.

the Son. Even the Arians did not deny the doctrine of *creatio ex nihilo*, and the Gnostics, who did deny it, were clearly recognized as archetypal heretics. One way to win a debate in this context was to paint your opponent as soft on *creatio ex nihilo*. In his debate with the Arians, Athanasius does not exactly charge them with denying *creatio ex nihilo*. Rather, he argues for the eternal generation of the Son and then argues that the meaning of the Son's eternal generation from the Father is that the Son must share in the uncreated, eternal, self-existent, necessary being of the Father. The function of the word ὁμοούσιον for Athanasius is to affirm that Christ must be understood to be on the side of creator in the creator-creature divide.

For us today, that conclusion may seem clear and obvious, but it is the fruit of the long, hard-fought war waged by pro-Nicenes throughout the fourth century against the dominant intellectual forces of their cultural context, which militated against a clear understanding of the creator-creature distinction. Greek mythology held that the cosmos is eternal and that the difference between divine and nondivine being was a matter of degree of purity. There was no clear dividing line between the divine and the human. So the idea of an emperor being divinized after death and, for later emperors, even during his lifetime was not that difficult to comprehend or fit into the Greco-Roman worldview. It was basically a promotion in being. Of course, this is where Jewish religious sensibilities clashed violently with Greco-Roman religion and politics. The absolute prohibition of idolatry and the mandate to worship only one God was indigestible to the Greco-Roman mind. Christianity struggled to maintain biblical monotheism in the face of a pervasive worldview that saw divinity as a matter of degree, extending from just above the human to the high and abstract oneness of the One.

Athanasius argued that if we agree that the Father is eternal, self-existent, and necessary in his being, then Scripture clearly teaches that the Son shares in the Father's essence. Therefore, it is necessary to view the Son as eternal, self-existent, and necessary in his being. If the Father is the transcendent Creator and the Son is of the Father's being, then the Son is also the transcendent Creator. Athanasius writes,

> For, whereas it is proper to men to beget in time, from the imperfection of their nature, God's offspring is eternal, for His nature is ever perfect. . . . But if He is Son, as the Father says, and the Scriptures proclaim, and "Son" is nothing else than what is generated from the Father; and what is generated from the Father is His Word, and Wisdom, and Radiance; what is to be said but that, in maintaining "Once the Son was not," they rob God of His Word, like plunderers, and openly predicate of Him that He was once without His proper Word

and Wisdom, and that the Light was once without radiance, and the Fountain was once barren and dry.[21]

Athanasius spends many pages going through one biblical text after another, doing detailed exegesis with the goal of showing how the Bible teaches that the Son is indeed one with the Father.

> They deny that the Son is the proper offspring of the Father's essence, on the ground that this must imply parts and divisions; what is this but to deny that He is very Son, and only in name to call Him Son at all? And is it not a grievous error, to have material thoughts about what is immaterial, and because of the weakness of their proper nature to deny what is natural and proper to the Father?[22]

Athanasius grounds his defense of the Nicene Creed's use of ὁμοούσιον in the fact that Scripture speaks of Christ as the Son of the Father. If it is illegitimate to utilize a material image to describe the immaterial relationship of the Son to the Father, then we are thereby criticizing Scripture itself. The point is that Scripture authorizes language drawn from the material world in calling the Father "Father" and the Son "Son." Thus we are following the pattern of biblical words in describing the relationship between them as ὁμοούσιον—oneness in being or substance—and if Scripture can use such language as father and son analogically to speak of the shared deity of the Father and Son, then we can do so as well. Essentially, Athanasius is arguing that the word ὁμοούσιον is biblical in the sense that it names a biblical concept. Athanasius says,

> When the Father says, "This is my beloved Son," and when the Son says that God is His own Father, it follows that what is partaken is not external, but from the essence of the Father. . . . What is from the essence of the Father, and proper to Him, is entirely the Son.[23]

So let us hear no more nonsense about the supposed imposition of Greek metaphysics on the Bible by the fourth-century fathers! They approach the subject with reverence and a determination to be biblical in all that they say about the Triune God. At the outset, they could not use language that unambiguously meant what the Bible means because that language had not yet been invented. They were taking concepts and breaking them apart by hammering them on the anvil of Scripture and then reforging them in the flame

---

21. Athanasius, *Four Discourses against the Arians*, discourse 1, 5.14 (*NPNF*[2] 4:315).
22. Athanasius, *Four Discourses against the Arians*, discourse 1, 5.15 (*NPNF*[2] 4:315).
23. Athanasius, *Four Discourses against the Arians*, discourse 1, 5.15–16 (*NPNF*[2] 4:315).

of truth until they were bent into a usable shape for proclaiming the gospel. They deserve better than being accused by moderns who are knee-deep in the liberal project of selling out their birthright of the gospel for a mess of philosophical porridge.

As mentioned above, Michael Haykin observed that the heretics against whom the fourth-century fathers argued were the ones guilty of conforming their thought to the Greek ideas of the culture around them. This point is asserted explicitly by Athanasius himself. He says that the Arians commit blasphemy when they say that there was a time when the Son was not. Then he writes,

> For if the Word is not with the Father from everlasting, the Triad is not everlasting; but a Monad was first, and afterwards by addition it became a Triad; and so as time went on, it seems what we know concerning God grew and took shape. . . . The Triad is discovered to be unlike Itself, consisting of strange and alien natures and essences. . . . It belongs to Greeks, to introduce an originated Triad, and to level It with things originate; for these do admit of deficiencies and additions; but the faith of Christians acknowledges the blessed Triad as unalterable and perfect and ever what It was.[24]

Note what Athanasius is doing here. He is accusing the Arians of having a doctrine of the Trinity that is more Neoplatonic than biblical. How strange it is that modern revisionists accuse the pro-Nicene fathers of the very fault that the pro-Nicene fathers criticized their heretical opponents of endorsing as they sought to correct the heretical theology that threatened the Nicene doctrine. Athanasius's most damning criticism of the Arian theology is that it compromises divine transcendence by admitting into God what comes into existence (see the phrase underlined in the quotation above).

Sometimes commentators on Genesis 1:1 say that the verse cannot possibly be teaching *creatio ex nihilo* because such a concept was unknown in ancient Near Eastern culture. The implication is that it must be in the general culture first in order for a biblical author to know of it. Then we are often told that the concept of *creatio ex nihilo* is first used in certain patristic authors, and the reader is left to assume that it must have been a Greek idea that the church fathers latched on to and read into the Bible. Some historical critics admit that the concept is found in New Testament texts such as John 1:3; Acts 14:15; Romans 4:17; and Hebrews 11:3, while others deny that the "full concept" is found in the Bible at all. But the idea of *creatio ex nihilo* is not found in

---

24. Athanasius, *Four Discourses against the Arians*, discourse 1, 6.17–18 (*NPNF*[2] 4:316–17, underlining added).

Greco-Roman mythology or in Greek philosophy. It is just as foreign to such contexts as it is to ancient Egypt, Canaan, or Mesopotamia. So where exactly did it come from? It did not come from any human culture. The concept of *creatio ex nihilo* is a biblical idea, received by biblical authors through special revelation from God under the inspiration of the Holy Spirit. It could just as easily have been given to Moses in 1500 BC as to Luke or the author of Hebrews in the first century AD. But if it were not in the Bible, it would not have been embraced by the fathers in the fourth century, because they would never have heard of it! What we find, however, is that by the fourth century this idea is not only known but *traditional*, as Anatolios notes above. It is a foundational building block in the concept of God that dominated fourth-century pro-Nicene theology. Athanasius got it from Isaiah, not Plato; Isaiah got it from Moses, not Babylon; and Moses got it from God, not Egypt. God revealed himself as the transcendent Creator to Israel, and pro-Nicene theology accepted it as authoritative doctrine and sought to elaborate it more precisely in the context of their culture.

The Completion of Philosophy by Prophecy

In chapter 5 we looked at the second major theme in Isaiah 40–48 regarding the nature of God: that Yahweh is the sovereign Lord of history, who is moving all things to their appointed telos through providence and miracle. For Isaiah, the main problem facing the people of God can be formulated in the phrase "the Holy One of Israel." Since God is holy and the people of Israel are unholy, how can there be any outcome other than the righteous fire of divine judgment falling on Israel? But then what becomes of the promises made to Abraham in Genesis 12:1–3 and to David in 2 Samuel 7:13? How can God use Israel to bring blessing to all the peoples of the earth and ensure that a descendent of David sits on the throne of Israel eternally? There is no logical solution to this dilemma; the only way to resolve the problem is through God's mighty acts in history. God must do something new.

The good news in the biblical worldview is that the future offers possibilities for something new; the story is not over. History is not cyclical but linear. Unforeseen plot twists may lie ahead that open up possible solutions not visible right now from our vantage point. The ultimate reason that predictive prophecy could never be eliminated from the Old Testament is that the subject matter of the Old Testament—our hope—is future. The problem with which the Old Testament writers wrestle cannot be solved apart from God doing something new, spectacular, and unprecedented in the future. If the future is just more of the same old thing endlessly repeated, then all hope is lost. This is why messianic prophecy gradually takes center stage in the Prophets, in the Psalter, in Chronicles, and generally toward the end of the Old Testament period. It is why prophecy develops into its apocalyptic mode in the classical Prophets, with the process intensifying in the Second Temple period. The Old Testament itself is essentially forward-looking and open-ended and becomes more so as time goes on. The expectation of what God is going to do only increases after the disaster of the exile.

In a way, Greek philosophy is similar insofar as it identifies the problem faced by human beings without having adequate resources within itself to solve the problem. For Plato, philosophy consisted mainly of three parts. First, metaphysics asks "What is reality like?" Second, ethics asks "How can I adjust myself to reality so as to live according to my nature and in harmony with the way the world really is?" Third, logic is the science of ensuring that we do not make mistakes in reasoning while answering the first two questions. Philosophy is wisdom, and wisdom is living in accord with reality. But philosophy is putting all its hopes in human reasoning abilities, and we humans are only partly rational in our behavior. We often act according to our bodily desires, and not infrequently we act irrationally. In the *Republic*, Plato argues that the goal of the philosophic life is to train ourselves to govern the passions by reason so that we always act according to the true good, rather than according to false conceptions of the good or without considering the good. But good luck with that; human nature is flawed. Very few people will ever have the combination of intelligence, leisure, and inclination necessary to become philosophers in the first place, and even those who do will often fail to do the good even when they know it and the opportunity to do it is right in front of them. Philosophy cannot get us to God or to the Good because it has no solution to the problem of human sinfulness.

The New Testament emphasizes the idea that Christ fulfills the Old Testament by providing what was missing under the old covenant. He is the Davidic King who reigns eternally. He is the Seed of Abraham who is the conduit for blessing to flow to the nations. He is able to be these things because he institutes in his blood the new covenant of Jeremiah 31. In Hebrews he is our great high priest through whom we gain access to God (4:14–16; 10:19–22). In Galatians Paul tells us that God provides his Spirit to fill us and empower us to overcome the downward drag of our old fleshly nature (5:16–26). In Romans Paul also tells us that Christ has kept the Law perfectly, thus enabling us to share in his righteousness, and that Christ dies as the perfect sacrifice for sin so that we might have our sins forgiven (3:21–26). The Gospels portray him as the perfect teacher (Matt. 7:28–29) and the greater prophet predicted by

Moses in Deuteronomy 18:15 (John 5:46; 7:40). He is the true Israelite, who is called out of Egypt (Matt. 2:14–15), resists temptation in the wilderness (4:1–11), and shows what it means to live out the spirit of the Law as well as obey it outwardly (5:1–7:29). As prophet, priest, and king, Jesus Christ is what the Old Testament predicted, modeled, hoped for, and required for its own fulfillment.

The church fathers emphasize the idea that Christ brings fulfillment to the philosophic quest undertaken by the noblest among the gentiles. The Jewish apostles who wrote the New Testament understood that the gospel was for the Jew first and also for the gentiles. But the fathers, as gentiles themselves, stressed that the gospel is the hope for the nations. In this section, we will examine *Dialogue with Trypho*, by Justin Martyr, one of the earliest of the church fathers, and then we will turn to one of the great theological classics of the fourth century, *On the Incarnation*, by Athanasius. These two works will highlight how seriously the fathers took predictive prophecy and how it was seen as the fulfillment of both the Old Testament and Greek philosophy. In Isaiah 40–48 we saw that one of the reasons the exiles could put their trust in the promises God was making to them through his prophet was because God's ability to predict the future demonstrated that he is the sovereign Lord of history. Since our only hope is the new thing God might do in the future, we must have confidence that he is the sovereign Lord of history in order to avoid despair. The early church took this aspect of God's nature very seriously and in the conversion of the nations saw the promises of God coming true before their very eyes.

Justin Martyr

Justin Martyr was a philosopher who converted to Christianity and eventually died as a martyr in Rome in the century following the apostles. He was born in Samaria around AD 114 to a Roman father, and he acquired a philosophical education. In his *Dialogue with Trypho*, he tells us that he esteemed philosophy as "the greatest possession, and most honourable before God."[25] He recounts how he studied in various philosophical schools—including Stoic, Peripatetic, and Pythagorean ones—before beginning to study with the Platonists. He progressed rapidly and tells us that "I expected forthwith to look upon God, for this is the end of Plato's philosophy."[26] In the next chapter, he tells about a chance meeting with a "certain old man, by no means contemptable in appearance," while walking along the seashore to

---

25. Justin Martyr, *Dialogue with Trypho*, chap. 2 (ANF 1:195).
26. Justin Martyr, *Dialogue with Trypho*, chap. 2 (ANF 1:195).

meditate in quietness and peace. In their Socratic dialogue about philosophy and the soul, they come to an agreement that the philosophers do not know what the soul is. The Platonists say the soul is immortal, but since it partakes in the changing world of flux, it cannot possibly be eternal. God alone is unbegotten and incorruptible. At this point, the old man begins to tell Justin about the Hebrew prophets.

> There existed, long before this time, certain men more ancient than all those who are esteemed philosophers, both righteous and beloved by God, who spoke by the Divine Spirit, and foretold events which would take place, and which are now taking place. They are called prophets. These alone both saw and announced the truth to men, neither reverencing nor fearing any man, not influenced by a desire for glory, but speaking those things alone which they saw and which they heard, being filled with the Holy Spirit. Their writings are still extant, and he who has read them is very much helped in his knowledge of the beginning and end of things, and of those matters which the philosopher ought to know, provided he has believed them. For they did not use demonstration in their treatises, seeing that they were witnesses to the truth above all demonstration, and worthy of belief; and those events which have happened, and those which are happening, compel you to assent to the utterances made by them, although, indeed, they were entitled to credit on account of the miracles which they performed, since they both glorified the Creator, the God and Father of all things, and proclaimed His Son, the Christ [sent] by Him: which, indeed, the false prophets, who are filled with the lying unclean spirit, neither have done nor do, but venture to work certain wonderful deeds for the purpose of astonishing men, and glorify the spirits and demons of error. But pray that, above all things, the gates of light may be opened to you; for these things cannot be perceived or understood by all, but only by the man to whom God and His Christ have imparted wisdom.[27]

This event leads to Justin's conversion. He finds what he has been seeking, not in Platonism, but in the Bible. Philosophy is completed by prophecy. Notice that Justin specifically mentions prediction as part of prophecy; he says that the prophets "foretold events which would take place." He expands on this point at length, taking the Old Testament messianic prophecies with the utmost seriousness as evidence that Jesus the Christ is really the Son of God, precisely because he did what was prophesied and thus brought to fulfillment the Old Testament hopes. In the course of his work, Justin quotes the entirety of Isaiah 53 as descriptive of the messiah and shows how Christ fulfilled this prophecy.[28]

27. Justin Martyr, *Dialogue with Trypho*, chap. 7 (ANF 1:198).
28. Justin Martyr, *Dialogue with Trypho*, chap. 13 (ANF 1:201).

One other way in which Justin agrees with the biblical perspective on history is his description of the origin of pagan mythology. He says that the myths common in Greco-Roman culture were uttered by "wicked demons, to deceive and lead astray the human race."[29] For Justin, the search for God undertaken by the Platonists was the closest any of the gentile nations came to the truth, and even they were unsuccessful in the end. Philosophy is superior to mythology but remains incomplete. One other point to note is that Justin continued to wear the philosopher's cloak after his conversion because he understood Christianity to be the true philosophy. If philosophy is a quest for wisdom and if Christ is the Wisdom of God, this makes perfect sense.

Athanasius

We now turn to a brief discussion of Athanasius's classic work *On the Incarnation*. This is the second part of a two-part work, the first part of which is titled *Contra gentes*. It was common for the church fathers to write polemically. They were a minority religion in a largely hostile environment, like Israel in the ancient Near East, and they had to explain to their flock why the culturally dominant assumptions about God, nature, and humanity were wrong and needed to be corrected by the Bible. Also like Israel, they did not hesitate to make use of images, words, ideas, and even doctrines held by the pagans around them when doing so helped to explain the distinctive truth of biblical theology. For example, Augustine's great work *The City of God* is divided into two main parts; the first (books 1–10) is aimed at refuting pagan religion, and the second (books 11–22) constitutes a biblical theology and its implications for doctrine, metaphysics, worship, politics, ethics, and much else besides. This pattern of attacking paganism followed by expounding the true faith is common in the fathers. In his *On the Incarnation*, Athanasius begins at exactly the same point that Augustine did in the beginning of book 11 of *The City of God*, namely, with the doctrine of creation. Both the Apostles' Creed and the Nicene Creed begin at the same point, which is where the Bible, considered as a unified book, also begins. The doctrine of creation is the logical foundation and presupposition of every other Christian doctrine.

Athanasius's work consists of fifty-seven sections grouped into nine chapters. Chapter 1 is titled "Creation and Fall" (secs. 1–5). Athanasius emphasizes that the Word by whom all things were made is the same Word by which all things are redeemed. He attacks the Epicureans, who were the Darwinists of their day. They denied that there is any Mind behind the universe, and

---

29. Justin Martyr, *First Apology*, chap. 54 (*ANF* 1:181).

Athanasius rejects this idea as nonsense. He speaks respectfully of Plato but criticizes him for holding that matter is eternal instead of believing in *creatio ex nihilo*. The Gnostics invent an "Artificer" other than the Father of our Lord Jesus Christ, and so they deny the truth. The fall consisted of breaking the one command God had given concerning the tree of the knowledge of good and evil, and it resulted in death. An ethical act had ontological consequences. The restoration of the fallen human race is the reason for the incarnation.

Athanasius expands on this last point in chapters 2 ("The Divine Dilemma and Its Solution in the Incarnation") and 3 ("The Divine Dilemma and Its Solution in the Incarnation Continued"), which constitute sections 6–18. The dilemma Athanasius has in mind is that God's work was in the process of being destroyed by corruption and death, because when humans are detached from the source of their life in God, they decay into nonexistence. The problem was deeper than simply disobedience, in that the sin (an ethical act) had caused the corruption of the creature's body (an ontological result). The only possible answer was the incarnation: "For this purpose, then, the incorporeal and incorruptible and immaterial Word of God entered our world."[30] Athanasius explains further: "The Word perceived that corruption could not be got rid of otherwise than through death; yet He Himself, as the Word, being immortal and the Father's Son, was such as could not die. For this reason, therefore, He assumed a body capable of death."[31] Prior to the incarnation, God had not abandoned his creation. He gave humankind general revelation in creation, and he also gave the Law and sent Prophets—all of which were ways by which he could be known. Yet none of these methods were sufficient to bring about the redemption of the human race. It was clear that "in order to effect this re-creation, . . . He had first to do away with death and corruption."[32]

The fourth chapter is titled "The Death of Christ" and consists of sections 19–25. For Athanasius, the purpose of the Word taking on flesh was to make it possible for him to die and "offer the sacrifice on behalf of all."[33] As Athanasius explains, "The death of all was consummated in the Lord's body; yet, because the Word was in it, death and corruption were in the same act utterly abolished."[34] Athanasius next answers objections from those who find the death of the Son of God distasteful or regrettable and affirms that it had to occur the way it did. Several atonement theories are combined in his thought without any attempt to separate them from one another. The theme

---

30. Athanasius, *On the Incarnation*, sec. 8, p. 33.
31. Athanasius, *On the Incarnation*, sec. 9, p. 35.
32. Athanasius, *On the Incarnation*, sec. 13, p. 41.
33. Athanasius, *On the Incarnation*, sec. 20, p. 49.
34. Athanasius, *On the Incarnation*, sec. 20, p. 49.

of Christ as a curse and a ransom sits side by side with a *Christus Victor* theory stressing Christ's triumph over the devil.[35]

Athanasius devotes the fifth chapter (secs. 26–32) to the resurrection, which he considers highly important. He stresses the reality and undeniability of Christ's real, physical death, and he has no doubt that it was a real, bodily resurrection. He sees the resurrection as a sign of the victory over death, for Christ has "robbed it of its power."[36] Interestingly, he points to the power of Christ exercised in his own day in the form of "expelling evils spirits and despoiling idols"[37] as evidence of the reality of Christ's resurrection.

Then in chapter 6 (secs. 33–40), Athanasius undertakes the "Refutation of the Jews." Athanasius says that he has already considered clear proof of the resurrection of Christ's body, but now he is concerned to investigate the unbelief and ridicule that the church faces from both Jews and gentiles regarding it. His basic approach to Jewish unbelief is to say that "their unbelief has its refutation in the Scriptures."[38] He talks of how the Prophets foretold the virgin birth (Isa. 7:14), and he quotes other texts predicting the birth, such as Numbers 24:5–7, 17; Isaiah 8:4; 19:1; and Hosea 11:1. Athanasius quotes Isaiah 53 extensively as a prophecy of Christ's death. He quotes other texts relating specifically to the cross, including Deuteronomy 28:66; Jeremiah 11:19; and Psalm 22. He stresses that none of the great messianic prophecies were ever fulfilled by figures in Israel's history, such as Moses and David. Athanasius points out many other prophecies in the Hebrew Bible, including the book of Daniel, as pointing forward to the messiah. Yet, he points out, when Christ came, prophecy and vision ceased in Israel.[39]

Chapters 7 and 8 (secs. 41–55) are titled "Refutation of the Gentiles" and "Refutation of the Gentiles Continued." Here Athanasius sounds like Isaiah as he excoriates the gentiles for not seeing "the shame and ridiculousness of their own idols."[40] He defends Christian belief in the incarnation as reasonable, if only one grants the truth of the basic premise that God exists. He is astute in pointing out that a great deal of the Christian faith makes no sense if there is no such thing as God but makes perfect sense if God really does exist. He argues that the creation of Christ's human body out of nothing (that is, out of no human father but a mother only) is no different from God's original creation of the universe out of nothing. There is no logical way to deny that

35. Athanasius, *On the Incarnation*, sec. 25, p. 55.
36. Athanasius, *On the Incarnation*, sec. 29, p. 59.
37. Athanasius, *On the Incarnation*, sec. 32, p. 63.
38. Athanasius, *On the Incarnation*, sec. 33, p. 64.
39. Athanasius, *On the Incarnation*, sec. 40, p. 73.
40. Athanasius, *On the Incarnation*, sec. 41, p. 75.

the creator of all things has the ability to perform miracles. If someone asks why God became a man rather than something more noble, such as the sun or fire, the answer is that he had to assume a human nature in order to heal it.[41] It is interesting to note that he appeals to Plato, who believed that the Author of the universe would come to the rescue and put things right.[42] He obviously believes that Plato's credibility is high, even if he did not know the gospel. Probably, like Augustine, Athanasius believed that if Plato could come back from the dead and hear of Jesus, he would become a Christian. Many of the fathers believed the same.

Athanasius admits that many Greeks believe that God should have communicated his will to instruct and save mankind, not by assuming a human body, but by simply speaking. Athanasius patiently answers this objection, but in the end it comes down to the fact that sin is not external to our being but a corruption of our very being. A change of mind or new understanding cannot change that basic fact.[43] For Athanasius, as for many of the early church fathers, people's abandonment of idols is one of the most dramatic and powerful evidences of the gospel's progress and the reality of the risen Christ's rule. This was closely related to the deliverance of people from demon possession. We can see the same kind of connection between idolatry and demon possession in the church in places where the power of paganism has not yet been totally broken. While teaching in northern Ghana, I personally met people who had been delivered by Christ's power from idol worship and demonic possession, and the local Christian leaders there informed me that the two deliverances must necessarily go together. Athanasius speaks frankly of how demons deceive people in pagan religion in much the same way that we see them doing in the Old Testament.[44] He writes, "His cross has vanquished all magic entirely and has conquered the very name of it."[45] Having spoken of the power of Christ in delivering people from the power of evil, Athanasius writes,

> The Greek philosophers have compiled many works with persuasiveness and much skill in words; but what fruit have they to show for this such as has the cross of Christ? Their wise thoughts were persuasive enough until they died. . . . But the Word of God, by strangest paradox, teaching in meaner language, has put the choicest sophists in the shade, and by confounding their teachings

41. Athanasius, *On the Incarnation*, sec. 43, p. 78.
42. Athanasius, *On the Incarnation*, sec. 43, p. 79.
43. Athanasius, *On the Incarnation*, sec. 44, p. 80.
44. Athanasius, *On the Incarnation*, sec. 47, p. 85.
45. Athanasius, *On the Incarnation*, sec. 48, p. 86.

and drawing all men to Himself He has filled His own assemblies. . . . For whose death ever drove out demons? . . . Who has ever so rid men of their natural passions that fornicators become chaste and murderers no longer wield the sword and those who formerly were craven cowards boldly play the man? . . . The Greeks told all sorts of false tales, but they could never pretend that their idols rose again from death.[46]

One of the many reasons why reading patristic theology is so relevant today is because it is written by people who were not mere armchair theologians but Christian pastors and leaders who were personally involved in evangelism and spiritual warfare. Their theology is never merely "academic" in the pejorative sense.

In the concluding chapter (secs. 56–57), Athanasius stresses the need for purity of life in order to understand the Scriptures: "One cannot possibly understand the teaching of the saints unless one has a pure mind and is trying to imitate their life."[47] This view is shared by all the church fathers. Theology is a spiritual discipline that leads to greater holiness for those who undertake it in a spirit of prayer, humility, and openness to the gentle correction and filling of the Holy Spirit.

What do Justin Martyr and Athanasius have in common? I suggest three points to take away from this glance at just two of their works. First, they are easier to understand than many of the academic textbooks that seek to describe their thought. In his introduction to the Popular Patristics series edition of Athanasius's *On the Incarnation*, C. S. Lewis makes this point vigorously. He says that a great mind, such as that of Plato or Athanasius, often produces great writing that can be understood by beginners, and that is part of its genius.[48] Lesson 1: We should read the fathers.

Second, both Justin and Athanasius strongly affirm the reality and value of predictive prophecy, especially messianic prophecy. This seems to be one of the weakest points of most modern academic biblical studies. When someone tells you that prediction is not a major part of what the Hebrew prophets were about, this is what poker players refer to as a "tell," an unconscious action that betrays an attempted deception. When someone trots out the old chestnut "The prophets were about forthtelling, not foretelling," you should brace yourself for a revisionist account of the meaning of the prophets that fits into a philosophical naturalist metaphysics. The fathers stressed mes-

46. Athanasius, *On the Incarnation*, sec. 50, p. 88.
47. Athanasius, *On the Incarnation*, sec. 57, p. 96.
48. C. S. Lewis, "Introduction," 3.

sianic prophecy as one of the main sinews holding the Testaments together. Lesson 2: Prophecy is foretelling as well as forthtelling.

Third, like Isaiah, the fathers believe that God's actions in history to fulfill the words of his prophets constitute sufficient evidence for putting our trust in him to keep his covenantal promises in the future. The first coming of Christ in fulfillment of prophecy makes it more certain that Christ will come again. Just as Isaiah used the exodus in chapter 40 to assure the exiles that God can save his people, so we look back to the birth, death, resurrection, and ascension of Christ and know that his second coming is certain. The theology of the church fathers is Isaianic, not just in details, but also in spirit. Lesson 3: The fulfillment of prophecy helps us see the unity of the Bible and the unity of truth.

Monotheism and Mystery

In chapter 6, we looked at the third major theme in Isaiah 40–48 regarding the nature of God, which is monotheism. We saw that biblical monotheism means that Yahweh alone is to be worshiped because he is utterly unique as the transcendent Creator and Lord of history. The Bible is not interested in denying the existence of the false gods of the nations; both the Old and New Testament writers know that these beings are real and that they pose as gods to deceive humans into worshiping them in pagan religions. But the fact that they are real does not mean it is legitimate to worship them, because they are creatures of the one true God of Israel. This is why the fundamental command in the Decalogue is to have no other gods before Yahweh.

The fourth-century church fathers were monotheistic in the biblical sense, but they were faced with the Arian controversy about the relationship of the Father and the Son. The problem was how to articulate a doctrine that was clearly monotheistic while doing justice to the full ontological equality in deity of the Son and Spirit. Although discussion focused on the Son, the implications of the ontological status of the Son for the status of the Spirit were obvious to all concerned. There was no point in addressing the problem of the subordination of the Spirit if the problem of the subordination of the Son remained unresolved. There was an obvious impetus to affirm the Son's full ontological equality in being with the Father (and the Spirit) because Christian worship was worship of the Triune God rather than of just the Father alone. So some form of trinitarian theology was the default position. But the doctrine needed to be formulated in a way that avoided both modalism and subordinationism. The Nicene ὁμοούσιον avoided subordinationism but was seen by many theologians between AD 318 and 381 as implying modalism.

Eunomius (d. AD 393) was a figure who thought it was necessary to bite the bullet and accept the ontological inferiority of the Son to the Father and affirm that the Son is *heteroousios* (ἑτεροούσιος), that is, of being that is other than or different from the Father. His strategy was to protect the uniqueness of the Father as ingenerate and therefore one of a kind. Like all fourth-century Christian theologians, he affirmed divine simplicity, but he believed that only the Father could be simple. He believed that once you introduced oneness of being of Father and Son, you could no longer affirm that God is simple. So he advocated subordinationism as the only solution compatible with monotheism. The Cappadocian fathers, especially Basil of Caesarea and Gregory of Nyssa, did more than anyone else to address this problem, and the solution they offered became the basis for the triumph of the Nicene ὁμοούσιον in AD 381. In what follows, I will focus on Basil's response to Eunomius.

The only legitimate difference between the Father and Son that can be admitted in Nicene formulations of the doctrine of the Trinity is that the Father is unbegotten, whereas the Son is begotten. But Father and Son are correlative terms that imply each other; that is, neither the Father nor the Son is what he is apart from the other. The Father has always been Father and the Son has always been Son. Augustine will use a reductio ad absurdum argument that if the Son is the Wisdom of God, how can there ever have been a time when the Father lacked his Wisdom? Was he then unwise?[49] But all pro-Nicene theologians recognize that here we reach the frontier of mystery. If the Father-Son relationship is eternal, how can we time-bound creatures comprehend it? They realized that when we contemplate the eternal Father-Son relationship, we understand that it is beyond our capacity to understand. So we realize that our proper response is not to dismiss it or to ignore it but to worship the Holy Trinity. This is where Nicene orthodoxy places the mystery.

Anatolios makes a good point by arguing that "perhaps every theology must ultimately invoke the ineffability of the divine mystery. But theologies, as well as the experiences they inculcate, are crucially determined by where the mystery is located."[50] But not everyone was ready to sign on to this position. As one of the most influential heretics of the fourth century, Eunomius was willing to go so far as to say that the Son is *heteroousios* to the Father. He was willing to say that the Son is like the Father in many ways, just unlike in essence. When many of the Eastern bishops, who were somewhat sympathetic

49. Augustine, *The Trinity* 7.1 (I/5, 219–20).
50. Anatolios, *Retrieving Nicaea*, 82.

to the concerns of the Arian side of the controversy, heard this statement that the Son is *heteroousios* to the Father, they realized that they were hearing the denial of the full divinity of the Son and they rejected it strongly. During the 360s and 370s, many such bishops moved steadily in the pro-Nicene direction as a result, and the basis was laid for the pro-Nicene consensus. Eunomius's willingness to say this, however, can be attributed to a rationalistic streak in his thinking that led him to be impatient with mystery. He insisted that "unbegotten," or "ingenerate" (both of which are translations of ἀγέννητος, *agennētos*), is a definition of the essence of God, which is given by revelation and which fully captures the essence of the divine nature.[51]

Anatolios points out that Eunomius was concerned to maintain the distinction of the Christian God from the world, over against the Greek tendency to make them coordinate. This of course is all well and good. (And it shows that even the fourth-century *heretics* were not guilty of the Hellenization thesis!) The problem was how Eunomius proposed to accomplish this worthy goal. Anatolios quotes Eunomius as follows:

> If we purify our notions of these matters with exactitude (*akribōs*), we will understand that God's mode of activity is not human but effortless and divine. We must not think that the [divine] activity is some kind of motion or division of his essence. This is in fact what those who have been led astray by pagan sophistries do have to suppose because they have united the activity to the essence and therefore present the world as coterminous with God.[52]

Eunomius's desire to preserve true transcendence and to emphasize the creator-creature distinction is commendable; the problem is not with the intention but with the execution. Eunomius insists that God's willing cannot be eternal, and if we were to understand God's will as eternal, then his causing of the world would be eternal, and the world would be eternally coordinate with God. In his being, God is free of all motion, including all causality, and this must be the case in order to preserve God's utter transcendence. Otherwise, God would be like Aristotle's First Cause, simply the first link in the great chain of being, and his being would differ from the being of the world only in degree. The upshot of all this for Eunomius is that God the Father cannot cause God the Son eternally, so he denies the eternal generation of the Son. Like the creation, the Son must then be the product of the Father's will.

Why is Eunomius so insistent that divine essence and divine willing not be conflated? Why does he insist that God cannot cause something by his

---

51. Anatolios, *Retrieving Nicaea*, 73.
52. Eunomius, *Apology* 22, as quoted by Anatolios, *Retrieving Nicaea*, 74.

nature? Well obviously he wants to rule out pagan theories of emanation of divine being as the source of the existence of the cosmos. He wants to uphold the creator-creature distinction and assert true divine transcendence. But he accomplishes these laudable goals by making the Son into a creature whose existence is contingent on an act of the Father's will. The Son thus becomes a being who, though the highest of all creatures, is not equal in being to the Father and certainly not eternal. Eunomius also thinks that because the Son is begotten, he cannot share the Father's simplicity.[53] Again, the goal of preserving divine simplicity is worthy, but the cost is too high. It creates an intolerable situation for the worshiping church, because to worship a creature who is not God is idolatry and a denial of monotheism.

Why would Eunomius allow himself to be backed into the corner of denying the full divinity of the Son, even in pursuit of such laudable goals? I think the key clue can be discerned in Ayres's summary of Eunomius's position:

> Eunomius deploys the same argument as Aetius to explain why the Son cannot come from the Father's essence. He distinguishes between generation from essence and generation by will. Anything generated from the essence shares the essence of that from which it is generated, and it is simply illogical to imagine that any generated thing shares God's ingenerate nature. As generated by will the Son has a clearly subordinate status; Eunomius assumes that ingenerate defines God in a unique way: God's unity and simplicity imply that ingenerate is the only characteristic of God.[54]

Ayres agrees with Anatolios that the subordinationists teach that the relationship between the Father and Son is one of will, while the pro-Nicenes teach that the relationship is one of essence or being. But the key phrase here is "ingenerate defines God," which is underlined in the quotation above. As Ayres notes, Eunomius claims "a strong degree of knowledge about God's essence through the name 'ingenerate.'"[55] This is the problem. It is ironic that by attempting to preserve the transcendence and uniqueness of God, Eunomius ends up dragging God down to a level at which he becomes comprehensible to the creature. Thus we see that not all major mistakes in theology are intentional attempts to denigrate the glory and majesty of the Lord. Sometimes a path taken in hopes of getting to a certain destination ends up taking one further and further away from the intended destination, and some paths turn out to be dead ends.

53. Ayres, *Nicaea and Its Legacy*, 146.
54. Ayres, *Nicaea and Its Legacy*, 147, underlining added.
55. Ayres, *Nicaea and Its Legacy*, 149.

Lewis Ayres's student, Andrew Radde-Gallwitz, has written a study of how the Cappadocian Fathers, especially Basil of Caesarea and Gregory of Nyssa, transformed the concept of divine simplicity in such a way as to make it possible to include the Son (and Spirit) within the simplicity of the Triune God, thus paving the way for the rejection of Eunomius's subordinationism and the triumph of the Nicene theology. Eunomius was condemned at the Council of Constantinople in AD 381, and the doctrine of the ὁμοούσιον of the Father, Son, and Spirit was accepted without sacrificing the doctrine of divine simplicity. In the process, we can see the key role played by mystery in the formulation of trinitarian doctrine. That role is not simply to invoke the category of mystery to make it possible to affirm contradictions. Rather, it is to use the category of mystery to guard the holiness of the essence of the Triune God from prying eyes and the acids of rationalism. What I am suggesting is that the Nicene affirmation of transcendence involves a mixture of rational analysis and humble faith that fit together harmoniously in the orthodox doctrine of God. Let us consider Radde-Gallwitz's argument.

Radde-Gallwitz argues that in trying to reconcile the doctrine of divine simplicity with the doctrine of the Trinity, Basil of Caesarea needed to reconcile simplicity with a "coherent theological epistemology."[56] Here Radde-Gallwitz is referring to an epistemological debate in ancient philosophy about the referent of words used to describe God, such as the word "ingenerate" used of God by Eunomius. Philosophy since Plato had been concerned to understand things by discovering their essences. To know something is to know what makes it the kind of thing it is, that is, its essence. So as Radde-Gallwitz puts it, what philosophers were looking for was

> not primarily definitions of words, but of realities, especially of natural "kinds" such as humanity or of forms such as justice. Knowing such definitions was held to be basic to knowing at all: in order to know something as beautiful, in order reliably and consistently to identify instances of beauty, one must know the essence of beauty. This is the thesis known as the epistemological priority of definition.[57]

Eunomius claimed to know God's essence because he was, on this point, an unreconstructed Platonist. Basil and Gregory, in seeking to refute Eunomius and avoid his subordinationist conclusions, found themselves having to correct Platonism at this point and articulate a theological epistemology in which God is not known in the same way as created things, that is, God

56. Radde-Gallwitz, *Transformation of Divine Simplicity*, 1.
57. Radde-Gallwitz, *Transformation of Divine Simplicity*, 3.

is not known by grasping his essence. They had other reasons for taking this approach, an approach taken by other church fathers as well; it was more than an ad hoc tactic to get around the problem posed by Eunomius. Rather, it was a significant intellectual move that had an enormous effect on the ability of pro-Nicene theologians to reconcile classical theism with the Christian understanding of the Trinity.

How did they do this? Radde-Gallwitz explains his thesis:

> My fundamental claim in this book is that Basil and Gregory transformed divine simplicity. They did so by articulating a version of the doctrine of divine simplicity that avoids the horns of total apophaticism and the identity thesis (as they encountered it in Eunomius), while still playing its by-then traditional role within the Christian tradition. It needed to serve as a way of sanctioning the attribution of contradictory properties to God.[58]

Now I would not have used the word "contradictory" in that last sentence; I would have said "apparently contradictory." But the gist is clear. We need to be able to say that God is merciful and that God is unchanging because Scripture says both, and we believe Scripture to be authoritative. The idea of simplicity functioned in early Christian theology (prior to the fourth century) as a way of affirming that God is one and unchanging and not complex, in flux, or evolving.

By articulating an epistemology in which one can know *that* something is without knowing *what* it is, Basil developed an alternative to the two errors described above. In other words, knowledge of something is a journey or a process, and that journey does not necessarily begin with knowing the definition of a thing's essence. This is especially true with respect to God. In fact, Basil thinks that we never know God's essence. Radde-Gallwitz puts it thus: "One never knows God's essence. However, progress in theological understanding is, like Aristotelian moral education, a process of moving from basic concepts to reflection upon those concepts."[59] We see here a genuine example of great progress in philosophical thought. It is not necessary to believe that one can easily know the essence of a thing in order to believe that a comprehensive knowledge of that thing would involve knowing its essence. So Platonism can be true, but knowledge can be nuanced so that it is not all or nothing.

Basil deploys the concept of *epinoia* (ἐπίνοια) in order to argue that we can develop genuine knowledge of God through analysis of concepts about his essence (theology) on the basis of his actions in history (the economy).

---

58. Radde-Gallwitz, *Transformation of Divine Simplicity*, 6.
59. Radde-Gallwitz, *Transformation of Divine Simplicity*, 123.

The distinction between theology and economy is related to the distinction between the immanent and economic Trinity. Strictly speaking, theology is knowledge of God as God is eternally in himself. Revelation of God's actions in history is not yet knowledge in this strict sense, but it can lead to true theology as we contemplate the actions of God in history and their implications for his nature. For example, it was a generally accepted Platonist principle that a cause must be greater than the effect, and so, in some way, the effect must be contained in the cause, because something cannot give what it does not have. In theology, this means that God must be great enough to do whatever it is that he in fact has done. So if God's power is enough to raise the dead, he must have life in himself and be greater than the power of death. If God can defeat the gods of Egypt and set the Israelites free, he must be greater in power than the gods of the nations. Since this process of deduction requires contemplation, it expresses the heart of what theology is. When one does theology, one is contemplating revelation in order to gain knowledge of the nature of God. One is studying God, not to master or control God by knowing his essence, but rather in a humble and contemplative way by being present to him and reverently focusing our attention on him. Understood in this way, theology is very close to worship.

In Greek philosophy prior to Basil, the word *epinoia* meant concepts in the mind that we devise in order to understand features of the things we are considering. For Eunomius, this is like saying that we do not really know God at all; we just make up concepts in our minds and apply them to God. Basil begs to differ. As Radde-Gallwitz puts it, Basil "introduces into the debate a *tertium quid* between bare names and objects."[60] Richard Vagionne gives a concrete example to illustrate what Basil is doing:

> There exists in any given case a "real" material object (a rock, say, or a piece of wood); this object really exists. On the other hand, there is also something which is "real" in the object which can be discerned by our minds (such as triangular or tetragonal shape), and of this we can form a concept or *epinoia*. This *epinoia* does not "exist" in the strict sense, but it does represent something that is "real."[61]

Basil is not just playing with words; he is arguing that we can have real knowledge of God without knowing the essence of God: "The term 'conceptualization,' however, is far from being restricted only to vain and non-existent imaginations."[62] Basil examines titles of Christ in Scripture, such as door,

60. Radde-Gallwitz, *Transformation of Divine Simplicity*, 145.
61. Vaggione, *Eunomius*, 241–42.
62. Basil of Caesarea, *Against Eunomius* 1.6, p. 98.

bread, vine, and light. Following Origen, Basil sees them as conceptualizations, and he argues that they are not all equivalent to each other in meaning. Something different is conveyed by Christ referring to himself as "door" than is conveyed by his referring to himself as "light." Yet, Basil contends, all these designations are referring to one being—Christ—and not to various things with different essences. Christ has one essence, and these various titles express various truths about the one essence. He then goes on to argue that what is true of Christ is also true of the Father.

Divine simplicity refers to the essence of God itself, not to the various true statements we make about that essence, none of which fully capture the definition of what God is. Basil presses home the point: this means that we cannot take "ingenerate" as the definition of God's essence even though it does express something true about God. As finite creatures whose minds are incapable of grasping the essence of God, we must speak of God by using *epinoia*; there is no other way for us to know God. As Radde-Gallwitz puts it, Basil's argument is that "the variety one encounters in one's mind should not be projected onto the object of one's thinking."[63]

When we read Scripture theologically, that is, when we read Scripture as the pro-Nicene fathers did, we read concepts that tell us something about the being of God, but we would never think of reducing what we mean by "God" to the concepts we read in Scripture. These concepts express something of God's nature in a true yet partial manner. And we find it necessary to contemplate these concepts (*epinoia*) and allow them to supplement each other, gradually purify our thinking, and lead our minds step by step up the ladder of the knowledge of God. The essence of God always remains higher than we can grasp, yet it is *there*, and it is real. This is part of the meaning of Hebrews 11:6: "Without faith it is impossible to please him, for whoever would draw near to God must believe that he exists and that he rewards those who seek him."

In chapter 4, I suggested that we understand Isaiah 40 by thinking about how Moses must have reflected on the events of the exodus as he contemplated the meaning of the mysterious divine name revealed in Exodus 3. As we thought about Isaiah combining exodus and creation language in chapter 40, I suggested that the meaning of Genesis 1:1 might be understood as the answer to a question raised by the overwhelming power of Yahweh displayed in his victory over the gods of Egypt—namely, just how powerful is Yahweh anyway? The answer in Genesis 1:1 is that Yahweh is not just the strongest of all the various gods by a matter of degree; he is something altogether dif-

---

63. Radde-Gallwitz, *Transformation of Divine Simplicity*, 153.

ferent in kind. Whereas everything in creation comes to be and passes out of being, Yahweh is the name of "He who is," the One who has existence as part of his essence, who does not need to be brought into being by another, and who has no beginning. Genesis 1:1 describes the beginning of everything except the Creator God. In engaging in such reflections, we contemplate the being of God by using what Basil would call *epinoia*, concepts that gradually move us up the ladder of understanding without ever defining God in a final or comprehensive manner.

A Triune God can be simple because Scripture reveals this One to be both one and three at the same time. In the development of pro-Nicene theology in the fourth century, the distinction was eventually made between the *ousia*, which refers to the oneness of God, and the *hypostases*, which refer to the threeness of God. But both refer to the essence of God. This is not contradictory, because God is not one and three in the same way at the same time. If we were saying that he was one and three in exactly the same sense, it would be a contradiction. But it is a paradox because *ousia* does not equal *hypostasis*. But, you ask, in what sense are they different? We do not know. And if one objects that if God is one in *ousia* and three *hypostases*, then God cannot be simple, the answer is that this would be true only if we were using the terms *ousia* and *hypostasis* to define God's essence comprehensively. But we are not. We are using these terms as *epinoia*, that is, as concepts that describe aspects of the essence of God truly but not exhaustively. This is where pro-Nicene theology places the mystery.

Isaiah seems to locate the mystery of God in a similar place when he says that Yahweh is an *'ĕlōhîm* but not like the other *'ĕlōhîm*, because he is absolutely unique. If Isaiah thought we could have absolutely no knowledge of God's being, he would refuse even to call him an *'ĕlōhîm*. But if he thought we could have comprehensive knowledge of God's being, he would define what it means for Yahweh to occupy his genus as a unique being. Isaiah speaks of Yahweh as an *'ĕlōhîm* on the way to speaking of his ineffability. In Exodus 3, Moses understands that God is the God of Abraham, Isaac, and Jacob, but there is more to the mystery than what that fact alone tells us. He is an *'ĕlōhîm*, but he is more than an *'ĕlōhîm*. When I said in chapter 2 that the God of the Bible is more than the god of the philosophers but not less (thesis 20), I was trying to follow the same pattern of reflection and speech on the being of God. Contemplative theology goes like this: "He is like X, but he is more than X—not less than X but more. . . . It is time to worship."

Pro-Nicene theology does not place the mystery at the point of the knowledge of God's being or essence, which would result in us having no real knowledge of God at all. Nor does it eliminate mystery altogether, which would result in reducing God to a part of the cosmos knowable in principle by creatures. Rather, it places the mystery between *epinoia* and definition, without losing the referent of language in the fog of unknowability. Thomas Aquinas will later insist that analogical language for God is different from univocal language (that is, what Eunomius used) and equivocal language.[64] For Thomas, analogical language allows us to say true things about the essence of God without capturing the essence of God in our definitions. He was systematizing the basic theological moves that were made in the fourth century and merely updating and clarifying the tradition.

Monotheism is a mystery. It must be a mystery if it is going to be biblical monotheism. There may be forms of philosophical monotheism that reject the epistemology developed by Basil and insist on having a clear and distinct definition of God. There may be philosophical monotheisms that insist on using univocal language for God, but these sorts of philosophical monotheism are not biblical monotheism. Biblical monotheism uses analogical language to speak of *epinoia* and make true statements about the being of God without presuming to define God's being or thinking that we can capture the totality of what God is in human definitions or terms. Biblical monotheism is not threatened by the fourth-century pro-Nicene doctrine of the Trinity, because like the Bible, Nicene talk about God is humble, modest, and reverent. It is rooted in faith, which according to Scripture is the prerequisite for true knowledge of God (Heb. 11:6). The Nicene doctrine of God is not merely compatible with the Bible, in the sense that it does not disturb or contradict the teaching of Scripture. The Nicene doctrine of God is profoundly and deeply biblical in the sense that it observes the revelation of God in the Bible, contemplates it reverently, and expresses it using every logical, conceptual, philosophical, and linguistic tool available in taking every thought captive to Christ.

In this chapter I have tried to show that despite the differences in language, historical period, and cultural situation, there is a similarity of spirit, method, and content between Isaiah 40–48 and fourth-century pro-Nicene theology. What this similarity boils down to is that both Isaiah and the pro-Nicene fathers worshiped the same God—the God of Israel, who created the heavens and the earth, revealed himself in the exodus, spoke through the prophets, and finally became incarnate in Jesus Christ. When I read Isaiah and Nicene theology, I get the distinct impression that for all the differences in terminology, philosophical background, and cultural challenges, they are talking about the same God. This is crucial for determining whether pro-Nicene theology is biblical.

64. See Thomas Aquinas, *Summa Theologica*, I, q. 13, arts. 1–12, esp. art. 10.

Eight

Creatio ex nihilo and the Rejection of Mythology

> Christian teaching about the creation of the world out of nothing is a cardinal doctrine: on this hinge turn all the elements of the second topic of Christian theology, which treats all things with reference to God, their beginning and end, the first topic being God's immanent life.
>
> John Webster[1]

Throughout this book I have argued that modern theology has lost its grip on Nicene orthodoxy because it has failed to challenge modern metaphysics at a fundamental level. Instead, many modern theologians have been preoccupied with trying to squeeze orthodox doctrines onto the Procrustean bed of modernist metaphysics. For them, the key question is "How much of the Bible can we fit into a philosophical naturalist framework?" This is a failing strategy that can lead only to compromise and heresy because it fails to recognize that the philosophical naturalism that has characterized the modern period is merely a temporary phase between the fall of Christendom and the rise of neopaganism. After scientific positivism destroys Christian faith, what comes next is not a rational, materialistic, science-based worldview. Rather, what comes next is neopaganism, which may include a philosophical pantheism for the intellectual elites but will also include polytheism for the masses, and for

1. Webster, "'Love Is Also a Lover of Life,'" 99.

237

many it also includes a fascination with magic, the occult, and the demonic. The line between technology and magic, the theme of the Faust legend, always was a bit of a blur for most people anyway.[2] Enlightenment-inspired philosophical naturalism is the means by which Western culture is sinking back into the kind of mythological thinking that characterized the Greco-Roman and ancient Near Eastern cultures, in the midst of which biblical revelation was given. It hardly needs to be said that this does not constitute "progress" by any rational standard.

The doctrine of *creatio ex nihilo* is the central metaphysical doctrine generated by the Christian doctrine of God as the transcendent Creator, and it is therefore at the heart of the clash between biblical faith and neopaganism. This was the case in the Old Testament period, in the New Testament period, in the postapostolic era of the second century, and in the fourth-century Arian crisis, and it is also the case today. In the opening quotation of this chapter, John Webster highlights the importance of this doctrine. The doctrine of *creatio ex nihilo* will affect every single doctrine about nature, humanity, sin, salvation, the person and work of the Holy Spirit, the nature and mission of the church, and eschatology. This is because accepting or rejecting *creatio ex nihilo* affects the nature of God, and the nature of God affects every single doctrine about the "all things" studied by theology "in relation to God." The doctrine of *creatio ex nihilo* marks off the kind of difference that perdures (1) between God and the world, (2) between uncreated and created being, and (3) between the relations among the three Persons of the Trinity (the processions) and the relation between the Persons and creation (the missions). Without a doctrine of *creatio ex nihilo*, we do not even have an actual doctrine of creation, at least not in the sense meant by historic Christian orthodoxy.

In this chapter we explore the Christian doctrine of *creatio ex nihilo* as the key metaphysical doctrine generated by the biblical doctrine of creation. I wish to show that understanding this doctrine is key to recovering a trinitarian classical theist doctrine of God. I do this in four stages. First, I show that the doctrine of *creatio ex nihilo* is under severe and unrelenting attack today, with the result that even conservative orthodox theologians shrink from defending it. Second, I show that it is nonetheless central to the Great Tradition of Christian theology down through the centuries, from the second century to the twentieth century. Third, I show that the tradition has been correct in

---

2. C. S. Lewis was onto this truth in the mid-twentieth century, as can be seen in his science-fiction trilogy, especially the third novel, *That Hideous Strength*. The depiction of N.I.C.E. in that book perfectly describes the combination of avidity, hubris, technological prowess, cruelty, and credulousness that we see in contemporary culture.

understanding this doctrine as the teaching of Holy Scripture in the sense of being a logical deduction from the plain sense of the biblical text. Fourth, in conclusion I itemize some of the doctrinal errors that a clear understanding of this "cardinal doctrine" rules out, and although there are many such errors, they can usefully be grouped into two categories: pantheistic heresies and polytheistic heresies.

Creatio ex Nihilo under Siege

David Burrell says that the main difference between the period of ancient philosophy and the medieval period is that "the presence of a free creator is all important to medievals and almost entirely neglected among the ancients."[3] He further notes that the modern desire to leave behind the "scholastics" led to a downplaying of the idea of creation in the modern period. He says, "Kant's strictures reinforced the predilections of scientific inquirers to relegate any discourse about origins of the universe beyond the pale of responsible thought."[4] He notes that this led to the presumption that both creator and creatures are part of the universe, which is what I mean by philosophical naturalism. This also is close to what J. G. Machen meant by the "pantheizing" tendency of modern liberal theology.[5] But having made this move, modern philosophy then found itself in need of foundations.

> A cursory look at the strategies whereby modern philosophers compensated for the absence of a creator, however, shows them to lead inescapably to foundational grounds, be they "self-evident" propositions or "sense-data" or whatever. Once these proved illusory, we cannot but enter a "post-modern" world. And if our presumptions regarding "philosophy" itself (a la Rorty) are inherently linked to such strategies, then we will inevitably regard a postmodern context as one in which "anything goes."[6]

The absence of a free creator in modernism eventually and inevitably leads to postmodern relativism.

This analysis is basically the same as the one I will offer in chapter 9, where I argue that postmodern skepticism and relativism are just the outworking in the late modern period of the nominalist assumptions baked into the very origins of modernity in the late Middle Ages and Enlightenment periods. This

3. Burrell, "*Creatio ex Nihilo* Recovered," 5.
4. Burrell, "*Creatio ex Nihilo* Recovered," 5.
5. Machen, *Christianity and Liberalism*, 63.
6. Burrell, "*Creatio ex Nihilo* Recovered," 5.

should push us back toward a recovery of the God of classical orthodoxy, but this has not yet happened. Burrell continues:

> So a singular result of this critique of the limitations endemic to the categories presumed by modern philosophy will suggest a benign and fruitful understanding of the ways "postmodernity" liberates us from the vain search for "foundations." Then we may be pointed towards a more flexible and subtle "foundation" in a free creator. But the very transcendence of a free creator can make modern philosophers nervous, leading them to find ways of eliminating "such a hypothesis." How else explain the paucity of reflection among current philosophers of religion regarding origination of the universe, even when these be Jews, Christians or Muslims, whose traditions avow a free creator?[7]

According to this analysis, the doctrine of *creatio ex nihilo* is in eclipse today because modernity, which is a cultural pathology caused by Christian European culture losing its belief in God, has left a gaping hole in the heart of the culture that has yet to be filled. But why is Western culture so reluctant to re-embrace the Christian God?

John Webster zeros in on the source of the "nervousness" to which Burrell refers. He describes the culture's "anxiety that the pure non-reciprocal gratuity of God's creation of all things out of nothing debases the creature, for a being so radically constituted by another as to be nothing apart from that other is a being evacuated of intrinsic worth."[8] Our creaturehood, which to the Christian seems to be the greatest comfort imaginable, seems to the pagan to be the most horrifying nightmare. We thus can understand the resistance put up against this doctrine in an age like ours. This is an example of what the fathers meant by viewing theology as a spiritual discipline leading to sanctification. To accept the doctrine of *creatio ex nihilo* involves bowing the knee before the Lord and confessing our need of him. But what if he turns out to be a tyrant? The gift of faith in this situation is a manifestation of divine grace, the first evidence of which is an understanding that the God who is the transcendent Creator of the Bible is different from the nominalist God of sheer will.

Once Western culture began to see the nominalist God of the late Middle Ages as arbitrary and unpredictable, the search was on for ways to secure human autonomy against a hostile nature that constantly threatens human life with destruction. This project was a strictly humanistic endeavor because no help could be expected from the nominalist God. In the European mind, the

7. Burrell, "*Creatio ex Nihilo* Recovered," 6.
8. Webster, "'Love Is Also a Lover of Life,'" 100.

idea of transcendence gradually became linked with the idea of arbitrariness, which is the source of the anxiety Burrell and Webster describe. The myth of the cosmos as a giant self-existent machine operating according to its own immanent laws made it easy to conceptualize God as hovering outside the cosmos and only occasionally, and seemingly randomly, injecting himself into the flow of history to do a miracle. The modern deistic worldview leads to a view of God as irrelevant to most of life and as acting randomly or arbitrarily, insofar as he can be said to work in the world at all. Moralistic therapeutic Deism arises in such a situation.

Because of the distortions produced by such a metaphysics, the doctrine of God as the transcendent Creator was perceived to be a threat to modern philosophy, which values autonomy above all else and sees individual freedom as the highest good. Yet it is unhelpful to reassure modern people not to worry because God is just there to help and will not interfere with their free will. Jesus did not say "Choose me, and I will be your cosmic butler." Rather, he said "Take up your cross and follow me" (Matt. 16:24). The paradox of faith is that only by losing one's life does one gain it (Matt. 16:25). In modernity this message is contradicted by the lie of the Serpent that only by jealously guarding your autonomy can you avoid being enslaved. In a misguided and unnecessary bid to preserve freedom, contemporary Western culture is willing to choose a mythological worldview that leads to the culture of death, only to lose that freedom in spiritual slavery to false gods. But David, who wrote "The fool says in his heart, 'There is no God'" (Pss. 14:1; 53:1), would have understood. Clarifying who God really is can thus be regarded as a spiritual battle, and the question of idolatry is, quite literally, a matter of life and death, as Paul explains in Romans 1.

Many of the voices advocating the abandonment of classical theism are involved in the science-religion dialogue, and they claim that the orthodox Christian view of God and the world does not accord well with what they perceive to be the unchallengeable findings of physics and biology. For example, the panentheist Philip Clayton describes how he builds a case for the superiority of panentheism over classical theism: "One might be convinced that panentheism is more compatible than traditional theism with particular results in physics or biology; or with common features shared across the scientific disciplines such as the structure of emergence."[9] The premise here seems to be that certain scientific theories make it impossible to believe in a transcendent Creator or that the universe had a beginning. So the choice is either to cling to outdated religious beliefs or accept science as our authority

---

9. Clayton, "Panentheism," 73.

on which religious and metaphysical beliefs we can hold going forward. But what exactly is "science," and who decides which views are "scientific" and on what basis?

Science as an institution has the kind of authority in the modern world that the church had in the medieval period and can wield its power as ruthlessly as the medieval church did at times. But are the kinds of metaphysical doctrines Clayton is talking about discovered by a neutral science at the bottom of a test tube or at the end of a telescope? Are they demonstrated by predictions validated by experiments, or are they metaphysical presuppositions used to organize the empirical data into theories and metatheories? "Science," as Clayton uses the term here, appears to mean the general consensus of metaphysical views predominant in a given society at a certain time. This sort of consensus differs widely from century to century and from culture to culture. But the connection of this sort of "science" to the successful technological applications that are generated from modern science (antibiotics, computer chips, aircraft, etc.) is vague. Do the highly successful technological advances made by modern Western culture "prove" the truth of the metaphysical views held by the dominant group in the post-Christian West today?

There is such a thing as a healthy respect for realism that assumes a relationship between true scientific descriptions of the world and the ability to make measurable predictions that can be used to prove the truth of these descriptions by means of repeatable experiments. But this differs from a pragmatism that says we should believe what the majority of our peers say is true because it seems to work. The difference is not always easy to discern, however, because sophists often try to clothe their personal philosophical views in the aura of "science."[10] Two things seem rather obvious, however: (1) the prestige of experimental science in our culture can be and often is exploited by ideologues for purposes unrelated to the disinterested pursuit of truth, and (2) the metaphysical belief that God is equal to the world (pantheism) or that God contains the world (panentheism) is not in any way derived from scientific theories that are testable by measurable predictions and verified by repeatable experiments.[11] For example, no scientific experiment could prove or disprove the eternality of matter. So it is pure sophistry and an abuse of science to claim that the inability to prove the idea of *creatio ex nihilo* should count against this metaphysical doctrine. That no empirical experiment can verify or disprove the eternality of matter is irrelevant to whether this metaphysical

---

10. Richard Dawkins, for example, has made a lot of money doing this with flair. When it comes to philosophy and religion, he is more of an entertainer than a serious thinker.

11. For a good discussion of these issues, see Bavinck, *Reformed Dogmatics*, 2:412.

doctrine is true or false. Its truth or falseness will be determined by means other than empirical scientific research; we can know that the cosmos had a beginning only by special revelation. If we do not accept special revelation, the best we can achieve is agnosticism.

Clayton clearly believes, with good reason, that some sort of panentheism accords better with the predominant metaphysical beliefs of modern philosophy. But this is not by any means the same thing as saying that panentheism accords better with physics itself or any other branch of science.[12] Instead, the real issue is that panentheism fits better within a metaphysical framework that presumes the truth of philosophical naturalism. This is actually a giant tautology. As individuals committed to philosophical naturalism, many modern scientists (such as Albert Einstein, for example) have found a view that sees God as part of the cosmos to be more congenial than believing in a transcendent Creator. But this is because they are modern people shaped by the metaphysics of modernity, not because they are scientists. It is about as remarkable as discovering that a certain native German speaker loves the sound of the German language. That fact may be true, but it certainly does not objectively prove that German is the most beautiful-sounding language in the world.

Creatio ex nihilo in the Great Tradition

So far in this chapter, I have discussed the doctrine of *creatio ex nihilo* as something one either believes or does not believe. But the situation is much more complex than that, especially in modernity. In this section and the next, we will examine this doctrine in the mainstream orthodox tradition of the church, and then we will look at how biblical texts related to it are interpreted. Before proceeding, however, I will lay out the complex range of possible positions one can hold on this doctrine. It is not easy to keep straight exactly what is being affirmed and denied by various writers about *creatio ex nihilo*.

In the following list, the working definition of *creatio ex nihilo* is the belief that the eternal Triune God brought all that is not God into existence by his Word out of no preexisting material at the beginning of creaturely time. Below is a list of possible positions to which we will refer:

1. It is possible to believe that *creatio ex nihilo* is a true doctrine about the relationship of God to the world.

12. For an elaboration of this argument, which I do not have space to pursue here, see Feser, *Last Superstition*.

2. It is possible to believe that this doctrine is taught in Genesis 1, either
    a. as the plain sense of the text or
    b. as deducible from the plain sense.
3. It is possible to believe that this doctrine
    a. is taught in Genesis 1 and also in other passages of Scripture, such as Psalm 33:6, 9; 90:2; John 1:3; Acts 14:15; Romans 4:17; Hebrews 11:3; and Revelation 4:11 or that
    b. it is not taught in Genesis 1 but is taught in certain other passages in the Bible.
4. It is possible to believe that Genesis 1 says nothing one way or the other about *creatio ex nihilo*.
5. It is possible to believe that Genesis 1 assumes the eternality of matter as other ancient Near Eastern myths do.
6. It is possible to believe that Genesis 1 does not explicitly teach *creatio ex nihilo* but does imply it to one degree or another.
7. It is possible to believe in *creatio ex nihilo* while also holding that it is not taught in Genesis 1.
8. It is possible to believe that the early church developed the doctrine of *creatio ex nihilo* in the second century as a result of the encounter with Gnosticism and/or Greek philosophy.
9. It is possible to believe that in developing the doctrine of *creatio ex nihilo* the early church was drawing a latent meaning out of the text that had been there all along, that is, a *sensus plenior*. In this case, it agrees with points 1, 2b, and 6 above.
10. It is possible to believe that in developing the doctrine of *creatio ex nihilo* the early church was inventing a doctrine without biblical support, so we should regard *creatio ex nihilo* as a matter of *adiaphora*. This position says that we can believe in all that the Bible teaches about creation without believing in *creatio ex nihilo*. In this case, it agrees with point 4 above.

Obviously this list does not exhaust all the possible combinations of beliefs about *creatio ex nihilo*, and there are many variations on these themes. These positions raise many questions about the relationship of the Old Testament to ancient Near Eastern mythology, the implications of the doctrine of inspiration for interpreting Genesis 1, the hermeneutical assumptions of those who focus solely on human authorial intent in interpreting the text, and so forth. We will discuss these issues in the rest of this section and the next one.

When we turn to the question of what the Great Tradition of Christian thought has said about the doctrine of *creatio ex nihilo*, we find a long tradition of agreement on certain fundamental points. The writers we consider below all believed that the doctrine of *creatio ex nihilo* is true (point 1) and taught in Genesis 1 (point 2a or 2b) and other parts of Scripture (point 3a). Historically, the view that Genesis 1 does not teach *creatio ex nihilo* was held by heretics and non-Christians, and it has been adopted by many historical critics in the modern era. The claim that we can revise the tradition on this point in order to adopt the cosmology of modernity and remain orthodox is highly tenuous at best and flagrantly heretical at worst. But I will reserve further discussion of this issue until the final section of this chapter.

We will begin our historical review with the postapostolic fathers in the second century, specifically the first two generations after the apostles, and progress toward the present. Ian McFarland opens his book on creation with the following statement:

> In about the year 180 a Christian bishop about whom we know very little, wrote the following to a pagan about whom we know even less: "God brought everything into being out of what does not exist, so that his greatness might be known and understood throughout his works." To contemporary eyes, these words of Theophilus of Antioch may seem thoroughly unexceptional as a piece of Christian teaching, but at the time they represented something new: a doctrine of creation from nothing.[13]

Really? This is something new? According to McFarland, the doctrine of *creatio ex nihilo* comes into existence "out of nothing" in AD 180! What are we to make of this claim?

First, McFarland acknowledges that Theophilus himself believed that the doctrine of *creatio ex nihilo* is taught in Holy Scripture. He quotes Theophilus as follows:

> Therefore, in order that God might be made known truly through [God's] works, and that [we should know that] God made the heaven and the earth and all that is in them by his Word, [Moses] says, "In the beginning God created heaven and earth." And then, after speaking of their creation, he explains to us, "The earth was invisible and unformed, and darkness was over the deep, and the Spirit of God moved over the waters." So Holy Scripture teaches this first of all: how the matter, from which God made and shaped the universe itself, came to be and was brought into being by God.[14]

13. McFarland, *From Nothing*, 1.
14. Theophilus of Antioch as quoted by McFarland, *From Nothing*, 2.

McFarland further admits that Theophilus gives expression to the main-stream Christian reading of Genesis 1 but then cites "many contemporary biblical scholars" who deny that *creatio ex nihilo* is taught in Genesis 1. McFarland claims that at this point in church history, it was not yet clear that the church would break from mythological accounts of the world's origin through "birth, manipulation, emanation, conflict, or chance rearrangement."[15] Other Christians prior to this point, McFarland says, had endorsed Plato's account in the *Timaeus*, which speaks of God forming preexisting matter into its current shape, and he cites Justin Martyr as an example. The clear implication of this argument is that the Bible has not broken free of the mythological account of world formation. We addressed this issue in part 2 above, but we need to probe further in this chapter because of its central importance.

First, we must consider McFarland's claim that the postapostolic fathers did not teach *creatio ex nihilo*. It would be hard to explain why the entire Christian tradition interpreted the Bible as teaching this doctrine if in fact it is not found in the Bible. But if between the end of the apostolic age and the beginning of the tradition of teaching *creatio ex nihilo* we can find a brief absence of the teaching, this would make it a little easier to believe that the tradition got the doctrine not from the Bible but from some other source. Let us see if a postapostolic period without any teaching of *creatio ex nihilo* actually exists.

Justin Martyr

The apologist Justin Martyr was born in 100 and died in the mid-160s. He studied in various schools of philosophy before being converted to Christianity.[16] According to McFarland, "Justin commended Plato's description of creation as God's shaping of pre-existing matter precisely on the grounds that it agreed with Genesis."[17] McFarland apparently thinks that Justin saw the *Timaeus* account of creation as compatible with Genesis 1 and that, therefore, Justin had no conception of *creatio ex nihilo*. In McFarland's mind, if Justin views the *Timaeus* as agreeing with Genesis 1, then Genesis 1 must say no more than the *Timaeus* says. It is true that the *Timaeus* has no account of the original matter on which the Demiurge worked being created out of nothing. Plato asks whether the things of this world had a beginning or not, and he affirms that they did, but the beginning is described as follows:

15. McFarland, *From Nothing*, 1.
16. See the discussion of Justin in chap. 7 above.
17. McFarland, *From Nothing*, 2.

Let me tell you then why the creator made this world of generation. He was good, and the good can never have any jealousy of anything. And being free from jealousy, he desired that all things should be as like himself as they could be. This is in the truest sense the origin of creation and of the world, as we shall do well in believing on the testimony of wise men: God desired that all things should be good and nothing bad, so far as this was attainable. Wherefore also finding the whole visible sphere not at rest, but moving in an irregular and disorderly fashion, out of disorder he brought order, considering that this was in every way better than the other.[18]

But just because Justin says that Plato agrees with Moses, is McFarland's assumption warranted that Justin did not believe that Genesis 1 teaches *creatio ex nihilo*?

In considering this question, we should note first of all the context of the passage from Justin's *First Apology* cited by McFarland. Justin is claiming that Plato is *dependent* on Moses. Moses, Justin points out, is of greater antiquity than Plato, and in the ancient world the common assumption was that an older source would normally be more authoritative than a later one. I quote the passage in full:

And that you may learn that it was from our teachers—we mean the account given through the prophets—that Plato borrowed his statement that God, having altered matter which was shapeless, made the world, hear the very words spoken through Moses, who, as above shown, was the first prophet, and of greater antiquity than the Greek writers; and through whom the Spirit of prophecy, signifying how and from what materials God at first formed the world, spake thus: "In the beginning God created the heaven and the earth. And the earth was invisible and unfurnished, and darkness was upon the face of the deep; and the Spirit of God moved over the waters. And God said, Let there be light; and it was so." So that both Plato and they who agree with him, and we ourselves, have learned, and you also can be convinced, that by the word of God the whole world was made out of the substance spoken of before by Moses. And that which the poets call Erebus, we know was spoken of formerly by Moses.[19]

There are several points to note here. First, Justin makes Plato dependent on Moses, whom Justin clearly regards as more authoritative. Moses gives the original and true story; Plato adapts part of the story for his own dialogue. Second, since Plato has great cultural prestige in Justin's day, Justin is trying to show that to agree with Genesis, one need not say that Plato was wrong. Third, Plato, in actual fact, was *not* wrong to say that God shaped the formless

18. Plato, *Timaeus* 29d–30a (p. 1162).
19. Justin Martyr, *First Apology*, chap. 59 (*ANF* 1:182).

matter of Genesis 1:2 into the world as we know it. Genesis itself says the same. Fourth, to avoid having to criticize Plato, Justin does not mention *creatio ex nihilo* here, since his purpose is to show that Plato is at least partly right. But he does quote Genesis 1:1 and must have assumed that his readers would notice that there is nothing in Plato to compare with that verse. The point McFarland seems to overlook is that Genesis teaches *both* the creation of formless matter out of nothing (1:1) and the shaping of formless matter into the universe as we know it (1:2–31). Belief in *creatio ex nihilo* does not entail believing that the universe was created instantaneously, without any intermediate stage of formless matter being shaped gradually into the present configuration of the universe. It simply entails not holding that anything that is not God exists eternally alongside God. It is possible to read the idea that matter is eternal into the *Timaeus*, since it does not contain a statement equivalent to Genesis 1:1. But to read it into Justin, who quotes Genesis 1:1 approvingly, is highly suspect. There are three options: (1) Justin believes in *creatio ex nihilo* but does not stress it in his *First Apology* because his purpose is simply to show that one need not deny Plato's doctrine in order to affirm Genesis; (2) Justin does not believe in *creatio ex nihilo* because he is a Platonist, who affirms the eternality of matter; or (3) we cannot conclude from the scant evidence before us whether Justin believed in *creatio ex nihilo*.

To help us decide among these alternatives, I suggest looking at Justin's *Dialogue with Trypho* and considering Irenaeus, another important second-century figure. First, in *Dialogue with Trypho*, Justin recounts his conversion to Christianity through being directed to the books of the Prophets by an old man he encountered on a beach and with whom he had an extended dialogue. In the course of this dialogue, we see the old man using the Socratic method to correct Justin on several points of Platonic philosophy. The old man convinces Justin that Plato's doctrine of the transmigration of souls is false. Then this section of the dialogue follows:

OLD MAN. These philosophers know nothing, then, about these things; for they cannot tell what a soul is.

JUSTIN. It does not appear so.

OLD MAN. Nor ought it to be called immortal; for if it is immortal, it is plainly unbegotten.

JUSTIN. It is both unbegotten and immortal, according to some who are styled Platonists.

OLD MAN. Do you say that the world is also unbegotten?

JUSTIN. Some say so. I do not, however, agree with them.

OLD MAN. You are right; for what reason has one for supposing that a body so solid, possessing resistance, composite, changeable, decaying, and renewed every day, has not arisen from some cause? But if the world is begotten, souls also are necessarily begotten; and perhaps at one time they were not in existence, for they were made on account of men and other living creatures, if you will say that they have been begotten wholly apart, and not along with their respective bodies.

JUSTIN. This seems to be correct.

OLD MAN. They are not, then, immortal?

JUSTIN. No; since the world has appeared to us to be begotten.[20]

The Greek word translated "begotten" here is *gennētos* (γεννητός). The interpretive problem is whether to understand "begotten" here in the sense of *creatio ex nihilo*. The point of the dialogue is that souls must have been created because the world as a whole was created. Part of what the old man means by "begotten" is that "perhaps at one time they were not in existence." In order to interpret the old man's correction of Platonic thought as meaning that the world is begotten out of the being of God, one would need to place the being of God on the same ontological plane as the being of the world and deny *creatio ex nihilo*. In context, this seems unlikely. In the earlier definition of God in chapter 3 of this dialogue, Justin defines God as "that which always maintains the same nature, and in the same manner, and is the cause of all other things."[21] God's being beyond all change and the cause of all things are two fundamental elements of the doctrine of transcendence (God as immutable and unactualized actualizer). Even if one resists the conclusion that Justin believed in *creatio ex nihilo*, it is impossible to prove from the texts available to us that he rejected the doctrine or believed anything incompatible with it. In this text, we see the word "begotten" (γεννητός) evolving from meaning "emanating out from the being of God" to the idea of the world of change being caused by an unchanging creator. This evolution of the meaning of the word will come to a climax in the Niceno-Constantinopolitan Creed of AD 381 in the following key words:

begotten	not made	being of one substance [essence] with the Father
γεννηθέντα	οὐ ποιηθέντα	ὁμοούσιον τῷ πατρί
gennēthenta	*ou poiēthenta*	*homoousion tō patri*

Source: Schaff, *Greek and Latin Creeds*, 59.

20. Justin Martyr, *Dialogue with Trypho*, chap. 5 (*ANF* 1:197).
21. Justin Martyr, *Dialogue with Trypho*, chap. 3 (*ANF* 1:196).

Just as the word ὁμοούσιον gradually acquires a technical (nonmaterialistic) meaning when used in trinitarian theology, so the distinction between γεννηθέντα and ποιηθέντα acquires a technical meaning, signaling the difference in the relationship between the Father and Son (γεννηθέντα) and the relationship between the Triune God and creation (ποιηθέντα). The former word refers to a unity of being, and the latter word refers to only an analogical relationship between two kinds of being that are ontologically distinct. The heart of that ontological distinction is found here in Justin Martyr's *Dialogue with Trypho*, where he contrasts the unchanging First Cause of all things with the world (ὁ κόσμος, *ho kosmos*).

In sum, I believe that Justin did not deny *creatio ex nihilo* and probably affirmed the concept, even if he did not say it explicitly.[22] If Justin's works are the only evidence one has that proves the earliest Christians did not hold the doctrine of *creatio ex nihilo*, one is leaning on a very thin reed.

Irenaeus

Irenaeus's (AD 130–202) dates overlap with those of both Theophilus of Antioch and Justin Martyr, and McFarland has to admit that Irenaeus clearly teaches *creatio ex nihilo*,[23] as the following quote from Irenaeus demonstrates:

> For, to attribute the substance of created things to the power and will of Him who is God of all, is worthy both of credit and acceptance. It is also agreeable [to reason], and there may be well said regarding such a belief, that "the things which are impossible with men are possible with God." [Luke 18:27] While men, indeed, cannot make anything out of nothing, but only out of matter already existing, yet God is in this point pre-eminently superior to men, that He Himself called into being the substance of His creation, when previously it had no existence.[24]

Paul Blowers identifies Irenaeus as representative of an emerging pre-Nicene consensus on the creator and creation, and the first of the five points of consensus he lists is *creatio ex nihilo*.[25]

We have now considered three figures in pre-Nicene theology. We could have examined others, such as Tertullian, who strongly affirms *creatio ex nihilo*

22. After reaching this conclusion on my own, I was pleased to find Herman Bavinck (*Reformed Dogmatics*, 2:416) affirming it as well.

23. McFarland, *From Nothing*, 6.

24. Irenaeus, *Against Heresies* 2.10.4 (*ANF* 1:370).

25. Blowers, *Drama of the Divine Economy*, 99. Blowers (77) also gives a handy list of quotations from Irenaeus on creation.

and argues for it against Hermogenes.[26] In Irenaeus of Lyons and Theophilus of Antioch we find strong arguments for *creatio ex nihilo*. In Justin Martyr we see that the situation is somewhat more ambiguous than many scholars claim in their zeal to identify a period of church history in which the doctrine of *creatio ex nihilo* was not taught. The evidence suggests that from the very beginning of the postapostolic period onward, the church read the Bible this way, and as soon as they were confronted with a denial of *creatio ex nihilo*— whether from heretical Christian teachers, Greek philosophers, or Gnostics like Marcion—they immediately affirmed *creatio ex nihilo* as the teaching of the Bible. The trajectory is clear, and by the fourth century it had become a strong consensus.

Fourth-Century Fathers

By the fourth century, the doctrine of *creatio ex nihilo* was considered to be foundationally important for Christian theology. As we noted in chapter 7, Khaled Anatolios lists *creatio ex nihilo* as one of the doctrines that fourth-century Christian theology was agreed on at the beginning of the Arian controversy.[27] A few citations will suffice to illustrate this point.

Basil the Great contrasted his view with that of the Manichaeans, who held that "matter came to the Creator from without; and thus, the world results from a double origin. It has received from outside its matter and essence and from God its form and figure."[28] As a fourth-century pro-Nicene theologian, Basil writes, "But God, before all things that now attract our notice existed, . . . created matter in harmony with the form that he wished to give it. . . . God created the heavens and the earth, but not only half—he created all the heavens and all the earth, creating the essence with the form."[29] This is interesting because it draws a link between the creation of matter itself with God's ability to create the world with "harmony." This is fundamental to the idea of the original goodness of creation; that God created the entire cosmos means that his will is reflected perfectly in what is created, unlike the ancient Near Eastern myths in which violence and struggle are part of the process of bringing order to the chaos.

Commenting on Genesis 1:1–2, Augustine says that the statement that God created the heavens and the earth means that God created the formless matter of verse 2 and then perfected it afterward with the action indicated

---

26. Blowers, *Drama of the Divine Economy*, 170–71.
27. Anatolios, *Retrieving Nicaea*, 36–38.
28. Basil the Great, *Hexaemeron* 2.2–3 (in Louth, *Genesis 1–11*, 2).
29. Basil the Great, *Hexaemeron* 2.2–3 (in Louth, *Genesis 1–11*, 2).

by "Let there be. . . ."[30] Augustine understands the words "without form and void" in verse 2 as "a convenient way of making clear to people what formless matter is."[31] But even this low-level kind of formless matter would not have any being at all if it did not receive being from God. Augustine stresses that God did not make the world from his own substance and that there is no other source of being. He then concludes as follows:

> Apart from yourself nothing existed from which you might make them, O God, undivided Trinity and threefold Unity, and therefore you made heaven and earth out of nothing—heaven and earth, a great thing and a small thing, because you are omnipotent and your goodness led you to make all good things, a mighty heaven and a tiny earth. You were; but nothing else was, from which you might make heaven and earth, two realities: one near to yourself, the other bordering on nothingness; one, to which you alone would be superior, the other, than which nothing would be lower.[32]

Augustine clearly sees Genesis 1 as teaching that God created the heavens and the earth and not just that God rearranged preexisting matter into a new form. Matthew Levering points out that for Augustine, God's ability to create out of nothing indicates that he is transcendent: "As Augustine is aware, only the transcendent God can give existence, as distinct from producing emergent realities or propagating new things. For giving and sustaining the *being* of things, a transcendent creator, infinite being (and not merely the infinite sum of all finite being), is necessary."[33] The doctrine of *creatio ex nihilo* as the teaching of Genesis 1 and other biblical texts was firmly established as the mainstream teaching of the church long before the beginning of the fourth century. Augustine's massive influence on the West ensured that this teaching was highly influential in medieval Western Christianity and on the Reformers.

One of the greatest Augustinians of the Middle Ages was Thomas Aquinas. He is sometimes portrayed as a mindless slave to Aristotelian philosophy, but he quotes Augustine more than Aristotle and does not hesitate to correct Aristotle when necessary. Thomas's goal was to integrate the valid insights of Aristotle into an Augustinian theological framework in order to show how Christian wisdom is comprehensive of all true science and makes use of both general and special revelation. In *The Silence of St. Thomas*, Josef Pieper writes that Aquinas has "a fundamental idea of creation, or more precisely, the

---

30. Augustine, *On the Literal Interpretation of Genesis*, in *On Genesis*, 171.
31. Augustine, *Confessions* 12.5 (I/1, 314).
32. Augustine, *Confessions* 12.7 (I/1, 315).
33. Levering, *Engaging the Doctrine of Creation*, 16.

notion that nothing exists which is not *creatura*, except the Creator himself; and in addition, that this createdness determines entirely and all-pervasively the inner structure of the creature."[34] Thomas knows that Aristotle denies that the cosmos had a beginning and he argues that the fact that the creation did have a beginning can be known only by special revelation. As Levering shows, Thomas does much more than pay lip service to the teaching of Genesis 1; he utilizes the doctrine of creation extensively in his theology. Levering quotes David Burrell as remarking, "We are directed to this rich metaphysical mode of reflection by the scriptures themselves. . . . So we should no longer be surprised to find scripture demanding philosophical clarifications to display its own coherence."[35] Then Levering comments,

> To some theologians, it has seemed that Aquinas's metaphysical profundity comes at the cost of separating the doctrine of creation from the history of salvation. In the *Summa theologiae*, however, metaphysically informed reflection on the Triune God's act of *creatio ex nihilo* forms the basis for reflection upon the unfolding of creation in history.[36]

Reformation Scholars

The Protestant scholastics of the seventeenth century followed in Thomas's footsteps as well.[37] Calvin comments on Genesis 1:1 as follows:

> To expound the term "beginning," of Christ, is altogether frivolous. For Moses simply intends to assert that the world was not perfected at its very commencement, in the manner in which it is now seen, but that it was created an empty chaos of heaven and earth. His language therefore may be thus explained. When God in the beginning created the heaven and the earth, the earth was empty and waste. He moreover teaches by the word "created," that what before did not exist was now made; for he has not used the term . . . *yatsar*, which signifies to frame or form, but . . . *bara*, which signifies to create. Therefore his meaning is, that the world was made out of nothing. Hence the folly of those is refuted who imagine that unformed matter existed from eternity; and who gather nothing else from the narration of Moses than that the world was furnished with new ornaments, and received a form of which it was before destitute. This indeed was formerly a common fable among heathens, who had received only an obscure

34. Pieper, *Silence of St. Thomas*, 47, as quoted in Levering, *Engaging the Doctrine of Creation*, 22.

35. Burrell, "*Creatio ex Nihilo* Recovered," 19, as quoted in Levering, *Engaging the Doctrine of Creation*, 23.

36. Levering, *Engaging the Doctrine of Creation*, 23.

37. Heppe, *Reformed Dogmatics*, 190–200.

report of the creation, and who, according to custom, adulterated the truth of God with strange figments.[38]

Calvin here unambiguously affirms *creatio ex nihilo* as the meaning of Genesis 1:1. Although he sees the meaning of the text as clear, he acknowledges that the heathen assert the eternality of matter due to having received an "obscure" report of creation. I think this a reasonable suggestion. From whom would the pagan nations have received a report on creation? It is likely that they were led astray by the fallen *'ĕlōhîm*, who conveniently omitted the part of the story where the transcendent Creator brought the heavens and earth into being out of nothing.

The Westminster Confession of Faith also affirms *creatio ex nihilo*: "It pleased God the Father, Son, and Holy Ghost, for the manifestation of the glory of His eternal power, wisdom, and goodness, in the beginning, to create, or make of nothing, the world, and all things therein whether visible or invisible, in the space of six days; and all very good."[39] In doing so, the Westminster Confession of Faith is typical of Reformation confessions.

Modern Witnesses

The *Catechism of the Catholic Church*, from the twentieth century, also affirms the doctrine. The entire paragraph IV ("The Creator") is well worth reading. In section 296 we read, "We believe that God needs no pre-existent thing or any help in order to create, nor is creation any sort of necessary emanation from the divine substance. God creates freely 'out of nothing.'"[40] The *Catechism* quotes Theophilus of Antioch and is a classic expression of the doctrine.

In the twentieth century, despite the tendency of historical criticism to deny that Genesis 1:1 (or any other verse in the Bible) teaches *creatio ex nihilo*, we see determined resistance from many theologians who seek to adhere to the traditional doctrine. I will cite just two examples: Herman Bavinck and Karl Barth.

Herman Bavinck recognized the growing influence of pantheism on modern philosophy and theology and identified Spinoza and Schleiermacher as two of the most important figures in promoting pantheism in the modern period.[41] He also saw how closely materialism and pantheism are related in

---

38. Calvin, *Genesis*, 70.
39. Westminster Confession of Faith, chap. 4: "Creation," art. 1 (Dennison, *Reformed Confessions*, 4:239).
40. *Catechism of the Catholic Church*, 87.
41. Bavinck, *Reformed Dogmatics*, 2:410–11.

the development of modern thought. They are two forms of philosophical naturalism, and which one a given thinker holds is less significant than the view that all "respectable" and "scientific" thought must fall into one or the other category. Against all forms of materialism and pantheism, Bavinck affirms what he understands to be the united Christian confession of "I believe in God the Father, Almighty, Creator of heaven and earth."[42] Bavinck argues that "all things in Scripture are described . . . as having been made by God and as being absolutely dependent on him."[43] God has created all things, and they exist only because of his will and remain dependent on him at all times. Bavinck also says,

> Moreover, at no time or place is there even the slightest reference to an eternal formless matter. God alone is the Eternal and Imperishable One. He alone towers above processes of becoming and change. Things, by contrast, have a beginning and an end and are subject to change. [In Scripture] this is expressed in anthropomorphic language.[44]

While Bavinck does not see the technical, metaphysical language of being in Scripture, he does believe the idea of *creatio ex nihilo* is there. For Bavinck, the clarity with which Scripture teaches a doctrine of creation leading to the deduction that *creatio ex nihilo* is true is the reason for the consensus of the orthodox tradition that this doctrine is both true and biblical.

In the second volume of his *Church Dogmatics*, on the doctrine of creation, Karl Barth devotes significant space to the exposition of Genesis 1. He considers the possibility that the "form and void" (*tōhû wābōhû*) of verse 2 might be formless matter that preexisted creation—that is, "a primeval reality independent of creation and distinct from God"—but rejects it decisively.[45] Barth assumes that the author of Genesis 1 knew the Babylonian myth and therefore was acquainted with the idea of eternal chaos as the primeval condition of the world. However, Barth concludes as follows:

> He definitely could not and would not appropriate or reproduce it. It would clash too much with the decisive concepts of v. 1, with the *bereshith*, with the *bara*, above all with the concept of *Elohim* in this later source. It is clear enough that there is a chaos. . . . But there is no such thing as a "reality of chaos" independently confronting the Creator and His works, and able in its own power as a matter or a hostile principle to oppose his operations. It may

---

42. Bavinck, *Reformed Dogmatics*, 2:416.
43. Bavinck, *Reformed Dogmatics*, 2:417.
44. Bavinck, *Reformed Dogmatics*, 2:417–18.
45. Barth, *Church Dogmatics* III/1, 102.

well be that the concept of a *creatio ex nihilo*, of which there is no actual hint in Gen. 1–2, is the construct of later attempts at more precise formulation. But its antithesis—the mythological acceptance of a primeval reality independent of God—is excluded in practice by the general tenor of the passage as well as its position within the biblical context.[46]

This view seems to be measured and reasonable. One way to sum it up is to conclude that everything said by the phrase *creatio ex nihilo* is found in Genesis 1 except the explicit declaration that God created out of nothing the earth described in verse 2. In the next section, I will argue in a manner similar to what both Bavinck and Barth have said. If you deny that Genesis 1 implies *creatio ex nihilo*, you are saying that the text is indifferent about whether matter is eternal or was brought into existence by the Word of God. The only alternative that does justice to the text as a whole is to say that even though it does not *say* that God created out of nothing, it strongly *implies* it, since the only logical alternative is incompatible with the text. Let us now turn to the interpretation of Genesis 1.

Creatio ex nihilo and the Bible

In chapter 4 we saw that there is great controversy in modern biblical studies over the question of whether Genesis 1 teaches the doctrine of *creatio ex nihilo*. This, however, is a modern controversy; the mainstream of the Christian tradition has unanimously taught that Genesis 1:1 speaks of God's creating out of nothing all that exists apart from God's own being. From the second century to the twentieth century, the predominant view has been that Genesis 1:1 speaks of the initial creation of the world in an unfinished form, described in verse 2 as being without form (*tōhû*) and void (*bōhû*) with darkness over the face of the deep (*təhôm*).

Modern historical-critical scholarship, however, begs to differ. As we saw earlier, according to Ian McFarland, many contemporary biblical scholars assert that *creatio ex nihilo* is not found in the text.[47] In his widely cited book on the development of the doctrine of *creatio ex nihilo* in the second and third centuries, Gerhard May is quite adamant that the doctrine of *creatio ex nihilo* is absent from Scripture. Matthew Levering explains that, for May, one cannot say that the biblical text teaches *creatio ex nihilo* unless it explicitly denies that God formed the world "out of eternal

---

46. Barth, *Church Dogmatics* III/1, 103.
47. McFarland, *From Nothing*, 1.

matter."[48] This is technically true but not nearly as important as it might be made to appear.

It would be tedious to scroll through commentary after commentary from the modern historical-critical tradition that say basically the same thing. Actually, they tend to vary between two closely related positions. Some interpret the text as a product of its time, and in most cases, that time is thought to be Babylon of the sixth or fifth century BC. They assume that the text must be saying something like what the Mesopotamian myths say, and in those myths, there is no concept of *creatio ex nihilo* and no concept of the world coming into existence or having a beginning. The chaos is simply there at the start of the story. Where it came from is not discussed, which leads one to suppose that it was always there in some form or other. If that were not the case, presumably the mythmakers would have come up with a story to explain how that was so. Their silence on the point seems to be a strong indication of their considered (or perhaps unconsidered) assumption that the world is eternal as far as anyone knows. So Genesis 1 is interpreted as another entry in the lineup of myths from that time and period, which of course rules out *creatio ex nihilo*.

Other interpreters offer a slight variation on this theme. They interpret Genesis in much the same way, but with more modesty and vagueness. We do not know where the writer might have thought the *tōhû wābōhû* came from; all we know is that it is assumed to be there at the start of the six days. I suggest that this position amounts to much the same thing as the first position, except that it lacks clarity compared to the first one.

What should we say about the historical-critical approach that reads Genesis 1 in light of the Mesopotamian myths—that is, the mythological reading of Genesis? I offer four criticisms of this reading of Genesis 1.

First, this reading makes Genesis 1 seem to contradict other passages in the Bible that speak of creation. Here are some biblical texts that we need to consider when deciding what Genesis 1 says: Psalms 33:6–7, 9 and 90:2; John 1:1–3; Acts 14:15; Romans 4:16–17; Hebrews 11:3; and Revelation 4:11. Let us look at each one briefly.

> By the word of the LORD the heavens were made,
>   and by the breath of his mouth all their host.
> He gathers the waters of the sea as a heap;
>   he puts the deeps in storehouses.
> . . . .

---

48. May, *Creatio ex Nihilo*, 7. See Levering's discussion in Levering, *Engaging the Doctrine of Creation*, 34.

> For he spoke, and it came to be;
> > he commanded, and it stood firm. (Ps. 33:6–7, 9)

Like many of the psalms, this one praises God for his work of creation, which it sees as displaying God's almighty power. The phrase "By the word of the LORD the heavens were made" seems to recall Genesis 1. The question is whether "and it came to be" (v. 9) can be interpreted as "it was reshaped into the shape it now has." This idea seems to refer to Genesis 1:3–25, but only awkwardly summarizes Genesis 1:1.

> Before the mountains were brought forth,
> > or ever you had formed the earth and the world,
> > from everlasting to everlasting you are God. (Ps. 90:2)

Here we see a faint echo of the contrast in Exodus 3 between the unchanging God (I AM) and the changing world. God is said to have no beginning or end.

> In the beginning was the Word [*Logos*], and the Word was with God, and the Word was God. He was in the beginning with God. All things were made through him, and without him was not anything made that was made. (John 1:1–3)

This text begins with a clear echo of Genesis 1:1 and then moves to place Jesus Christ (cf. v. 14) in the beginning, closely identified with God the Father in the work of creation. Those who criticize the fathers for reading Christ into Genesis need to reckon with the fact that the inspired author of the Gospel of John did it first. This poses a serious theological problem: Can an inspired writer's interpretation of an earlier passage of Scripture be considered wrong? I think not. Either we must argue that John is not identifying Christ with the Word in Genesis 1, or we must accept that Christ is the Word through whom the Father created and so is present in Genesis 1. This passage seems to support *creatio ex nihilo* in saying all things were made through him and then emphasizing that without him nothing that exists was made.

> Men, why are you doing these things? We also are men, of like nature with you, and we bring you good news, that you should turn from these vain things to a living God, who made the heaven and the earth and the sea and all that is in them. (Acts 14:15)

This passage is interesting because the main topic is not the nature of creation but rather the difference between pagan idolatry and Christianity. The crowds of Lystra mistook Paul and Barnabas for gods after Paul healed a crippled man. "Barnabas they called Zeus, and Paul, Hermes, because he was the chief speaker" (Acts 14:12). In attempting to set them straight, Paul draws a contrast between the idols and the living God, who, he says, "made the heaven and the earth and the sea and all that is in them." Did Paul mean "reshaped preexisting matter into the shape we see around us" or "brought the world into existence"? It is difficult to be absolutely sure, but nothing in these words rules out the possibility that Paul meant both "brought into existence" and "formed into the present configuration."

> That is why it depends on faith, in order that the promise may rest on grace and be guaranteed to all his offspring—not only to the adherent of the law but also to the one who shares the faith of Abraham, who is the father of us all, as it is written, "I have made you the father of many nations"—in the presence of the God in whom he believed, who gives life to the dead and calls into existence the things that do not exist. (Rom. 4:16–17)

Here Paul says that God "calls" things "into existence," which strongly suggests *creatio ex nihilo*. If Paul had in mind the fashioning of preexisting matter into a new shape, this would be an odd way to express it. It is simply not credible to say that a man like Paul could not have held a view that no one around him held. As the previous quote from Acts shows, Paul had a worldview that was unique in his time, and he had a tendency to challenge quite a number of fashionable claims and practices (like idol worship, for example).

> By faith we understand that the universe was created by the word of God, so that what is seen was not made out of things that are visible. (Heb. 11:3)

If this verse does not teach *creatio ex nihilo*, it comes as close as one can without actually doing so. It refers to the universe and not just the earth, and it speaks of not making visible things out of other visible things. Would it be natural to take this to mean that God made what is visible out of special invisible stuff? That seems to read in an idea that is just not there. The contrast seems to be between fabricating something out of previously existing material and making something altogether new out of nothing.

> Worthy are you, our Lord and God,
>   to receive glory and honor and power,
>   for you created all things,
>   and by your will they existed and were created. (Rev. 4:11)

This text explicitly says that God created "all things," which reiterates what Genesis 1:1 means by the Hebrew idiom "the heavens and the earth." The tradition has typically expressed it by saying that God created all that is not God. It seems that even the formless matter was created by God.

What are we to make of these intriguing texts? None of them explicitly use the words "out of nothing" that later interpreters desire. But is *creatio ex nihilo* the clear implication of what the texts do say? Let me suggest a way to avoid having to accept these two as the only possible alternatives.

As I said in chapter 4, exegesis is a matter of first reading the text very carefully to determine what it says. When two people are having a civilized debate, it often happens that one will take what the other has said, summarize it by putting it in their own words, and then say to the first person, "Have I correctly stated your position?" When the first person agrees that the second person has accurately and acceptably summarized that person's position, then and only then can real debate begin. If I constantly describe your position in a way that you deem unfair, selective, or distorted, then the debate tends to degenerate into ad hominem attacks and name-calling. But if I restate your position in terms you are comfortable owning, then we can make progress, even if the nature of the progress is simply clarity about where we disagree. I suggest that the first step in exegesis is restating or summarizing what the text says in a fair and accurate manner. The original human author is not here to defend himself, so other interpreters will need to stand in for Paul or John or whomever and assess the accuracy of the restatement.

The second step in exegesis is to contemplate the meaning of the plain sense of the text. The kind of contemplation I have in mind here is prayerful contemplation, that is, contemplation undertaken in the presence of God. The goal is to hear what God is saying to us today through the text. The premise here is that the true Author of the text is God, because we are dealing with inspired Scripture. God is therefore the primary Author, and what God says through the text must be taken into account. If the human intention of the text determines the literal sense, the divine intention constitutes an extended or expanded literal sense. But the literal sense is what God is saying through it. The most practical way to arrive at the literal sense is to contemplate the text in its canonical context to gain clues about what the divine author may be saying. Lest we be guilty of accusing God of contradicting himself, we must assume that one text of Scripture will not contradict another.

Would denying *creatio ex nihilo* as the meaning of Genesis 1 make it contradict the other texts we have surveyed here? The answer is both no and yes. It is no on a narrow technical level. But it is yes if we follow the Westminster Confession in holding that the meaning of a biblical text includes both the plain sense (what it says) and what can be deduced from the plain sense. I think *creatio ex nihilo* can be deduced from the plain sense of the texts listed above, because unless we assume the truth of *creatio ex nihilo*, we make the texts contradict what can be deduced from other texts. For example, I believe that it can be deduced from "the heavens and the earth" (*haššāmayim wə'ēt hā'āreṣ*) in Genesis 1:1 that nothing exists except what God created, and Hebrews 11:3 says that what is visible was not made out of visible things. So if we were to interpret Hebrews 11:3 to mean that maybe they were made out of invisible things, we would be saying that some things (that is, some invisible things) were not made by God, and this would contradict Genesis 1:1. Is this argument airtight? Could one suppose that both Genesis 1 and Hebrews 11 are talking about working with preexistent matter? I personally do not think so. But even if such a supposition were possible, we must ask why the Great Tradition never came to this conclusion.

Second, denying that Genesis 1 teaches *creatio ex nihilo* is incompatible with the Great Tradition. In the previous section, we saw that the mainstream of Christian theology from the second century to the twentieth century— including Eastern, Western, Roman Catholic, and Protestant theology— agrees that the doctrine of *creatio ex nihilo* is the teaching of Holy Scripture. The question that arises is not why the tradition interpreted the Bible this way, but rather why historical criticism challenged the tradition.

Third, the mythological reading of Genesis 1 is clearly a product of its time. It presupposes that the text must be a product of its time and that its historical context was dominated by mythological thinking. During the Enlightenment, a period in which there was a huge upswing in materialism, Spinoza launched historical criticism as a movement. And during the nineteenth century, when Darwinism was shifting the view of the universe from that of a giant machine to a self-existent organism, the mythological reading of Genesis really gained ground in Christian theology. The mythological reading of Genesis did not make Genesis strange or odd in such a context; rather, it made Genesis reinforce the fashionable prejudices of the age. Evolutionary metaphysics and pantheism were becoming the dominant worldview among Western intellectuals, and Genesis was being domesticated and turned into a tract for the times rather than being allowed to function as a prophetic challenge to the cultural religion of liberal Protestantism. But Genesis 1 is not just about the creation; it is also about the creator.

Fourth, this mythological reading of Genesis 1 undermines the doctrine of God in the rest of Scripture and the classical orthodox tradition by diminishing or perhaps even erasing real transcendence. There has been a lot of pressure from evangelical scholars who have been influenced by evolutionists in the scientific disciplines to adopt the mythological reading of Genesis and thus "harmonize" Genesis and "science."[49] The current flashpoint is the historicity of Adam. Was there a first human pair who sinned and through whom sin entered the world? Was there a historical fall? These questions are pressing, and the pressure seems to be coming from those who wish to make the Bible accord with the spirit of their own age. But this is nothing new; the ancient Israelites felt pressure to join their Canaanite neighbors in idolatrous pagan worship—even human sacrifice—because of their proximity to the idolatrous nations around them.

The questions of primary interest to me in this book concern relational theism. How does God relate to the world? Is God transcendent in the sense that the classical theist tradition has claimed? Does God change and evolve in his being along with the world? Is the world his partner (or foe)? Is God completely sovereign, or is he in some sense limited by the natural world? *Creatio ex nihilo* is a key doctrine in answering such questions. You won't find a process theologian or a panentheist advocating *creatio ex nihilo*, and maybe we should draw a lesson from this fact. Perhaps this is why the orthodox tradition viewed *creatio ex nihilo* as so useful in combating heresy. Because it was so useful in distinguishing the heretics from the orthodox, the fourth-century pro-Nicene fathers could not get away from using the word ὁμοούσιον, even though the word itself (like *creatio ex nihilo*) does not occur in Scripture. I think the tradition displayed great wisdom in this matter.

I conclude that the mythological reading of Genesis 1 advocated by the historical-critical approach over the past two centuries or so is inadequate. It does not allow the unique, powerful, revealed portrait of God as the transcendent Creator to emerge from the Bible. Instead, it obscures the nature of the biblical God as we see it described in the trinitarian classical theism of historic orthodoxy and opens the door to nature-worship, pantheism, and polytheism. Given this conclusion, how can we respond with a better reading, and what resources from the Great Tradition can we use to develop such a reading? Let me briefly suggest three points and then refer readers to my book *Interpreting Scripture with the Great Tradition* for a fuller treatment.

First, we must approach the text contemplatively, expecting mystery and depth and allowing the text to speak for itself. Rather than viewing Genesis 1 as a product of its age and limiting its meaning to what the surrounding ancient Near Eastern culture could imagine, we should approach Genesis 1 as a text inspired by God and given to us in the Holy Scriptures as the teaching God deems important for us to know. We therefore approach the text asking

49. See, e.g., Lamoureux, *Evolutionary Creation*.

what it is that God wants to say to us through it. The human author's conscious intention is foundational to the literal sense, but the divine author's intention in speaking through the human author is the extended literal sense. The literal sense is what God reveals through the text, not the constricted sense of what an uninspired human author could legitimately be expected to say given his historical limitations.

Because all Scripture is inspired, it is all full of depth and mystery, but Genesis 1 is especially significant and mysterious for two reasons. First, it is the very beginning of the Bible. In my view, Genesis 1:1 is the most powerful and revolutionary sentence in the history of world literature. If it is true, then everything changes. To attribute it to an accident of scroll management that this chapter begins the five books of Moses, the Old Testament, and the Bible fails to recognize God's providence right in front of our eyes. Whatever comes at the beginning of the sacred Scriptures must be of great importance. Second, Genesis 1 is significant because it describes a miracle. The Bible begins with a miracle: "In the beginning, God created the heavens and the earth." Philosophical naturalism is refuted by the very first verse of the Bible. There is no point in thinking "Oh well, at least they are not denying the bodily resurrection of Christ when they deny *creatio ex nihilo*." Be patient, they will. It is illogical to read Genesis 1 naturalistically and Matthew 28 supernaturally. Patterns of interpretation are established in Genesis that will eventually spread throughout the Bible. (If you don't believe me, read Bultmann.)

Second, we need to allow our doctrine of inspiration to check the reckless tendency to proliferate contradictions between the plain sense and logically deduced meanings of various texts. Here I think we stand at a crossroads: in one direction lies the possibility of doing good biblical theology, and in the other lies the death of biblical theology. If we deny that Genesis 1:1 means that God created all things, then we have introduced a contradiction into the Bible, with the inevitable result that the Bible ceases to function authoritatively in theology. If the Bible contradicts itself, it cannot be our primary authority in theology.

The historical-critical approach is rooted in, and inextricable from, the evolutionary metaphysics of the nineteenth century. The evolutionary approach to the development of the doctrine of God that we examined in part 2 sees Israel's monotheism as developing from Canaanite polytheism by a process determined by social experience. In this understanding of theology, doctrines of God are symbols of communal experience and bubble up from society by a process of abstraction. In such a worldview, there is no room for revelation or a transcendent God speaking truth into human community through a prophet. There are profound and deep theoretical connections between the liberal theology of the nineteenth century and historical criticism, and neither Spinoza's heirs nor Schleiermacher's disciples could ever uphold the orthodox tradition of Nicene trinitarianism.

Third, we must ask what the text contributes to our understanding of God. The worst feature of both liberal theology and historical criticism is that they are anthropocentric rather than theocentric. In the classical tradition, theology is not about human experience of God; it is about the being of God and God's acts in history. Shifting the focus away from God to human experience replaces theology with religious studies or the history of religion. The value of theology lies precisely in its ability to call us out of ourselves and away from a preoccupation with our own ideas, experiences, and feelings to an encounter with our Creator. If it does not do this, it is not theology. This is why many biblical scholars today are not theologians and should therefore be regarded with suspicion by the church. They may purport to tell us what the Bible means, but they often reveal only the fashionable prejudices of the elites who dominate the academic culture of contemporary universities.

Creatio ex nihilo and Modern Mythology

Modernity is a cultural pathology caused by Christendom losing its faith in God, leaving a huge vacuum at the heart of the culture. Every society in human history has a worldview of some sort. The basic worldview questions are perennial and arise anytime people reflect on the meaning of life. Who am I? Where am I? What is wrong? What is the solution? These basic worldview questions can be asked and answered in any culture, no matter how primitive it may be, and they must be asked and answered by every society, no matter how advanced and scientific it may be. Prior to the emergence of natural philosophy in ancient Greece, all human cultures were mythological, including Greek society itself. In a mythological society, the worldview questions are answered by stories. Such stories may be invented from human imagination, but if they are, they still must cohere with humanity's experience of reality if they are to become central to a culture.

In chapters 3–6, we saw that some myths, or at least some twists in the plots of myths, are the result of demonic forces—called fallen 'ĕlōhîm in Scripture—deceiving human beings and distorting reality. We should not regard it as coincidental or accidental that all myths either totally exclude the transcendent Creator or diminish his being and distort his character. Despite our much-vaunted modern skepticism and hardheaded scientific mentality, we are perhaps too credulous in this area. The Bible's role as revelation is to correct and polemicize against mythical distortions of reality, especially idolatry.

In ancient Greece, the rational search for scientific answers to the worldview questions led to the rise of philosophy. Philosophy generated both physics and metaphysics. Physics studies bodies in motion by conceptualizing theories and then testing these theories with experiments that bring the theories into contact with empirical reality via prediction and measurement. Metaphysics deals with questions about what lies beyond the physical, or material, reality that makes the physical world exist as it is. Why can material reality be described in mathematical terms, making it possible to formulate theories that can be tested empirically? Why does mathematics work? This is a metaphysical question, and in the Platonic tradition it led to formulating various doctrines of universals and becoming utterly convinced that universals must exist in some form in order for the world to be as we know it to be. The question of change is a basic metaphysical question. Parmenides's belief that change is an illusion was found to be as unsatisfactory as Heraclitus's view that everything is change. The former theory contradicts the basic experience of life, growth, and death and cannot explain the change we live through as humans. The latter view cannot account for the constancy of identity through change. The baby, the child, the adult, and the old man are all one person. How is that possible?

Plato's genius was to propose his theory of forms as a way of drawing together both Parmenides's and Heraclitus's insights into one "theory of everything" in order to explain the world as a combination of change and permanence. One of the implications of such a theory was developed by Aristotle and later taken over by Thomas Aquinas as a proof of the existence of God. Put simply, the argument went like this. We observe change occurring, and change is the actualization of potential. But potential does not actualize itself; it requires an actualizer (a cause). So every change in the world is caused by something external to the thing that is changing, and this cause results in the thing's potential being actualized. Working your way up the causal chain, you eventually come to a First Cause, which itself must be uncaused. In order for a First Cause (that is, a First Actualizer) to be uncaused, it must be pure actuality with no potentiality whatsoever. This means that it does not change and cannot change but actualizes change in other things. The point is not that there had to be such a First Cause to get the series started in the first place. Rather, the point is that no change would be occurring now if such an Unactualized Actualizer were not at this moment acting at the head of a series of intermediate causes to actualize potential and thus cause change. The most basic philosophical question—"Why is there something rather than nothing?"—is more precisely formulated as "Why is there change and development in the world?" Why is there life, death, growth, and so on? God is the Unactualized Actualizer and the underlying cause of all that exists.

Existence is not a static state; it is life and change and growth. The divine being is purely actualized or fully actualized life. This is what Thomas Aquinas perceived and is the basis of his integration of philosophy and theology and of general and special revelation. Thomas stood in the patristic tradition of the Nicene doctrine of God, and he understood what John means when he reports Jesus as saying "For as the Father has life in himself, so he has granted the Son also to have life in himself" (John 5:26). God is life. This is why Jesus prayed "This is eternal life, that they know you, the only true God, and Jesus Christ whom you have sent" (John 17:3). To know and worship the one and only true God is to have life. This is why the question asked in the title of chapter 9 of this book is so vital. It also is why the first commandment in the Decalogue is to have no other gods before Yahweh. Thus Jesus sums up the Law by quoting Deuteronomy 6:5, saying, "You shall love the Lord your God with all your heart and with all your soul and with all your mind" (Matt. 22:37).

In chapter 2 I said that the Great Tradition of Christian orthodoxy has always affirmed that God is more than the god of the philosophers but not less (thesis 20). God is the Unactualized Actualizer, the First Cause of the universe. So God is the God of the philosophers. God is the simple, immutable, eternal, self-existent, First Cause of the universe. But God is also the Father who sends the Son to become incarnate and works to redeem creation through the Holy Spirit. God is eternally Triune, and so all that is true of God is true of Father, Son, and Spirit equally. The immanent Trinity is God in himself as he is eternally. The economic Trinity is God as he reveals himself through his mighty acts in history: creation, reconciliation, and redemption. Most heresies involve subtracting from God's glory by denying one or another of his attributes or acts. Most heresies also involve using univocal language for God, which tends to collapse the immanent Trinity into the economic Trinity and lower God to being a comprehensible creature instead of the mysterious transcendent Creator. God is sovereign over history, able to work by providence or miracle according to his absolute will. He alone is worthy to be worshiped (Rev. 4:8, 11).

The classical tradition of Christian orthodoxy consists of a coming together of the best of the Greek metaphysical tradition with the revealed truth of Holy Scripture, which chastises and corrects pagan mythology. Christian metaphysics is true because it combines general and special revelation into a synthesis of reason and faith so as to give the most comprehensive account of reality possible for human beings to give. This is what I mean by Christian Platonism. For this reason, to give up on either revelation or metaphysics is to relapse into mythological thinking and the sometimes gross and sometimes subtle idolatry that grows naturally and inevitably out of mythology.

One of the main forms of theological error today is the widespread tendency to reduce God to the level of the creature by viewing God as another name for nature. This is done, for example, in Spinoza's pantheism, but it is also done in Moltmann's dynamic panentheism. Here we see God conceptualized within the limits of the space-time continuum as the soul of the universe or as the universe itself. Very often we see people led unwittingly to embrace some sort of pantheism by scholars who are trying to reconcile Christian theology with naturalistic evolution. Sometimes, as in process philosophy, the universe is viewed as a living organism. But ancient humans got there first with the concept of the Mother Earth goddess, a mythology that is found globally over millennia of human history. In many ways, we could consider this to be the perennial philosophy, the default position of the human mind that is either ignorant of the transcendent Creator or unwilling to bow to him in worship.

The other main form of theological error today is the increasingly common tendency to reduce God to the level of the creature by viewing God as a being among beings, one of the existing things in the universe and therefore subject to change. We are close to this error whenever we unthinkingly refer to God as "a person." Because of the danger of reducing God to the level of a creature, I tell my students that we should say that God is personal but not that God is a person. Of course, Jesus Christ is a person, but he is a person unlike any other person in the history of the world; he is absolutely unique because he is one person with two natures. Every other person has only one nature, and we have no experience of what it means to be a person with two natures simultaneously. We need to be very careful in how we talk about Jesus Christ as a person. All univocal language should be zealously rejected, and the analogical nature of all the language we use should be highlighted and kept constantly in mind. When it comes to social trinitarianism, we multiply the potential for error by three. The relation of three persons to each other has no analogy in human or family life. We simply have no experience of what it means for three persons to have one common essence. For Peter, James, and John all to have a human nature is not the same as the Father, Son, and Spirit being one in essence. Peter, James, and John have three human natures; God has one nature. Peter, James, and John have three human wills; God has one unified will. Peter, James, and John can act in concert or singly; all three persons of the Godhead act inseparably. The most conservative version of this error is known as theistic personalism, and it is embraced by many analytic philosophers today and even by the most conservative Christians among them.

The idea that the cosmos is an eternal, self-existent, self-moving entity that evolves on its own and is alive is a myth. To worship the cosmos is idolatry. To identify it as God is a heresy. The idea that God is a being within the cosmos who interacts with other beings in such a way as to change them and be changed himself in the process is also a myth. To think of God this way is to reduce him to the status of a creature. It also is heresy. Both of these false concepts of God—pantheism and theistic personalism—are widely held as true today. Both are compatible with the metaphysics of philosophical naturalism that is so dominant in the modern West. Rejecting this false metaphysics and the concepts of God that fit within it makes one a dissenter to modernity and out-of-step with contemporary culture. It is to reject modern mythology, just as the early church rejected Greco-Roman mythology and the Old Testament prophets rejected ancient Near Eastern mythology.

Just as it was in the fourth century at the time of the Arian crisis, the doctrine that is absolutely determinative for the rejection of mythology today is the doctrine of *creatio ex nihilo*. This doctrine defines the relationship between God and the world in a way that preserves the genuine transcendence of God and ensures his sovereignty in providence and history as the unique creator of all things. The doctrine of *creatio ex nihilo* has come under constant attack in the past two centuries, but it remains centrally important to the Christian doctrine of God.

Nine

Do We Worship the God
of the Bible?

My argument is not that theologians do not treat the fourth century
as authoritative, but that the fourth century is only allowed to be
authoritative within modern systematics in ways already shaped
by particular modern and supposedly necessary constructions of
authoritative argument and thus only in ways that hide the true
challenge of those models of authoritative argument present in the
fourth-century texts themselves.

Lewis Ayres[1]

Just because a person worships a god does not mean that the god being worshiped is the one true living God of the Bible. Therefore, God commands his
people, "You shall have no other gods before me" (Exod. 20:3). This most
basic command in the Bible—to worship the one true and living God and only
him—implies that it is possible to worship other gods and thus disobey this
command. "Who is the true God?" is therefore the most important question
any human being can ask. It is a question that each of us must answer in order
to realize our human nature most fully, for as Augustine famously put it, "You
have made us and drawn us to yourself, and our heart is unquiet until it rests
in you."[2] Who God is determines who we are. To obey the Socratic injunction

---

1. Ayres, *Nicaea and Its Legacy*, 403.
2. Augustine, *Confessions* 1.1 (I/1, 39).

to know ourselves, we must first know God. Our single most fundamental task in life, therefore, is to know what and who God is.

In this book, we have sought to retrieve the answer that the historic Christian church has given throughout its existence to the question "Who is God?" We have seen that this answer is best expressed by the phrase "trinitarian classical theism," which captures the essence of the Nicene doctrine of God that crystallized in the fourth-century debates over Arianism. In chapter 1, we saw that the pro-Nicene fathers of the fourth century incorporated the simple, immutable, eternal, self-existent, transcendent God, who is knowable through general revelation, into the biblical narrative of the Triune God, who speaks and reveals himself in his mighty acts in history as Father, Son, and Holy Spirit. They identified the God of classical theism as the Triune God of the Bible, and they insisted that there is only one God and that he alone is worthy of worship. They contemplated the mighty acts of God in history in order to learn what these acts reveal about the eternal being of God in himself. For them, biblical exegesis and the development of sound doctrine based on those exegetical results went hand in hand with philosophical speculation about the mysteries of God's relationship to the world. The goal in my first chapter was to recover the classical method of doing theology by contemplating the results of exegesis and seeking to formulate doctrines that can guide us in a deeper "second exegesis," in which we try to listen to God's voice speaking to us through the text. Contemplative exegesis presumes that the Bible is a unity inspired by the Holy Spirit, with the central theme of Jesus Christ and redemption. As we contemplate the meaning of Scripture, we attempt to allow God to modify, correct, and refine our doctrines, including the metaphysical ones we use as we approach the task of exegesis. Theology never leaves the Bible behind but constantly seeks to understand its depths to a greater and greater extent.

In chapter 2, we summarized the contents of trinitarian classical theism in twenty-five theses. The historic orthodox doctrine of God was confessed and proclaimed by the church for over fifteen centuries—from the Council of Constantinople in AD 381 all the way up to the European Enlightenment of 1650–1800 and beyond. There is a continuous tradition running from the Old Testament Scriptures through the apostolic writings of the New Testament to the church fathers, coming to a climax in the writings of Augustine. Through his highly influential writings, that consensus was passed on to the great thinkers of the medieval period. The first forty-three questions of Thomas Aquinas's *Summa Theologica* constitute the locus classicus of the orthodox Christian doctrine of God. This doctrine of God, which can be termed "trinitarian classical theism," is presupposed by the Protestant

Reformers, expounded in detail by the Protestant scholastics, and embedded in the Reformation confessions such as the Augsburg Confession, the Thirty-Nine Articles, and the Westminster Confession. It is taken as fundamental truth as much by the Puritans and evangelicals as by Eastern Orthodoxy and Roman Catholicism and is expressed faithfully in the *Catechism of the Catholic Church* in the latter part of the twentieth century. This summary of the historic Christian doctrine of God is catholic in the sense of being universally held by all orthodox Christians.

Using the contemplative approach to exegesis described in chapter 1 above, we then examined Isaiah 40–48 in some depth in chapters 3–6. We saw that when interpreted within its canonical context, this important section of Isaiah teaches that God is the transcendent Creator and the sovereign Lord of history, who alone is to be worshiped. In chapter 7, we turned to the pro-Nicene theologians of the fourth century who developed the Nicene doctrine of God enshrined in the Niceno-Constantinopolitan Creed of AD 381 and found that they were using the same themes of transcendence, sovereignty, and monotheism to elaborate the same doctrine of God as Isaiah. In chapter 8, we saw that the doctrine of *creatio ex nihilo* is a key component of the identity of God both in Isaiah and the Bible as a whole and also in the Nicene tradition. The uniquely biblical doctrine of *creatio ex nihilo* serves to highlight the creator-creature distinction. The God of the Bible is totally other than creation, and his being is unique and mysterious. We cannot rationally define the nature of this God; all we can do is respond to his self-revelation in Scripture with faith and worship. The God of historic Christian orthodoxy is the transcendent Creator, and this understanding of God is found in Scripture, in the great ecumenical creeds, and in most theology up to the beginning of the modern period.

The purpose of this final chapter is to evaluate major trends in the doctrine of God in the twenty-first-century Western world. The most common theological approach today is to start with the assumptions of modernity and evaluate traditional Christian theology in an attempt to see how much of it can reasonably be made to fit within modern metaphysical assumptions and to cohere with modern cultural values. The purpose of this chapter is to turn the tables and do precisely the opposite. How should modern theology and ethics be evaluated in light of the trinitarian classical theism we have retrieved from the history of orthodox Christianity? What do current trends mean, and where will they lead if unchecked? In what specific ways does the church need to resist the spirit of the age? How can pure biblical doctrine be preserved to hand on intact to another generation? These are the questions that animate this discussion.

The church, after all, is weak and forgetful. Both liberal denominations and conservative evangelicals have little sense of being rooted in historic orthodoxy or the Bible. Everywhere we look we see novelty and startling departures from the classical tradition, such as the process theology widespread in liberal Protestantism, the dynamic panentheism of Moltmann, and the open theism of Pinnock and Sanders. Even in evangelical circles, God is often viewed as a person like us only bigger, older, and stronger, and he is said to be in time and thus subject to emotions and change just like human beings—things strenuously denied by historic Christian orthodoxy. Theistic personalism and social trinitarianism continue to make inroads, as do various forms of theistic mutualism. Concepts like immutability, impassibility, simplicity, eternity, and aseity are dismissed as Greek metaphysical ideas that are not found in Scripture. It seems obvious to many people today that the God of traditional classical theism is not the God of the Bible. We are told that we now know that God is made up of three persons who love each other like family members and that God changes his mind from time to time, gets angry, and does not know the future. Furthermore, we are told that this is what anyone who reads the Bible with an open mind will conclude that it means.

What makes these claims so astonishing is that they imply that the entire Christian tradition—including all of the leading pastor-theologians of the past fifteen centuries—missed the plain meaning of Scripture and did so by a rather wide mark. They presume that not only the church fathers but even the Protestant Reformers (in the name of *sola Scriptura*, no less) enshrined within their confessions and catechisms a doctrine of God derived not from the Bible but from pagan Greek philosophy. Is it really possible that Christian teachers and ecclesiastical bodies representing Eastern Orthodoxy, Roman Catholicism, and all the major Protestant churches—including the Anglican, Lutheran, and Reformed branches—all unanimously built the ecumenical creeds of the undivided church of the first five centuries and the confessions of the churches of the Reformation not on the rock of Holy Scripture but on the flimsy reed of Aristotelian metaphysics? There is, frankly, an air of unreality about much of what is going on in theology today.

Were all readers of the Bible for the first two millennia of the church just incompetent and illogical, or should we look to the modern cultural context for clues? The nineteenth-century "theory of theology's fall into Hellenization"[3] has been advanced as evidence that the church fathers unwittingly incorporated a Greek philosophical concept of God into their theology, but as we saw

---

3. This phrase comes from Paul Gavrilyuk (*Suffering of the Impassible God*, chap. 1), who argues persuasively against it.

in chapter 7, competent scholars have argued that this theory is overstated and obscures more than it illumines.[4] I prefer an alternative explanation. It is not the church fathers (and the entire tradition up to the eighteenth century) that fell into the trap of cultural captivity; it is modern Protestantism that came under the sway of pagan metaphysics.

We must admit that the church is never untouched by the culture around it in every age. And it is hardly a secret that contemporary Western culture is in crisis. Our culture is characterized by a pluralism so extreme that it is best described as debilitating confusion; it resembles a mental illness more than a philosophy. Both epistemological and moral relativism corrode tradition and morality. Nothing seems solid or permanent. Truth is seen as relative, and tradition is viewed as inferior. Even theology seems liquid. All is in flux and supposedly "progressing," although one struggles to understand how "progress" is the best description of a culture that is failing to reproduce itself and is characterized by the breakdown of the family, the devaluing of human life in abortion and euthanasia, skyrocketing suicide rates, an epidemic of drug abuse, and rapidly increasing rates of mental illness. If this is progress, we need less of it. And I think our skepticism should also extend to theological matters. Should we blithely accept that our doctrine of God must also "progress" along with the culture, or should we perhaps remember that not all change is positive? We all know that things are always changing throughout history, but sometimes they change for the worse and not for the better. The "caveman to spaceman" narrative of progress is a myth of the Enlightenment that only naive ideologues can take seriously at this point in history. Are we not supposedly living in a postmodern age that has left the Enlightenment behind? Whence arises this touchingly naive faith in progress?

This final chapter attempts to build on the previous ones in order to give an answer to the following questions: Why is the doctrine of God in such disarray today? What drives the revisionist impulse in twentieth-century theology? Why does the revisionist impulse extend even to evangelical theologians, and even to the conservative Calvinists among them, rather than being confined to liberal theologians? How do we make sense of the fragmentation of a mature, stable, and living tradition of theology over the past two centuries? We begin with an examination of the supposed revival of trinitarian theology in the twentieth century.

---

4. In addition to Gavrilyuk, see Wilken (*Spirit of Early Christian Thought*) and Pope Benedict XVI ("Regensburg Lecture," 130–48). Pope Benedict XVI's analysis of what he calls "dehellenization" is brilliant and repays careful reading.

The Doctrine of God Today: Revival or Revision?

Stephen Holmes notes that the conventional wisdom in the textbooks is that the twentieth century was a period of the revival of Nicene trinitarian theology. But Holmes thinks that this conventional wisdom is contradicted by the facts:

> I see the twentieth century renewal of Trinitarian theology as depending in large part on concepts and ideas that cannot be found in patristic, medieval, or Reformation accounts of the doctrine of the Trinity. In some cases, indeed, they are points explicitly and energetically repudiated as erroneous—even occasionally as formally heretical—by the earlier tradition.[5]

Academics generally do not toss the word "heretical" around lightly, so Holmes's use of it in this context is quite striking. In chapter 1 of his book, Holmes discusses the work of Barth, Rahner, and Zizioulas as foundational to the rest of twentieth-century trinitarian theology. Prior to Barth's break with liberal theology during World War I, the doctrine of the Trinity had been in eclipse since the rise of Enlightenment Deism. The most famous symbol of the way the doctrine of the Trinity had been decentered in Christian theology was Schleiermacher's placement of it at the very end of his dogmatics, in a separate section of its own.[6]

Schleiermacher holds that the doctrine of the Trinity is not really part of dogmatics because it cannot be derived directly from the Christian consciousness.[7] As B. A. Gerrish points out, Schleiermacher does not view Christian dogmatics as containing either natural science or metaphysics.[8] For Schleiermacher, dogmatics is not, as it is for traditional theology, "the study of God and all things in relation to God"[9] but rather "accounts of the Christian religious affections set forth in speech."[10] For Schleiermacher, the idea of God is the expression of the "feeling of absolute dependence."[11]

> If however, word and idea are always originally one, and the term "God" therefore presupposes an idea, then we shall simply say that this idea, which is nothing more than the expression of the feeling of absolute dependence, is the most direct reflection upon it and the most original idea with which we are here

5. S. Holmes, *Quest for the Trinity*, 2.
6. Schleiermacher, *Christian Faith*, 738–51.
7. Schleiermacher, *Christian Faith*, 740.
8. B. A. Gerrish, "Foreword" to Schleiermacher, *Christian Faith*, vii.
9. This is John Webster's definition in *God and the Works of God*, 3.
10. Schleiermacher, *Christian Faith*, 76.
11. Schleiermacher, *Christian Faith*, 17.

concerned and is quite independent of that original knowledge (properly so called), and conditioned only by our feeling of absolute dependence.

Although Schleiermacher presents his work as a dogmatics of the newly unified Protestant church in Germany, his idea of how theology talks about God is very different from, say, the definition of God given in the Westminster Shorter Catechism's answer to question 4: "God is a Spirit, infinite, eternal, and unchangeable, in his being, wisdom, power, holiness, justice, goodness, and truth."[12] Advocates of the older theology may have been self-deceived or wrong, but obviously they thought that they were talking about the being and attributes of *God*, not merely about human religious experience.

Since for Schleiermacher the *res*, or thing studied, in dogmatics is not the being and attributes of God but rather the feelings (or affections or experience) of the members of the Christian community, natural science and metaphysics are not part of revealed truth nor any part of Christian theology. As a Christian, I am therefore able to affirm Christian doctrines while allowing my views on the nature of the world to be shaped by the contemporary science of my particular age, and there is no possibility of conflict between the two. There can be no conflict because my theological beliefs are entirely subjective constructions of my mind and do not need to correspond to anything in extra-mental reality. Some form of post-Kantian constructivist epistemology is presupposed. The reality outside my mind, on the other hand, is the domain of natural science, and there is no need for theological doctrines to shape, correct, or inform my beliefs about the real world outside my mind. God, immortality, and the soul are not empirically or logically demonstrable; they are postulates of the practical reason.[13]

This might sound like a wonderfully clever scheme for protecting theology as a viable enterprise in an age of science, but we are naive if we think that this will allow our theological beliefs to continue undisturbed indefinitely. The more the "scientific worldview" (which is just materialist metaphysics in a white lab coat) takes hold of our imagination, the more belief in traditional Christian doctrines of creation, sin, and redemption slowly fades away and ceases to be operative. We have seen this process unfold in the history of liberal Protestantism over the last century as orthodox doctrines are not exactly refuted and rejected but just gradually erode as different worldviews take control of the imagination of theologians. It might be Marxism, environmentalism, or progressivism that is embraced instead, but one way or

---

12. Westminster Shorter Catechism, q. 4 (Dennison, *Reformed Confessions*, 4:353–54).
13. Kant, *Critique of Practical Reason*, 126–36.

another, Christian orthodoxy slowly loses its power to shape the Christian mind, and something else takes its place.[14]

The liberal theology against which Barth revolted is rooted in the Enlightenment's supposed demolition of natural theology and the theological metaphysics of classical orthodoxy. Kant said that it was Hume's treatment of causation that had "interrupted my dogmatic slumber,"[15] and what he meant was that he became convinced that Hume had refuted natural religion once and for all and had made classical metaphysics untenable. Hume, of course, did no such thing, but Kant and the mainstream of Western philosophy after him (including liberal theologians like Schleiermacher) believed that he did.[16] Schleiermacher's understanding of theology as the naming of human experience using religious symbols fits within the constraints of Kant's antirealist epistemology.[17] Admission to the club of modernity, however, comes at the price of having to abandon the tradition of classical orthodoxy. We must ask whether twentieth-century theology ever managed to break free from this sort of antirealist skepticism. If any major theologian of the twentieth century managed to do so, it would have to be Karl Barth. And, as Holmes points out, it is significant that Barth was the most important figure in the twentieth-century revival of trinitarian theology.[18]

Barth placed the doctrine of the Trinity at the very beginning of his massive *Church Dogmatics*, in his prolegomena in volume 1, the traditional location for the proofs for God's existence. Barth believed that our knowledge of God could be derived from Jesus Christ, and he based his entire dogmatics on that idea. This entailed, for him, rejecting the traditional proofs for the existence of God. J. Gresham Machen, however, speaks for the Great Tradition when he writes that "rational theism, the knowledge of one Supreme Person, Maker and active Ruler of the world, is at the very root of Christianity."[19] Machen points out that a knowledge of God was presupposed in all that Jesus said. Both Jesus and his contemporaries had a conception of God derived from

14. In at least one liberal Protestant church in Toronto, this process has advanced to the point where belief in God itself has faded away, and the church has an atheist for a pastor. Just when you think liberalism cannot erode any more of the faith, the creative genius of liberal theology finds a way to depart even further from the faith. See Dempsey, "Meet the United Church Minister."

15. Kant, *Prolegomena to Any Future Metaphysics*, 5.

16. Feser, *Last Superstition*, 213–14.

17. Stephen Hicks (*Explaining Postmodernism*, 58–83) sees Kant's antirealist epistemology as undermining metaphysical realism and argues that Kant opened the door to postmodernism in the twentieth century.

18. S. Holmes, *Quest for the Trinity*, 3–9.

19. Machen, *Christianity and Liberalism*, 56.

the Old Testament, which affirms that only the fool does not believe in God (Pss. 14:1; 53:1). The issue under debate was not God's existence but whether Jesus was the way to God. The controversies in the Gospels all revolve around this point. Jesus was related, Machen says, to a real Person, "whose existence was just as definite and just as much a subject of theoretic knowledge as the existence of the lilies of the field that God had clothed."[20]

For Schleiermacher, God is the word we use for the feeling of absolute dependence and thus not necessarily an actually existing being in the sense meant by classical theology. For Barth, God is known through Jesus Christ, who is the self-revelation of God. But Barth rejects natural theology and the idea that one can prove the existence of God by reason or that one can have any knowledge of God through conscience, intuition, or nature. He thus offers no resistance to the claims of Hume and Kant. But even though Barth does not directly challenge the Enlightenment demolition of Christian metaphysics, he does try to do an end run around the problem by evading the question of whether God can be said to exist independently of our beliefs about Jesus Christ. Therefore, there are two ways to interpret Barth's project as a whole. What we might call the *orthodox interpretation* of Barth thinks he means that we really do have access to extra-mental reality through the Word of God as witnessed in the words of Holy Scripture. Jesus Christ, not natural science or metaphysics, is actually the ultimate means of knowing the truth about reality. But those holding what we might call the *modernist interpretation* of Barth think he is denying that we can have any knowledge of reality outside of what our own minds construct, and therefore theological doctrines are not necessarily statements about reality itself.[21] The former view aligns Barth with Thomas Aquinas and the Great Tradition on the issue of metaphysical realism, while the latter view aligns Barth with Schleiermacher and the Enlightenment. Both interpretations are widespread today in Barth studies, but the two interpretations cannot both be right.

I do not propose to solve this long-standing, highly complex, and fiercely contested problem of historical theology in this book; I have other priorities. However, I do wish to point out one undeniable fact that may be relevant to the question of how Barth should be interpreted. We can see that in the twentieth-century theology that came after Barth, the idea of how God relates to the world deviated in increasingly serious ways from the theological metaphysics of the Great Tradition. Already in 1923 Machen observed that "modern liberalism,

20. Machen, *Christianity and Liberalism*, 57.
21. For more on this issue in Barth interpretation, see McCormack, *Orthodox and Modern*, esp. the introduction.

even when it is not consistently pantheistic, is at any rate pantheizing. It tends everywhere to break down the separateness between God and the world."[22] As we read through chapter 1 of Holmes's book, we can see that this tendency to break down the distinction between God and the world is the thread that binds together post-Barthian, twentieth-century doctrines of God. This means that theology after Barth did not manage to break free of the pantheizing tendency of the liberal theology against which Barth supposedly rebelled. What is the significance of this historical fact for interpreting Barth? Again, my purpose here is not to settle the question of the proper interpretation of Barth's project; it is rather to try to understand why and how twentieth-century theology deviated so radically from historic Christian orthodoxy. One thing is clear; even if Barth is not the cause or source of the revisionist theology that followed him, he certainly failed to prevent it from becoming the dominant stream of twentieth-century theology despite his massive influence.

To illustrate this point, we have time to look briefly at only a couple of examples of post-Barthian theology. The first is Wolfhart Pannenberg's decision to base the doctrine of the Trinity on the history of the Son's relation to the Father.[23] Pannenberg reads the Gospel accounts of the relationship between the incarnate Son and the Father not as descriptive of the relationship of the human Jesus to the Father, as the tradition had done, but as descriptive of the trinitarian relations, as the tradition had repeatedly refused to do. Pannenberg uses Rahner's rule—that the economic Trinity is the immanent Trinity and the immanent Trinity is the economic Trinity[24]—in a way that effectively reduces the immanent Trinity to the economic Trinity. This is a theme that runs throughout twentieth-century theology: once the theological metaphysics of the Great Tradition is gone, it is impossible to speak of God apart from history. There are three options: (1) God is history (Hegelianism), (2) the iron laws of history replace God (Marxian atheism), or (3) God is absent (plain old atheism). Regardless of what path modern revisionist theology takes, the result is always a loss of divine transcendence, aseity, and mystery. Pannenberg takes Barth's and Rahner's ideas and works them out to their logical conclusion in a version of the first option (Hegelianism).

Pannenberg says explicitly that he is deliberately building on Barth's decision to base the doctrine of the Trinity on the revelation of God in Christ but is using Rahner's rule to do more consistently what Barth accomplished only partially:

22. Machen, *Christianity and Liberalism*, 63.
23. S. Holmes, *Quest for the Trinity*, 17
24. Rahner, *Trinity*, 22.

Karl Barth demanded that we base the doctrine of the Trinity on the revelation of God in Jesus Christ. He did not succeed in meeting his own demand, but Karl Rahner has taken it up and sharpened it with his thesis of an identity between the immanent and economic Trinity.[25]

Pannenberg thus rushes in where Barthians fear to tread and affirms in a no-nonsense manner that "God has made himself dependent upon the course of history."[26] If one is going to read Barth in an orthodox way as being in harmony with the Great Tradition, one needs to explain why Pannenberg is wrong to think that he is merely making Barth more logically consistent by driving Barth's thought in this direction.

As a second illustration, we can examine another German theologian of the generation following Barth, Jürgen Moltmann. As Holmes rightly points out, Moltmann begins by insisting on the Gospel history, especially the passion of Christ, as *an event in the divine life*, which is, as Holmes puts it, "more self-consciously radical" than Pannenberg.[27] Moltmann develops a social doctrine of the Trinity in which the three Persons are mutually interrelated with no hierarchy, and the result is that they are like a family of individuals. Holmes notes that, as in Pannenberg's theology, Moltmann's God is dependent on the world in the sense that God binds himself in love to the creation so that "created events are events in the life of God."[28] As Moltmann puts it, "We shall start from the assumption that the relationship between God and the world has a reciprocal character."[29] In this sort of relationship, the world is changed by the action of God, and God is changed by the action of the world; it is exactly like a relationship between two creatures. This contrasts with classical orthodoxy in which God has aseity and independence so that although the world is acted upon by God and changed by God as a result, the creation is not capable of acting on God and changing God. Observe how far Moltmann is willing to go:

> The unity of Jesus the Son with the Father is a unity which preserves their separate character, indeed actually conditions it. Moreover it is not a closed unity; it is an open union. That is why we can read in the High Priestly prayer (John 17:21): "that they may all be one; even as thou, Father, art in me, and I in thee, that they also may be in us. . . ." The fellowship of the disciples with one another has to resemble the union of the Son with the Father. But not only

25. Pannenberg, *Systematic Theology*, 1:327–28.
26. Pannenberg, *Systematic Theology*, 1:329.
27. S. Holmes, *Quest for the Trinity*, 19–20.
28. S. Holmes, *Quest for the Trinity*, 22.
29. Moltmann, *Trinity and the Kingdom*, 98.

does it have to resemble that trinitarian union; in addition it has to be a union within this union. It is a *fellowship with God* and, beyond that, a *fellowship in God*. But that presupposes that the triunity is open in such a way that the whole creation can be united with it and can be one within it. The union of the divine Trinity is open for the uniting of the whole creation with itself and in itself.[30]

It is little wonder that John Cooper has written that Moltmann has developed "the most extensive explicitly panentheistic Christian theology of the late twentieth century."[31] There is a radical difference between what Moltmann is saying here and what the Augustinian-Thomist tradition has said about all beings participating in divine being and only being capable of existence by doing so. For the tradition, participation is an analogical relation in which divine being is never collapsed without remainder into creaturely being, which always remains dependent and contingent. But in Moltmann's thought, the being of God blends with creaturely being so that *both* are dependent and contingent. As Vanhoozer points out, the result is a Trinity so open as to be threatened by a "loss of transcendence."[32] For Moltmann, God and the world are so interrelated that it is difficult to discern where one ends and the other begins. The pantheizing effects of liberalism, noted by Machen, are clearly on display here.[33]

In the rest of chapter 1 of *The Quest for the Trinity*, Holmes discusses a range of major twentieth-century figures. He describes Robert Jenson as one who self-consciously develops "a radically revised metaphysics."[34] He describes John Zizioulas as offering a revisionist account of the fourth-century development of Nicene theology, which amounts to "a stress on the personal, volitional nature of God's existence."[35] Using the concept "person" in a univocal manner as having the same meaning when applied to God as when applied to humans, Zizioulas stresses personal freedom or will as the real essence of God. This view has a powerful appeal to modern people, who worship freedom from constraint as the highest good. In the work of a number of prominent analytical philosophers of religion in the Anglo-Saxon world, including Alvin Plantinga and Richard Swinburne, Holmes sees the same theme of God as a person like us only greater, older, wiser, and more powerful.[36] In various branches and types of twentieth-century theology, the

---

30. Moltmann, *Trinity and the Kingdom*, 95–96, italics original.
31. Cooper, *Panentheism*, 237.
32. Vanhoozer, *Remythologizing Theology*, 111.
33. Machen, *Christianity and Liberalism*, 63.
34. S. Holmes, *Quest for the Trinity*, 23. See also Swain, *God of the Gospel*.
35. S. Holmes, *Quest for the Trinity*, 13.
36. S. Holmes, *Quest for the Trinity*, 30–32. Dolezal (*God without Parts*, 136–47) also evaluates these philosophers as departing from classical theism and falling prey to univocism.

pantheizing effects of nineteenth-century liberal theology persist and gain momentum, while in other branches there is a tendency toward seeing God as a being like us within the cosmos.

Brian Davies uses the term "theistic personalism" to describe a widespread tendency in twentieth-century theology.[37] For Davies, "theistic personalism" stands in contrast to "classical theism." Some theistic personalists think of God as a being within time, learning as he goes along and acting and being acted upon. Most deny that God is impassible and immutable. They tend to downplay mystery, and they use language about God and humans univocally, rather than analogically as the Great Tradition has done. It might seem odd that theistic personalism and social trinitarianism would flourish alongside pantheism and panentheism. However, after reflection we see that this is not really so strange: pantheism and polytheism go together in other contexts, such as ancient Greco-Roman mythology and philosophy and also in Hinduism. What all these sets of ideas have in common is the absence of the concept of transcendence as characterizing the relation of God to the world. The idea of a personal transcendent God is a uniquely biblical and Christian idea, and once trinitarian classical theism is left behind, the sense of mystery and wonder over the astonishing fact of the creator and First Cause of the universe *speaking* to us is lost. Either God is regarded as less than the transcendent Creator (that is, as a mere person differing from us only in degree), or God is seen as less than personal (that is, as one with nature and/or history). But the one way he is never understood in modernity is as both transcendent and personal simultaneously, which is the central point of classical orthodoxy.[38]

As I discussed in chapter 1, this new kind of theism so prevalent in twentieth-century thought is what James Dolezal calls "theistic mutualism."[39] The key feature of this kind of theism is that God and the world are involved in a mutual give-and-take relationship. In what Dolezal terms "hard theistic mutualism," God is portrayed as needing the world in some respect: the world affects God necessarily and causes actual change in him. Process theology is an example of hard theistic mutualism. In "soft theistic mutualism," on the other hand, God does not need to create and cannot be affected by the world except as he sovereignly permits it to happen. But soft theistic mutualists contend that God does allow real change in his being and that if he did not do so, he would not really be in a genuine relationship with us. Thus they use

37. Davies, *Introduction to the Philosophy of Religion*, 9–16.
38. For an elaboration of this point, see chap. 2 of my *Interpreting Scripture with the Great Tradition* and chap. 2 of the present book, where I elaborate on the nature of trinitarian classical theism with regard to freedom and inspiration.
39. Dolezal, *All That Is in God*, 1–8.

univocal language to conceive of the relationship between God and humans in the same way they conceive of a relationship between two creatures. Open theism is an example of soft theistic mutualism, although Dolezal shows that less-extreme versions of the same idea can also be found in a large number of evangelical and Reformed theologians, as we shall see in the last section of this chapter. The difference between the soft and hard versions of theistic mutualism is simply how much change occurs in God and how much power the world has over against God. But in the end, it is all just a matter of degree. In both hard and soft theistic mutualism, God's being is neither immutable nor independent of creation. Divine transcendence is radically redefined if not denied altogether. The creator-creature distinction is placed in grave jeopardy or denied outright. All of this constitutes a radical revision of the classical orthodox doctrine of God. At some point, it clearly descends into soul-destroying heresy.

What we see in the purported revival of trinitarian theology in the twentieth century, therefore, is not a revival of Nicene orthodoxy or a recovery of the trinitarian classical theism confessed by the church for over 1,500 years. Rather, what we see is a series of radial departures from the entire tradition. This is why Lewis Ayres offers this stark analysis: "In many ways the argument of my last chapter is not that modern Trinitarianism has engaged with pro-Nicene theology badly, but that it has barely engaged with it at all. As a result the legacy of Nicaea remains paradoxically the unnoticed ghost at the modern Trinitarian feast."[40] What we see in the so-called revival of trinitarian theology in the twentieth century is not a revival but a revision, not a recovery of orthodoxy but an accommodation of the faith to the spirit of the age. In the next section, I offer a possible explanation of how this astonishing development came about.

The Origins of Modern Revisionist Theology

Classical orthodoxy was nearly unanimous in affirming what I call "trinitarian classical theism" from the fourth to the eighteenth centuries, but twentieth-century theology departed radically from this doctrine in the name of reviving the doctrine of the Trinity. My explanation for how this occurred lies in understanding the role of metaphysics in the history of theology.

In order to understand contemporary theology, we must understand the intellectual culture in which it is embedded, and this entails understanding

---

40. Ayres, *Nicaea and Its Legacy*, 7.

what modernity is and how it came to be. I define modernity as a pathological condition caused by the rejection of the Christian God by a culture whose soul was shaped by belief in that God. By this I mean that Western culture is essentially Christendom, and Christendom is now dying because Western culture has lost its faith in God. Without faith in God, Western culture is Christendom without Christ, an empty shell without a soul.[41]

The West gradually emerged in the Middle Ages after the collapse of the western half of the Roman Empire; pagan Rome fell into decay and rotted from within. As that happened, however, Christian biblical revelation fused with certain Greek philosophical ideas to produce a new, vigorous, and innovative civilization that rose quickly in the early Middle Ages in Europe. Christendom was a dynamic force that gave the world such magnificent accomplishments as the university, the hospital, limited government, the rule of law, freedom of religion, Gothic architecture, polyphony, the art of the Dutch masters, modern medicine, and modern science. Politically, intellectually, and militarily Europe rose to world dominance in the modern era.

The reasons for the rise of Western Christendom are many and various, but any explanation is incomplete without recognizing that so much beauty and scientific truth and so many useful inventions could not have been attained unless the architects of that culture were in touch with reality, at least to some degree. Of Western culture's many accomplishments of world historical significance, none would have been possible for a culture that was totally out of touch with reality and living in a dream world or driven by false religion or ideology. This of course does not mean it was anywhere near perfect; after all, the whole project was run by fallen descendants of Adam, who were crippled by original sin. Violence, military conquest, colonial exploitation, and greed were also integral parts of the story, as has been the case with every civilization in human history. But Western European culture was in touch with reality because of Christianity. The theology derived from the Bible corrects, extends, and completes the knowledge of God derived from reason operating on its own, and the result is knowledge of the true and living God and his creation.

41. In his many books, Christopher Dawson has developed an extensive critique of Western culture centered on this basic point. A good entry point into Dawson's thought is his collection of essays *Christianity and European Culture*. In particular, see the essay "Civilization in Crisis" in that book, where Dawson writes the following: "In the last resort every civilization depends not on its material resources and its methods of production but on the spiritual vision of its greatest minds and on the way in which this experience is transmitted to the community by faith and tradition and education. Where unifying spiritual vision is lost—where it is no longer transmitted to the community as a whole—the civilization decays. 'Where there is no vision, the people perish'" (78; cf. Prov. 29:18 KJV). This analysis is what a non-Marxist theory of culture looks like.

Part of that knowledge of God involves a self-knowledge, which includes an acknowledgment of our sinfulness as sons and daughters of Adam. But Christianity not only recognizes sin as part of our reality; it also has ways of dealing with it. Therefore, such a culture could both engage in the sin of slavery on a massive scale and yet also eventually become the first great civilization in world history to abolish slavery. Any adequate account of Western culture has to explain *both* of these facts, and the currently fashionable view that Western culture is totally evil is simply incapable of explaining all the relevant facts because it is merely ideology.[42] In any case, only a knowledge of the true God could allow a culture to get its arms around reality to the extent that Western culture did. However, the harbingers of the decline of Western culture were discernable in it early on, for every human culture since the tower of Babel has carried within it the seeds of its own destruction. This is part of what the story of the tower of Babel tells us, as great thinkers from Augustine of Hippo to J. R. R. Tolkien have recognized.

My analysis of the etiology of the decline of Western culture as primarily metaphysical in nature is informed by a large number of sources: I mention in particular the work of C. S. Lewis, John Milbank, Hans Boersma, Hans Frei, Alasdair MacIntyre, Michael Allen Gillespie, and Peter Kreeft.[43] The beginnings of the decay of the West can be located in several movements in late medieval scholastic thought, including nominalism (William of Occam) and voluntarism (Duns Scotus). To place the origins of the decline so far back in time may seem counterintuitive. Does it really make sense to attribute cultural decline in the twentieth century to intellectual movements in late-medieval scholasticism? And did not many of the greatest advances of the

---

42. Just to be clear, I am using the word "ideology" here in the sense of one of the secondary definitions of the word: "Ideal or abstract speculation; in a depreciatory sense, unpractical or visionary theorizing or speculation." *Shorter Oxford English Dictionary*, 2nd ed. (1989), s.v. "ideology."

43. Everything written by C. S. Lewis is important, but see especially his scintillating little book *Abolition of Man*. His fiction is also important, esp. *Silver Chair* and *That Hideous Strength*. Kreeft's book *C. S. Lewis for the Third Millennium* is extremely helpful. It contains a clear and concise account of the rise of modernity and how Lewis offers an alternative. Milbank's *Theology and Social Theory* is highly stimulating, although I cannot follow him in rejecting classical philosophical realism, which is a very serious problem for his work (5). He is most helpful, however, in his critique of modernity. Boersma's *Heavenly Participation* is excellent, and Frei's *Eclipse of Biblical Narrative* has been widely influential. I read MacIntyre's brilliant book *After Virtue* many years ago, and it remains formative for my thinking as an insightful critique of modernity. Gillespie (*Theological Origins of Modernity*) offers remarkably clear insights into the changes in the doctrine of God at the beginning of modernity. Kreeft's *Platonic Tradition* contains a portrayal of Christian Platonism that is remarkably similar to mine, all the more remarkable because I did not read it until my *Interpreting Scripture with the Great Tradition* had already been published.

West come *after* the fourteenth century? Much of the material prosperity and military power of the West emerged only in the seventeenth and eighteenth centuries, and it is true that the nineteenth century was the era of European world dominance, when the sun never set on the British Empire. But European world dominance in the nineteenth century was built on a house of cards, as the events following 1914 clearly demonstrated.

The sack of Rome in 410 was preceded by centuries of decay. In fact, many thoughtful Romans, including Augustine, held that removing Rome's only serious rival by the defeat of Carthage in the Third Punic War in 146 BC opened the door to the decline of morality and discipline that led to the fall of Rome half a millennium later, in AD 410. Augustine writes of how "Asiatic luxury, worse than any armed enemy," crept into Rome and how "it became obvious that Carthage's sudden overthrow did Rome far more harm than its previous hostility had ever done."[44]

Like the ancient Roman Republic, the moral and intellectual foundations of the West were cracked. After the "long nineteenth century," the events of 1914 ushered in the manifold disasters of the twentieth century: the Great War, the rise of Fascism and World War II, the Holocaust, the rise of Communism, the Gulag, nuclear war, the Cultural Revolution, and the Sexual Revolution. The scale of the disasters was unprecedented, and the rapidity of the change was practically unmanageable. Traditions dissolved, governments fell, and the basic social unit, the family, began to disintegrate as postmodernism and nihilism spread throughout the Western world. In June 1978, Solzhenitsyn tried to warn the West in his famous Harvard commencement address, "A World Split Apart."[45] He saw the same rotten religious and moral foundations in the West that he had seen in the Soviet Union. His analysis of how a disaster such as Stalinism was possible was simple but profound. In another very significant speech, he put it this way: "Men have forgotten God, that's why all this has happened."[46] In his post–World War II book *Ideas Have Consequences*, Richard Weaver locates the origins of moral and epistemological relativism and the loss of belief in the dignity of humankind way back in

---

44. Augustine, *City of God* 3.21 (I/6, 98–99).

45. This speech is often known by the title "A World Split Apart," which, after some preliminary remarks, are the opening words of the speech proper. However, it was published in *Harvard Magazine* under the title "The Exhausted West," which can be accessed online. It was reprinted in Solzhenitsyn, *Solzhenitsyn Reader*, 561–75.

46. Solzhenitsyn, "Men Have Forgotten God." This was his address in 1983 when he was awarded the Templeton Prize for Religion. It can be accessed online but is also reprinted in Solzhenitsyn, *Solzhenitsyn Reader*, 576–84. For more of his speeches during this period, see Solzhenitsyn, *Warning to the West*.

late-medieval nominalism.[47] Conservative thinkers from C. S. Lewis to Russel Kirk and from T. S. Eliot to Peter Kreeft offered the same analysis: there is no future without a return to the past, because truth is truth no matter when it is first discovered and articulated.

Nominalism is the denial of philosophical realism, which is an implication of the Christian doctrine of God's creation of the world. Belief in the existence of universals (realism) was part of what allowed people in the Middle Ages to understand that nature is not just booming, buzzing confusion but rather an orderly and structured entity governed by laws that can be expressed mathematically. Numbers are universals, and without mathematics, modern natural science would not be possible. So science depends on universals, and to deny universals brings science itself into question.

For medieval thinkers, hierarchy in society was meant to mirror the hierarchy found in nature, which was believed to mirror the hierarchy in the heavens. The world was created by a good God through his *Logos* in such a way that order and structure was imprinted on the world through the act of creation. Moreover, the same Creator made us humans in his own image, and part of what that meant to the theologians of Christendom was that we are rational creatures with the capacity to comprehend the logical structures inherent in creation. This set of background beliefs was necessary for the emergence of natural science. Order is not simply appearance; it is inherent in reality as such, and the mind is capable of grasping it. This set of metaphysical beliefs makes natural science possible.[48] Yet in late modernity, order in nature is dismissed as mere illusion. Darwinism stares at order and purpose in nature and denies that it is really there.

When you put together a belief in the classical concept of God as the all-wise and all-loving Creator with the concept of nature as an ordered cosmos, you have the foundation for all sorts of great cultural achievements, including natural science. But what happens if you lose confidence in the goodness and predictability of God? Michael Allen Gillespie suggests that the impact of nominalism on the Western concept of God was greatly magnified by the series of disasters that befell Europe in the fourteenth century and led to just such a loss of confidence. Early modern Europe felt the impact of a crisis of faith. Two things came together at just the right moment to produce this crisis: a dangerous idea and a set of events that magnified the impact of the idea.

---

47. R. Weaver, *Ideas Have Consequences*, 3ff.

48. Burt makes this case in *Metaphysical Foundations*. Pope Benedict XVI's "Regensburg Lecture" also makes this case very lucidly and beautifully, and the editor, James Schall, expertly explains the context of Benedict's speech. That book contains the full text of the lecture.

The idea was nominalism. William of Occam wanted to affirm the total and complete sovereignty of God, and he thought that in order to be completely sovereign or free, God must be unpredictable.[49] So he engaged in thought experiments such as wondering if God could change the Ten Commandments. Could he command us to commit adultery? If so, would adultery then be right? If you said no, would that not imply that there is a law higher than God to which God must adhere? And if so, would that not de-throne God from being sovereign? And if you said yes, would that not preserve God's total freedom? Thus, the idea of a constant natural law that we could know apart from God's command became problematic: how could such an idea be consistent with divine sovereignty? But as the idea of God being predictably good became more difficult to accept, the degree of uncertainty we face as humans in an unpredictable universe increased exponentially. Now all this scholastic, intellectual speculation might have remained at the theoretical level but for some social circumstances that plunged Europe into a terrifying state of chaos.

During the fourteenth century, a perfect storm of disasters engulfed Europe and caused great anxiety, fear, and loss of cultural confidence. First, there was the Black Death, which eradicated one-third of the population with an accompanying decline in town life, international travel, and trade. Second, there was the Little Ice Age and the decline in arable land together with an increase in hunger and poverty. Third, there was the Hundred Years' War between France and England, which meant that the age was characterized by constant upheaval and violence. Fourth, there were the social dislocations caused by the Crusades, including the draining off of much of the best leadership and wealth of the continent into a lost cause in foreign lands. Fifth, just to make everything worse, the church was weak and undergoing the "Babylonian captivity" of the papacy, and for a time there were two, and for a while even three, popes. When you put it all together, the fourteenth was a very bad century; in fact, it was the worst period Europe would see until the horrors of the twentieth century. In this situation, the nominalist God of sheer will was of no comfort to suffering people; in fact, such a God was a threat. As Gillespie writes,

> Nominalism sought to tear the rationalistic veil from the face of God in order to found a true Christianity, but in doing so it revealed a capricious God, fearsome in his power, unknowable, unpredictable, unconstrained by nature and reason, and indifferent to good and evil. This vision of God turned the order

49. Kreeft, *Platonic Tradition*, 67–83.

of nature into a chaos of individual beings and the order of logic into a mere concatenation of names. Man himself was dethroned from his exalted place in the natural order of things and cast adrift in an infinite universe with no natural law to guide him and no certain path to salvation. It is thus not surprising that for all but the most extreme ascetics and mystics, this dark God of nominalism proved to be a profound source of anxiety and insecurity.[50]

In a situation characterized above all by uncertainty, danger, and suffering, believing in the nominalist God only made matters worse. This new and dark concept of God is the source of modern atheism, or to put it differently, modern atheism rejects this type of God and assumes that there is no other God in which to believe.

This concept of God also led Western thinkers to a new correlative concept of the human in which *will* is the essence of man just as *will* is the essence of God. In the opening sentences of his great work *Institutes of the Christian Religion*, John Calvin notes that the knowledge of God is intertwined with our knowledge of ourselves:

> Nearly all the wisdom we possess, that is to say, true and sound wisdom, consists of two parts: the knowledge of God and of ourselves. But, while joined by many bonds, which one precedes and brings forth the other is not easy to discern. . . . Again, it is certain that man never achieves a clear knowledge of himself unless he has first looked upon God's face, and then descends from contemplating him to scrutinize himself.[51]

In early modernity, thinkers descended from contemplating the face of the nominalist God of sheer will to scrutinize themselves as creatures characterized by the will to conquer nature in the name of making an inhospitable world safe for human habitation.

After the fourteenth century, we see the rise of early modern science and technology, and it is in this cultural context that we see the rejection of teleology and final causation, which only get in the way of the task of gaining mastery over nature and subjecting it to human will. The concern of early modern thinkers such as Francis Bacon was to gain power over nature through technology, using technological power to master the chaos of nature or at least stem its most pernicious effects.[52] The emphasis was on power, not wisdom, and on theory only as a means to technological application. This ushered in

---

50. Gillespie, *Theological Origins of Modernity*, 29.
51. Calvin, *Institutes*, 1.1.1 (1:35); 1.1.2 (1:37).
52. See Grant, *Technology and Justice*.

the era of invention, technological innovation, and machines, which gathered steam in the Enlightenment era (1650–1800) and continued through the nineteenth and twentieth centuries. Until the mid-twentieth century, technological progress functioned for many Western intellectuals as practically a substitute religion and source of meaning in life. Auschwitz and Hiroshima, therefore, were not only human tragedies; they were also the destruction of meaning for many post-Christian Western progressivists. The Gulag similarly destroyed the faith of many Marxists. Technology was the god that failed spectacularly to deliver on its promises of utopia and of providing meaning for humans. The human will is an inadequate source of meaning precisely because it is just as arbitrary and unpredictable as the nominalist God.

The Great Tradition of Christian theology defines not only God but also God's relationship to creation, that is, to nature and to us. The classical orthodox view of God stresses that God is metaphysically ultimate, the First Cause and source of all things, and that God is transcendent Being itself. The "god" of modernity, on the other hand, is a person in time like us, only bigger and more powerful, and he is entirely unpredictable and beyond good and evil. Trinitarian classical theism regards God as goodness itself and grounds the moral law and scientific laws in the very being of God, thus evading the pernicious choice of regarding law as either above God (which robs God of his sovereignty) or below God (which makes God arbitrary and unpredictable). Modern people need to hear of the God of the Bible and Christian orthodoxy, a God who is goodness itself and therefore always acts in harmony with his own nature, but modernity is precisely the rejection of the metaphysical implications of the orthodox Christian doctrine of God.

Modernity's Rejection of the Theological Metaphysics of Nicaea

The church fathers interacted with the best philosophy of their day and extracted certain ideas from it that they saw as compatible with the revelation given in the Bible, and they utilized these ideas in the articulation of what they saw as the metaphysical implications of revealed theology. Here I want briefly to sketch out a framework for understanding the relationship between the theological metaphysics of Nicaea and modernity. The goal is to understand what has been lost and what needs to be recovered.

In *Interpreting Scripture with the Great Tradition*, I suggested that the theological metaphysics of the Great Tradition can usefully be labeled "Christian Platonism." Some readers reacted with suspicion to any positive use of the term "Platonism." It is important to restrain one's instinctive hostility to this term until it is defined clearly enough to make meaningful debate possible. Once the following set of definitions has been considered, it should be apparent why there is such unrelenting, unnuanced, and uncompromising antagonism to this term from those in thrall to modernity. Modernity hates both Platonism and Christianity, and putting elements of both together in one phrase is to poke the beast in the eye with a hot stick. Nietzsche, for example, could never make up his mind whether he hated Platonism or Christianity more.[53] Those interested in being biblical and orthodox should perhaps take note that at least "Christian Platonism" has all the right enemies and therefore deserves a hearing.

Lloyd Gerson, a historian of ancient philosophy, has spent a lot of time thinking about how best to understand the history of Greek philosophy. He notes that prior to the nineteenth century, Platonism was defined quite broadly to include the teachings of Socrates, Plato himself, Aristotle, the Middle Platonists, the Academics, and the Neoplatonists up to Porphyry and Proclus. Platonism thus constituted the central tradition in Greek philosophical thought for eight centuries and is to be contrasted mainly with naturalism or materialism. Platonists believed in a nonmaterial reality to which this material cosmos is related and on which it actually depends. Given this fact, it is not hard to see why the church fathers would view Platonism as a more promising conversation partner than, say, Epicureanism or Stoicism or, God forbid, the Sophists. Platonists believed in truth and objective science and accepted the reality of a moral law that is not mind-dependent but rather is built into the nature of reality. But the Platonists disagreed among themselves on many issues; Platonism was a living, breathing debate, not a fossilized set of ideological talking points. This led Christian theologians to see value in engaging Platonism in dialogue.

Gerson proposes a five-part framework of ideas that he calls "Ur-Platonism" as a kind of skeleton that fits all sorts of Platonist thinkers who differ on many points but agree on these five main points. In a brilliant move, Gerson expresses his five points as negatives so as to provide as much room for disagreement as possible within a common framework. The five points are antimaterialism, antinominalism, antimechanism, antiskepticism, and antirelativism.[54] Gerson is not claiming that all Platonist philosophers consciously and explicitly emphasized these five points as such; it is a heuristic reconstruction of a general philosophical position that can be viewed as the framework of Platonism as a philosophical tradition.

---

53. See his famous gibe about Christianity being merely "Platonism for the people" (often translated "Platonism for the masses"). Nietzsche, *Beyond Good and Evil*, 14.
54. Gerson, *From Plato to Platonism*, 9–19.

Gerson defines *antimaterialism* as "the view that it is false that the only things that exist are bodies and their properties."[55] A Platonist, for example, typically believes that humans are made up of souls as well as bodies. Christians know that this doctrine is taught in the Bible. Gerson defines *antimechanism* as "the view that the only sort of explanations available in principle to a materialist are inadequate for explaining the natural order."[56] When people are materialists, the usual route they follow in science is to accept only mechanistic explanations for change. As a Christian, I view this as transferring an attribute of God as pure actuality (with the power of self-motion) to the creation and regarding the creature as if it were God, a form of idolatry according to Romans 1. So we again see how the fathers might view Platonism as better than the alternative. Gerson defines *antinominalism* as "the view that it is false that the only things that exist are individuals, each uniquely situated in space and time."[57] Nominalism says that each existing thing is unique, but antinominalists contend that two things can be unique individuals and still have the same nature, because their natures are universals that inhere in individually existing things. The nominalist, on the other hand, has difficulty explaining how there can be both sameness and difference; if two things are not identical, they must be unique. Antinominalism can thus be regarded as a basic metaphysical concept necessary for science. Nominalism therefore is antiscience. Gerson defines *antirelativism* as the denial of the view attributed to Protagoras by Plato that "man is the measure of all things, of what is that it is and of what it is not that it is not."[58] There are two kinds of relativism—epistemological and ethical—and both are prevalent in the postmodernism of contemporary culture. As Gerson points out, ethical relativism is virtually hedonism, which we see in the sexual revolution of the twentieth century. Epistemological relativism defines truth as what is true for me or my group, and we see this in postmodernism. But relativism based on antirealism tends to destroy the possibility of knowledge as a cultural possession and degenerates into the will to power. Modernity prefers the hedonism of Epicureanism and the antirealism of the Sophists over Platonism. Gerson defines *antiskepticism* as "the view that knowledge is possible."[59] He shows that if either materialism or nominalism were true, skepticism would follow. Plato attacks the sophists with vigor for denigrating the necessity and possibility of knowledge, and he would have a field day attacking the target-rich environment of late modern Western academia.

55. Gerson, *From Plato to Platonism*, 11.
56. Gerson, *From Plato to Platonism*, 11.
57. Gerson, *From Plato to Platonism*, 12.
58. Gerson, *From Plato to Platonism*, 13.
59. Gerson, *From Plato to Platonism*, 13.

Gerson contends that there is a large (though certainly not infinite) range of possible positions one could hold and still be operating within the framework of Ur-Platonism. His basic reason for holding to Ur-Platonism is its explanatory power: only such a set of metaphysical views makes it possible to explain the phenomena that the philosopher must explain. Human knowledge of the world cannot be explained by materialism, and a culture that has had such tremendous success with science and technology should laugh at the suggestion that genuine human knowledge of the world is impossible. Yet this is exactly what is implied by materialism and nominalism, which can be seen, for example, in David Hume's denial of causality.[60] One way to conceptualize how Ur-Platonism relates to Western culture is to think of our culture's rise and success as being caused by the acceptance of Ur-Platonism and the decline and crisis of our culture as being caused by the subsequent rejection of Ur-Platonism.

This is why I gave an account of the rise of nominalism in the previous section. The fourteenth century was the turning point in the story; it was the crack in the metaphysical foundations of the West. The reason the church fathers found it worthwhile to make an alliance with Platonism was that the metaphysical framework of Ur-Platonism is true and consistent with the teaching of Scripture, even if individual Platonists hold many wrong doctrines. Christian Platonism is Ur-Platonism fleshed out and corrected using biblical theology. In the world of late antiquity, Neoplatonism was the main rival to Christian Platonism, and the latter eventually triumphed over the former. For example, the fathers found it necessary to make the crucial creator-creature distinction using the key doctrine of *creatio ex nihilo* in order to correct Platonism and make it compatible with biblical revelation. When Ur-Platonism is placed within the framework of the biblical doctrine of creation, it does a serviceable job of expressing key metaphysical truths that follow from the doctrine of creation. The Bible does not merely teach that universals exist; it explains why and how they exist. For Augustine and Aquinas, universals are ideas in the mind of the Creator God, and this is how they can exist in reality without existing anywhere in the material cosmos except in individually existing things. Thus scholastic realism solves the problem raised by Aristotle's critique of Plato's theory of the forms. Creation through the divine Logos explains rational structure in nature. The correspondence, the fit, between the order of nature that we express in scientific laws and the human mind,

---

60. For a refutation of Hume's attack on the concept of causation, see Feser, *Five Proofs*, 40–42. Feser shows how contradictory and inappropriate it is for an empiricist, of all people, to question the principle of causality.

which grasps those laws, is something that materialistic Darwinism is utterly incapable of either explaining or grounding. But the Christian doctrine of God as Creator does both.[61]

The decline of the West, which is part of what I mean by "modernity," is simply the systematic, point-by-point rejection of the theological metaphysics of the Great Tradition, which I refer to as "Christian Platonism," that is, Ur-Platonism fleshed out and corrected by biblical theology. In the late Middle Ages, we see the rise of *nominalism* in the thought of William of Occam. In the thought of the pioneers of early modern science, such as Descartes and Bacon, we see the rise of *mechanism*. The Enlightenment takes up the cause of *materialism* with a quasi-religious fervor to complete the destruction of realism, the supernatural, God, creation, and providence. After the end of the Enlightenment, *skepticism* comes to a high point in the writings of David Hume. Then, following the constructivist thought of Immanuel Kant, we see a rapid descent into *epistemological relativism* in Nietzsche and the postmodernists and *ethical relativism* in the sexual revolution of the twentieth century. At the same time, Darwin's thought was undermining the Christian doctrine of creation that undergirded the theological metaphysics derived from the Nicene doctrine of God. It was then just at that point that the peace, prosperity, and cultural complacency of the Victorian Age was shattered by the Great War. In an eerily similar way to the perfect storm of the fourteenth century, a series of gigantic cultural disasters hammered Europe in the twentieth century, and the result was a massive loss of cultural confidence, the collapse of Christianity, and the rise of Nietzschean will to power in the great totalitarian systems of the twentieth century. The impact of bad ideas was magnified by a perfect storm of civilizational disasters. As Solzhenitsyn warned, we cannot forget God and expect not to become inhuman in our relationships to one another. If we forget God, totalitarianism follows.

Evangelical Theology as the Conservative Wing of the Liberal Project

In modernity, the rejection of Ur-Platonism results in the rise of a set of metaphysical beliefs consisting of materialism, nominalism, mechanism, relativism, and skepticism, which one might call "Ur-Modernism." These beliefs

---

61. For a dismantling of scientism, the doctrine that science is the only and self-sufficient source of truth, see Feser, *Last Superstition*, 83–85, 191, and all of chap. 6. For arguments against the view that science is the only genuine source of knowledge, see Feser, *Five Proofs*, 273–85. His arguments show not that scientism is probably not true but that we can be rationally certain that it is not true. In chap. 6 of *Last Superstition*, Feser shows how consistent scientism clearly and necessarily devolves into nihilism.

are often associated with postmodernism, but they were actually baked into modernity from the beginning of the modern project in the fifteenth century, and they flourished during the Enlightenment (1650–1800). Postmodernism should really be called "hypermodernism," for it is merely the logical outworking of modernist metaphysical assumptions. Modernity puts this nihilistic worldview into practice one step at a time. The theological metaphysics of Nicene Christianity shaped Christendom, but modern metaphysics shapes the modern West. The change from one metaphysical system to the other is the fundamental difference between the two, and the differences go all the way down. Christianity was at home in Christendom, and Christian Platonism fit well with the Nicene doctrine of God. But when modernity arose, the entire classical theological system was shaken to the core.

Whether Christian theology had any place in modernity was a serious question confronted by theologians, philosophers, and scientists in the nineteenth century. Did Christian theology have any place, for example, in the emerging research universities of the nineteenth and early twentieth centuries? If so, what concept of theology would be appropriate in an academy built on modern metaphysics? The liberal project was found to be necessary in order to seek answers to such questions. The liberal project consisted of historical criticism of the Bible stemming from Spinoza and of revisionist theology stemming from Schleiermacher.[62] I treat the rise of historical criticism extensively in chapter 4 of *Interpreting Scripture with the Great Tradition*, but here I want to focus on the revisionist views concerning God and his relationship to the world that stem from Schleiermacher. In an earlier section of this chapter, I argued that twentieth-century theology is a continuation (with a possible hiatus in the massive work of Barth) of nineteenth-century liberal theology and its pantheizing tendencies. Now it is possible to explicate the exact nature of the liberal project, both in its nineteenth- and its twentieth-century forms.

An attempt is being made to restate all Christian doctrines on the basis of, and in the context of, modern metaphysics. This is what the liberal project is all about. In commenting on the shift in modern theology that Hans Frei spoke of as "the great reversal," Kevin Vanhoozer describes it as "that fateful moment when theologians began to see their task as fitting the biblical story of God and the gospel into the world as understood by modern science and

---

62. In *Interpreting Scripture with the Great Tradition*, I used the supplanting of Christian Platonism's metaphysical analysis by modern metaphysics to explain why modern hermeneutics has gone off the rails so drastically. In the present book, I am using the same historical analysis to explain why the modern doctrine of God has departed so radically from classical orthodoxy. Theology and hermeneutics are integrally related.

philosophy."[63] They do not affirm one particular way of stating the doctrine of God; arguments can take place about the relative merits of process theology and theistic personalism *within* the context of the liberal project. However, the modern metaphysical beliefs described above ("Ur-Modernism") are used as the framework within which all Christian doctrine must fit. To the extent that a given doctrine does not fit, it must be trimmed, revised, and changed to make it fit. Theology cannot be allowed to speak of a God who is completely transcendent and free of influence from the creation so as to be immutable and impassible. The proofs for the existence of God cannot be regarded as logically valid. The Bible cannot be regarded as inerrant and infallible when it comes to history or science. In short, no Christian doctrine can be permitted to have implications for metaphysics or natural science if those implications pose a direct challenge to materialism, mechanism, nominalism, relativism, or skepticism.

The only kind of Christian theology that can be allowed to exist within the modern secularized university is whatever is left after it has been revised along these lines. It seems inevitable that whatever ends up being left over after the "acids of modernity"[64] have done their work will not even faintly resemble historical Christianity. In fact, what is left over will be the paganism that existed in the world before Yahweh revealed himself to Abraham. In other words, if pursued to its logical end, the liberal project must necessarily lead to the utter destruction of the Christian faith and to the rise of a new paganism.

In the quotation that heads this chapter, Lewis Ayres says,

> My argument is not that theologians do not treat the fourth century as authoritative, but that the fourth century is only allowed to be authoritative within modern systematics in ways already shaped by particular modern and supposedly necessary constructions of authoritative argument and thus only in ways that hide the true challenge of those models of authoritative argument present in the fourth-century texts themselves.[65]

I agree with Ayres that modern systematics is "shaped by particular modern and supposedly necessary constructions of authoritative argument" and that fourth-century pro-Nicene theology is not really allowed to challenge modern systematic theology. In this chapter I have tried to explain why this is the case. Whether Ayres would agree with all the particulars of my argument is

---

63. Vanhoozer, *Remythologizing Theology*, 29. See Frei, *Eclipse of Biblical Narrative*.

64. This phrase comes from Lippman, *Preface to Morals*, 8. This book was first published in 1929.

65. Ayres, *Nicaea and Its Legacy*, 403.

beside the point. The main point is that participation in the liberal project is fraught with peril, and in order for *ressourcement* to succeed, it is necessary to refuse the presuppositions of modernity and to challenge the very rules of the game rather than trying to play it more skillfully than one's opponents.

Many contemporary evangelical theologians are trying to play the game called the liberal project without understanding what game they are playing or what its rules actually are. A great deal of contemporary evangelical theology is trapped within modernist metaphysical assumptions without understanding either the origin or the trajectory of those assumptions. The biggest weakness of evangelical theology today is that it lacks a profound grasp of the history of metaphysics, and this deficiency arises not because evangelical biblical scholars and systematic theologians are not intelligent. Rather, there is a lack of competence across the range of subdisciplines in theology. Overspecialization means that Old Testament scholars do not understand enough about metaphysics to be competent in biblical theology. Systematic theologians do not understand enough about patristic theology to see where they are departing from the tradition.

No one can be an expert in everything, but statements about God constitute theology, and theology is a single activity. Anyone who wishes to do theology of any sort—from Old Testament exegesis to systematic theology—needs basic competence in all of the following areas: the history of philosophy and theology, biblical languages, biblical hermeneutics, biblical introduction, the history of biblical interpretation, biblical theology, and dogmatic theology. To ask that it be made easier is to ask the impossible; it cannot be less complicated than it is. Asking that theologians without competencies in all these areas be allowed to do theology is like demanding that a person with only high school biology be allowed to perform surgery. It can be done, but the results will not be pretty.

To delineate the problem more precisely, observe this curious fact: most evangelicals would see the need for systematic theologians to make use of the results of biblical exegesis in doing their work, but most would *not* see the need for biblical exegetes to make use of systematic theology in doing their work. In fact, they would be more likely to see the use of systematic theology in exegesis as a liability. This reflects the modern prejudice against dogma and the influence of the liberal project being carried out in the secular academy. In an effort to secularize the interpretation of the Bible, historical criticism rejects the regulative role of dogma in biblical interpretation because it desires to substitute modern metaphysics in the place of the dogmatic and creedal heritage of the church. If we do not realize this, we do not understand what is really going on. In this book, I have tried to model a way of doing systematic theology that refuses to play the game according to the rules of modernity.

Geerhardus Vos is an example of a theologian who did understand that biblical theology needs to make use of systematic theology in order to be faithful.[66] In the introduction to his *Biblical Theology*, he traces the changing definitions of the term "biblical theology" in Protestant scholasticism, pietism, and then in the Enlightenment thought of J. P. Gabler.[67] He notes that Gabler's oft-quoted definition is influenced by the rationalism of his school, and he discusses the impact of rationalism on the discipline of biblical theology. He notes the naturalism inherent in nineteenth-century "philosophy of evolution," which

> teaches that nothing can be known but phenomena, only the impressionistic side of the world, not the interior objective reality, the so-called "things in themselves." Such things as God, the soul, immortality, a future life, etc., cannot enter into human knowledge, which in fact is no knowledge in the old solid sense. Consequently all these objective verities come to be regarded as lying beyond the province of Theology. If the name *Theology* is still retained, it is a misnomer for a classification and discussion of religious phenomena.[68]

Clearly Vos has Kant and Schleiermacher in his sights here. He is aware of the importance of metaphysics for biblical interpretation and the nature of theology, and he knows that modern metaphysical doctrines have shaped nineteenth-century historical criticism and liberal theology.

In response, some evangelical biblical scholars and theologians say that they are trying to evangelize the culture and trying to win a hearing in the secular academy and that this is why they employ "methodological naturalism" in their scholarly work. But it is highly dangerous to reduce all theology to apologetics. There is, of course, a place for apologetics; I do not wish to be dismissive of it. But to reduce all of theology to apologetics is like reducing the marriage relationship to courtship. Courtship is essential, but there is much more to marriage than that. Apologetics oversteps its bounds when it becomes determinative of theological method.

Theology should be primarily exegetical and contemplative and should lead first and foremost to worship. The title of this chapter—"Do We Worship the God of the Bible?"—is the basic question that theology must address. And

66. In addition to the work in biblical theology for which he is famous, Vos also authored a multivolume systematic theology. See Vos, *Reformed Dogmatics*.

67. Vos, *Biblical Theology*, 9.

68. Vos, *Biblical Theology*, 11.

often the best apologetic is deep truth expressed without compromise and put into practice, which is what the church does every Lord's Day in worship. Worship is our first priority, because if we take our eyes off the One who is high and lifted up and who alone is to be worshiped, we can easily fall into error. When the surrounding culture is pagan and dismissive of God and the Bible, the temptation is strong to put a little water into the wine of revelation in an attempt to make the doctrine of God more palatable to non-Christians. Throughout Israel's history the people were tempted to make Yahweh more like the other gods—to worship him in the way the other gods were worshiped, to think of him as being like the other gods, and even to fall into the trap of thinking he could be manipulated like the other gods. But the LORD says, "To whom then will you compare me, that I should be like him? says the Holy One" (Isa. 40:25). If the Bible is right in saying that the LORD is incomparable, then we must acknowledge that we cannot bring others to faith in God by making him seem more familiar and less strange to the children of this world. In light of these reflections, let us consider some of the trends and teachings common in evangelical theology today.

In the final section of this chapter, I want to examine evangelical theology. In James E. Dolezal's penetrating work *All That Is in God: Evangelical Theology and the Challenge of Classical Christian Theism*, he makes the surprising statement that even confessional Calvinists are succumbing to the charms of theistic mutualism.[69] As he discusses divine immutability in chapter 2, he names those he feels have been influenced by theistic mutualism, and it reads like a "Who's Who" of the Evangelical Theological Society and Evangelical Philosophical Society: Donald MacLeod, J. Oliver Buswell, Ronald H. Nash, D. A. Carson, Bruce Ward, Rob Lister, J. P. Moreland, William Lane Craig, Wayne Grudem, and even J. I. Packer.[70] It is surprising to see Bruce Ware on this list, because Ware has written so vigorously against open theism.[71] Dolezal, who is unfailingly polite, does not accuse his fellow conservative evangelicals of heresy. Rather, he argues that these theologians are well-meaning but confused. He believes, as do I, that they are sincerely attempting to be biblically sound and historically orthodox in their work, but they do not completely succeed in achieving what they intend.

For example, in the book *God Is Impassible and Impassioned: Toward a Theology of Divine Emotion*, Rob Lister, one of Ware's students, develops a monograph-length case for viewing God as both impassible and

---

69. Dolezal, *All That Is in God*, 3.
70. Dolezal, *All That Is in God*, 21–35.
71. Ware, *God's Lesser Glory*.

impassioned. The book does not say that the orthodox tradition is wrong about impassibility; rather, it says that the patristic tradition taught that God is both. Lister then proceeds to develop his own view of God as both. Where Lister goes wrong is not in his intention to remain orthodox but in his misunderstanding of the patristic tradition and, particularly, the significance of the distinction between the immanent Trinity and the economic Trinity.

Because the fathers followed the pattern of biblical language in saying that God loves, has mercy on, and is wrathful toward creatures in the course of history, Lister concludes that the fathers taught that God is impassioned. And from the creaturely perspective, this is true. When I repent of my sins, God forgives me (1 John 1:9). For me as a creature, this is a perfectly true statement. The Bible says it, and we should not be afraid to say it. But the Bible also presents God as perfect and unchanging, and this is also true (Mal. 3:6; James 1:17). Scripture does not contradict Scripture, and we must interpret these verses so that one does not contradict the other. Lister does not distinguish clearly between passages in the fathers where they are simply following the pattern of biblical speech in stating that God (from our perspective) changes in some way and other passages in the fathers where they are reflecting on how the two strands of biblical teaching can be reconciled as noncontradictory and even mutually illuminating.

He does deal with one of the latter kind of passages from Augustine's *The Trinity*, but Lister fails to understand that Augustine's doctrine of God's eternity is not incompatible with Augustine's ability to say that God is loving, merciful, and so forth. He seems not to grasp that Augustine is attempting to explain why it is legitimate to say that, from the creature's perspective, God changes, while also affirming that God in himself does not change. Here is part of the passage in which Augustine discusses this point:

> Thus when he is called something with reference to creation, while indeed he begins to be called it in time, we should understand that this does not involve anything happening to God's own substance, but only to the created thing to which the relationship predicated of him refers. *Lord*, says the psalm, *you have become our refuge* (Ps. 90:1). God is called our refuge by way of relationship; the name has reference to us. And he becomes our refuge when we take refuge in him. Does this mean that something happens then in his nature, which was not there before we took refuge in him? No, the change takes place in us; we were worse before we took refuge in him, and we become better by taking refuge in him. But in him, no change at all. So too, he begins to be our Father when we are born again by his grace, because He gave us the right to become sons of God (John 1:12). So too our substance changes for the better when we are

made his sons; at the same time he begins to be our Father, but without any change in his substance.[72]

Augustine obviously thinks that he has explained why the language of Scripture is stating the truth that God does become our refuge and we do become his sons. This does justice to the meaning of the texts involved, but Augustine does not interpret them as saying that God's being changes because of our human decisions. Yet Lister claims that "Augustine's doctrine of divine eternity appears to hinder his case for God's emotional expression."[73] But Augustine never said that God's expressing emotion was a change in his being. The issue is whether Augustine's explanation of the meaning of the scriptural text is correct. I would say that Augustine has explained how the texts identify a change in our status, and I believe that Augustine's interpretation correctly gets at the meaning of the texts. Lister, however, is not satisfied.

Lister insists that Augustine should read a meaning into the text that I do not believe is there—namely, that God "is capable of having actual in-time relations with his creatures,"[74] which in context appears to mean that God changes as a result of the actions of his creatures. Lister must mean this, because otherwise he has nothing to complain about in Augustine's statements in this passage. Augustine explains how the creature changes and how the creature's relation to God changes (he becomes our refuge, we become his sons). But this does not satisfy Lister, and he accuses Augustine of inconsistency because "Augustine's doctrine of divine eternity appears to hinder his case for God's emotional expression." What else could Lister mean but that he is unhappy that Augustine does not believe God's being changes even as the relationship of the creature to God changes?

Lister fails to see that in the depths of God's own being (that is, God considered as immanent Trinity), God is *more* than what is revealed in God's actions in history (that is, God considered as economic Trinity). The immanent being of God is partially but not completely revealed in the divine acts in history, because the ability of the creature to comprehend the divine nature is limited. What is revealed is all true, and nothing in the depths of the divine nature could ever contradict what is revealed, but what is revealed does not provide an *exhaustive* account of the depths of God's being. It is this "something more" in the immanent divine nature that makes God ultimately unknowable to the creature.[75]

---

72. Augustine, *Trinity* 5.4.16–17 (I/5, 204).
73. Lister, *God Is Impassible and Impassioned*, 106.
74. Lister, *God Is Impassible and Impassioned*, 106.
75. Lister (*God Is Impassible and Impassioned*, 244–45) quotes John Thompson, who accuses Moltmann of collapsing the immanent Trinity into the economic Trinity and failing to

Actually, God is both knowable and unknowable in different ways. God is unknowable in that the creature cannot comprehend the totality of what God is. But God is knowable in that God can take a bit of his own self-knowledge and communicate it to the creature so that the creature can have true but limited, creaturely knowledge of God. This is why the immanent Trinity cannot be collapsed into the economic Trinity, which often happens in modern theology. Failing to distinguish between the immanent Trinity and the economic Trinity results in a loss of divine mystery and transcendence and the downgrading of God to the level of a creature.

When we compare the accounts of Augustine and Lister, we find that Augustine is able to understand the divine immutability and divine action in history as paradoxical because Augustine does not collapse the immanent Trinity into the economic Trinity. Without this key distinction, divine immutability and divine action in history become a contradiction rather than a paradox. A paradox, we recall, is only an apparent contradiction, not a real one. For Lister, either God has emotional experiences that change his being, just as our emotional experiences change our beings, or else God cannot be said to be loving or merciful or wrathful. For Augustine, God's actions in history are compatible with his eternity, immutability, and impassibility because he is not a creature in time like us, and his being is different from ours, not just in degree but also in kind. He does not *have* experiences in the way we do because his being is qualitatively different from our creaturely being. So while analogies are valid at certain points, we cannot speak of God's action and our action in univocal terms; nor can we speak of God's being and our being in univocal terms.

Ironically, Lister criticizes the tradition for affirming a paradox while he himself appears to affirm a contradiction. Augustine does not teach that God both changes and does not change in exactly the same way at exactly the same time, which would be a contradiction. Rather, he affirms God's mysterious eternity and immutability at the same time as he affirms the reality of the change in the creature's relationship to him. The difference between the divine being and created being is where the mystery is located, and this is what prevents the paradox from being a contradiction. But Lister places the mystery within the divine being itself in a univocal manner:

---

make a proper distinction between creator and creature when he asserts that God suffers on the cross, but Lister does not himself criticize Moltmann for speaking of the being of God in univocal terms as if it were just like creaturely being. Instead, he criticizes Moltmann's doctrine of the cross as being only a revelation of the nature of God and not the means of redemption for sinners. Lister is quite right to level this latter criticism against Moltmann, but Moltmann's historicizing the being of God is an even more fundamental problem.

God's ontological immutability gives rise to his ethical immutability, and both of those in turn secure God's relational mutability toward his creatures in the appropriate moral contexts. . . . God's ontological impassibility (by which, again, we mean invulnerability, not impassivity) makes certain, in virtue of his constant character, that God will respond not only with the appropriate volition, but also with the perfectly fitted affective response to his creatures' in-time moral and personal fluctuations. . . . God's relational passions accord completely with his will, but this passion is no less passionate for being perfectly voluntary.[76]

From what Lister writes here, I can only conclude that he is, in Dolezal's terms, a soft theistic mutualist, who locates the inconsistency between God's being impassible and impassioned within the being of God himself, which constitutes a contradiction, not a paradox.

Lister is not the only evangelical theologian who thinks he is making only a minor modification to the doctrine of God and not really departing from the tradition.[77] This sort of "minor modification" is widespread today, and this kind of misunderstanding of the patristic tradition is equally common. A good question to ask at this point is "Why is it so hard for modern theologians to understand the patristic position?" If the medieval schoolmen could do it and the Reformed scholastics and Puritans could do it, why can modern evangelicals not do it? Well, of course, many modern evangelicals do understand it, but given the origins of modernity described above and the pervasiveness of the liberal project, we see that our historical context militates against understanding, let alone defending, the historic orthodox doctrine of God. Modern metaphysical assumptions are widely taken for granted, seldom challenged, and hardly ever competently refuted. In such an intellectual context, it is not surprising that many theologians become convinced that the only viable way forward is some sort of compromise with modernity. They despair of ever overturning the metaphysics of modernity. But I believe that the intellectual structure of modernity is rotten, and one of these days it is going to topple over on its own. Standing firm while the surrounding culture self-destructs was how the early church conquered the Roman Empire, and all we need to do is imitate that example.

I conclude, therefore, that a great deal of contemporary evangelical theology seems to be merely a conservative wing of the liberal project. As conservatives, evangelicals do not seek change for the sake of change, and they are never as radical as they could be. They seek to purchase a respected

76. Lister, *God Is Impassible and Impassioned*, 242–43.
77. One prominent and influential theologian who takes the same sort of line is Oliphant, *God with Us*.

place in the secular academy for the cheapest possible price by attempting to make as few changes to received doctrine as possible in order to fit into the modern metaphysical framework. They often make the alterations only in their narrow area of specialization, and in this way, overspecialization facilitates the illusion of continuity even as compromise occurs. They succeed in convincing themselves that they are remaining faithful to the Bible and the Great Tradition even though they have had to do a bit of trimming and tucking here and there to get things to fit well enough to pass inspection in the academy. However, the bigger question is whether there is any future in the liberal project and anything to gain from being preoccupied with it. If it is just going to end in neopaganism, why bother with it? What about the cost in time and energy that is drained away from the primary exegetical-contemplative task of theology? We need to be less interested in passing fads in a decadent and declining culture and much more concerned with the permanent things.

Epilogue

Why the Church Does Not Change Its Mind

I began this book by recounting how my mind has changed over the past two decades. My journey has been against the grain of modernity, but it has been a journey into the heart of the unchanging faith of those who know the God of the Bible. "Jesus Christ is the same yesterday and today and forever" (Heb. 13:8), and the saints rest securely in his unchanging love. Since God has come among us by miraculous actions in history and, in these last days, in the person of his Son, the Lord Jesus Christ, our knowledge of God arises from the contemplation of his action in history.

What we seek in our contemplation of his action is certain knowledge of his eternal being. We want to know God as God is in the depths of his perfect nature. This is what drives theology forward. But we do not see history itself as the revelation of God; we see divine self-revelation in the providential and miraculous history of redemption as interpreted by the prophets and apostles of Holy Scripture. History itself is often inscrutable; in Jesus Christ we find the key to comprehension. The witness of the church focuses on Christ and the gospel, not on current events or the immediate past and imminent future. History contains many false starts, wrong turns, and much regress as well as progress. But we know *whom* we have believed (2 Tim. 1:12).

Sometimes we preserve past progress just by standing still while the flood sweeps away those whose grasp of the truth is weak. In certain historical situations in the past, the church has survived by refusing to panic and give up the truth of Scripture in the face of seemingly overwhelming challenges from those who embody the spirit of the age. One such historical situation stands out above all others. In AD 360, with an Arian emperor on the throne of Rome, things looked bleak for Nicene orthodoxy. Jerome famously wrote, "At that moment the term *Usia* [*Ousia*] was abolished: the Nicene Faith stood condemned by acclamation. The whole world groaned, and was astonished to find itself Arian."[1] Officially, the empire was Arian, with an Arian creed and an Arian emperor. The Nicene faith was illegal, on the ropes, and apparently doomed. Yet despite all this, within twenty years the Nicene doctrine of God would be established as orthodoxy at the Council of Constantinople, the Nicene ὁμοούσιον would be restored to the creed, and the church would be saved from heresy. Things may look bad for the orthodox doctrine of God right now, but this is not the first time in history that this has happened.

Now is not the time for compromise but for standing fast in the truth: "Let us hold fast the confession of our hope without wavering, for he who promised is faithful" (Heb. 10:23). As Paul instructed the Thessalonians, "Test everything; hold fast what is good" (1 Thess. 5:21). We must resist the temptation to feel ashamed of historic orthodoxy as though it is somehow outdated. In the ninth century BC, King Ahab probably told Elijah that he was not on the "right side of history"! This is what heretics always say, but it is just wishful thinking on their part. The Bible makes clear that history is in the hands of the transcendent Creator of the cosmos, who is guiding and directing all things to their destiny in Christ. We have the promise of our Lord: "I am coming soon. Hold fast what you have, so that no one may seize your crown" (Rev. 3:11).

In this book, I have called on Christians to find new hope by engaging in the work of *ressourcement*—that is, the recovery of treasures from the past that can enrich our witness and common life in the present and the future. It may seem paradoxical that in order to be more biblical, we must acknowledge that God is the simple, immutable, eternal, self-existent, First Cause of the cosmos. But if we are to bear faithful witness to the God who speaks and acts in the Bible, this is what we must do. For the God of the Bible is not less than the god of the philosophers, but more. There is no God behind the God of the Bible, because the God who speaks and acts to judge and save in Israel and finally in Jesus Christ is not merely the tribal god of the Jews and Christians but the only true God—the transcendent Creator and sovereign Lord of history, who alone is worthy of worship by the entire rational creation, both human and angelic.

---

1. Jerome, *Dialogue against the Luciferians* 19 (NPNF[2] 6:329).

Appendix

Twenty-Five Theses on Trinitarian Classical Theism

Thesis 1: Christian theology consists of the doctrine of the church of Jesus Christ derived from Holy Scripture, not from the opinions of mere human beings.

Thesis 2: Theology is the study of God and all things in relation to God.

Thesis 3: Theology can be divided into two parts: (1) what is taught explicitly in Scripture and (2) what may be deduced from what is taught explicitly in Scripture.

Thesis 4: Christian theology consists of exegesis, doctrines, and metaphysical implications of doctrine, which form the context for further exegesis.

Thesis 5: God's existence is evident to reason, even though fallen human beings, because of sin, either deny God's existence or refuse to be grateful to him and worship him (Rom. 1:20).

Thesis 6: God is the First Cause of all that exists but is not himself caused, since existence is part of his own essence (Exod. 3:14).

Thesis 7: God has aseity, or independence from creation; while creation is dependent on God, the reverse is not true.

Thesis 8: God is eternal, which means that he has neither beginning nor end as all creatures do.

Thesis 9: As the First Cause of all that exists other than himself, God is immutable.

Thesis 10: As pure act, God is simple.

Thesis 11: God is transcendent, which means that he is not a being within the universe but the sovereign Lord of all that exists.

Thesis 12: The language we use for God is analogical rather than either univocal or equivocal.

Thesis 13: God is omnipotent, which means that his act fulfills his nature perfectly in all things.

Thesis 14: God is omnipresent in the sense that all things are present to him, and "in him all things hold together" (Col. 1:17).

Thesis 15: God is omniscient, which means that he knows all things—past, present, and future—in one eternal act.

Thesis 16: God's transcendence does not prevent him from acting in history to speak, judge, and save.

Thesis 17: God is holy, just, and wrathful, but God is also loving, merciful, and gracious.

Thesis 18: The immutable First Cause of all things, who speaks and acts, is a paradox, not a contradiction; this is a mystery, which is what the major paradoxes of the faith are called.

Thesis 19: God is incomprehensible to the creature; although we can have true knowledge of God, we can never have comprehensive knowledge of God, which means that we can know God without comprehending God.

Thesis 20: The God of the Bible is more than the god of the philosophers but not less.

Thesis 21: The created order bears the imprint of the divine Logos, and humans are created in the image of God, which means that the human mind can apprehend the order and structure in the creation, which is the basis of natural theology, natural moral law, and scientific laws.

Thesis 22: The transcendent Creator of the universe has revealed himself to Israel and climactically in Jesus Christ, which is the First Mystery of God.

Thesis 23: The Nicene doctrine of the Trinity expresses the unity of the Father, the Son, and the Spirit—three persons (*hypostases*) but one being (*ousia*), which is the Second Mystery of God.

Thesis 24: The Second Person of the Trinity, the Son, has assumed a human nature into a hypostatic union with himself in the incarnation, which is the Third Mystery of God.

Thesis 25: The purpose of theology is neither to dissolve nor to explain the mysteries of the faith; rather, the purpose of theology is to define what the church believes, teaches, and confesses about these mysteries to enable contemplation and worship of God while avoiding heresy.

Bibliography

Works cited in the footnotes or mentioned in the text are listed here, as well as a few other works of particular importance for the argument of this book. All items are written in, or translated into, English. We are increasingly well served by the wide availability of patristic, medieval, and Reformation works in English translation. Although historians of theology will always need to work in the original languages, especially Latin and Greek, pastors and generalists can now gain a firsthand acquaintance with the rich heritage of the Christian tradition. To cite only three prominent examples, the Works of Augustine series from the New City Press and the Ancient Christian Commentary on Scripture series and the Reformation Commentary on Scripture series from InterVarsity Press are of great value to biblical and systematic theologians.

Ahlström, Gösta W. *The History of Ancient Palestine from the Palaeolithic Period to Alexander's Conquest*. Sheffield, UK: JSOT Press, 1993.

Allen, Michael, and Scott R. Swain. *Reformed Catholicity: The Promise of Retrieval for Theology and Biblical Interpretation*. Grand Rapids: Baker Academic, 2015.

Allis, Oswald T. *The Unity of Isaiah: A Study in Prophecy*. Philadelphia: Presbyterian & Reformed, 1950. Repr., Eugene, OR: Wipf & Stock, 2000.

Anatolios, Khaled. *Retrieving Nicaea: The Development and Meaning of Trinitarian Doctrine*. Grand Rapids: Baker Academic, 2011.

Arnold, Bill T., and Brent A. Strawn, ed. *The World around the Old Testament: The People and Places of the Ancient Near East*. Grand Rapids: Baker Academic, 2016.

Athanasius. *On the Incarnation*. Translated by a religious of CSMV. Popular Patristics 44a. Crestwood, NY: St. Vladimir's Seminary Press, 1993.

Augustine of Hippo. *City of God, Books 1–10.* Translated by William Babcock. Edited by Boniface Ramsey. The Works of St. Augustine I/6. Hyde Park, NY: New City Press, 2012.

———. *City of God, Books 11–22.* Translated by William Babcock. Edited by Boniface Ramsey. The Works of St. Augustine I/7. Hyde Park, NY: New City, 2013.

———. *The Confessions.* Translated by Maria Boulding. Edited by John E. Rotelle. The Works of St. Augustine I/1. Hyde Park, NY: New City, 1997.

———. *On Genesis: Two Books on Genesis against the Manichees; and, On the Literal Interpretation of Genesis: An Unfinished Book.* Translated by Roland J. Teske. Fathers of the Church 84. Washington, DC: Catholic University of America Press, 1991.

———. *The Trinity.* Translated by Edmund Hill. Edited by John E. Rotelle. The Works of Saint Augustine I/5. Hyde Park, NY: New City, 1991.

Ayres, Lewis. *Nicaea and Its Legacy: An Approach to Fourth-Century Trinitarian Theology.* Oxford: Oxford University Press, 2004.

Baltzer, Klaus. *Deutero-Isaiah: A Commentary on Isaiah 40–55.* Translated by Margaret Kohl. Edited by Peter Machinist. Hermeneia. Minneapolis: Fortress, 2001.

Barth, Karl. *Church Dogmatics.* Vol. II/1, *The Doctrine of God.* Translated by J. W. Edwards, O. Bussey, and H. Knight. Edited by G. W. Bromiley and T. F. Torrance. Edinburgh: T&T Clark, 1957.

———. *Church Dogmatics.* Vol. III/1, *The Doctrine of Creation.* Translated by J. W. Edwards, O. Bussey, and H. Knight. Edited by G. W. Bromiley and T. F. Torrance. Edinburgh: T&T Clark, 1958.

Basil of Caesarea. *St. Basil of Caesarea: Against Eunomius.* Translated by Mark Delcogliano and Andrew Radde-Gallwitz. Fathers of the Church 122. Washington, DC: Catholic University of America Press, 2011.

Bavinck, Herman. *Reformed Dogmatics.* Translated by John Vriend. Edited by John Bolt. 4 vols. Grand Rapids: Baker Academic, 2003–8.

Benedict XVI, Pope. "The Regensburg Lecture." Pages 130–48 in *The Regensburg Lecture.* Edited by James V. Schall. South Bend, IN: St. Augustine's Press, 2007.

Beyer, Bryan E. *Encountering the Book of Isaiah: A Historical and Theological Survey.* Grand Rapids: Baker Academic, 2007.

Block, Daniel I. *Israel: Ancient Kingdom or Late Invention?* Nashville: B&H Academic, 2008.

Blowers, Paul. *Drama of the Divine Economy: Creator and Creation in Early Christian Theology and Piety.* Oxford Early Christian Studies. Oxford: Oxford University Press, 2012.

Boersma, Hans. *Heavenly Participation: The Weaving of a Sacramental Tapestry.* Grand Rapids: Eerdmans, 2011.

———. *Nouvelle Theologie and Sacramental Ontology: A Return to Mystery.* Oxford: Oxford University Press, 2009.

———. *Sacramental Preaching: Sermons on the Hidden Presence of Christ*. Grand Rapids: Baker Academic, 2016.

———. *Scripture as Real Presence: Sacramental Exegesis in the Early Church*. Grand Rapids: Baker Academic, 2017.

Boethius. *The Consolation of Philosophy*. Translated with introduction and notes by Richard Green. Library of Liberal Arts. Indianapolis: Bobbs-Merrill, 1962.

Bright, John. *A History of Israel*. 4th ed. Louisville: Westminster John Knox, 2000.

Burrell, David B., CSC. "*Creatio ex Nihilo* Recovered." *Modern Theology* 29, no. 2 (April 2013): 5–21.

Burt, E. A. *The Metaphysical Foundations of Modern Science*. 1924. Repr., Mineola, NY: Dover, 2003.

Calvin, John. *Genesis*. Translated from the original Latin and compared with the French edition by John King. Calvin's Commentaries 1. Grand Rapids: Baker Books, 2005.

———. *Institutes of the Christian Religion*. Translated by Ford Lewis Battles. Edited by John T. McNeill. 2 vols. Library of Christian Classics. Philadelphia: Westminster, 1960.

———. *Isaiah*, vol. 1. Translated from the original Latin by William Pringle. Calvin's Commentaries 8. Grand Rapids: Baker Books, 2005.

Carter, Craig A. *Interpreting Scripture with the Great Tradition: Recovering the Genius of Premodern Exegesis*. Grand Rapids: Baker Academic, 2018.

———. *The Politics of the Cross: The Theology and Ethics of John Howard Yoder*. Grand Rapids: Brazos, 2001.

———. *Rethinking Christ and Culture: A Post-Christendom Approach*. Grand Rapids: Brazos, 2007.

Catechism of the Catholic Church. New York: Doubleday Dell, 1995.

Childs, Brevard S. *The Struggle to Understand Isaiah as Christian Scripture*. Grand Rapids: Eerdmans, 2004.

Clayton, Philip. "Panentheism in Metaphysical and Scientific Perspective." Pages 73–93 in Clayton and Peacocke, *In Whom We Live and Move and Have Our Being*.

Clayton, Philip, and Arthur Peacocke, eds. *In Whom We Live and Move and Have Our Being: Panentheistic Reflections on God's Presence in a Scientific World*. Grand Rapids: Eerdmans 2004.

Coogan, Michael D., ed. *Stories from Ancient Canaan*. Philadelphia: Westminster, 1978.

Coogan, Michael D., and Mark S. Smith, eds. *Stories from Ancient Canaan*. 2nd ed. Louisville: Westminster John Knox, 2012.

Cooper, John W. *Panentheism—the Other God of the Philosophers: From Plato to the Present*. Grand Rapids: Baker Academic, 2006.

Copleston, Frederick C., SJ. *Greece and Rome*, part 2. Vol. 1 of *A History of Philosophy*. New York: Image Books, 1946.

Currid, John D. *Against the Gods: The Polemical Theology of the Old Testament.* Wheaton: Crossway, 2013.

Darwin, Charles. *The Descent of Man.* In *Darwin: A Norton Critical Edition.* Edited by Philip Appleman. New York: Norton, 1970.

Davies, Brian. *An Introduction to the Philosophy of Religion.* 3rd ed. Oxford: Oxford University Press, 2004.

———. *The Thought of Thomas Aquinas.* Oxford: Oxford University Press, 1992.

Dawkins, Richard. *The God Delusion.* New York: Houghton Mifflin, 2008.

Dawson, Christopher. *Christianity and European Culture: Selections from the Work of Christopher Dawson.* Edited by Gerald J. Russello. Washington, DC: Catholic University of America Press, 1998.

Day, John. *God's Conflict with the Dragon and the Sea: Echoes of a Canaanite Myth in the Old Testament.* University of Cambridge Oriental Publications 35. Cambridge: Cambridge University Press, 1985.

Dempsey, Amy. "Meet the United Church Minister Who Came Out as an Atheist." In *Toronto Star*, February 21, 2016. https://www.thestar.com/news/gta/2015/03/16/atheist-minister-praises-the-glory-of-good-at-scarborough-church.html.

Dennison, James T., ed. *Reformed Confessions of the 16th and 17th Centuries in English Translation.* 4 vols. Grand Rapids: Reformation Heritage Books, 2008–14.

Dever, William G. *What Did the Biblical Writers Know and When Did They Know It? What Archaeology Can Tell Us about the Reality of Ancient Israel.* Grand Rapids: Eerdmans, 2001.

Dixon, Thomas. *From Passions to Emotions: The Creation of a Secular Psychological Category.* Cambridge: Cambridge University Press, 2003.

Dolezal, James E. *All That Is in God: Evangelical Theology and the Challenge of Classical Christian Theism.* Grand Rapids: Reformation Heritage Books, 2017.

———. *God without Parts: Divine Simplicity and the Metaphysics of God's Absoluteness.* Eugene, OR: Pickwick, 2011.

Dorner, Isaac August. *Divine Immutability: A Critical Reconsideration.* Translated by Robert R. Williams and Claude Welch. Minneapolis: Fortress, 1994.

Duby, Steven J. *Divine Simplicity: A Dogmatic Account.* London: Bloomsbury T&T Clark, 2016.

———. *God in Himself: Scripture, Metaphysics, and the Task of Christian Theology.* Studies in Christian Doctrine and Scripture. Downers Grove, IL: IVP Academic, 2020.

Durkheim, Émile. *The Division of Labor in Society.* Translated by G. Simpson. New York: Free Press, 1960.

Feser, Edward. *Five Proofs of the Existence of God.* San Francisco: Ignatius, 2017.

———. *The Last Superstition: A Refutation of the New Atheism.* South Bend, IN: St. Augustine's Press, 2008.

Fesko, J. V. *Reforming Apologetics: Retrieving the Classic Reformed Approach to Defending the Faith*. Grand Rapids: Baker Academic, 2019.

Feuerbach, Ludwig. *Lectures on the Essence of Religion*. Translated by Ralph Manheim. New York: Harper & Row, 1967.

Frei, Hans. W. *The Eclipse of Biblical Narrative: A Study in Eighteenth and Nineteenth Century Hermeneutics*. New Haven: Yale University Press, 1974.

Garrett, Duane A. *Rethinking Genesis: The Sources and Authorship of the First Book of the Pentateuch*. Fearn, Ross-shire, UK: Focus, 2000.

Gavrilyuk, Paul L. *The Suffering of the Impassible God*. Oxford Early Christian Studies. Oxford: Oxford University Press, 2004.

Gerson, Lloyd P. *From Plato to Platonism*. Ithaca, NY: Cornell University Press, 2013.

Gillespie, Michael Allen. *The Theological Origins of Modernity*. Chicago: University of Chicago Press, 2008.

Goldingay, John, and David Payne. *Isaiah 40–55: A Critical and Exegetical Commentary*. 2 vols. International Critical Commentary. London: Bloomsbury T&T Clark, 2006.

Grant, George P. *Technology and Justice*. Toronto: Anansi, 1986.

Grudem, Wayne. *Systematic Theology: An Introduction to Biblical Doctrine*. Grand Rapids: Zondervan, 1994.

Hamilton, James M., Jr. *God's Glory in Salvation through Judgment: A Biblical Theology*. Wheaton: Crossway, 2010.

Hanson, R. P. C. *The Search for the Christian Doctrine of God: The Arian Controversy 318–381*. Grand Rapids: Baker Academic, 2005.

Harnack, Adolf von. *What Is Christianity?* Translated by T. B. Saunders. Introduction by Rudolf Bultmann. Fortress Texts in Modern Christianity. Philadelphia: Fortress, 1957.

Hart, David Bentley. *The Experience of God: Being, Consciousness, Bliss*. New Haven: Yale University Press, 2013.

Haykin, Michael A. G. *Rediscovering the Church Fathers: Who They Were and How They Shaped the Church*. Wheaton: Crossway, 2011.

Hegel, G. W. F. *Hegel's Philosophy of Right*. Translated with notes by T. M. Knox. Oxford: Oxford University Press, 1952.

Heiser, Michael S. *The Unseen Realm: Recovering the Supernatural Worldview of the Bible*. Bellingham, WA: Lexham, 2015.

Heppe, Heinrich. *Reformed Dogmatics*. Revised and edited by Ernst Bizer. Translated by G. T. Thomson. Eugene, OR: Wipf & Stock, 2007.

Hicks, Stephen R. C. *Explaining Postmodernism: Skepticism and Socialism from Rousseau to Foucault*. Expanded ed. Roscoe, IL: Ockham's Razor, 2017.

Hill, Andrew E., and John H. Walton. *A Survey of the Old Testament*. 3rd ed. Grand Rapids: Zondervan, 2009.

Holmes, Arthur. *The Idea of a Christian College*. Grand Rapids: Eerdmans, 1975.

Holmes, Christopher R. J. *The Lord Is Good: Seeking the God of the Psalter*. Studies in Christian Doctrine and Scripture. Downers Grove, IL: IVP Academic, 2018.

Holmes, Stephen R. *The Quest for the Trinity: The Doctrine of God in Scripture, History and Modernity*. Downers Grove, IL: IVP Academic, 2012.

Kant, Immanuel. *Critique of Practical Reason*. Translated by Lewis White Beck. Library of Liberal Arts. Indianapolis: Bobbs-Merrill, 1929.

———. *Prolegomena to Any Future Metaphysics*. Translated by Paul Carus. Extensively revised by James W. Ellington. Indianapolis: Hackett, 1977.

Keller, Catherine. *Face of the Deep: A Theology of Becoming*. London: Routledge, 2003.

Kim, Hyun Chul Paul. *Reading Isaiah: A Literary and Theological Commentary*. Macon, GA: Smyth & Helwys, 2016.

Kreeft, Peter. *C. S. Lewis for the Third Millennium: Six Essays on the Abolition of Man*. San Francisco: Ignatius, 1994.

———. *The Platonic Tradition*. South Bend, IN: St. Augustine's Press, 2018.

Lamoureux, Denis O. *Evolutionary Creation: A Christian Approach to Evolution*. Eugene, OR: Wipf & Stock, 2008.

Leith, John H., ed. *Creeds of the Churches: A Reader in Christian Doctrine from the Bible to the Present*. Rev. ed. Atlanta: John Knox, 1973.

Levering, Matthew. *Engaging the Doctrine of Creation: Cosmos, Creatures, and the Wise and Good Creator*. Grand Rapids: Baker Academic, 2017.

———. *Scripture and Metaphysics: Aquinas and the Renewal of Trinitarian Theology*. Malden, MA: Blackwell, 2004.

Lewis, C. S. *The Abolition of Man*. New York: HarperCollins, 2001.

———. "Introduction." In Athanasius, *On the Incarnation*.

———. *The Silver Chair*. New York: Macmillan, 1953.

———. *That Hideous Strength*. London: John Land the Bodley Head, 1945.

———. "The World's Last Night." Pages 65–85 in *Fern-Seeds and Elephants and Other Essays on Christianity*. Edited by Walter Hooper. Glasgow: William Collins & Sons, 1977.

Lienhard, Joseph T., ed. *Exodus, Leviticus, Numbers and Deuteronomy*. Ancient Christian Commentary on Scripture 3. Downers Grove, IL: InterVarsity, 2001.

Lippman, Walter. *A Preface to Morals*. 1929. Repr., New York: Routledge, 2017.

Lister, Rob. *God Is Impassible and Impassioned: Toward a Theology of Divine Emotion*. Wheaton: Crossway, 2013.

Louth, Andrew. *Discerning the Mystery: An Essay on the Nature of Theology*. Oxford: Oxford University Press, 1983.

———, ed. *Genesis 1–11*. Ancient Christian Commentary on Scripture 1. Downers Grove, IL: InterVarsity, 2001.

Machen, J. Gresham. *Christianity and Liberalism*. Grand Rapids: Eerdmans, 1923.

MacIntyre, Alasdair. *After Virtue*. 3rd ed. Notre Dame, IN: University of Notre Dame Press, 2007.

Marx, Karl. "*The German Ideology*, Volume One." Pages 162–96 in *The Portable Karl Marx*. Edited by Eugene Kamenka. New York: Viking Penguin Books, 1983.

May, Gerhard. *Creatio ex Nihilo: The Doctrine of "Creation out of Nothing" in Early Christian Thought*. Translated by A. S. Worrall. Edinburgh: T&T Clark, 1994.

McCormack, Bruce L. *Orthodox and Modern: Studies in the Theology of Karl Barth*. Grand Rapids: Baker Academic, 2008.

McFarland, Ian A. *From Nothing: A Theology of Creation*. Louisville: Westminster John Knox, 2014.

McLaren, Brian. *A New Kind of Christianity: Ten Questions That Are Transforming the Faith*. New York: HarperCollins, 2010.

Middleton, J. Richard, and Brian J. Walsh. *Truth Is Stranger Than It Used to Be: Biblical Faith in a Postmodern Age*. Downers Grove, IL: InterVarsity, 1995.

Milbank, John. *Theology and Social Theory: Beyond Secular Reason*. Oxford: Blackwell, 1990.

Moberly, R. W. L. *Old Testament Theology: Reading the Hebrew Bible as Christian Scripture*. Grand Rapids: Baker Academic, 2013.

Moltmann, Jürgen. *The Crucified God: The Cross of Christ as the Foundation and Criticism of Christian Theology*. Translated by R. A. Wilson and John Bowden. Minneapolis: Fortress, 1993.

———. *The Trinity and the Kingdom: The Doctrine of God*. Translated by Margaret Kohl. Minneapolis: Fortress, 1993.

Motyer, J. Alec. *The Prophecy of Isaiah: An Introduction and Commentary*. Downers Grove, IL: IVP Academic, 1993.

Muller, Richard A. *Post-Reformation Reformed Dogmatics*. 2nd ed. 4 vols. Grand Rapids: Baker Academic, 2003–8.

Nietzsche, Friedrich. *Beyond Good and Evil: Prelude to a Philosophy of the Future*. Translated with an introduction and commentary by R. J. Hollingdale. New York: Penguin Books, 1973.

Oden, Thomas C. *After Modernity . . . What? Agenda for Theology*. Grand Rapids: Zondervan, 1990.

———. *Classic Christianity: A Systematic Theology*. San Francisco: HarperOne, 1992.

———. *The Rebirth of Orthodoxy: Signs of New Life in Christianity*. New York: HarperSanFrancisco, 2003.

———. *Requiem: A Lament in Three Movements*. Nashville: Abingdon, 1995.

Oliphant, K. Scott. *God with Us: Divine Condescension and the Attributes of God*. Wheaton: Crossway, 2012.

Oswalt, John N. *The Bible among the Myths: Unique Revelation or Just Ancient Literature?* Grand Rapids: Zondervan, 2009.

———. *The Book of Isaiah: Chapters 1–39.* New International Commentary on the Old Testament. Grand Rapids: Eerdmans, 1986.

———. *The Book of Isaiah: Chapters 40–66.* New International Commentary on the Old Testament. Grand Rapids: Eerdmans, 1998.

———. "*Creatio ex nihilo*: Is It Biblical, and Does It Matter?" *Trinity Journal,* n.s., 39 (2018): 165–80.

———. *The Holy One of Israel: Studies in the Book of Isaiah.* Eugene, OR: Wipf & Stock, 2014.

Pannenberg, Wolfhart. *Systematic Theology.* Translated by Geoffrey Bromiley. 3 vols. Grand Rapids: Eerdmans, 1991–98.

Pelikan, Jaroslav. *The Emergence of the Catholic Tradition (100–600).* Vol. 1 of *The Christian Tradition: A History of the Development of Doctrine.* Chicago: University of Chicago Press, 1971.

Pieper, Josef. *The Silence of St. Thomas: Three Essays.* South Bend, IN: St. Augustine's Press, 1999.

Pinnock, Clark H. *Most Moved Mover: A Theology of God's Openness.* Grand Rapids: Baker Academic, 2001.

Pinnock, Clark H., et al. *The Openness of God: A Biblical Challenge to the Traditional Understanding of God.* Downers Grove, IL: InterVarsity, 1994.

Plato. *Republic.* Pages 575–844 in *The Collected Dialogues of Plato.* Edited by Edith Hamilton and Huntington Cairns. Princeton: Princeton University Press, 1961.

———. *Timaeus.* Pages 1151–1211 in *The Collected Dialogues of Plato.* Edited by Edith Hamilton and Huntington Cairns. Princeton: Princeton University Press, 1961.

Polkinghorne, John. *Science and the Trinity: The Christian Encounter with Reality.* New Haven: Yale University Press, 2004.

Pritchard, James B., ed. *The Ancient Near East: An Anthology of Texts and Pictures.* Princeton: Princeton University Press, 2011.

Provan, Iain. *Discovering Genesis: Content, Interpretation, Reception.* Grand Rapids: Eerdmans, 2015.

Provan, Iain, V. Philips Long, and Tremper Longman III. *A Biblical History of Israel.* 2nd ed. Louisville: Westminster John Knox, 2015.

Radde-Gallwitz, Andrew. *Basil of Caesarea, Gregory of Nyssa, and the Transformation of Divine Simplicity.* Oxford Early Christian Studies. Oxford: Oxford University Press, 2009.

Rahner, Karl. *The Trinity.* Translated by Joseph Donceel. Tunbridge Wells, Kent, UK: Burns & Oates, 1970.

Robertson, Owen Palmer. *The Christ of the Prophets.* Abridged version. Phillipsburg, NJ: P&R, 2008.

Sagan, Carl. *Cosmos*. New York: Ballentine Books, 1980.

Sandys-Wunsch, John, and Laurence Eldredge. "J. P. Gabler and the Distinction between Biblical and Dogmatic Theology: Translation, Commentary, and Discussion of His Originality." *Scottish Journal of Theology* 33 (1980): 135–58.

Schaff, Philip, ed. *The Greek and Latin Creeds, with Translations*. Vol. 2 of *The Creeds of Christendom, with a History and Critical Notes*. New York: Harper & Brothers, 1890.

Schleiermacher, Friedrich. *The Christian Faith*. Edited by H. R. MacIntosh and J. S. Stewart. Edinburgh: T&T Clark, 1999.

Seitz, Christopher R. *The Elder Testament: Canon, Theology, Trinity*. Waco: Baylor University Press, 2018.

Smith, Christian, with Melinda Lundquist Denton. *Soul Searching: The Religious and Spiritual Lives of American Teenagers*. Oxford: Oxford University Press, 2005.

Smith, Mark S. *The Early History of God: Yahweh and the Other Deities in Ancient Israel*. 2nd ed. Grand Rapids: Eerdmans, 2002.

———. *The Memoirs of God: History, Memory, and the Experience of the Divine in Ancient Israel*. Minneapolis: Fortress, 2004.

———. *The Origins of Biblical Monotheism: Israel's Polytheistic Background and the Ugaritic Texts*. New York: Oxford University Press, 2001.

———. "Ugarit and the Ugaritians." Pages 139–67 in Arnold and Strawn, *The World around the Old Testament*.

Solzhenitsyn, Alexander. "The Exhausted West." *Harvard Magazine* (July–August 1978). Reprinted as "A World Split Apart: 1978 Harvard Commencement Address." Pages 561–75 in *The Solzhenitsyn Reader*.

———. "Men Have Forgotten God: The Templeton Address." Pages 576–84 in *The Solzhenitsyn Reader*.

———. *The Solzhenitsyn Reader: New and Essential Writings, 1947–2005*. Edited by Edward E. Ericson Jr. and Daniel J. Mahoney. Wilmington, DE: ISI Books. 2006.

———. *Warning to the West*. Translated by Harris L. Coulter and Nataly Martin. Edited by Alexis Klimoff. New York: Farrer, Straus & Giroux, 1976.

Soskice, Janet Martin. "Athens and Jerusalem, Alexandria and Edessa: Is There a Metaphysics of Scripture?" *International Journal of Systematic Theology* 8, no. 2 (April 2006): 149–62.

Steinmetz, David C. "The Superiority of Pre-critical Exegesis." Pages 3–14 in *Taking the Long View: Christian Theology in Historical Perspective*. Oxford: Oxford University Press, 2011.

Stendahl, Krister. "Biblical Theology, Contemporary." Vol. 1, pages 418–32 in *The Interpreter's Dictionary of the Bible*. Edited by George A. Buttrick. Nashville: Abingdon, 1962.

Stevenson, Leslie. *Seven Theories of Human Nature*. Oxford: Oxford University Press, 1974.

———, ed. *The Study of Human Nature: A Reader*. 2nd ed. Oxford: Oxford University Press, 2000.

Stevenson, Leslie, and David L. Haberman. *Ten Theories of Human Nature*. 4th ed. Oxford: Oxford University Press, 2004.

Swain, Scott R. *The God of the Gospel: Robert Jenson's Trinitarian Theology*. Downers Grove, IL: IVP Academic, 2013.

Swinburne, Richard. *The Christian God*. Oxford: Oxford University Press, 1994.

Thomas Aquinas. *Summa Theologica*. Translated by the Fathers of the English Dominican Province. 5 vols. Notre Dame, IN: Ava Maria, 1920.

Trueman, Carl R. *The Creedal Imperative*. Wheaton: Crossway, 2012.

Turretin, Francis. *Institutes of Elenctic Theology*. Translated by George Musgrave Giger. Edited by James T. Dennison Jr. 3 vols. Phillipsburg, NJ: P&R, 1992–97.

Vaggione, Richard Paul. *Eunomius of Cyzicus and the Nicene Revolution*. Oxford Early Christian Studies. Oxford: Oxford University Press, 2000.

Vanderkam, James, and Peter Flint. *The Meaning of the Dead Sea Scrolls: Their Significance for Understanding the Bible, Judaism, Jesus and Christianity*. San Francisco: HarperOne, 2002.

Vanhoozer, Kevin J. *Remythologizing Theology: Divine Action, Passion and Authorship*. Cambridge: Cambridge University Press, 2010.

Vos, Geerhardus. *Biblical Theology: Old and New Testaments*. Grand Rapids: Eerdmans, 1948.

———. *Reformed Dogmatics*. Translated by Richard B. Gaffin Jr. 5 vols. Bellingham, WA: Lexham, 2012–14.

Walsh, Brian J., and J. Richard Middleton. *The Transforming Vision: Shaping a Christian Worldview*. Downers Grove, IL: InterVarsity, 1984.

Ware, Bruce A. *God's Greater Glory: The Exalted God of Scripture and the Christian Faith*. Wheaton: Crossway, 2004.

———. *God's Lesser Glory: The Diminished God of Open Theism*. Wheaton: Crossway, 2000.

———. "A Modified Calvinist Doctrine of God." Pages 76–120 in *Perspectives on the Doctrine of God: 4 Views*. Edited by Bruce A. Ware. Nashville: B&H Academic, 2008.

Weaver, J. Denny. *The Nonviolent God*. Grand Rapids: Eerdmans, 2013.

Weaver, Richard M. *Ideas Have Consequences*. Chicago: University of Chicago Press, 1948.

Webster, John B. *Confessing God: Essays in Christian Dogmatics II*. Edinburgh: T&T Clark, 2005.

———. "God, Theology, Universities." Pages 157–72 in Webster, *Virtue and Intellect*.

———. *God and the Works of God*. Vol. 1 of *God without Measure: Working Papers in Christian Theology*. London: Bloomsbury T&T Clark, 2016.

———. "'Love Is Also a Lover of Life': *Creatio ex Nihilo* and Creaturely Goodness." Pages 99–114 in Webster, *God and the Works of God*.

———. "*Non ex Aequo*: God's Relation to Creatures." Pages 115–26 in Webster, *God and the Works of God*.

———. *Virtue and Intellect*. Vol. 2 of *God without Measure: Working Papers in Christian Theology*. London: Bloomsbury T&T Clark, 2016.

Wellhausen, Julius. *A Prolegomena to the History of Ancient Israel*. Translated by W. Robertson Smith. Eugene, OR: Wipf & Stock, 2003. First published in German in 1878 under the title *History of Israel*, vol. 1, and then in 1883 under the title *A Prolegomena to the History of Ancient Israel*.

Wesley, Charles. "Love Divine, All Loves Excelling." Hymn 2 in *Great Hymns of the Faith*. Edited by John W. Peterson. Grand Rapids: Singspiration of Zondervan, 1968.

Whitelam, Keith W. *The Invention of Ancient Israel: The Silencing of Palestinian History*. London: Routledge, 1996.

Wilken, Robert Louis. "The Church as Culture." *First Things* (April 2004). https://www.firstthings.com/article/2004/04/the-church-as-culture.

———. *The Spirit of Early Christian Thought: Seeking the Face of God*. New Haven: Yale University Press, 2004.

Wittman, Tyler R. *God and Creation in the Theology of Thomas Aquinas and Karl Barth*. Cambridge: Cambridge University Press, 2019.

Yeago, David S. "The New Testament and the Nicene Dogma: A Contribution to the Recovery of Theological Exegesis." *Pro Ecclesia* 3, no. 2 (1994): 152–64.

Yeats, William Butler. "The Second Coming." 1919. https://www.poetryfoundation.org/poems/43290/the-second-coming.

Index of Scripture

Index of Persons

Index of Subjects

Printed in Great Britain
by Amazon

66436029R00210